The Apostolic Church

The Apostolic Church

EVERETT F. HARRISON

GRAND RAPIDS, MICHIGAN
WILLIAM B. EERDMANS PUBLISHING COMPANY

Copyright ©1985 by Wm. B. Eerdmans Publishing Co.
255 Jefferson Ave. S.E., Grand Rapids, Mich. 49503

Reprinted, October 1986

Library of Congress Cataloging in Publication Data

Harrison, Everett Falconer, 1902–
  The apostolic church.

  Bibliography: p. 237
  1. Church history—Early and primitive church, ca. 30–600.
  2. Bible. N.T.—Criticism, interpretation, etc.
  I. Title.
  BR162.2.H32 1985   270.1   84-26061

ISBN 0-8028-0044-0

Contents

INTRODUCTION   ix

I. THE BACKGROUND OF THE APOSTOLIC AGE   1
1. The Political and Cultural Background   1
2. The Religious Background   9

II. THE BOOK OF ACTS   19
1. History of Criticism: A General Overview   19
2. History of Criticism: The Speeches in Acts   26
3. The Historical Value of Acts   33

III. THE EXTERNAL HISTORY OF THE APOSTOLIC CHURCH   41
1. Pentecost   41
2. The Gentile Mission   53
3. Persecution and the Break with Judaism   61
4. The Extension of the Gospel during the First Century   72
5. Church and State   80
6. Church and Society   89

IV. THE INTERNAL DEVELOPMENT OF THE CHURCH   100
1. The Concept of the Church: Its Organization   100
2. Theology (Gleaned Mainly from the Preaching)   109
3. Incipient Creeds   115
4. Baptism   122
5. Worship (including the Lord's Supper)   130
6. Christian Life   140
7. Ministry   149
8. Teaching   157
9. Discipline   166

V. THE INDIVIDUAL CHURCHES   176
1. Jerusalem   176
2. Antioch   183
3. Philippi   190
4. Thessalonica   195
5. Corinth   201

6. Ephesus   208
7. Colosse   216
8. Rome   219

ENDNOTES   229

SELECTED BIBLIOGRAPHY   237

Author's Note

THIS volume has been prepared in the hope that those who are looking for a text that deals comprehensively, though not exhaustively, with developments in the early years of the life of the Christian Church will find in it at least a modicum of help. References to pertinent literature are restricted almost entirely to works in English.

Introduction

THE materials of the New Testament can be grouped into two divisions bearing the labels "Gospel History" and "Apostolic History," the first unit covering the four Gospels and the second including the remainder of the New Testament. This division answers readily to the twofold classification often cited in patristic references to the New Testament books—Gospel and Apostle.

Apostolic History, then, includes the book of Acts and all that follows in our English Bible. But the term can serve in a more limited sense to refer to the contents of the book of Acts. Our use of the designation will differ somewhat from both of these in that it is intended to cover the life and work of the early church as reflected in these sources. The method of study will be basically topical rather than chronological.

THE RELATION BETWEEN APOSTOLIC HISTORY AND GOSPEL HISTORY

The division between the history of the earthly life of Jesus and the history of the life of the church he created by his redemptive work is natural. But it would be wrong to draw such a hard and fast line between them that their organic relationship is obscured. Writers who begin their discussion of the rise of Christianity with John the Baptist are simply recognizing the practical impossibility of beginning with Pentecost. The continuity between the period covered by the Gospels and the apostolic age is not strictly a modern insight. It is reflected in the work of Luke, who set before himself the task of writing an account of the events that centered in the historic Jesus and had their issue in the formation and development of the church. Our habit of thinking of the Gospel by Luke and the Acts as two separate entities (a perception encouraged by the fact that in our Bibles they are physically separated) obscures the sense of continuity that Luke felt and tried to express. If his Gospel stood last in the fourfold collection rather than third, it would be followed immediately by Acts, which would help us to think in terms of a single work in two parts. We could then see at a glance how Acts is intended to tie into the close of the Gospel of Luke.

In writing a twofold work Luke was apparently following the custom of his time. Josephus, for example, begins Book II of his *Against Apion* by saying, "In the first volume of this work, my most esteemed Epaphroditus, I demonstrated the antiquity of our race. . . . I also challenged the statements of Manetho. . . . I shall now proceed to refute the rest of the authors who have attacked us." To put both books on a single roll was impracticable; it would have made the roll altogether unwieldy. The Gospel that is credited to Luke eventually took its place beside the other three, leaving Acts to stand alone. Yet modern students sense the legitimacy of speaking of "Luke-Acts" in order to emphasize the continuity. There is no consensus as to the interval involved in the writing of the two books. One fact is clear, however: whereas Luke had predecessors in Gospel production, as he himself acknowledges (Luke 1:1), in writing the Acts he had to break new ground. Consequently, whereas his Gospel can be compared with and supplemented by the others, such a course is not possible in dealing with Acts.

The relation of Gospel History to Apostolic History is one of *causality*. To put the matter simply, without Christ there would be no church. Without his ministry, there would be no ministry in his name. The events of the apostolic age presuppose the events recorded in the Gospels, even though the Gospels were not yet in existence as written records during that period. It is helpful to think of the materials in the Gospels as being of three types, according as that material looks to the past, or reflects the standpoint of the present, or anticipates the future. Type one includes Old Testament quotations and the presentation of the mission of Jesus as fulfilling the prophets. Type two reflects the contemporary scene involving the words and works of Jesus. Type three includes the material that anticipates the age to follow, when Jesus will no longer be on earth but will have a witness maintained by those whom he has chosen and trained. These three elements sometimes lie side by side, as in Mark 1:1–8. In verses 1–2 a quotation is used to explain the emergence of John the Baptist in terms of Old Testament prophecy. Then comes the contemporary emphasis, the description of John and a summary statement of the impact of his ministry. Finally, in verse 8, John's prediction regarding the coming one is cited: "I baptize you with water, but he will baptize you with the Holy Spirit." This carries us forward to the beginning of the apostolic age. The greater part of the type three material, however, comes from the lips of Jesus, such as his prediction of the establishing of the church, his eschatological discourse, and his farewell message in the upper room. The evaluation one gives this latter type of material reflects one's basic viewpoint. If we are able to see a truly revelational element in the unfolding of the events of the Gospels, we will have little trouble in accepting the legitimacy of the predictive element found there. If not, we will resort to the expedient of explaining it as a reading back of the outlook and understanding of the early church into the records of the ministry of Jesus. This is a device calculated to give authority to the de facto position of the church. But it is an enfeebled theism that declines to accept the responsibility for prediction, to say nothing of the ethical problem in the church's assigning to Jesus utterances that really originated (so the theory contends) with his followers at a later time. We are on more secure ground if we suppose that Jesus did in fact come with a program that included the future and was willing to talk about it, even when it mystified his disciples.

THE RELATION BETWEEN THE APOSTOLIC AND THE OLD CATHOLIC CHURCH

We have seen that the apostolic age depends on and grows out of Gospel History and that the latter, in turn, is the organic development of Old Testament prophecy. But if we take our position at the point of the emergence of the church and look forward rather than backward, we see a long unfolding of church history. It is worth asking what the relation is between the apostolic church and the church in the second century. The apostles are no longer present in this later era. Is it possible that the character of this period is already reflected in the literature of the New Testament? Some scholars think that this is the case. They profess to detect things here and there in Acts and the epistles that are akin to the characteristic elements of the postapostolic era. F. F. Bruce has assembled a comprehensive list of these items that supposedly indicate the presence of incipient catholicism: "the shift of emphasis from the local church to the church universal, the replacement of the charismata by an institutional ministry, the recession of the hope of glory at an early parousia in favour of dependence on the present means of grace dispensed through the church and its ministry, and the adoption of a codified confession of faith."[1]

A natural consequence of adopting this viewpoint will be an inclination to use these items as criteria for a late dating of the New Testament documents in which they are alleged to be present, a questionable procedure unless the dating can be supported by other data. An illuminating statement from the pen of Leonhard Goppelt can provide needed perspective on this issue:

> The teachers of the passing apostolic age (with the exception of the Gnostics) attempted in two ways to render possible the historical existence of the church: The one stressed the proclamation of the word, indeed, a proclamation which was concretized in the sacrament and carried by the entire community by admonition, intercession, and church discipline. The other developed a pedagogical system of repentance, a natural-legal ethos, a stabilization of the church office by legal means, and a qualification of worship as well as the church office by means of the mystery—altogether, an adaptation of the church to forms of life which have been tested in history. One cannot say that the second way

completes the first simply through more definite needed forms of church life. Indeed, for the most part, the first way is not completed by the second but rather supplanted by it; that part of the church which emphasized the pneumatic-eschatological element by means of the word was, for the most part, eliminated. We call the first type "apostolic" and the second "early Catholic." As we retrospectively summarize the evidence, we see the first was developed from later New Testament writings, the second from the so-called apostolic fathers.[2]

In assessing the transition from apostolic Christianity to later stages of the life of the church it is well to note the pivotal importance of Asia Minor, because it was in this area that the transmission of the faith was most faithfully accomplished. During the second century the leaders of the church in this region frequently referred to the elders and what they handed down. As Bornkamm observes, with these church leaders *presbyteros* "is not a title for office-bearers in the local congregation but a term for members of the older generation who are regarded as mediators of the authentic tradition and reliable teachers."[3]

Adolf Schlatter has pointed out that in late Judaism the famous teachers of Israel, such as Shammai, Hillel, and Gamaliel, were called elders.[4] The church in Asia Minor was obviously influenced by this Jewish background.

Another facet of the problem of the relationship between the church of the apostolic age and the church of the following period pertains to orthodoxy and heresy. Here two antithetical positions have been defended. One is the view of Walter Bauer, expounded in his *Orthodoxy and Heresy in Earliest Christianity* (ET, 1971), that various doctrinal positions coexisted in the early days of the church and that orthodoxy as we know it won out only gradually and was finally able to erect its monuments in the ecumenical creeds. On the other hand, H. E. W. Turner (*The Pattern of Christian Truth* [1954]) argued for the position that under the influence of the apostles the tradition that constituted the foundation for belief was faithfully handed down and maintained by the great mass of Christians, whereas heresies were later deviations from this pattern and were recognized as such by the church and for this reason were condemned.

A supplementary word by I. Howard Marshall is helpful: "Granted that there is diversity and development in the theologies expressed in the New Testament, the question is whether this is the same thing as saying that no distinction between orthodoxy and heresy was being made, or that this concept did not exist prior to the development of a vocabulary to describe it."[5]

Turner's position is surely the more defensible of the two. It receives support when one notes the church's attitude toward Gnosticism. As Goppelt puts it, "Contrary to Bauer, the emergence of the Gnostic movements was not debated as though they were schools of thought, but they were directly repudiated as pseudo-Christian."[6]

CHAPTER I

The Background
of the Apostolic Age

1. THE POLITICAL AND CULTURAL BACKGROUND

For a survey of this kind it is desirable to go back to the era of Alexander the Great in the fourth century B.C. His father, Philip of Macedon, had brought the city-states of Greece under his control. For his own part, Alexander, a great military strategist despite his youth, determined to challenge Persia and its sprawling empire to the east with a view to retaliating for earlier Persian invasions of Greece. At this time Rome was busy consolidating its hold on Italy and dealing with the threat of the Gauls. It was not yet a world power.

Beyond his military objective Alexander had a vision of hellenizing the Orient. For this purpose he brought to the territories he had conquered Greek colonists and technicians of various kinds to establish centers where the Greek language and way of life would be transplanted. He had the concept of a new humanity—the Asiatic peoples infused with the civilizing influence of the Greeks. This was not so much imposed as offered. The Levant, where nationalism had grown old and feeble, was ripe for a change. It was probably fortunate that the inspiration for the hellenizing of the Orient came not from the Greek peninsula proper but from Macedonia. If the Greek outlook was acceptable to the conqueror of Greece, why should it not be also to those under his rule?

For Palestine, hellenization involved two phases. Following the death of Alexander and the division of the empire among his generals, the land of the Jews came first under the control of the Ptolemaic kingdom of Egypt. For the most part there was little pressure to impose Greek influences. Those who migrated to Egypt naturally adopted the Greek tongue and became more or less familiar with Greek thought and civilization. But when Palestine came under the sway of Syria, which was part of the Seleucid kingdom claimed by another of Alexander's generals, its tardiness in adjusting to the hellenizing spirit irritated its overlords, especially Antiochus IV (Epiphanes). This man was not averse to using violence to force the people to give up their peculiar and exclusive ways so as to become like the rest of his subjects. His tactics evoked resistance accompanied by a great upsurge of national feeling infused with zeal for the faith of the fathers. Under their Maccabean leaders the Jews won their religious freedom and eventually their independence.

Understandably there was considerable resentment on the part of the majority against those Jews who had become infected by the hellenizing trend, but it proved impossible to root out entirely the use of the Greek language or to banish Greek thought. Greek cities abounded on the fringes of the Jewish commonwealth. Complete isolation from Greek influence was impossible. It is well to note in passing that one aspect of the Maccabean struggle was destined to have a strong influence on the nation some two centuries later. When Jewish opposition to Roman control increased around the middle of the first century A.D. it was easy for some patriots to assume that if God had brought deliverance from Syria he would do the same with respect to Rome, even though the latter was a much more powerful adversary. So it came about that reason was abandoned under the impact of propaganda for a holy war in which God was expected to come to the aid of his covenant people.

After Alexander there was no strong centralizing power able to keep the eastern Mediterranean area politically unified, but Greek language and civilization continued to influence and mold great masses of people, especially in the free cities. (Hellenization was much weaker in the rural areas.) Meanwhile, a new master was about to emerge out of the west whose hold on the Levant would be more permanent than that of Alexander and his successors. Rome was heavily committed in its own area by a series of wars with Carthage, which finally came to a close around 200 B.C. But scarcely had military operations come to an end in North Africa when Rome became involved in the eastern Mediterranean, where Philip V of Macedon and Antiochus III of Syria combined forces to strengthen their position at the expense of Egypt, which was now too weak to hold its territory. On invitation from Egypt, not only Athens and some other city-states of Greece, but Rome also, despite war weariness, answered the call for help. First the Romans subdued Philip, then Antiochus, thereby giving themselves a foothold in Greece and Asia Minor. That foothold became a virtual stranglehold when the Romans returned to Greece to crush a rebellion led by Perseus, son of Philip V of Macedon. Reprisals were taken against communities in Greece that were deemed sympathetic to Perseus.

The settlements made with Carthage and Greece did not last. Roman envy of the Carthaginian commercial revival led to a determination to destroy this rival. Opposition to the Romans in Greece centered in the Achaean Confederacy, which now defied Rome. The response of the Romans was savage and final. In the same year (146 B.C.) Carthage and Corinth were demolished, the destruction amounting to notice that rebellion anywhere would not be tolerated. The Greek historian Polybius witnessed the sacking of Corinth and was horrified to see Roman soldiers playing dice on the pictures of famous artists (see *The Histories of Polybius*, LCL, 6.39.2).

Although the Romans respected Hellenism, they could appreciate it only in an amateurish way. Consequently, even though they became heirs of Alexander in the sense that they eventually came into power over much of the territory he had controlled, they lacked the capacity to appreciate fully the Greek spirit and genius, and did much to crush its hopes for revival. The Roman upper classes did adopt the Greek language, but they were not very successful in absorbing the intellectual contribution of the Greeks in literature and philosophy. Rome was too busy practicing the arts of war and administration, too busy satisfying its lust for power and riches, to devote much energy to culture. And in the whole process the Roman character suffered serious deterioration. On the other hand, the combination of Roman military might and administrative skill did provide stability in an age that contained the seeds of anarchy. In general, the Romans took the commonsense approach of doing as little as possible to disturb the status quo among peoples they subjugated. Subject nations were permitted to retain local administration, customs, and religion as long as these offered no threat to the welfare of the state. In pre-Christian times these peoples were not overly burdened with taxation, but this situation did not last. Eventually, as the supervision of officials relaxed, permitting local abuses, and the needs of the imperial exchequer increased because of the necessity of maintaining a large army and providing food and entertainment for the masses in the city of Rome, financial burdens became heavier and created hardship for the provinces. Meanwhile, for a time the immense treasure drained from Greece as punishment for rebellion enabled the Roman authorities to relieve their own citizens of taxation.

The final century of the republic, which came to an end in 27 B.C., was marked by internal struggles within the Roman state. Whereas the Senate was in nominal control, the rise of dictators imperiled the structure of government. An increase in professional soldiery was favorable to the making and undoing of these dictators. Three who attained some prominence were Sulla, Pompey, and Julius Caesar, although Pompey spent nearly all his time in the field enjoying the power of his extraordinary command. Displaying unusual military and administrative ability, he did much to advance and consolidate Roman power in the east, including ridding the Cilician coast of the plague of piracy and restoring autonomy to many small city-states, including some that had been taken over by the Jews through their Hasmonean rulers. Pompey also established new cities and organized the Decapolis, a league of ten cities to the east and north of Israel that was anti-Semitic in character and united for commercial advantage.

Pompey was introduced to Jewish politics in 63 B.C., when he was asked to arbitrate between two Hasmonean aspirants to the throne, the brothers

Hyrcanus and Aristobulus. The situation was complicated by the fact that an embassy of the people sought to have both men set aside so that the nation might return to theocracy. Because of the treachery of Aristobulus, Pompey used force in entering Jerusalem. Some of the people were killed and several thousand were carried off captive to Rome. Thus the beginning of Roman control in the country was marked by considerable bitterness. An additional element of vexation for the Jews was the fact that the Romans soon turned to the Idumeans to provide leadership in the land in order to forestall the threat of a Jewish revolt to gain independence. From the Roman standpoint it was a wise move, for these descendants of Esau knew the Jews far better than they did. Also, the Idumeans could be counted on to remain loyal to Rome, for it was to their advantage to do so. The most prominent of these rulers was Herod the Great, son of Antipater. His qualities of leadership were displayed when he was still a young man, and during his long reign Jewish aspirations for freedom were held in check as the country grew more prosperous in spite of Roman taxation. At the same time, population kept rising during this era of peace. Herod had a large family, several of whom are mentioned in the New Testament.

After returning to Italy, Pompey joined with Caesar and Crassus to form the First Triumvirate. The three men hoped to consolidate their power at the expense of the Senate. Crassus lost his life, however, and Caesar, after a falling out with Pompey, marched on Rome to seize the reins of government. The Senate decided to throw in its lot with Pompey, which necessitated its flight from Rome. Pompey was killed in 48 B.C., leaving Caesar as sole dictator. The Senate, though not abolished, now had a secondary role in affairs of state.

Caesar is particularly important for an understanding of Roman-Jewish relations. An initial agreement had been made by the Romans with Simon, the Maccabean ruler in the second century B.C., guaranteeing religious liberty to all Jews in Roman territory. This agreement was now underscored and enlarged by a decree of Caesar that made this recognition perpetual. His decree was honored by later Roman rulers with the exception of Caligula. He granted other privileges to the Jews as well: the right of Sabbath observance, freedom from military service (since this could conflict with Sabbath observance), the right to maintain the temple and observe the stated festivals, and provisions to safeguard their Scriptures against such abuses as had marked the campaign of Antiochus Epiphanes to destroy Judaism. The Jews were expected to revere the head of the Roman state but not required to worship him, and they were excused from participation in pagan religious observances.

Apparently Caesar was fully aware that it was in the interest of Rome to avoid antagonizing the Jews. For one thing, they had already demonstrated their patriotism and readiness to give their lives in defense of their faith. Furthermore, they were now divided into two groups, the Palestinian

Jews and those in the Diaspora, but they remained united by such ties as the law, the Sabbath, the synagogue, the temple, the annual festivals, circumcision, and the dietary laws. This meant that if the Jews in the homeland became disaffected, their brethren in the Dispersion might also make trouble for Rome. The situation was particularly touchy in the east, where a large community of Jews had remained in Babylon when their brethren returned to the land of their fathers. If their descendants should turn against Rome and link up with the Parthians, a people who had recently come into prominence along the eastern flank of the empire, Rome would have its hands full. So it was politic to placate the Jews as much as possible.

Before resuming our account of external events, it is well at this point to consider the Jewish Dispersion. Several causes operated to effect the scattering of this nation: divine action designed to chasten the covenant people for their disobedience (hence the Assyrian and Babylonian captivities, leaving many of them in the lands to which they had been removed); deliberate transplantation by hellenistic rulers, such as the removal of two thousand families from Babylon and the eastern regions to Lydia and Phrygia; the taking of prisoners in time of war, notably Pompey's transfer of thousands to Rome after his capture of Jerusalem; and voluntary emigration to other lands where it was easier to make a living than in Palestine. Many flocked to Syria and Egypt in post-Alexandrian times.

The Dispersion was widespread. Agrippa's letter to Caligula when the latter was emperor reads as follows:

> As for the holy city, I must say what befits me to say. While she, as I have said, is my native city, she is also the mother city not of one country, Judaea, but of most of the others in virtue of the colonies sent out at divers times to the neighbouring lands, Egypt, Phoenicia, the part of Syria called the Hollow and the rest as well, and the lands lying far apart, Pamphylia, Cilicia, most of Asia up to Bithynia and the corners of Pontus, similarly also into Europe, Thessaly, Boeotia, Macedonia, Aetolia, Attica, Argos, Corinth and most of the best parts of Peloponnese. And not only are the mainlands full of Jewish colonies but also the most highly esteemed of the islands, Euboea, Cyprus, Crete. I say nothing of the countries beyond the Euphrates, for except for a small part they all, Babylon and of the other satrapies those where the land within their confines is highly fertile, have Jewish inhabitants.[1]

Again, Josephus gives the testimony of Strabo the geographer: "This people has already made its way into every city, and it is not easy to find any place in the habitable world which has not received this nation and in which it has not made its power felt."[2] The evidence from inscriptions points in the same direction—and since it was the Jewish habit to take Greek names, this evidence is probably even more extensive than it appears on the surface. Luke's account of Paul's missionary activities indicates that it was rare to find a city without a synagogue (see Acts 9:2; 15:21). Acts 2:9–11 indicates several other areas inhabited by Jews prior to the day of Pentecost that marked the beginning of the church.

Estimates of the number of Jews in the Dispersion vary considerably, from about four million to six million in New Testament times. One thing is certain: there were more Jews in the Dispersion than in the homeland. Population increase following the captivity period was due primarily to two factors. One was natural growth, since the Jews often had large families, in keeping with their understanding of the will of God, and they did not expose their infants. The other factor was their proselytizing activity, in which they were often successful, despite the disfavor they incurred among pagans who resented their exclusive manner of life, which kept them apart from non-Jews. To balance this, however, was their high view of God, their solid morality, their domestic peace and happiness, and their reliable, industrious character. Hellenistic rulers found it to their advantage to have communities of Jews in their realms, for in that era of great flux and jostling of cultures these people proved to be a stabilizing influence.

They were not always appreciated by their neighbors, to be sure. Resentment was aroused because the Jewish faith was a permitted religion that carried with it the right to maintain the temple in Jerusalem by paying an annual per capita tax as well as by making gifts. The sight of large sums being siphoned from local communities to be sent to Judea was hardly welcome. Also the Jews had the right of jurisdiction over their own members, so that they did not appear in the courts unless they became involved with pagans. At some places they were given local citizenship (e.g., at Alexandria and Antioch), which brought some discontent to the non-Jewish masses in these centers. In fact, we read of attempts at Antioch to have Jewish citizenship revoked.[3] On the whole, the Jews in the Dispersion were well behaved. As a minority group they realized that it was to their advantage not to give provocation to their adversaries. In the homeland, however, where they predominated, they could prove obstreperous, giving the representatives of Rome (e.g., Pilate) some anxious moments.

Conspiracy against Caesar led to his assassination in 44 B.C., but the conspirators had to flee when Mark Antony, by the force of his funeral oration, aroused the wrath of the public against them. This opened the way for the formation of the Second Triumvirate, consisting of Antony, Lepidus, and Octavian, the nephew of Caesar. Eventually Octavian became dominant, just as Caesar had been in the First Triumvirate. The Idumeans who controlled Palestine were quick to shift their loyalty to the new masters. Although the Jews tried to persuade Antony to jettison the Idumeans, he refused. This led the Jews to revive efforts to regain their independence by rallying around their Hasmonean leaders, but Herod, with Antony's support, was declared king of Judea by the Roman Senate and went on to crush the independence movement and establish himself as ruler of the land and vassal of Rome. Although he rebuilt the temple in Jerusalem, he remained a pagan at heart, more intent on pleasing the Romans than pleasing his subjects.

During Herod's reign Roman affairs took a drastic turn in a new direction. Antony, infatuated with Cleopatra of Egypt, allowed himself to be drawn into her ambitious scheme to set up an independent kingdom, a scheme in which he and the forces under his command would be used to gain control of the eastern Mediterranean area. Realizing the danger, Octavian marshaled a large force and defeated the opposition. Antony and Cleopatra committed suicide and the Egyptian kingdom was added to the Roman domain.

Now the strong man in the situation, Octavian sensed the necessity of bringing an end to the rivalries and divisions that had weakened Rome for a century. As the conqueror he was able to assume control of the state, including the military, although the Senate was not abolished. He was wise enough to retain some of the forms of republican government in order to obviate a charge of despotism. His assumption of the title Augustus, which held sacred associations for the Romans, probably expedited the growing acceptance of the view that he was worthy of being accorded honor as a divine figure. People were grateful for the peace that he had brought to society. These developments brought new opportunities for the spread of the gospel, which was soon to be launched in Palestine. It was under Augustus that the decree went out to enroll the people for taxing purposes, which in the providence of God effected the fulfillment of Scripture that the Messiah would be born in Bethlehem (see Luke 2:1–7).

The reign of Augustus was in many ways a golden age, marked not only by peace but also by the construction of roads and buildings, the fostering of trade, and the development of administration throughout the empire. The provinces were divided into senatorial and imperial jurisdictions. The former group, forming an inner ring around Italy, were ruled by proconsuls responsible to the Senate, their normal term of office being a year. Gallio was such an official (see Acts 18:12). The imperial provinces, lying toward the frontiers of the empire, were under the jurisdiction of the emperor, who governed them through legates. Most of the legions, also under his control, were concentrated in these provinces, guarding the borders. Judea was an imperial area, whether under a client king, as during the Herodian era, or under a governor during other periods (see Luke 3:1).

At Herod's death his son Archelaus succeeded him, but there was trouble over the succession. Antipas, another son of Herod, who received Galilee and Perea as his domain, was dissatisfied because an earlier will had given him Judea. Both men pleaded their cause before Augustus, who retained Herod's final disposition. Subsequently a delegation of Jews asked that direct Roman rule be instituted over their land. This finally took place in A.D. 6, when popular feeling against Archelaus ran so high that Augustus banished him. Henceforth, except for the brief reign of Herod Agrippa I, Judea was ruled by a procurator who had his seat of government at Caesarea (see Acts 23:23–24). After years of Herodian rule the Jews were convinced that they were better off under direct Roman control, in which case they supposed they would be given more freedom to pursue their religion and their way of life. But in the long run the Jews did not gain, for a series of governors distinguished mostly by cruelty and rapacity tried the patience of the nation beyond endurance.

There was a hint of trouble when Judas of Galilee led a revolt in A.D. 6 against the enrollment of the Jews as Roman provincials and the inevitable taxation that would follow. The revolt was crushed, but it planted seeds of bitterness and determination to resist the tyranny of Rome. From this incident grew the Zealot party, which advocated the use of force to regain independence. The tide was moving strongly in this direction during the ministry of Jesus, creating a problem for him: he found it necessary to refuse to identify himself with this movement even though his refusal was bound to make enemies for him among his own people. He had to choose whether he wanted to be regarded as a traitor or a patriot. He made his attitude clear in the incident of the tribute money (Matt. 22:15–22).

The Roman administration in Palestine was obliged to keep continually on the alert for possible uprisings that might challenge its authority and bring on open revolution. In time, some of the Zealots began to resort to terrorism. These were known as Sicarii—dagger-wielding assassins. Recall that when Paul was set upon by the Jews in Jerusalem and was rescued by the Roman guard stationed at the castle of Antonia, he was mistaken by the chiliarch for a revolutionary (Acts 21:38). Although it is customary to date the outbreak of the Jewish War against Rome at A.D. 66, a virtual state of war existed for years prior to that time.

The Herods understood the Jews better than the Romans did and sometimes counseled Rome as to the course to be taken, but not all Romans were prepared to accept advice. A notable example is the emperor Caligula. The Roman governor in Egypt, Flaccus by name, became obsessed by the notion that it would please Caligula if he were to embark on a campaign of persecuting the Jews. When Agrippa, who had not yet come to power in Palestine as Herod Agrippa I, visited Egypt, he was publicly insulted. Moreover, an image of Caligula was brought into the synagogues, touching off a riot as the mob turned on the Jews, who naturally resented and resisted any attempt to make them acknowledge the divinity of a man, even though he be the ruler of the empire. Venting their dislike on the Jews, the mob killed and plundered. Caligula, apparently more displeased with the Jews than with the pagans, and moved by an insane egotism, determined to test the loyalty of Jews in their homeland by introducing his statue there. The Roman governor tried to delay the execution of this plan, knowing that the Jewish nation would prefer mass extermination to compulsory idolatry. Agrippa used his friendship with Caligula to persuade him to countermand the order.

Agrippa's part in this episode put him in high favor with the Jews. This grandson of Herod the Great may well have been the best liked of all the Herodian clan. When Claudius succeeded Caligula, he thought well enough of Agrippa to set him over nearly all the domain once governed by his grandfather. But this interlude of kingship lasted only three years, ending with Agrippa's death (see Acts 12). After this, direct Roman rule was instituted over Palestine by means of procurators. Agrippa II, before whom Paul made his defense (see Acts 26) was a son of Agrippa I. He was given the title king as a courtesy, but his territory was limited.

Of the remaining governors sent by Rome to Judea, one of the most infamous was Felix. The book of Acts is in agreement with other sources concerning his character and administration. He was shameless in accepting bribes, but got nowhere with his prisoner Paul on this score. Festus was a man of higher caliber, but the damage done by his predecessors was irremediable. The Jews were disgusted and permanently alienated. Events moved rapidly toward a break with Rome and the terrible carnage that engulfed the land, especially in the siege and fall of Jerusalem in A.D. 70.

Sporadic revolts against Rome continued in later years, notably the one under Bar Cochba in the second century. These attempts at resistance were inspired by the hope of supernatural intervention on behalf of the people of God, but all these messianic pretenders perished and their followers with them. Judaism had to learn to accommodate itself to the status quo and seek consolation in its spiritual heritage. The effort to do so became enshrined in the Talmudic literature of later centuries.

In *The Book of Acts in History* (1955), H. J. Cadbury performs a service by pointing out the various strands that intermingle in this Lukan work. The Christian movement began in a strictly Jewish setting, yet even here an element of Greek influence is discernible (the Hellenists in the Jerusalem church). In the Gentile mission of Paul the setting is hellenistic, with Jews in a minority and Roman elements cropping out here and there. But the Jewish, Greek, and Roman elements are crowned by still another factor, the Christian, which adapts itself to these elements but transcends them. The distinctive ingredient is the Christian. The rest constitute the foil. Yet the success of Christianity owed much to the providential preparation found in Jewish teaching and hopes, in Greek language and culture, and in Roman peace, justice, administration, and communication.

2. THE RELIGIOUS BACKGROUND

Our chief concern here is to deal with pagan religion as found among the Greeks and Romans, although developments among the Hebrews should be taken into consideration also.

Whereas with the Hebrews religion and philosophy were so blended as to make a separation between them virtually impossible (religion was an integral part of their view of the world), this was not true of the Greeks. They derived their worldview from philosophy, but their religion was part of their relation to the city-state. This changed somewhat in the hellenistic period, when religion tended to become a more personal thing. But the separation between religion and philosophy is important for the student of Greek life, for it means that ethics and morals belonged to the field of philosophy rather than religion. This tended to produce what F. J. A. Hort has called the fatal chasm between religion and morality among the Greeks, and it constituted a serious limitation on the Greek character. One can understand, then, how Greek philosophy could so powerfully influence the course of civilization while Greek religion had little effect.

The type of religion disclosed in the Homeric poems is familiar. We meet the Olympian deities, headed by Zeus, mythological beings more powerful than men yet possessing all the foibles that belong to human nature. They can be envious, angry, vindictive, or immoral as occasion offers. Only Zeus seems to maintain strict justice and impartiality. In the struggle over Troy, the gods are ranged on both sides of the conflict. Human beings may have a rather precarious existence, for their appeals to one deity as a kind of patron may make them the target of hostile action on the part of another. Every undertaking must have the blessing of the gods, and care is taken to propitiate them by appropriate sacrifices. Religion is a businesslike affair; the gods are sought after for the benefits they can bestow. Undeniably this anthropomorphic depiction of the gods confers on them a naive simplicity that charms the reader, but on the side of ethics and spirituality there is much to be desired. Then, too, the distribution of functions among the gods makes the pantheon a practical necessity, forestalling ready receptivity to the idea of the unity of God. The worship of the Olympians "could offer no real explanation of the mystery of life, no sense of purpose in human existence, no real comfort in adversity; nor did it provide an incentive for conduct, nor an assurance of immortality."[4]

Something should be said about two figures whose influence was nevertheless considerable in the lives of their devotees. One is Apollo, reputed son of Zeus, whose cult centered in Delphi, where the priestess of the oracle gave guidance to those who sought it. As late as the time of Plutarch, who belongs to the same period as the apostles, people were building temples to this deity. Plutarch himself held a priesthood at Delphi. In the classical period and even into the hellenistic age there were groups of people in the various Greek communities who were known as interpreters or exegetes of Apollo. If we ask, then, what human need this cult endeavored to fill, we are obliged to say that Apollo was the prophetic voice designed to provide guidance for frail humanity. In the context of the New Testament this need was supplied, of course, first by John the

Baptist, then by Jesus, and in the early church by those with the spirit of prophecy. This is not to say that the Greek phenomenon and the biblical are on the same basis. As with pagan religion in general, there is a tendency, at times almost diabolical, to manipulate the needs and aspirations of men in the interest of those who dominate the cult. "The more widespread and the more deeply ingrained was the uneasy dread of an invisible all-powerful spirit-world, the greater became the authority of the oracle that alone could give guidance in this confused turmoil of ghostly activities."[5]

The other figure to be noted is Asklepios (variously spelled). He is the great healer deity of Greek religion. Although the breakup of the city-states that began with Alexander's conquest of the Greek peninsula brought a new importance to individual life, it also created a greater sense of loneliness and personal need than people had felt before when they were by birth and experience a part of a close-knit community. More play was given to the emotions. A keener appreciation of the suffering of man and of the need to heal it emerged. Medical science was fairly well advanced, but it did not hold the field unchallenged. There was widespread belief in faith healing, and the healer par excellence was the god Asklepios.

The Asklepios cult was strongest in Epidaurus, a community on the Saronic Gulf southeast of Corinth. Patients usually came to sleep in the temple there in the hope of being granted a dream of oracular nature that would give direction for their cure. How much manipulation and fraud entered into the situation is difficult to say, but at any rate many people felt that they were healed or greatly helped. When confronted by testimonies of this kind, the Christian response was usually that cures could be admitted but were to be attributed to demonic agency.

We mention Asklepios here in order to emphasize that the ancients were alive to the desirability of a salvation that would include healing for the body. We can understand, then, that the ministry of our Lord and after him of the apostles had a double-edged appeal, offering something both to the body and to the spirit, a service to the whole person. But it should be noted that neither Jesus nor the missionaries of the apostolic age advertised themselves as healers when they came into a community. As a rule, the gospel was preached first.

Homer had a place for fate as well as for the gods, though no clear guidelines to distinguish them. Later on, the tragic poets disclosed a strong pessimistic outlook because of their acceptance of the doctrine of fate. It is even daringly suggested that Zeus himself is subject to this rather impersonal power. Among the philosophical schools the Stoics were notable for their endorsement of this doctrine. What the divine being determines will surely follow. The only options open to men are compliance, which will bring its measure of satisfaction, or resistance, which can bring only a state of wretchedness.

In the works of Aeschylus and Sophocles there is an awareness of human failure and corresponding punishment. A favorite theme is the folly of insolent behavior (*hybris*), which is sure to bring retribution (*nemesis*) from the gods. But emphasis on man's sin was not congenial to the Greek outlook, which was one of indifference and even levity. It is no wonder that Paul had his difficulties in trying to inculcate simple, basic Christian morality in the Gentile churches. Their Greek inheritance had not provided much preparation for such teaching.

A strain quite different from the popular mythology comes to the fore in the worship of Dionysus, the god of wine and frenzied celebration associated with Thrace and northern Asia Minor. It is generally assumed, though the matter cannot be stated positively, that Orphism was a reformation and refinement of the wilder Bacchic type of this religion. Orphism taught that the soul was imprisoned in a material body, necessitating ascetic practices aided by purgatorial purification after death. This movement influenced Pythagoreanism, but did not become a missionary force. In fact, no phase of Greek religion succeeded in doing that. In the hellenistic age, when men were so intent on becoming Greek in thought and custom and language, the poverty of Greek religion was so great that it did not spread to other lands along with the cultural infusion. Instead, hellenistic rulers adopted local worships and faiths. As Tarn observes, "Had Ptolemy I enthroned Zeus in Alexandria and persecuted Osiris, Egypt would have fought but would have understood; that the Ptolemies built temples to Egyptian deities meant to Egyptians not toleration but weakness—the invader had no faith in his own gods."[6]

By the time of Alexander the old popular Greek religion had long since lost its hold, eclipsed by the rise of the scientific temper, which in turn was the result of the work of the early philosophers, who were physicists and materialists. And just as popular religion collapsed under this attack and was replaced by skepticism, so the political failure of Greece, revealed in the conquest of the city-states by Macedonia, effected the virtual collapse of the state religion. If the cultus could not insure the continued freedom of the city-state, it was judged no longer worthy of perpetuation. The state religion was largely ceremonial anyway. Understandably the result was a gravitation to a type of religion that was more personal and would satisfy individual needs. So we are confronted with the so-called mystery religions.

Although Greece did have its own native mystery religions, notably the Eleusinian, in the hellenistic age, there was also a great influx of such religions from the Orient. The considerable travel of those days brought foreigners and their religions with them to the Greek cities. This type of worship became popular throughout the Greco-Roman world, the Roman policy of religious freedom facilitating its spread. As these resident aliens banded together to observe their peculiar rites, other people developed a curiosity about them that often blossomed into active interest, since these cults seemed to offer deliverance from the ills of life. Moreover, men in the hellenistic age were gripped by the fear of death (see Heb. 2:15) and were ready to turn to anything that offered the prospect of a blessed immortality.

The best-known and most widely adopted of these mystery cults was the worship of Isis and Osiris, which had its origin in Egypt. But the motif common to the cults as a whole was the centrality of the experience of death and resurrection on the part of the god or goddess who dominated the cult. Through initiation the individual could look forward to being so identified with the deity as to attain a blessed immortality. But this was an expensive process, which meant that the rank and file had to be content with such ceremonies as were open to them short of initiation.

As to their basic character, the mystery religions were nature cults intended to dramatize the annual decay of vegetation and the revival of life in the spring. This annual repetition of the death-life motif stands quite apart from the once-for-all character of the death and resurrection of Christ. The mythological character of the cult deities also placed a great gulf between them and Jesus Christ, an actual historical person. Furthermore, Christianity does not countenance a doctrine of absorption into deity. The line between the Lord God and his people is never erased, even in eternity. It must be granted that early Christian teaching made use of certain terms (including *mystery*) that were current in the mystery religions, but such borrowing of religious terminology signifies little in light of the intrinsic differences involved.

Any survey of religion in the hellenistic age should include consideration of the Hermetic writings. These derive their name from the Greek god Hermes, the closest Greek counterpart to the Egyptian god Thoth, the actual subject of these tractates. Thoth is characterized as the very, very great one, the revealer of truth. The most prevalent view concerning these writings is that they comprise a mixture of native Egyptian lore, Oriental mysticism, Greek philosophy, and even Judaism. This appraisal is in line with the fact that the most prominent feature of religion in the hellenistic period is syncretism. Fairweather comments, "The leading notes in the Hermetic faith are those of illumination, regeneration, and deification."[7] The principal tractate is called *Poimandres,* which is understood to mean "the mind of the sovereignty." One of the earlier workers in the field, R. Reitzenstein, wrote a book by this title in which he deals with the Hermetic materials. Walter Scott and C. H. Dodd are two of the later researchers. The essence of the movement was an emphasis on knowledge as the key to the religious life. Little cultic development is observable, since stress fell on personal intellectual aspiration. These writings date from a time somewhat later than that of the New Testament, so they should not be thought of as exercising a formative influence on the Christian faith, but they do help to provide an understanding of the climate in which people sought meaning in an intellectual approach to the spiritual world.

Hermetism is one phase of a large and somewhat diverse movement characteristic of the hellenistic period that bears the label Gnosis or Gnosticism. This attempt to yoke philosophy and religion began to challenge the church in the first century as it took on Christian elements. In the following century it became an even more serious threat. Modern man finds it somewhat difficult to comprehend the type of thought associated with Gnosticism. It contains a worldview that is quite different from ours. The following statement by R. McL. Wilson provides a helpful summary.

> The Hellenistic world considered the universe to be a system of concentric spheres, rising above and around the earth. Each was ruled by a minor divine being associated with one of the planets, and human destiny was believed to depend in some way upon these powers. The Platonic distinction between the ideal world and that perceptible to the senses was widely current; the ideal world to which man really belongs— or at least to which some men really belong—was set above the spheres, where also the transcendent God had his abode. The Stoic doctrine that the soul was a spark of the divine fire enclosed in matter was also prevalent, and the combination of all these doctrines led to the conclusion that the soul was essentially a fragment of the divine imprisoned in an alien medium, from which it sought to gain release. Return to its true abode in the higher regions was secured either by purification from fleshly lusts, by ascetic practices, by regulation of the whole life in accordance with the dictates of the higher element within, or by a magic knowledge of the names of the ruling powers and of the passwords which were the keys to unlock the gates which barred the way, or by a mystic vision and enlightenment which raised the fortunate recipient above the limits of human nature and made him a god himself. Sometimes there is some idea of a redeemer sent from above to lead the soul upon its journey; elsewhere man is left to himself to struggle upwards towards the light by holy living. Sometimes the soul is condemned to endure a round of reincarnations in atonement for past errors, or again there is as in Stoicism a reabsorption of the several sparks into the one divine fire from which they came.[8]

In this statement one notices that in contrast to the fairly uniform worldview that governed men of the period there was wide diversity as to the method to be employed in extricating oneself from the toils of human existence under the oppressive control of higher powers. This diversity runs the gamut from Hermetism, which might be described as a kind of intellectual mysticism, down to astrology and magic. The book of Acts testifies to the prevalence of this lowest aspect of hellenistic religion (see 8:9ff.; 13:6ff.; 16:16ff.; 19:18ff.). In the use of magic, instead of an approach to God through prayer, there is a resort to various devices regarded as sufficiently potent to compel the deity to act according to the dictates of one's own will. It was thought that by the use of secret words, especially in the combination of strange syllables, one could tap the mysteries of the divine realm and open the resources of divine power. It is curious to find in the magical papyri of Egypt, along with the names of various Oriental deities used in these formulae, the names of Israel's God—Yahweh, Sabaoth, Kurios, and the like—another testimony to the syncretism of the period. But for the most part the formulae are made up of what seem to us mere nonsense syllables. The claims made in the papyri are high-sounding—guaranteed to win the affection of any fair lady, to ward off disease, to bring success to a business venture, and so on. They begin to sound like a patent medicine advertisement. Sometimes there are prayers and hymns in these papyri, attesting a readiness to glean from any source that might prove efficacious in solving the problems of life.

It should be noted that amid the welter of commingled religious ideas that formed the mosaic of hellenistic religion there was at times a reaching out for a more unitary conception of God. This groping toward monotheism was aided by the collapse of the old Homeric mythology and encouraged by the abler Greek philosophers, especially Plato. But it could not be expected to have the clarity and nobility of the Old Testament presentation of God that was founded on revelation. Its limitation is well stated by Otto Piper:

> Hellenistic civilization . . . was built upon an idea of man, according to which his individual life was all-important. . . . While theoretically it held monotheistic views, belief in one supreme principle was practically only the acceptance of a philosophical theorem, which was not infrequently coupled with all kinds of superstitions. Similarly, the insight into the moral aspect of truth was interpreted in a humanistic way. The idea of a God-given law was deemed to be incompatible with man's freedom. Even the highest type of morality, namely, Stoicism, was therefore a glorification of man's natural existence rather than an attempt to raise man above nature and to place him directly before God.[9]

In this survey, only a brief statement can be made on Roman religion. In the early days of Rome, when the community was agricultural, Numa was the deity, the name being derived from a traditional lawgiver. There were various household deities such as the Genius, representing the lifeblood of the family; Lar (pl. Lares), definable as the luck of the family; the Penates, or embodiment of the storehouse; and Vesta, the spirit of the hearth. The emphasis fell on the family unit rather than on the individual. In line with this, reverence for ancestors was a powerful factor in Roman life. This subordination of the individual to the larger unit was also evident in public life. The state was regarded as of far greater importance than the individual, whose good must be sacrificed, if need be, for the sake of the good of the many. W. Fairweather comments,

When a Roman went forth to battle he had always in view the protection of hearth and home. This was his watchword, and it embodied all that was most sacred to him. The ashes of his fathers were as dear to him as the temples of his gods; they *were* indeed his gods, the Lares and Penates at whose shrine his household worshipped. The reverence for his ancestors was the most deeply rooted principle in the Roman heart, the most powerful factor in Roman life.[10]

The second phase of Roman religion involved the assimilation of other religions. Greek deities were introduced through the Etruscans and the Greek colonies in Sicily. The Greek pantheon received Roman names—Zeus became Jupiter, Artemis became Diana, and so on. The names were different but the functions were the same. During the Second Punic War (218–202 B.C.) the Romans grew somewhat despondent over the successes of Hannibal, the Carthaginian general who invaded Italy and stayed for fifteen years without losing a battle. In this crisis, Oriental religions were welcomed for the help they might bring in this situation. Later on some of them were forbidden because of scandal, as in the case of the Isis cult, or because of the fear of detrimental effects on the Roman character, as in the case of the worship of Cybele. Nevertheless, this openness to other religions was extended to Judaism and Christianity as well when their turn came.

A third stage in Roman religion is associated with emperor worship, which became the crux of disagreement between Rome and the Christians. There are indications in the book of Acts, particularly in connection with Paul's ministry at Thessalonica, that the preaching of Christ as Lord was already tending to bring suspicion of disloyalty to Caesar (see Acts 17:7). Part of Luke's purpose in writing Acts, in all probability, was to show that the followers of Christ were not disloyal to the Roman government and were not a threat to the peace and unity of the empire.

There are intimations from very early times that the deification of rulers was fairly common. Its roots are not too difficult to trace. "Imperial apotheosis was the result of flattery, gratitude, policy, and historic precedent."[11] Although this was written with the Roman situation in mind, there is a biblical precedent in Nebuchadnezzar, as reported in Daniel. Another instance is the reception of Alexander the Great into the Egyptian pantheon following his conquest of Egypt. He was declared the adopted son of the god Re. His successors, the Seleucids, tried to make use of the same device. Antiochus IV, for example, took the title Epiphanes, which denoted divinity. As the power of Rome began to be felt in the east, communities seeking the protection and help of the conqueror from the west began to add to their religious venerations the worship of Rome, its spirit, or more accurately, its *tychē* or Fortune, corresponding to what the Romans spoke of as their Genius. Perhaps it could equally well be called Rome's destiny, the evident favor that providence had bestowed on this people whose armies were sweeping through much of the world and whose administration honeycombed every conquered district. It was only a step to the position that public acknowledgment of Rome's living representative as somehow worthy of divine honors was in order. And so, throughout the East, in pre-Christian times, ever and again Roman generals and proconsuls were accorded divine honors as spokesmen for mighty Rome.

After his death, Caesar was deified by official Senate decree. As already noted, Octavian was given the title *Augustus*. Other titles followed, adding to his dignity. "The emperor was even the human manifestation of Zeus, king of heaven, or Helios the sun-god."[12] Augustus appeared reluctant to accept divine honors for himself, but the more he demurred, the more he was overruled by popular demand. Perhaps this is what he secretly hoped for, and he was clever enough to realize that the best way to get it was to protest his unworthiness to receive it.

Worship of a deceased emperor had become established, but then there arose the complication of extending such honor to a living individual. To combine the two was not easy. Both phases seem to have continued side by side to some extent, but the tendency was to forget about the dead rulers as divine persons and concentrate on the living one as the exponent of the power of Rome. Emperor worship was a straightforward political expedient as far as the state was concerned, akin to the mark of the beast in the book of Revelation. To be sure, it was not an exclusive thing. Those who conformed to the imperial cult were free as private citizens to engage in whatever religion they chose. The Jews, as already noted, were in a separate category. Their obligation toward the emperor fell short of actual worship. Daily sacrifices were offered in the temple *for* him but not *to* him.

As the Christian movement became less and less Jewish in its character by reason of the influx of Gentile converts, it increasingly loomed as a threat to Rome. The death of Peter and Paul and the destruction of many other Christians in the time of Nero give a clear indication of what was to come. Rome felt it could not countenance a religion that refused to accord divine honors to its sovereign. It saw in Christianity, whose refusal to do so was especially obvious in light of the willingness of other religions to conform, a mark of singular perverseness that must be punished. Doubtless there were other factors also. Roman officials were not always well informed about this new religion, judging by Pilate, Festus, Pliny, and others, and so they were the more vulnerable to the insinuations made by enemies of the faith that Christian gatherings were the setting for awful crimes such as cannibalism and incest. The Christian proclamation of a future kingdom, universal in character, over which *their* king would preside, must have sounded dangerously competitive in Roman ears, and the predicted destruction of the present order (see, for example, 2 Pet. 3) could only be viewed as a challenge to the stability and permanence of the empire. From the time of Nero, Rome drew a distinction between Jews and Christians.

The former had a national faith; the latter claimed a universal following that knew no national boundaries. The upshot of all this was that the protection that Christianity enjoyed in its early days when it was predominantly a Jewish-Christian entity was withdrawn. The new faith was now viewed as a dangerous rival deserving suppression and extinction. But the same providence that gave it official protection under the umbrella of Judaism at the beginning, so that it could grow strong, now aided it in the fires of persecution when that protection was withdrawn.

Brief attention should be given to the situation in Judaism during the period prior to the emergence of Christianity, with an eye to the specifically religious factors. On the cultural side, as already observed, Palestinian Judaism could not isolate itself completely from hellenizing influences, but its hold on the Jewish population in matters of religion continued to be firm. In the Dispersion the Jews were under far more pressure from their environment, even though the synagogue served as as oasis in the desert of paganism. Philo admits some apostasy from Judaism in the Dispersion, dividing deserters into three groups: those who succumbed to the weakness of the flesh and sought gratification outside the restrictions of the Jewish law; those who could be classed as social climbers, people who sought a place for themselves in pagan society or in the political arena and found their Jewish inheritance a liability; and those who could be labeled free-thinkers, who desired to roam without restraint in the literature and the concepts of the pagan world, with the result that they were drawn away from the faith of their fathers. An example of the second type is Tiberius Alexander, Philo's nephew, who renounced Judaism and rose to great prominence in Egypt and then in Palestine as the aide of Titus at the siege of Jerusalem.

A modern reseacher, E. R. Goodenough, relying heavily on archeological finds (see his *Jewish Symbols in the Greco-Roman Period*), concludes that a considerable number of Jews became syncretistic from the fact that they were willing to adopt pagan symbols for their synagogues. But one should beware of reading too much into such evidence. The Jews were adept at accommodation without giving up anything vital. Harry A. Wolfson writes,

> With the example of Scripture before them they were not afraid to make use in the description of their own religion of terms used in the description of other religions, but whatever common terms they used, the difference was never blurred for them between truth and falsehood in religious belief and right and wrong in religious worship. For the understanding of the nature of Judaism throughout its history, and especially during the Hellenistic period, this twofold aspect of its attitude toward other religions is of the utmost importance. Those who seem to see evidence of religious syncretization in every use of a pagan term by a Hellenistic Jew simply overlook this one important aspect in the attitude of Judaism toward other religions.[13]

CHAPTER II

The Book of Acts

BECAUSE the history of criticism of the book of Acts is fairly complex, we will be considering it in two parts. In the first we will take up a general overview, considering the broad lines of development in this area of study. In the second part we will give special consideration to the treatment of the speeches in Acts, which have become the object of an important critical debate.

1. HISTORY OF CRITICISM: A GENERAL OVERVIEW

Although we will to some extent attempt to reconstruct and explain developments in the apostolic age, our chief concern in this section is the book of Acts itself, inasmuch as it constitutes our principal source of information on the rise and early progress of the church. A review of the history of the treatment of this subject shows that interest has periodically shifted from one critical preoccupation to the next, variously addressing such problems as authorship, date, and purpose.

Early investigators were perplexed by the unevenness of the material, which is full in some places and sketchy in others. Another problem is the virtual restriction of the account to the labors of Peter and Paul to the neglect of other apostolic figures. The heading of the book anticipates this difficulty somewhat, "Acts of the Apostles" rather than "The Acts of the Apostles" being the better attested wording. The Canon of Muratori (latter part of the second century), by using the caption "The Acts of All the Apostles," was probably making a deliberate attempt to shut the door on apocryphal Acts.

The author's omission of material has to be reckoned with, but in the very nature of the case Luke was unable to include all that happened. Selectivity was essential. With reference to the majority of the Twelve, it is possible that in the period following Pentecost there was nothing distinctive to report about them as individuals, and that they are for this reason referred to as a group (see 4:33; 6:2; 8:1; 11:1; 15:2; etc.).

Some critics have complained that Luke's summaries (6:7; 9:31; 12:24; 16:5; 19:20; 28:31) are "cover-ups" to hide lack of information. There does not seem to be any justification for such a judgment. If Luke realized that he could not report all developments, the use of summaries was the most satisfactory way to indicate the general progress of the faith without going into detail and consuming precious space.

Prior to 1835, several writers dealt with Acts and were especially interested in its purpose. Rather strangely they took the position that only one purpose could have operated in the composition of the book. If the purpose was historical, it could not have been apologetic, and vice versa. This is an arbitrary limitation to impose on an author, and it is seldom insisted on today.

In 1836 two works appeared, Karl Schrader's *The Apostle Paul* and F. C. Baur's *Paul: His Life and Works*, which set the tone of investigation for years to come. Schrader observed that the presentation of Paul and his work in Acts differs substantially from that which can be gleaned from Paul himself in his letters. Since this problem faces each generation of scholars, something should be said about it here. If Luke's account is clearly at variance with Paul's, the traditional view that Luke was his companion and colaborer becomes more difficult to accept. In his own writings Paul insists on his apostleship, bearing down particularly hard on this issue in his more controversial letters, but in Acts Luke practically ignores his apostolic rank. Again, Paul strongly opposes the legalism of the Judaizing teachers who disturbed his converts, especially in Galatia, but in Acts Luke seems to be intent on showing how loyal Paul was to Judaism, noting that he was willing to take vows upon himself (see 18:18; 21:24–26) and to circumcise Timothy (see 16:3). Also, whereas Paul in his letters magnifies the importance of the fund for the poor believers in Judea, sponsoring a strong effort among his churches, Luke practically ignores the whole matter (Acts 24:17 contains the sole reference). Then there is the item of Paul's intention to visit Spain (Rom. 15:24, 28) about which Luke is silent. It is natural that the critic should be disturbed over such matters, but they do not appear to be crucial when considered in the light of the different vantage points from which the two men wrote. Luke was concerned largely with the external phenomena rather than with the theological implications of events, though he was by no means indifferent to the latter.

Schrader detects a tendency on Luke's part to play down anything that might be offensive to Rome. There is, for instance, no account of Paul's death at the end of Acts. Schrader suggests that to have included it would have been to disturb the impression created up to this point of offical Roman toleration of Christians.

"Tendency" criticism was more highly developed in Baur's work— *tendency* meaning a particular slant on the part of an author that tends to color the facts in the case. Baur thought that the writer of Acts was guilty of this. His own interpretation of the book is an attempt to fit it into a reconstruction of the course of early church history worked out along philosophical lines. He was heavily influenced by Hegelianism and adopted its formulas for application to biblical study. Starting with a certain situation as thesis, he looked for opposing factors that would constitute the antithesis, and then sought to determine the attempted synthesis or harmonization. His conclusion was that Acts is best understood as a harmonistic work, probably written by a Paulinist who sought to show that Paul tried valiantly to minister to the Jews but was thwarted by their unrelenting opposition.

Baur also contends that the author of Acts covered over the deep rifts between Peter and Paul and between their followers, surmising the existence of this deep-seated division from the early chapters of 1 Corinthians, in which we read of those who were attached to Peter and of those who followed Paul (1:12). He sought substantiation for this idea of cleavage by appealing to Galatians 2, in which Paul is said to have publicly upbraided Peter for his conduct at Antioch in relation to Gentile believers (vv. 11ff.). In Baur's estimation, the sharper the antagonism reflected in a book (thesis and antithesis), the greater is its claim to authenticity. To support his opinion, he makes use of the Clementine literature, a series of documents emanating from the third century but which could fairly be assumed to reflect second-century tradition. Peter is the hero in these writings, and his great antagonist is Simon Magus (cf. Acts 8:9–21). Baur considered the latter to be simply a veiled allusion to Paul. He concluded that if Paul had been so bitterly hated in the second century, he could well have been hated even more in the first. But the appeal to the Clementines is ill-founded. As H. Lietzmann notes, "only quite recently have penetrating researches recognized the Clementine writings as a freely composed romance without any significance for research in the early Christian and Judaistic period."[1]

In order to argue that Acts was a harmonistic writing, Baur was forced to assume that it was composed at a late date, when the sharp antagonism between the Peter/Paul factions had died out. His reconstruction has two outstanding weaknesses. First, his effort to find basic opposition between Peter and Paul is exegetically unsound. It is clear that the two men stood shoulder to shoulder on the nature of the gospel and the issue of receiving Gentiles into the church. The real cleavage was not between Peter and Paul but between the two of them together on the one hand, and the Judaizers on the other. The Judaizers insisted that Gentile believers had to be circumcised before they could be received into Christian fellowship, that without it they could not be saved (see Acts 15:1). As already noted, Baur appeals to Galatians 2:11ff.—despite the fact that Galatians 2:1–10 makes it clear that the two apostles were in solid agreement on the gospel and sealed this agreement by extending the right hand of fellowship.

One might ask, however, whether Baur did not have a point, since Galatians 2:11 does indicate disagreement. Could this mean that there was underlying friction despite the earlier agreement? Baur does not ask why this disagreement flared up. All he does is to imply that the understanding recorded in Galatians 2:1-10 was a half-hearted affair on the part of the Jerusalem apostles.[2] One can readily gather from Paul's account that when Peter was rebuked for the inconsistency between the convictions he expressed in Jerusalem and his conduct in Antioch, he acknowledged that he had done wrong. He made no defense. It should be noted also that in the Corinthian situation Paul did not hold Peter responsible for the faction that insisted on rallying behind his name.

The second weakness in Baur's reconstruction is his assumption that the collision between Judaizers and Paulinists continued for a long time after Paul's death. There simply is no evidence for such an assumption. It can be granted, however, that Judaizing activity did not readily cease, despite the decision of the Jerusalem Council (see Acts 15)—for evidence of which, see Philippians 3:2-3.

Researches into patristic literature carried on by Zahn and Lightfoot also seriously damage the credibility of Baur's position. These men establish that the composition of the books of the New Testament could not have been strung out through the first and second centuries, since patristic sources often show knowledge of the books in question at a time prior to the date suggested by the Tübingen school.

In fact, Baur's theory has been rejected by men on both sides of the theological fence. Conservatives have insisted that Acts was not written from a partisan viewpoint. On the other hand, Bruno Bauer, a radical, has suggested that Baur was not radical enough, because he accepted certain of Paul's epistles as authentic when he should have rejected all of them. Bauer held that Acts has more claim to be considered historical than the epistles because it presents a gradual and reasonable development and contains a more faithful picture of Paul than the epistles do!

The greatest weakening of the Tübingen hypothesis, however, comes from Albrecht Ritschl, who had been Baur's disciple. His position, as we have noted earlier, is that the Old Catholic Church was characterized by legalism, that it viewed Christianity as a new law—which is understandable in light of the influence of the Old Testament on the church, plus the practice and teaching of Jesus (see Matt. 5:17). The Master did not set aside the law but allowed his followers to come to a proper understanding of its role as they were guided by the Spirit through the apostles. According to Ritschl, the legalistic party actually became a distinctly minor factor and Jewish Christianity faded into insignificance by the time of the Old Catholic Church, so that legalistic pressure from such a source could not have accounted for much in the shaping of the church of the latter part of the second century. Rather, he argues, this church was the result of the rise of Gentile Christianity, but a type that had lost much of the original touch of Paul. By that time the church was unable to understand Paul and his advocacy of freedom from the law, and so it drifted into a practical legalism.

Ritschl's view of Acts naturally became more favored than that of Baur. He saw that the conflict was not between Peter and Paul, but between the two apostles and the legalists.

During the latter part of the nineteenth century criticism moved further and further from the extreme position of Baur and the Tübingen school. In Pfleiderer, Holtzmann, and Jülicher the general point of view one finds with regard to Acts is not that of tendency criticism—namely, that the author consciously perpetrated a fiction—but rather that the author unconsciously introduced fiction into his narrative. Holtzmann puts it this way: "Where, according to the Tübingen criticism, the author of Acts *would* not see, according to the newer interpretation he *could* not see."[3] Though the later critics give up the philosophy behind the Tübingen reconstruction, they tend to retain a late date for the book, maintaining that it was written so long after the events it records that a faithful account could not be expected. This is a somewhat condescending approach: the writer, poor fellow, did the best he could, but the circumstances were against him.

A change in the approach to Acts is discernible early in the twentieth century, largely due to the labors of Harnack in Germany and Sir William Ramsay in Britain. Harnack worked particularly in the area of literary criticism, touching philology and sources, and giving considerable attention to matters of date and authorship. He finally came to the conclusion that Acts was written by Luke while Paul was still a prisoner at Rome. McGiffert finds fault with Harnack on the ground that his earlier writings on Acts allow for inaccuracies that he attributes to the distance between Paul and the time of the writer, but when he shifts to the earlier date for Acts he leaves himself without any such basis on which to handle historical problems—and that as a result he glosses over them rather than facing them. Harnack's work in the Lukan writings still has considerable value, especially in the area of philology (e.g., his study of Luke's medical terms).

Before turning to the contribution of Ramsay, we should say a word about J. B. Lightfoot, a leading British scholar whose labors in the area of the early church, reflected in his commentaries on Paul's epistles and in various essays, cut the ground from beneath the Tübingen hypothesis. As J. W. Hunkin puts it, "By a more thorough exegesis, and by a more faithful adherence to the actual sources, Lightfoot constructed a picture of the development of the early Church which was plainly more reliable than anything the Tübingen school had been able to produce."[4] Lightfoot did some masterly work in the Apostolic Fathers as well as in the New Testament.

Sir William Ramsay's research is diversified, but it lies principally in the area of archeology and geography as well as in the history of the hellenistic era. As in the case of Harnack, he started out heavily prejudiced against the book of Acts as a reliable account of Christian beginnings. He finished up with an almost idolizing devotion to Luke. In his student days he accepted without question the conclusions of Baur. What changed his mind was his own diligent research in the Near East. We have his statement of the change of attitude concerning Acts that resulted:

> The present writer, starting with the confident assumption that the book was fabricated in the middle of the second century, and studying it to see what light it could throw on the state of society in Asia Minor, was gradually driven to the conclusion that it must have been written in the first century and with admirable knowledge. It plunges one into the atmosphere and the circumstances of the first century; it is out of harmony with the circumstances and spirit of the second century.[5]

More recent study in Acts by those steeped in the critical tradition has been marked by a less favorable attitude toward the book. One finds the criticism that Harnack's work was hurried and ill-considered, and that Ramsay became almost partisan in his devotion to Luke. Though the five-volume set entitled *The Beginnings of Christianity* is the work of several people, and so one cannot speak of its having a uniformity of attitude on crucial questions, the general position of its authors appears to be that Acts has marks of carelessness in its composition, that the discrepancies between it and Paul's acknowledged writings are too numerous and too serious to be passed over lightly, and that even the "we" sections bear marks of having been utilized by someone other than the author of these diary notes. So we end up with an unknown author writing sometime around the close of the first century. D. W. Riddle, writing in *The Study of the Bible Today and Tomorrow* (ed. H. R. Willoughby), advocates giving up the attempt to harmonize Acts and the Pauline letters, insisting that the latter must be accorded the place of authority. If the book of Acts corroborates the epistles, well and good, but if they are silent on a certain matter, we should not assume that the information provided by Acts is necessarily sound. Riddle's position relegates Acts to an entirely subordinate position in relation to the Pauline data. A judgment regarding this assessment must wait until we have considered the historical value of Acts.

More recently two German scholars have made significant contributions to the study of Acts. In 1951 Martin Dibelius published a series of essays (subsequently translated into English under the title *Studies in the Acts of the Apostles*) in which he notes that Acts is different from the Gospel according to Luke in that the author stood on different ground: he did not have material to draw upon, to edit and arrange in the same way he had used Mark and Q in producing his Gospel. Having no predecessor for the period covered by Acts, he was obliged to gather such material as was available from various quarters and add to it his own contribution. So Dibelius finds two strands running through Acts, which may be distinguished by the terms *tradition* and *composition*. It is the latter element that originated with Luke, and it shows up especially in the speeches sprinkled through the book. As Dibelius construes the matter, Luke is not so much a historian as a preacher telling his own generation what he thinks it needs to hear in the messages purporting to come from Peter, Paul, and others. This viewpoint has become influential, especially in Germany, and has colored much of the work done on Acts in recent years.

Following closely on the heels of Dibelius and sympathetic to his general position came Hans Conzelmann, whose book *Die Mitte der Zeit* (1954) was translated in 1960 under the title *The Theology of St. Luke.* Whereas Dibelius emphasizes Luke's role as preacher, Conzelmann stresses his contribution as a theologian. It is his contention that the delay in the Parousia of Jesus was a decisive factor in shaping Luke's thinking, apparently leading him to alter the primitive eschatology of the church so as to enable it to accept its position in the world and carry on its work of evangelism, content to let the end come in accordance with the wisdom of God. As previously noted, Conzelmann finds three stages prior to the arrival of the *eschaton:* (1) the law and the prophets, terminating in the person and work of John the Baptist; (2) the ministry of Jesus; and (3) the ministry of the church in the present age. He understands the ministry of Jesus to be related to the end in the following way:

> The truth is that in the life of Jesus in the center of the story of salvation a picture is given of the future time of salvation—a picture that is now the ground of our hope: his life is an event which procures for us forgiveness and the Spirit, and thereby entrance into a future salvation. Yet this in no way alters the fact that the period of Jesus, like the present, is not yet the End. The Good News is not that God's kingdom has come near, but that the life of Jesus provides the foundation for the hope of the future Kingdom. Thus the nearness of the kingdom has become a secondary factor.[6]

A difficulty with Conzelmann's treatment is his failure to demonstrate that the so-called delay of the Parousia was actually a problem. This should be demonstrated rather than assumed. Furthermore, Acts 1:1 makes a clear-cut distinction between the period of Jesus' ministry and the period of the church's ministry precarious. The teaching of Jesus contains elements both of imminence and of a required process—the unfolding of redemption history.

Mention should be made also of Ernst Haenchen, whose commentary on Acts appeared in 1959 and was translated into English in 1971. He stresses not only the importance of eschatology but also the concept of the Gentile mission which occupies such a large place in Acts. By the time Luke wrote, the Gentile character of the church was apparent, but at the beginning it was a Jewish-Christian movement. How is the shift to be explained? Luke seeks to show (in line with his basic understanding of the outlines of God's plan for the salvation of his people—what we moderns have come to call *Heilsgeschichte*) that this was the will of God for the New Israel and that the apostles carried out this shift to Gentile predominance

under divine leading. Haenchen thinks that Luke was not wholly success-
ful, for he was obliged to grant that the real source of inspiration for the
Gentile mission came not from the apostles but from the Hellenists.
Haenchen, like Baur, feels that Luke has glossed over the element of
conflict within the church itself on this matter of the acceptance of the
Gentiles.

We have referred to Baur and the Tübingen school. It is refreshing to
discover that a more recent voice from this institution warns about extremes
in criticism. Martin Hengel states:

> In our business we all too often come up against the limits of "historical-
> critical" work. Furthermore, when it is wrongly applied, this work does
> not revive past events, but dissolves them in the clouds of vague hypoth-
> esis. Sometimes it would be more appropriate here to talk of an unhistor-
> ical-uncritical method. Awareness of his own limitations and the constant
> lack of source material should therefore make the historian modest, and
> always open to correction in his attempts at reconstruction. However, he
> should not become a sceptic, since the texts with which he is dealing as
> a theologian and a New Testament scholar resist destructive scepticism
> as much as they resist unbridled fantasy. He has to approach them in a
> responsible fashion, in the awareness that the evidence about Jesus and
> earliest Christianity which has been entrusted to him conveys a power
> which has shaken mankind to the core and which continues to be
> influential today in creating faith and bringing about community.[7]

2. HISTORY OF CRITICISM: THE SPEECHES IN ACTS

As I noted earlier, it seems wise to include with the brief overview of the
criticism of Acts some special consideration of the reception that has been
accorded to the speeches, a body of material that constitutes about one
fifth of the total text. F. F. Bruce has noted that this material comprises four
basic types: (1) evangelistic (e.g., Peter's Pentecost sermon); (2) deliberative
(e.g., the report of the Jerusalem Council in chap. 15); (3) apologetic (e.g.,
Stephen's address before the Sanhedrin in chap. 7); and (4) hortatory (e.g.,
Paul's farewell message to the Ephesian elders in chap. 20).

From the literary standpoint the presence of speeches in Acts should
occasion no surprise. In the Old Testament historical books, and even in
the prophets, events are interlarded with speeches or dialogues. Likewise,
in the canonical Gospels, we find intermingled with the record of the
movements of Jesus and his deeds reports of his sayings, sometimes in the
form of detached utterances but at other times in the form of fairly lengthy
discourses. As Cadbury observes, such speeches help to relieve monotony
that might otherwise be imposed on the reader by the continuous recital
of events. Secular literature abounds with this sort of thing, even in history
writing, at least in the ancient period.

One cannot avoid raising the question of the relation of the written report to the content of the speeches as originally given. Three possibilities emerge. First, they could be verbatim reports of what was said on the various occasions. This is unlikely for several reasons. For one thing, it is artificial to suppose that on every occasion someone was present to take down the address word for word. Indeed, on some occasions it is hard to see how Luke could have obtained a full report of what was said (e.g., the speech of Gamaliel before the Sanhedrin in Acts 5). Most important is Luke's own testimony that he has not recorded all that was spoken, for after reporting Peter's Pentecost sermon he states, "And he testified with many other words and exhorted them, saying . . . " (Acts 2:40).

A second, equally dubious possibility is that Luke invented the speeches and put them into the mouths of the men to whom they are credited in his account. Seldom is this postulated in bald form, but some scholars do give the impression that they presume Luke's thought to be back of the speeches more than that of the personalities to whom they are attributed. To support this contention they point out that different mission-ary sermons addressed to Jews follow the same pattern and cite some of the same Scriptures, that Paul says just about what Peter says. They see this as evidence that in the last analysis one author is responsible for these addresses. But since the *kerygma* is the same no matter who declares it, a great amount of sameness ought to be expected. Sermons to Jews, for instance, make considerable use of Scripture. It should be expected that some passages would have been regarded as standard proof texts that would naturally be used in the proclamation of the gospel no matter who was speaking. This applies especially to the subject of the resurrection of Jesus (see Acts 2:27; 13:35). Back of this use of *testimonia* is the Savior's postresurrection teaching to his disciples (Luke 24:44–47).

A third possibility regarding the content of the speeches—indeed, the most probable—is that the sermons and addresses are digests summarizing what was spoken on the various occasions indicated in the text. One can read Peter's Pentecost sermon in five minutes or less. We can be sure that on such a momentous occasion much more was actually spoken—and, in fact, Luke says that such was the case (see v. 40).

Current study of the speeches is obliged to take into consideration the view of Dibelius that Luke's own creative touch (as distinct from his use of traditional material) is to be discerned in the speeches, where he turns preacher and speaks to his own generation through the mouths of apostles and others. His contention is that Luke was greatly influenced by the hellenistic pattern of writing history, which had its classic expression in the methodology of Thucydides. This famous Athenian historian informs his readers about his procedure in the following passage:

As to the various speeches made on the eve of the war, or in its course, I have found it difficult to retain a memory of the precise words which I had heard spoken; and so it was with those who brought me reports. But I have made the persons say what it seemed to me most opportune for them to say in view of each situation; at the same time I have adhered as closely as possible to the general sense of what was actually said. As to the deeds done in the war, I have not thought myself at liberty to record them on hearsay from the first informant, or on arbitrary conjecture. My account rests either on personal knowledge, or on the closest possible scrutiny of each statement made by others. The process of research was laborious, because conflicting accounts were given by those who had witnessed the several events, as partiality swayed or memory served them.[8]

This quotation deals with the two broad classifications of material that entered into the history—words and events. We are concerned chiefly with the former. It is clear that Thucydides is not admitting a speech into his record where none was actually made. He repudiates the idea of creating speeches out of his imagination. And he is careful to say that the truth rather than dramatic effect is his objective.

It is altogether likely that Luke was familiar with Greek historiography. He may well have been influenced by it. But even if this were the sole influence behind his work in the matter of reporting speeches, one would not be justified in supposing that he took great liberties in making his characters say what he wanted them to say. Beyond this, we might note that the Greek historians provide no examples of the missionary sermon that is so prominent in Acts, and so it can hardly be argued that Luke was dependent on them in this area. As Bertil Gärtner observes, the speeches in Acts are brief and not stylistically elaborated as are the Greek models. Those who are familiar with Josephus, the Jewish historian who was greatly influenced by Greek writers, will recall that in his rendition of the story of Abraham preparing to sacrifice his son Isaac, he has Abraham delivering a long speech at the climactic moment. Such a treatment is clearly psychologically unsound, but Josephus was following convention in handling it in that way. There is nothing of this sort in Luke's work. Also, as Gärtner has emphasized, Luke shows a heavy indebtedness to the Old Testament in his extensive use of quotations from that source. His basic motif of *Heilsgeschichte* constrained him to include the Old Testament in his sweep. It is reasonable to conclude that he was most heavily influenced by the Hebrew conception of historiography, which, as Gärtner notes, "becomes a divine interpretation of the course of events."[9]

Our chief concern should be with the reliability of the speeches. First, the element of sameness in the evangelistic sermons addressed to Jews ought not to be construed as suspicious, as though Luke were laboring to make his characters say the same thing. In his book, *The Apostolic Preaching and Its Developments*, C. H. Dodd demonstrates that there is an underlying unity as to what constitutes the gospel, whether one looks into the Gospels or the Acts or the epistles. Bible scholars—even F. C. Baur—have uniformly accepted 1 Corinthians as Pauline, and Galatians as well. In 1 Corinthians 15:11, after having stated the elements of the gospel, Paul goes on to say, with evident reference to the apostles, "Whether, then, it was I or they, this is what we preach, and this is what you believed." Similarly, in Galatians 2:9 Paul reports the extending of the right hand of fellowship between himself and Peter and the others who were present. This passage shows that the basis for this display of unity was a common understanding and acceptance of the gospel of grace. Consequently, it is only natural to expect that any faithful reporting of their proclamation of the gospel—Acts included—would find these leaders in agreement rather than sounding discordant notes.

Second, along with this agreement on the basics of the gospel—the death, resurrection, and exaltation of Jesus and the necessity for repentance and faith—we find that there are some distinctives. One of the complaints made by Dibelius is that there is little if any setting forth of distinctly Petrine and distinctly Pauline theological elements in the speeches. It may be granted that such distinctives do not stand out sharply—but then we must recall that Luke's principal interest was in the consentient testimony of the leaders of the church, and naturally so. But for this very reason the distinctives that do appear are important. Peter's message in Acts 3 is decidedly Jewish in its thrust (see 3:13, 26; cf. 4:27, 30). Here he speaks of Jesus as the Servant of God in rather obvious dependence on the Servant songs of Isaiah, which also entered into Jesus' awareness of his mission (see, for example, Mark 10:45). It is probable that this line of teaching was prominent in the postresurrection instruction given by our Lord to the apostles. On the side of Paul, the allusion to justification in his Pisidian Antioch sermon (Acts 13:39) has the appearance of having been faithfully reported. If someone were minded to say that this reference is deliberately injected by Luke to give a Pauline flavor to the sermon, then it is appropriate to ask why he did not do this more often. His restraint is hard to understand except in terms of faithful reporting.

Third, the fact that Peter is represented as placing some emphasis on the earthly ministry of Jesus (see Acts 2:22; 10:37–39) is logical in light of his presence with the Lord during that time. On the other hand, in the account of Paul's preaching at Pisidian Antioch nothing is said about the earthly ministry, which is understandable in light of the fact that Paul had not been a follower of Jesus in those days.

Fourth, confidence that Luke is giving a faithful report is created by the agreement between Peter's addresses in Acts and the content of his first letter. Some of these agreements are striking:

1. The foreknowledge of God (cf. Acts 2:23 and 1 Pet. 1:2, 20)

2. Silver and gold (cf. Acts 3:6 and 1 Pet. 1:18)

3. The faith that comes through Christ (cf. Acts 3:16 and 1 Pet. 1:21)

4. The term *wood* used for the cross (cf. Acts 5:30; 10:39 and 1 Pet. 2:24)

5. Presence of the word *athemitos*—"unlawful" (the only New Testament occurrences are in Acts 10:28 and 1 Pet. 4:3)

6. God as impartial (cf. Acts 10:34 and 1 Pet. 1:17)

7. The divine judge of the living and the dead (cf. Acts 10:42 and 1 Pet. 4:5).

A similar comparison can be made between Paul's address in Acts 20 and his letters:

1. Compare "God can build you up and give you an inheritance (Acts 20:32) with "the Father . . . has qualified you to share in the inheritance" (Col. 1:12).

2. Compare "I have not coveted anyone's silver or gold or clothing" (Acts 20:33) with "we worked night and day in order not to be a burden to anyone" (1 Thess. 2:9).

3. Compare "We must help the weak" (Acts 20:35) with "We who are strong ought to bear with the failings of the weak" (Rom. 15:1).

In dealing with the address of Paul to the Ephesian elders (Acts 20), Dibelius complains that it is strange to have Paul defend his conduct and his ministry to men who were not charging him with anything. He interprets the situation as a case of Luke's seizing an opportunity to glorify his hero Paul. But is this proper and sufficient ground for denying the speech to Paul? In his letters the apostle is compelled to defend himself again and again. Although the elders did not themselves find fault with Paul, it is likely that there were some at Ephesus who had become critical of him, just as there were some at Corinth (note, for instance, the many passages of self-defense contained in 2 Corinthians). Why should it be thought improbable that Paul would review his labors among the Ephesians, where he had spent an unusually long time? After all, this was a farewell message, a propitious time for such a review. The recital need not be considered an attempt by Luke to glorify Paul when it might just as plausibly be an effort by the apostle to sharpen the memory of his audience and provide them with an example for the conduct of their own life and witness in the days to come when he would no longer be available to them in person.

We should also give some special consideration to Paul's speech at Athens (Acts 17), since it has been the subject of intensive research and divergent evaluation. Years ago Eduard Norden wrote a book entitled *Agnostos Theos* in which he argued that the writer of Acts had taken as a model for this speech an account of the pagan philosopher and wonderworker Apollonius of Tyana. If this were true, we could not have an accurate knowledge of what transpired at Athens. Eduard Meyer, who regarded Luke as the greatest historian between Thucydides and Eusebius, confronted Norden in this matter and finally persuaded him that he had been in the wrong. It is not surprising, then, to find Harvard professor Werner Jaeger stating for the record that "I no longer believe in Norden's brilliant thesis that the author of Acts must have used as his literary pattern a work about . . . Apollonius."[10]

Jaeger reminds us of the importance of the account of Paul's visit to Athens, or rather the importance of what it represents. The future of Christianity depended on the encounter of Greeks and Christians. This marks the beginning of the intellectual struggle between Christianity and the classical world. "This discussion required a common basis, else no discussion would be possible. As such a basis Paul chose the Greek philosophical tradition, which was the most representative part of that which was alive in Greek culture at the time."[11]

W. L. Knox had this to say: "I see no reason to change the view expressed in *Gentiles*, c. i, that we have a genuine record of the occasion of St. Paul's first meeting with serious Gentile philosophy, and that the speech embodies the kind of philosophical commonplaces that he was likely to know and use."[12]

According to Dibelius, however, Luke's account is merely an imaginative speculation as to what Paul might have said on such an occasion to a pagan audience. Moreover, he contends that the speech is in fact quite out of keeping with Paul's teaching in his epistles, in two points especially: the views on idolatry and the knowledge of God it presents. Dibelius finds in Acts 17 a lenient view of idolatry quite foreign to Paul (cf. Rom. 1:18ff., for example). He is thinking particularly of Acts 17:30—"In the past God overlooked such ignorance." And yet we might note that it was grief over the idolatry of Athens that stirred the apostle to action to begin with (see v. 16), a fact corroborated by the urgent call for repentance at the close of the address (v. 30). Paul shows the same concern that he exhibited at Lystra, when he tore his garments in protest of the attempt to worship him (see Acts 14:14). It is true that Paul uses the term *ignorance* (v. 30), but one should not gather from this word the idea that he regards this ignorance as excusable (cf. Eph. 4:18). Forgiveness is indeed possible, but we are all still responsible for our wrong actions. Further, the word *overlooked* (v. 30) does not have connotations of condoning something but rather of longsuffering in view of the plan to bring the Lord Jesus into the world via incarnation.

With reference to the other matter, the knowledge of God, Dibelius holds that the speech admits the validity of such knowledge as paganism is capable of without the aid of special revelation, that God is near man in his natural state, as certain Greek poets had also affirmed (v. 28). But we need the total picture here in order to understand the situation. The very fact that the Athenians were prepared to acknowledge an unknown God, on which Paul capitalizes at the beginning of his speech, is sufficient in itself to demonstrate that these men had not discovered God. We can surely grant that the tenor of the speech makes room for the possibility that man in his natural state may be impressed with his need for God and that he may grope to find him, but the conclusion of the speech makes it evident that only in Christ has God revealed himself to the end of salvation.

Gärtner's appraisal of the Areopagus address is quite different from that of Dibelius. He finds it to be in keeping with Romans 1 in its rebuke of idolatry and in its characterization of sinful man as being ignorant of God, as well as in the emphasis it gives to natural revelation. Gärtner's concluding remarks show how close Acts 17 is to characteristic Jewish apologetic dealing with paganism (although of course it goes beyond the Jewish tradition with its distinctly Christian note):

> If there is reason to allege that the Areopagus speech belongs to a tradition going back to Paul, it may also be correct to say that, in its Diaspora preaching, it also links up with a Jewish pattern. This pattern is found in several places in Jewish literature, but is particularly prominent in the *Wisdom of Solomon* 13-15. As we have seen earlier, there is a close relationship between this portion of *Wisdom of Solomon* and Acts 17 in respect to their theology. The reference to nature has the same function, namely, to reinforce an attack on a false conception of God and a forceful polemic against idolatry. As has often been pointed out, Paul's letters contain ideas which have their counterparts in the *Wisdom of Solomon;* this is particularly true of Romans, where we see the same structure of ideas as is found in *Wisdom of Solomon* 13-15 and Acts 17. It is quite easy to detect an intimate connection between all three texts, which need not be ascribed to any interdependence between the different authors, but rather suggests a tradition common to all. This tradition can, in all essentials, be classified as Jewish Diaspora propaganda."[13]

In conclusion, objections to the position of Dibelius can be summarized as follows:

1. His claim that it was customary for ancient historical writers to introduce speeches into their narratives is only partially true. The best men, such as Thucydides and Polybius, when they lacked direct access to a speaker, did all in their power by way of research, including consulting with witnesses, in order to be able to reproduce the substance of what was said. Not all historians were similarly motivated, including Josephus.[14]

2. If Luke had really been occupied in inventing speeches, it must be said that he missed some opportunities (e.g., Acts 5:20-21).

3. If Luke freely composed the speeches, we could hardly expect to find the nuances that appear here. As we have noted with respect to the addresses of Peter, there are distinctives that Luke does not include in the other speeches he records. As C. F. D. Moule observes, "One cannot help thinking that, if Luke had been composing freely as a dramatist, he might have used this *pais*-language again quite suitably in Pauline speeches."[15]

Moule is alluding to Acts 3:13, 26 and 4:27, 30, where this word for servant occurs.

4. The Aramaisms in the speeches found in the early part of Acts present a formidable problem to the viewpoint of Dibelius. In these instances, Luke was obviously dependent on source material rather than on personal observation. Aramaisms include matters of vocabulary, syntax, and style. For examples, see Acts 3:16 and 4:25. Such items were presumably not a part of Luke's equipment as a Gentile. Their presence argues for faithful reporting on his part.

5. Dibelius would have a better case if he could demonstrate that the speeches are unsuitable for the middle of the first century, at which time they purport to have been given. This he is unable to do.

3. THE HISTORICAL VALUE OF ACTS

Some modern writers hesitate to use the word *historian* in reference to Luke, not necessarily because they rate his workmanship as poor or untrustworthy, but because he did not provide the sort of thing we expect of a history in the modern sense. For example, he does not indicate his sources, and his account is far from being a complete record of the apostolic age. Nor does he give any explanation for the obvious gaps.

Luke does not use the word *history* to describe his own work. It was clearly his intent to provide a continuation of the story begun in the Gospel that bears his name, aiming to describe the origin and progress of the Christian church as a supernatural, spiritual movement carried on by certain men who had a personal relationship to Jesus Christ. Overarching this is the unseen activity and leadership of the Holy Spirit.

Certainly we do not find history here in the merely annalistic sense. There are many gaps and no dates. Among the significant omissions are the following:

1. There is no description of congregational life in the mission churches. Jerusalem, the mother church, is treated briefly, but nothing is noted about divisions in the Corinthian church or any other. We ought however to note that Luke's purpose was to deal with the founding of congregations rather than with their development. Many of the things that Paul found it necessary to deal with in his letters occurred after he had left for other areas. Luke always kept himself at the growing edge of the new movement.

2. There is no account of how the gospel came to Rome and Alexandria, two of the most important centers of the faith in the subapostolic age. In light of Acts 1:8, this may seem unwarranted. However, as already noted, Luke is largely concerned with the work of Peter and Paul, which may account for these omissions.

3. There is no account of what happened to Peter following the Jerusalem Council. One can only guess as to why this should have been omitted. It does seem that Luke's preoccupation with Paul's work led to his passing over the labors of many others.

4. The abrupt close of Acts leaves unanswered the problem of the outcome of Paul's trial. Various explanations have been offered concerning this, including the view that Luke wrote and published his account before the trial was concluded.

In addition to gaps in Luke's work, there are also repetitions. The most obvious are these: the threefold account of the conversion of Paul and the twofold account of Peter's ministry at Caesarea. A similar explanation may suffice for both cases, namely, that Luke's chief concern was for the mission to the Gentiles. Perhaps a similar explanation can be given for the repetitious treatment of the warnings communicated to Paul on his last trip to Jerusalem concerning what awaited him there (Acts 20:23; 21:4; 21:11). This had a bearing on his mission, for as matters worked out he not only went to Rome but went as a prisoner, which gave him opportunity to witness in situations that otherwise would not have been open to him (i.e., to the Praetorian guard and officialdom in the capital).

Our concern here, however, is not so much with the choice of material as with the quality of what is included. What evaluation are we to make of its historical accuracy?

Although Acts has no prologue of the sort that is provided for Luke's Gospel, it is no doubt reasonable, in view of the close relationship between the two books, to take what Luke says in Luke 1:1–4 as a guide to the author's spirit and methodology in his second work. In this connection, two items are arresting. One is the importance he attaches to eyewitness testimony as the basis for information concerning events of the Gospel period. This suggests that when he came to write about the church he made every effort to get in touch with those who participated in the events of the early days. Barnabas, Silas, and Philip belonged to the Christian community in Jerusalem, and Luke had opportunity to consult with each of them. The same is true of James, the head of the Jerusalem church, for Luke was with Paul on his final visit to the holy city. During the apostle's two-year confinement at Caesarea Luke could have laid the groundwork for the writing of Acts by utilizing the many sources of information that were open to him. He was not idle for those two years. Nor should we rule out the use of written sources, at least in part, especially for the early chapters.

The second item in the prologue that invites attention is the objective Luke holds before himself as a writer—namely, to convey such knowledge as will bring certainty to Theophilus concerning the things he has learned about Christian beginnings. This is a clear intimation that Luke intends to hew to the line of truth rather than resort to fable or the use of the imagination. That he remained faithful to this purpose in writing the Gospel is apparent, for he can be checked against the parallels with Matthew where both depend either on Mark or Q. To be sure, there is some material that is unique to Luke's Gospel, but that material is intrinsically sound, comparing favorably with what is found in the double tradition (Mark and Matthew). This reliability creates an expectation that in the Acts, where no parallel material is available for comparison, he can be trusted to maintain the same scrupulous care.

That he had a genuine historical instinct is apparent in the fact that he alone among New Testament writers mentions a Roman emperor. He does this three times, referring to Augustus (Luke 2:1), Tiberius (Luke 3:1), and Claudius (Acts 18:2). On one occasion he goes so far as to fix the event he is describing in terms of a certain year in an emperor's reign (see Luke 3:1). Biblical scholars agree that Luke aims to connect the Christ-event and the rise of the church with events in the secular world, at least in a way sufficient to indicate the historical setting.

In addition to his historical interest, the fact that he was a Christian would entail that he had a sense of responsibility to abide by the truth and look to the Spirit of truth for a right understanding of the things with which he was dealing.

Historians should be judged not only by what they say but also by what they do not say. Restraint is one of the most marked characteristics of Luke. F. C. Burkitt notes that it would have been very easy, in recording the postresurrection ministry of Jesus, to have reported that he had given directions to his followers that tallied with the actual program of developments as pictured in the book of Acts. Luke did not succumb to any such temptation. Burkitt remarks on this same general theme that "the writer who planned the speeches in Acts could easily have extemporized instructions to Peter about the admission of Gentiles into the church, to name but one among the pressing questions of the Apostolic Age. It is only right that we should remember this abstention when we come to consider what sort of weight should be assigned to the historical statements in Acts."[16]

It is necessary to evaluate the historian's work as a whole in addition to checking it in details. Uncertainty about details stemming from a lack of available information need not bother us if we are persuaded of the writer's ability and diligence and honesty. Sir William Ramsay has put the matter well:

We might ask whether it is a probable or possible view that the author can be unequal to himself, that in one place he can show very high qualities as an accurate historian, and that in another place, when dealing with events equally within the range of his opportunities for acquiring knowledge, he can prove himself incompetent to distinguish between good and bad, false and true. He that shows the historic faculty in part of his work has it as a permanent possession.[17]

In this connection, Luke's dedication of his work to Theophilus ought to be considered. As Ernst Haenchen notes, "An ancient book was not specially for the person to whom it is dedicated. . . . The person to whom the book was dedicated would give permission for copies to be made and see to its dissemination."[18] The bearing of this fact on the matter of accuracy is obvious: surely Luke would have been solicitous for the feelings and reputation of Theophilus, careful to include nothing that would embarrass his sponsor.

Historical accuracy has a close relationship to the purpose for writing in Luke's case: if one of his objectives was to demonstrate that Roman officials time and again judged that Christianity was not deserving of condemnation but should be allowed to continue its work of evangelism, then it was absolutely essential that his record of events be unimpeachable from the standpoint of historical accuracy. He was writing with an audience in mind which was in position to know most of the facts that pertained to Roman affairs, and could make inquiry about the rest (viz., items bearing on Roman-Jewish relations). Luke could not afford to risk exposure if he wanted his material to carry weight and accomplish its purpose. Haenchen is open to challenge when he asserts that Luke "writes not for a learned public which would keep track of all his references and critically compare them, but rather for a more or less nonliterary congregation which he wants to captivate and edify."[19] Was the most excellent Theophilus not a learned man? Luke had to consider the entire spectrum of his readership.

We might note at this point that there are a number of examples in Acts that provide positive evidence of the author's accuracy:

1. He always gives the proper designation for Roman officials. He also understands the difference between the two types of provinces, the senatorial and the imperial, and in each case the proper term for the official in charge: he uses *anthupatos* (proconsul) in references to Sergius Paulus (13:7) and Gallio (18:12), and he uses *hegemon* in a reference to the imperial governor of a province (23:24). As Lightfoot points out, the status of a province could change, so a writer would have to be in close contact with the situation to know such information at any given time:

> If disturbances broke out in a senatorial province and military rule was necessary to restore order, it would be transferred to the Emperor as the head of the army, and the Senate would receive an imperial province in exchange. . . . A very few years before St. Paul's visit to Corinth, and some years later, Achaia was governed by a propraetor. Just at this time, however, it was in the hands of the Senate, and its ruler therefore was a proconsul, as represented by St. Luke.[20]

Luke identifies the rulers at Thessalonica as *politarchai* (rulers of the city), a usage that was once considered dubious, until its currency was confirmed by inscriptions found on the site. He identifies the town clerk at Ephesus as the *grammateus*. Moulton and Milligan comment, "The importance of the office at Ephesus, to which Acts 19:35 points, is now abundantly confirmed by the inscriptions."[21] When Luke mentions the leading official on the island of Malta, he uses a term that may sound to our ears like a general expression, for we use "head man" in that way. But Malta inscriptions have shown that *ho prōtos* was a technical term for the governor of the island (28:7).

2. The attitude of Roman officials toward Christianity and its representatives has already been noted. Repeatedly these officials exonerated the missionaries of charges of disloyalty or disruption. But this attitude changed at the time of Nero and became more or less fixed as one of opposition during the reign of Domitian and then of Trajan, who belongs to the early part of the second century. If Acts had been written late in the first century or early in the second, as many suppose, it may well be doubted that this earlier state of things would have been described at all, let alone repeatedly. Luke's account is best understood in the light of contemporary experience. As R. P. C. Hanson remarks, "The later we place Acts in the first century the more difficult it becomes to reconcile its language about the Roman Government with the contemporary situation; and . . . if we place it in the second century (and as late as 130), we cannot reconcile the two at all."[22]

3. The references to Roman citizenship in Acts accurately reflect its characteristics during the period it covers. A. N. Sherwin-White notes that this is so in two particulars. First, Claudius Lysias is reported as being able to buy Roman citizenship (22:28), which means that he had to advance a considerable sum of money as a bribe to the men strategically placed in the administration who could secure this favor for him. This was very much the situation during the time of Claudius, whereas during Nero's reign there was a clamping down on such practices.[23] Second, Sherwin-White notes that a Roman citizen in the provinces was officially immune from personal punishment and in Paul's day it would have been quite natural for those who ordered such punishment for him to have been alarmed when they discovered their error (see Acts 16:37–39; 22:25–29), whereas "the force of this feeling ultimately petered out with the large extension of the citizenship through the provinces, just as the privileges of Romans came to be whittled down at a similar rate. Acts breathes the climate of the earlier phase."[24]

4. The failure of Felix to send Paul to his own province for trial is also noted and explained by Sherwin-White. No sooner had the Roman governor read the letter of Claudius Lysias regarding Paul than he asked the prisoner what province he belonged to (23:34). Paul responded with the information that he was from Cilicia, yet Felix did not pursue the matter. Why not? Noting that such a practice in the case of a Roman citizen was optional on the part of the governor, and might have been welcomed by Felix in order to rid himself of the trouble of taking jurisdiction, Sherwin-White goes on to say, "The answer may well lie in the status of Cilicia,

which even more than Judaea, though a separate administrative area, was a dependency, of the Legate of Syria in the early Principate."[25] In other words, Felix realized that the Legate of Syria would probably not relish taking on a case that pertained to a minor part of his jurisdiction.

5. Paul's appeal to Caesar, as described in Acts, fits the Roman law of that period, but it does not fit the procedure that became current in the second century. The difference is that in Paul's time the officiating judge (the provincial governor in his case) did not try the case; at most he would hold a preliminary hearing (as did Felix and Festus), leaving the disposition to the emperor. In later times, however, sentence *was* given in the provincial court, after which appeal could be made to the emperor.[26]

To such evidences of the historical accuracy of the author of Acts we could add examples of accuracy in geographical references. Sir William Ramsay details examples of this sort in his book *St. Paul the Traveller and the Roman Citizen*.

All of this is not to say that there are no problems with the text of Acts, however. Without attempting a complete listing, we will note a few of these problem areas and try to evaluate them.

1. Some scholars decline to accept Acts as thoroughly reliable because of the emphasis it places on the miraculous. Of course the significance of this complaint depends on one's theological presuppositions. It is in any case not a problem peculiar to Acts; the emphasis on miracles is also substantial in the Gospels. A good place to start grappling with it is in Paul's letters. He wrote to the Galatians, "Does God give you his Spirit and work miracles among you because you observe the law, or because you believe what you heard?" (Gal. 3:5). It would be pointless to appeal to the phenomenon of miracles in these churches if Paul and his readers did not believe that any had occurred. Likewise, in writing to the Romans and summarizing his missionary labors up to that time, he says, "I will not venture to speak of anything except what Christ has accomplished through me in leading the Gentiles to obey God by what I have said and done—by the power of signs and miracles, through the power of the Spirit" (Rom. 15:18–19; cf. 2 Cor. 12:12). Moreover, those who are familiar with the Apocryphal Acts readily admit a qualitative difference between the wonders reported there and those that are recorded by Luke.

2. Somewhat puzzling is Luke's use of the Septuagint for Old Testament quotations contained in the sermons recorded in the early chapters of Acts. We might suspect that Aramaic would have been a more natural choice in this context, since speaker and listener alike would presumably have been very limited in their knowledge of the Greek Old Testament. It is possible, but not certain, that he himself shifted the quotations from an originally Semitic text to the Greek form because he presumed that the audience for whom he was writing Acts would be more familiar with the latter.

3. An objection has been raised to the figures Luke gives for the membership of the Jerusalem church—three thousand at Pentecost, rising to five thousand shortly thereafter, and increasing still more later (see Acts 5:14; 6:7). It has been thought that these figures are too high for a place the size of Jerusalem and that they represent an idealizing of the actual situation. In truth, the size of the population of the city remains largely a matter of conjecture, but its normal population at this period, on a conservative estimate, was about twenty-five thousand.[27] But one must realize that at festival time (in this case, Pentecost) that figure must have been increased many times over. Some of the pilgrims would remain for a time, especially those who had relatives in or near the city. It is expressly intimated that the converts at Pentecost remained for some time (2:42). In fact, it appears that most of them were actually residents of Jerusalem (2:5).

4. Doubt has been expressed about the reliability of Luke's statement that Barnabas and Paul appointed elders over the churches in the cities they evangelized on their first missionary journey (14:23) on the ground that Paul fails to speak of elders when writing his various congregations. In Philippians 1:1 he mentions bishops (overseers) and deacons, but does not use the term *elder*. But throughout his writings Paul seems disinclined to make any references to church officers. His failure to mention elders is somewhat understandable in light of the fact that he scarcely ever mentions any officers. He was more concerned with the functioning of persons gifted by the Holy Spirit to perform certain services in the congregation than with office as such. We will return to this problem later in the text.

5. A genuine difficulty is presented by the data of Gamaliel's speech, in which Theudas is mentioned before Judas the Galilean (see 5:36–37), thus reversing the historical order of these two men. Some would explain the matter by saying that Luke was drawing on Josephus, who mentions the revolt of Theudas and then goes on to mention the execution of two sons of Judas.[28] This might explain Luke's order, but it would also signal a blunder on his part. Since Luke lists the followers of Theudas as four hundred in number and Josephus speaks of a very great multitude, it is in any case unlikely that Luke is dependent on the Jewish historian. The most plausible solution is that both writers had access to a common source which mentioned the two revolutionaries together, even though they were half a century removed from each other. It is also possible that the Theudas of Luke and the Theudas of Josephus were different individuals, though it seems unlikely, especially since the name was not common.

6. It is frequently alleged that the picture of Paul in Acts is so different from that which he himself provides in his letters that Luke's presentation can hardly be considered reliable. This is too large a problem to consider in detail at this point, but we might just note that a difference in emphasis among those who are basically in accord is not uncommon. Paul's interest

in theology was undoubtedly greater than Luke's, but Luke was far from being antitheological in his outlook.

It is noteworthy that a leading historian of our time is ready to conclude that when Luke touches on Roman matters he is thoroughly trustworthy. Sherwin-White asserts that "for Acts the confirmation of historicity is overwhelming. . . . Any attempt to reject its basic historicity even in matters of detail must now appear absurd. Roman historians have long taken it for granted."[29]

CHAPTER III

The External History of the Apostolic Church

1. PENTECOST

We are following the plan of dealing first with the rise and extension of the church, then turning back and looking at it from within, considering its congregational life and activity (as distinct from its outreach). This arrangement may have some disadvantage from the chronological stand-point, but it is hoped that by using this method we will be able to investigate the two phases, the external and the internal, more effectively. It is to be expected in a book such as Acts that the external features will predominate over the internal, whereas in the epistles one naturally expects the reverse. Nevertheless, both Acts and the epistles will be useful to some extent in both areas.

Understandably there are gaps in Luke's account, but this should make us all the more grateful for the material he has given us. When his account ends, our knowledge of the progress of Christianity suffers a tremendous loss. The sense of incompleteness is greater in the first half of the book than in the remainder, for Luke was not a participant in the events of the early period. He has compensated somewhat for the scarcity of information by supplying summaries that indicate in a general way that the gospel was making progress. They also serve the purpose of preparing the reader for the next development in the story (see 6:7; 9:31; 11:21; 12:24). Some are found in the latter part of the book also (16:5; 19:20; 28:30–31).

Luke's own method of narration is to alternate pictures of the believing community with descriptions of the contacts of the church with those who were without, whether hostile or noncommitted. A review of the contents of Acts 1:1 to 8:3, where the story of the witness in Jerusalem concludes, makes this apparent:

1:1–26	Believers alone are in view
2:1–41	Pentecost—witness to unbelievers
2:42	Brief picture of converts
2:43	Public reaction
2:44–47	A glimpse of the life of the church

3:1–4:22   Testimony to the unsaved by miracle and message, leading to imprisonment of two apostles and their defense before the Council
4:23–32   The church's reaction to the apostles' release
4:33   Further witness by the apostles to the public
4:34–5:11 The church's care for its own people
5:12–42   More contact with the public and further confrontation with the Sanhedrin
6:1–6   The church's effort to solve the problem of its own needy
6:7–8:3   Further testimony to the unsaved, with special emphasis on the ministry of Stephen, his martyrdom, and the persecution of the church

Chapter one provides a running start for the study of Pentecost. The chapter divides naturally into two parts: the events that took place before the ascension and the activities of the believing community in the ten days that followed.

Over a forty-day period Jesus manifested himself from time to time to his own (1:3). These appearances fulfilled his promise to the Eleven (see John 14:19) and were restricted to believers (in keeping with the statement recorded in Matt. 23:39). For the disciples the value of this contact with the risen Lord must have been incalculable. Since he had predicted the resurrection (see Mark 8:31; 9:9, 31; 10:34; 14:28), when it occurred their confidence in him was restored after having been dashed by the crucifixion. From this time forth, whatever he would predict would have been taken with the utmost seriousness. If Jesus had spoken the content of Acts 1:8 during the precross ministry, it could not possibly have made the impression it did when he set his program before the disciples prior to the ascension. These meetings with the risen Lord were times of genuine joy and refreshment. From the very first one, marked as it was by his comforting salutation, "Peace be with you" (John 20:19), all sense of strangeness was dissipated. As Schlatter notes, the Lord did not upbraid them for their failure and desertion; his willingness to come to them in this direct, personal way was in itself a declaration of forgiveness and restoration.[1] Their calling and their responsibility to represent him before the world remained intact. Though the Lord appeared on occasion to individual disciples (see the close of the various Gospels), what is emphasized in Acts 1 is his contacts with the whole group. These meetings were a miniature of the church that was to be—the Lord in the midst of his own (Matt. 18:20). As far as one can tell from the narrative, the sense of unity was not diminished between appearances, serving as a foretaste of the days when the Savior would not be with his followers in bodily presence but nevertheless would be actually present by the Spirit.

In seeking a rationale regarding the location of the appearances,

Schlatter makes the suggestion that by appearing in Galilee our Lord was emphasizing that the movement centering in himself was distinct from Judaism, which focused on Jerusalem, whereas his appearances in the Jerusalem area served to make it clear that witness to him as the risen Lord must be borne in that area so as to challenge the nation at its center with the fact of his resurrection.[2]

The second activity of the risen Lord noted in the text (Acts 1:3) is his instruction of the Eleven concerning the kingdom of God. This expression occurs half a dozen times in Acts, a sharp drop from its frequency in the Synoptic Gospels. That it occurs at all is significantly helpful in offsetting the objection that Jesus promised a kingdom but what came into being instead was a church. This observation suggests a failure of plan. However, inasmuch as the expression "the kingdom of God" *is* used in Acts, it would seem to be quite adaptable to the concept of the church (cf. 20:25; 28:31). In the kingdom teaching of Jesus reported in the Synoptic Gospels there are three major strands: its current existence by virtue of the coming and activity of Jesus of Nazareth; its eschatological realization; and the form it would take in the interval between these two, having spurious as well as genuine adherents (see Matt. 13). Early Christians found themselves in the midst of what was obviously a mighty operation of God, from which they looked back to the impetus given to it by the historic Jesus and from which they looked forward to the consummation.

Possibly one could say that the future aspect of the kingdom was not central to our Lord's teaching during the forty days, since the disciples do ask, "Lord, are you at this time going to restore the kingdom to Israel?" (1:6). This impression is confirmed by the closing chapter of Luke's Gospel, in which we are informed that Jesus' discussions with the disciples following the resurrection centered on the fact that his death and resurrection in light of the prophetic Scriptures constituted the necessary orientation for his followers who would be carrying out the commission he had given to them (see Luke 24:27, 44–48). Nothing is said about the consummation of the kingdom. That phase is not altogether lacking from Acts 1, however, since it is noted that the ascension of Jesus was accompanied by the angelic promise that he would come again (1:11).

The more immediate future was the major thrust in our Lord's teaching at this time. It concerned two items: the apostles' baptism with the Spirit and the program of evangelism set before them, which would be realized by the Spirit's enablement (1:5, 8). With these utterances we find ourselves virtually on the threshold of Pentecost.

The baptism with the Spirit has some perplexing aspects. From the Lord's statement in 1:5 it is evident that the experience was to take place shortly after his departure—in other words, at Pentecost. If 1:8 is intended to be linked with this fulfillment, then it would appear that the baptism with the Spirit is to be viewed as an experience of the Spirit's empowering that enabled the recipients to make an effective witness for Christ. But two questions must be faced. How can this be squared with the teaching about the baptism with the Spirit in 1 Corinthians 12:13, where it is equated with being given a place in the body of Christ (i.e., the church) and nothing at all is said about power for witness? Further, if the baptism with the Spirit in 1:5 speaks of an experience, how does this differ from the later experiences of the apostles wherein they were filled with the Spirit (4:8, 31)? If the two expressions have the same meaning, why is the baptism mentioned only in Christ's prediction (1:5) whereas "filling" is the terminology for later experiences? Interestingly enough, when Peter preached to the household of Cornelius, the Holy Spirit fell on the audience and they spoke with tongues just as the apostles had done at Pentecost. When Peter rehearsed this event to the leaders at Jerusalem, he linked it to our Lord's words in Acts 1:5, and yet he made no mention of power for witness.

Two conclusions can be drawn with some degree of confidence. One is that baptism with the Spirit is a once-for-all matter (cf. 1 Cor. 12:13) and should be distinguished from the filling with the Spirit, which can clearly occur repeatedly. The second is that even though baptism with the Spirit is the act of the Spirit whereby those who believe in Christ are placed into the body of Christ (i.e., the church, which was realized at Pentecost), on this occasion the element of power for witness receives special attention (cf. Luke 24:49). At Pentecost the two things happened at once.

We should not suppose that baptism with the Spirit invariably involved this impartation of power. Scripture does not state this at all in connection with other receptions of the Spirit involving Saul of Tarsus (9:17); Cornelius and company (10:44–48); the Samaritans (8:14–17); or the Ephesians (19:1–7). In view of the silence of Scripture about the dynamic effects of the reception of the Spirit, it is precarious to insist that the baptism with the Spirit entails power for witness as an inevitable result. The primary function is to place the recipient into Christ and his church. This occurs at the beginning of Christian experience. In this respect the apostles occupied an extraordinary place, since they were believers for some time before they received the Spirit's baptism. It is dubious procedure to take them as exemplars for the seeking of the experience of the baptism with the Spirit at some point in Christian life. Spirit baptism as well as water baptism belongs to the inception of the salvation experience. At least this is so ordinarily. There may be circumstances under which water baptism is delayed.

In contrast to this once-for-all character of baptism with the Spirit is the constant obligation of the child of God to be filled with the Spirit (note the present tense in Eph. 5:18—"be continuously filled with the Spirit"). One should bear in mind that the book of Acts evidences an amazing freedom on the part of the Spirit in his operations. It is therefore difficult to establish theological norms on the basis of this book alone. Wisdom dictates that we should be satisfied to find the norm in the epistles and make such adjustment of the materials in Acts to that norm as will establish the closest harmony. An example of congruence is the fact that the passive voice is used for "baptize" both in Acts 1:5 and in 1 Corinthians 12:13. It is notable also that in Acts 1:5, when Jesus indicated what would take place in a few days, he said nothing about a need for the disciples to prepare their souls for the experience, thus underscoring the fact that the baptism was a sovereign provision of God, independent of human qualification except for a saving relationship to Jesus Christ.

Several things in connection with the Lord's commission (1:8) invite attention:

1. We note, with Goppelt, a similarity of pattern between Acts and Luke's Gospel. Luke 4 pictures Jesus in his synagogue message at Nazareth as outlining the nature and scope of his ministry based on Isaiah 61:1-2. Correspondingly, at the beginning of Acts we find our Lord laying down the master plan for his disciples to follow in terms of their equipment (the same as his), what they are to do, and where they are to go.

2. The degree of spiritual preparation in the geographical areas to be covered lessens as one moves outward. Jerusalem was the heart of Judaism, and Judea its outlying sphere of special influence. Samaria, though antagonistic to the Jews, had its own Pentateuch and shared many concepts with its neighbors. Finally, the outer perimeter was either slightly conditioned (through the influence of the Diaspora) or was entirely ignorant of the spiritual heritage of Judaism.

3. Each of the places mentioned in 1:8 had its own latent challenge, its own obstacle, requiring the aid of the Spirit to overcome it. Jerusalem was the city that crucified the Lord of glory; sullen opposition could be expected there. Judea was the home of the traitor; that alone could make the apostles reluctant to minister there. Samaria had no love for the Jews; it had refused hospitality to Jesus (see Luke 9:51ff.), and at an earlier point he had warned his disciples explicitly to avoid Samaria (see Matt. 10:5). As for the ends of the earth, there was little incentive to go that far, not only because those regions were so distant but also because they harbored the Gentile "dogs," the unclean with whom the pious Jew should not associate.

4. To offset these disadvantages, Jesus had prepared the way for his own. (a) He had visited the holy city on numerous' occasions and had taught in the temple courts, expressing his longing to gather its people to himself (see Matt. 23:37). (b) Jesus had been born in Bethlehem of Judea. His forerunner had ministered there, as had the Master himself (see Matt. 19:1; John 3:22). (c) Samaria was not neglected by the Savior (see John 4; Luke 17:15-19). (d) Though he had been sent to the lost sheep of the house of Israel, he anticipated the coming era by turning aside now and then to minister to Gentiles (see Matt. 8:5ff.; 15:21ff.), and he had predicted

a mighty influx of Gentiles into the kingdom (Matt. 8:11) as well as indicating what would make this possible (John 12:20–24).

5. The failure of the Lord to mention Galilee in his Great Commission is somewhat puzzling, since nearly all the apostles (perhaps all but Judas) were from this area (see Acts 1:11). Probably Jesus felt confident that these men would not neglect their native places, despite his own cool reception in Nazareth. His confidence was justified by later developments (see Acts 9:31). It is just possible that his reference to "all Judea" was intended to include Galilee (as is the case in Luke 23:5, for example).

Between the ascension and Pentecost the followers of Jesus were occupied with two things: a ministry of prayer and the choosing of a successor to Judas. During our Lord's ministry his followers had expressed an interest in learning to pray and had received instruction from him (see Luke 11:1–4), but virtually nothing is said about their actual prayer life. In fact, we get a negative impression from their failure in the Garden of Gethsemane. But they are now described as being capable of sustained and intensive prayer, even though the Lord is no longer with them. Furthermore, a spirit of equality is evident in the fact that the faithful women who accompanied Jesus to Jerusalem and ministered to his needs (Luke 8:2–3) were incorporated into the circle of prayer. The members of Jesus' family were there also. "Brothers" (1:14) may be too narrow a rendering in this passage. Walter Bauer says, "There is no longer any doubt in my mind that *adelphoi* can mean brothers and sisters in any number."[3] It is thrilling to think of the possibility that Jesus' whole family was there, brought to faith by his resurrection. Schlatter notes the importance to be attached to the presence of Jesus' family on this occasion.[4] The appeal of the gospel to the nation Israel, a nation that emphasized the solidarity of the family, would be weakened if that message were spurned by Jesus' own family through continued rejection of his claims. That the brothers became workers as well as pray-ers is evidenced by Paul's testimony (see 1 Cor. 9:5).

No explanation is given for this prayer activity, but since the apostles had been warned not to leave Jerusalem (1:4) and since their witness was not to begin till the Spirit had come upon them, prayer seemed the most natural thing for them. Possibly they knew that before Jesus received the Spirit at his baptism, he was engaged in prayer (see Luke 3:21–22).

The latter half of the chapter is taken up with the choosing of Matthias as replacement for Judas. Several things stand out:

1. The leadership of Peter, in agreement with the prominence he had attained during Jesus' ministry. His denial of the Master had been forgiven. No one questioned his right to act as spokesman for the group.

2. Peter's use of Scripture (1:20). He shows the benefit of Jesus' instruction in this area after the resurrection.

3. His restraint in speaking of the traitor (he avoids using this word). Probably his own failure in denying the Savior made him realize how frail

mankind is and how susceptible to sin. Judas's sad end was enough in itself to bring home the impact of the wages of sin.

4. The need for a replacement for Judas seems to have been dictated by the importance of the number twelve. There were twelve tribes in Israel. The church, as the new Israel, had to express its completeness by retaining the same number of men in its leadership as Jesus had provided by his original choice.

5. As to qualifications, the ability to witness to the fact that Jesus had risen from the dead was primary, but also essential was that the new man should have been with him from the beginning of the ministry, from the time of the preparatory ministry of John. In all probability, only two men in the company of 120 met these requirements (see Acts 1:23).

6. The use of the lot was a recognized Old Testament practice and should not be regarded as an inappropriate method for choosing the successor in this case. Moreover, to argue that God showed his displeasure with the selection of Matthias by rejecting him (since he is not mentioned by name after this) is entirely inconclusive, since nearly all the apostles are treated with the same silence. The notion that God had in mind Saul of Tarsus as Judas's replacement is not supported by Scripture, for although Paul insisted on his apostleship (on the ground that he had seen the risen Lord and received his commission from him), he never included himself as one of the Twelve but always stood in distinction from them as an independent who had been specially chosen by the risen Lord (see Gal. 1:17; 1 Cor. 15:9–11). Men had nothing to do with his selection (see Gal. 1:1).

The Events of the Day of Pentecost

Pentecost is a Greek word meaning "fiftieth," serving to indicate that the feast of Pentecost came on the fiftieth day after Passover (Lev. 23:15), which means that it fell on the first day of the week.

Jewish teaching maintained that when the Spirit completed his task of inspiring the writers of the Old Testament his activity ceased, to be resumed in the messianic era. There is evidence from the intertestamental period that the Hebrews felt the lack of inspired guidance in their time. After the battle of Beth-zur, in which Judas Maccabeus and his men defeated the Syrians, they marched to Jerusalem to cleanse the sanctuary that the pagan Syrians had defiled. We read that they pulled down the altar and laid up the stones in the mountain of the house in a convenient place, until there should come a prophet to give an answer concerning what should be done with them (1 Macc. 4:46; cf. 14:41–42).

To speak of the Spirit as coming is scriptural (see John 16:8; cf. 7:39). But this should not be understood as denying the presence and activity of the Spirit in the Old Testament era and in the period covered by the Gospels. In accordance with the nature of progressive revelation, however, we recognize that God dominates the Old Testament epoch, the Son of God dominates the Gospel period, and the Spirit dominates the segment covered by Acts and the epistles together with the age of the church, which has continued to the present time. Most of the New Testament functions of the Spirit are anticipated in the Old. He is the Spirit of life (Gen. 1:2), the Spirit of wisdom and understanding (Ex. 31:1–3), the Spirit of counsel (Neh. 9:20), the Spirit of power (Judg. 3:10), the Spirit of conviction (Gen. 6:3), the Spirit of conversion (Zech. 12:10), the Spirit of prophecy (Zech. 7:12), the Spirit of the sovereign LORD who would anoint the Messiah (Isa. 61:1), and so on.

The advent of the Spirit, coupled as it was with the ascension of the Lord Jesus and dependent on that event, gave evidence that the work of redemption that the Son of God had come to achieve was now accomplished. Likewise, the order of these events emphasized that the work of the Holy Spirit was dependent on and intimately connected with the salvation Christ had won. To use familiar theological terminology, the Spirit was to apply the work of Christ to human lives in saving and transforming power.

Since Pentecost was one of the three major feasts observed annually in Israel, on this occasion as in other years Jerusalem must have been filled with people from far and near. The normal population was swollen to many times its usual size, with some pilgrims obliged to find lodgings in the environs of the city. Nowhere in the epistles do we find an extended discussion of Pentecost, which may appear to be a strange omission, yet the fact that Paul could write to Gentiles and mention Pentecost (1 Cor. 16:8) suggests that the theological significance of the day was recognized by his readers and needed no elaboration. One would like to know the reaction of Jewish Christians to this day of festival as it was observed from year to year. We know that Paul, in planning a trip to Jerusalem with a gift from his churches for the poor saints in that city made a great effort to reach his destination by Pentecost (see Acts 20:16).

The place where the Spirit's manifestation occurred is not specified (see 2:1). It may well have been the upper room mentioned in 1:13, but if so there must have been an exodus from these quarters, probably to the temple area, in order to have space for the mass of people that began to congregate.

Dramatic tokens of the Spirit's advent were provided, the sound making its appeal to the ear and the fiery tongues to the eye. As far as the Twelve were concerned, these phenomena served to assure them that the promise of Jesus (1:4) was being fulfilled. The tokens were too obvious and too striking to be dismissed as subjective elements induced by desire on their part to have the Spirit come. No sooner had the Spirit fallen on them than they began to speak in tongues, as the Spirit enabled them (2:4). From the close connection of 2:1–4 with the material in the latter half of chapter one, it is likely that the whole company of 120 participated in this experience.

It is clear from 2:6 that on this occasion tongues involved intelligible speech. "Each one heard . . . in his own language." The same cannot be certified for the other occasions when tongues are mentioned in this book (10:46; 19:6). Nothing is said one way or the other to clarify the matter. As to the content of the message conveyed, Luke's explanation is that the mighty works of God were recounted in a spirit of praise. One can only hazard the supposition that these works included not only the gift of the Spirit but the prior gift of Christ and the whole movement of God in providing salvation. The symbolic value of tongues is the assurance given to the church that in the essential task of communicating the gospel the Spirit is the great enabler.

A large audience was quickly assembled, described as devout men, Jews, who had come from many places outside the land (2:5) as well as Judea (2:9). For the most part, it seems, they had been born and raised in the Dispersion (2:8). Some scholars contend that they were pilgrims attending the feast and so were residing only temporarily in the city. However, Luke states that these Jews were living in Jerusalem. He does not say that they were sojourning, but on the contrary uses a form that expresses permanent habitation. (For other examples in Acts, see 2:14; 4:16; 9:22; 11:29; 13:27; 17:24; 19:10; 22:12—in all cases the same word is used.) It was the wish of pious Jews of the Dispersion to spend their last days on the soil of the holy land and to be buried there. Furthermore, we gather from 2:42 that those who became believers at Pentecost did not leave the city but continued there as part of the Christian community. Whether some of them returned later to the areas where they had previously lived in order to preach the gospel, one can only conjecture. The possibility should not be ruled out. Neither can the possibility that pilgrims to the festival were in the crowd that Peter addressed.

If it is in fact the case that those Jews were permanent dwellers at Jerusalem (be assured that Luke knew how to use the word *sojourning* if that is what he intended to say), some consequences necessarily follow. Because they would have been devout, familiar with the Messianic predictions of Scripture, it is extremely likely that they would have been in Jerusalem at Passover that year, when Jesus was crucified. They would have been exposed to the debate and heartfelt questioning that this event provoked, especially when rumors began to circulate that the grave of Jesus was empty. It all adds up to the conclusion that Peter had a prepared audience (cf. 2:22).

Luke says that these devout Jews were from every nation under heaven (2:5). Judaism had begun to associate Pentecost with the giving of the law by considering it an anniversary memorial of that great event. (In its original context it marked the offering of the firstfruits of the wheat harvest, which has its own special relevance here, the three thousand being the firstfruits of the harvest of converts to Christ.) In connection with the giving of the law, Jewish tradition held that it was supernaturally carried to people all over the world. It is recounted in Midrash Tanchuma 26c as follows: "Although the Ten Commandments were promulgated with a single sound, it says, 'all people heard the voices'; it follows then that when the voice went forth it was divided into seven voices and then went into seventy tongues, and every people received the law in their own language." This tradition may have been current in the days of the early church (some scholars find it in the book of Jubilees and in the Qumran literature). Luke may be picturing Peter's audience as representatives of the lands from which they had come, lands to which the gospel would be going forth to reach Jew and Gentile alike.

We have already noted the suspicion in late Judaism that the Spirit had departed. The contrast here with early Christianity, then, is striking—the Jewish community making the Feast of Weeks the anniversary of the giving of the law and the Christian community making it the anniversary of the giving of the Spirit. Paul felt the deadening effect of the letter of the law, contrasting it with the Spirit (Rom. 2:29; 7:6; 2 Cor. 3:6). Schlatter remarks, "The Jewish community was now bound to the Word once written in the Spirit, and the sacred Book had become her lord. Yet however great their gratitude and veneration for it might be, the Jews were acutely aware that something was lacking. They were waiting for something new; they needed a new manifestation of God's grace. . . . They were waiting for the Spirit."[5]

Another connection between Pentecost and the Old Testament naturally suggested by the narrative is the confusion of tongues at Babel, leading to the dispersal of the nations. Disobedience led to confusion of tongues. Now, at Pentecost, God in grace indicates his purpose that by the enablement of the Spirit the many linguistic and national units (cf. Gen. 10) will be unified by the power of the gospel as the Spirit directs the dissemination of the word of truth.

Peter, the spokesman on this occasion, was one of those to whom the Lord had promised the gift of the Spirit of truth. His sermon reveals the fact that he had indeed been taught during the intervening period. The Spirit had given him understanding of the import of Messianic prophecy and led him to magnify Jesus as the Christ (cf. John 16:14).

Peter's sermon falls into three divisions: his explanation of the phenomena that had excited the crowd (2:14–21); his proclamation of Jesus in terms of his ministry, death, resurrection, and exaltation (2:22–36); and his counsel for those who responded to his message (2:37–40).

In the first section the apostle quickly disposes of the notion that he and his companions are drunk, and he goes on to cite the true reason for these unusual manifestations. Prophecy has been fulfilled (he quotes Joel

2:28–32). Profiting from the Lord's postresurrection teaching, Peter is able to affirm that what has happened that day is in keeping with what God had promised through the prophet long ago. The reference to "all flesh" may be adequately explained by what follows—namely, old and young, men and women.

Peter gives prominence to the word *prophesy*. He does not quote Joel to explain the tongues, for the word does not occur there, but rather to explain what was communicated thereby. In biblical usage at least three ideas attach themselves to prophesying. One is to foretell, which does not apply here (cf. vv. 17–18), for although Joel is predicting, the same is not said of those about whom he speaks. Another meaning of the word is "to forthtell," which is the most common nuance. The Old Testament prophets had far more to declare to their own day and generation than they were called on to declare by way of prediction. This second meaning can possibly apply here, since prophesying can be a synonym for preaching. It was the very thing Peter was doing. There is also a third sense: prophesying can mean to engage in praise to God (see 1 Chron. 25:3). This agrees well with Acts 2:11 and seems to fit Acts 19:6 also, where speaking in tongues and prophesying are distinguished. The two are distinguished in 1 Corinthians 12–14 also. By his use of the Joel passage, Peter is saying that the messianic age has come (i.e., has begun). Its consummation, whether it be near at hand or remote, is made certain.

In the central portion of his message Peter deals only lightly with the ministry of Jesus (2:22) before moving on to his death, which he views from two standpoints: the guilt of those who caused that death and the divine purpose that was accomplished through it. Chief attention, however, is given to the resurrection, and again Scripture is quoted (Ps. 16) for support. Rather surprisingly, he does not appeal to his experience or that of his comrades in being privileged to see the risen Lord and have fellowship with him. We can derive from this the lesson that in our preaching, our experience is no substitute for Scripture. If God had spoken of the coming of the Spirit and the audience could attest the fulfillment, the same word of God was worthy of trust respecting the Christ-event, especially the resurrection. Verse 33 is crucially important here. The crowd had witnessed the phenomena related to the Spirit's coming. How was this event to be explained? The one explanation that would suffice is the exaltation of Christ, at whose behest the Spirit had been poured out. In order to be exalted to glory, Jesus had first to be raised from the dead. As to the meaning of the resurrection with respect to the person of Jesus, Peter summarizes by saying that this event set him apart as Lord and Christ (2:36).

Does this mean that Jesus was not properly viewed as Lord and Christ prior to the resurrection and exaltation? By no means, even though one must grant that the precross use of these titles is quite limited in relation to the much more frequent use after the resurrection. If it could properly be said that the Christ should suffer (Acts 3:18; Luke 24:46), and if Jesus was indeed the Christ, then he did not become the Christ by virtue of his exaltation. (Cf. Rom. 1:3–4, where the sonship of the Lord Jesus is mentioned before his earthly connections are mentioned, and then the heightened aspect of sonship is linked with his resurrection.)

We should look at the results of Peter's sermon. Many of his hearers were "cut to the heart" (2:37). Jesus had told the apostles that when the Spirit came he would convict the world respecting sin, righteousness, and judgment (John 16:8). At Pentecost the conviction of sin was obvious. These people knew the Old Testament and its prophecies. They were familiar also with the life and ministry of Jesus (2:22). They had not protested when their leaders delivered him over to Pilate and to death. To think that they had allowed themselves to be implicated in the national rejection of Israel's Messiah must have been a devastating thought! Jesus had also said that the Spirit would convict of righteousness because he himself would go to the Father. The exaltation of Christ that accounted for the outpouring of the Spirit also proclaimed the righteousness of Jesus in making his great claims while on earth. "He appeared in a body, was vindicated by the Spirit" (1 Tim. 3:16). Jesus indicated that the Spirit would also convict of judgment. This is hinted at in the present situation, as Peter warns, "Save yourselves from this corrupt generation" (2:40). It was ripe for judgment.

To his anxious inquirers Peter prescribes repentance and baptism (2:38). He is able to assure them that when they thus express their faith in Christ crucified and risen, the Spirit will be given to them. Though faith is not expressly mentioned, it is clearly involved in repentance (cf. 11:18). The prominence of repentance is appropriate here. If this requirement was in the forefront of the preaching of John the Baptist even before Jesus was the issue, how much more must it be central now, in view of the rejection of the Nazarene.

Three thousand responded to the invitation. This was probably only a fraction of the crowd that heard Peter speak, but it represented a great victory for the gospel. Several factors account for this large ingathering. As previously noted, these people were Jews familiar with prophecy. They were also devout, God-fearing persons. They were familiar with Jesus' earthly ministry and probably with his claims. The advent of the Spirit proved to be the catalyst as the whole complex of events was set in perspective by the preaching of Peter.

It is quite possible that more people were brought to Christ at Pentecost than responded to him during his entire earthly ministry. He had many followers, but the following was poorly grounded and often turned out to be superficial (see, for instance, John 6:60, 66). The largest number of disciples that we read of is a group of five hundred, to whom Jesus appeared, probably in Galilee, after his resurrection (1 Cor. 15:6). But it would be a mistake to conclude that the Spirit is more effective than Jesus in winning people. After all, the Lord continues to work through the Spirit and through his followers, so the results in fact belong to him (see 1:1). The great task of the Lord Jesus was to provide salvation by his death and resurrection. Conversion in large numbers could hardly be expected before the cross. Jesus did not publicly proclaim the death and resurrection except occasionally, in enigmatical language (e.g., John 12:32).

After Pentecost the number of believers kept increasing from day to day (2:47), no doubt largely through the witness of the apostles but also through the joyful testimony of the new converts. Luke mentions two other factors that should be taken into account: the signs and wonders wrought by the apostles (2:43) and the manner of life of the new believers (2:44–47). These things will be discussed when the Jerusalem church is examined in more detail in Chapter V.

2. THE GENTILE MISSION

In discussing this subject one is confronted by an initial problem. As G. B. Caird puts it, "It is difficult to explain the reluctance of the Jerusalem church to embark on a mission to the Gentiles, if they had received from Jesus an explicit command to do so."[6] Many others share this point of view, going so far as to suggest that the church put the Great Commission (Matt. 28:18-20) into the lips of Jesus after the Gentile mission was an accomplished fact. This, of course, raises the question of truthfulness in reporting on the part of the Gospel writers. It also involves the assumption that the Jerusalem church was in fact reluctant to take the gospel to Gentiles, a conclusion that has not been shown to be warranted. Unfortunately the Lukan account does not provide us with any certainty concerning the exact interval of time covered by the early chapters of Acts. At best we can infer that much happened in a relatively short period. Probably not more than two or three years intervened between Pentecost and the conversion of Saul of Tarsus, the chief human instrument in the expansion of the testimony to the Greco-Roman world. The apostles could have reasoned that their first responsibility was to establish a strong base in Jerusalem before moving out to the rest of the world, so that their localized success could serve as a recommendation to prospective believers elsewhere.

In fact, there would be something decidedly unnatural in an effort to reach out to the Gentiles before the intermediate steps were taken—namely, the evangelizing of Judea and Samaria. That the gospel was taken to Samaria at all would be remarkable unless there had been an express command from the Lord Jesus. The existence of Christian communities in Judea is attested in Acts 9:31ff., but no indication is given of the time during which such churches were established. However, the fact that the gospel made its way as far as Damascus prior to the conversion of Saul (see Acts 9:1ff.) demonstrates the outreach of the church at a fairly early time. That Paul was called to minister to Gentiles is affirmed both in Acts 9:15 and in his own testimony (Gal. 1:16), another corroboration of a prior pronouncement of the Great Commission. To suppose that the Jerusalem church had an aversion to evangelizing Gentiles is to overlook the fact that Judaism had long been reaching out to Gentiles in the Dispersion through its synagogues. Furthermore, it is stated that those who began to preach the gospel to Gentiles in Antioch were Hellenists from the Jerusalem church (Acts 11:20). It is quite possible that many who responded to the message in the Jerusalem setting voluntarily returned to areas of the Dispersion where they had formerly resided following a period of instruction in the elements of the faith. (Acts 11:20 may contain a hint to this effect.)

Furthermore, the Jerusalem church was able to expand by means other than sending out missionaries. People from near and far came to the city and returned to their homes with a knowledge of the gospel (Acts 5:16; 8:26ff.).[7]

Christianity received something by way of example from Judaism, for in the last century before Christ many Gentiles had been won to the Jewish faith in the Dispersion, and this activity was continuing when the church began to reach out to the same field of opportunity. "It was only because the Diaspora synagogues were spread like a thick net over the entire area of the Mediterranean that Christianity could expand over the whole *oikoumene* within one generation, and only because Diaspora Judaism had always had missionary contact with her environment that Gentiles beyond her limits could be won so quickly for the message of Jesus."[8]

Judaism laid three requirements on its Gentile converts. The first was circumcision, a rite required of Abraham and his descendants as the mark of the covenant relationship (see Gen. 17:11–12) and necessary also for the *ger* (stranger) who desired to have a share in Israel's Passover observance (see Ex. 12:48). The second was baptism, self-administered and properly witnessed, which carried with it the obligation to assume the yoke of the Torah. The third was the offering of an appropriate sacrifice (though this requirement was discontinued when the temple was destroyed).

Some Gentiles resented and resisted the demand that they be circumcised. This was particularly true of Greeks, since they almost idolized the human body. To them circumcision appeared degrading and humiliating. Consequently, many who might otherwise have become proselytes because of their attraction to Judaism were content to retain the status of God-fearer (see Acts 13:16). Women did not have to face this problem and so were more open to assuming proselyte status.

One who reads the book of Acts gets the distinct impression that Christian success in winning God-fearers to the new faith became a sore point with the Jews. After all, they had been cultivating these people, hoping all the while for their advancement into the ranks of the proselytes. The fruit that seemed ripe for the plucking was suddenly picked off by Christian missionaries. Under these circumstances it is easy to understand the rise of Jewish agitation against the church.

Although we are accustomed to thinking of the Gentile mission as having been primarily carried on by Paul (not without reason), yet it is clear that he was not the pioneer in this development. From Acts 6 we learn that in the Jerusalem church there were already two groups, identified respectively as Hebrews and Hellenists (v. 1). Luke does not explain these terms. It is commonly held that the difference was a matter of language. Werner Jaeger writes that the term *Hellenists* refers to

> the Greek-speaking element among the Jews, and consequently also among the early Christian community in Jerusalem at the time of the apostles. It does not mean Jews born or brought up in Jerusalem who had adopted Greek culture, but people who no longer spoke their original Aramaic at home, even if they understood it, but Greek, because they or their families had lived abroad in Hellenized cities for a long time and later had returned to their homeland. Those of them who had not become Christians had their own Hellenistic synagogues in Jerusalem, and we find a Christian Hellenist like Stephen involved in long religious discussions with them.[9]

Others think we must go beyond the criterion of language, suggesting that possibly this group had absorbed paganizing tendencies or were characterized by opposition to the temple worship, since Stephen belonged to this group and spoke out along this line (see Acts 7:47–50). Whatever may be the solution to this problem, it is clear that the Hellenists were responsible for initiating Christian testimony to the Gentiles.

The neglect experienced by needy hellenistic widows in the Jerusalem church came to an end with the appointment of the Seven, all of whom could have been Hellenists, judging on the basis of their Greek names. At any rate, Luke indicates that certain of the Seven became active in public preaching, especially Stephen. When he was martyred, persecution flared against believers, with the Hellenists as the principal target, and as a result this segment of the congregation was scattered to other areas. Instead of taking cover, they became active in spreading the message of the gospel. The verb that can be rendered "scattered throughout" (8:1) is the verb used to denote the scattering of seed at planting time. So evangelism was promoted by the persecution. Caird observes that during this period many Aramaic-speaking Christians apparently fled into Judea, where they established churches.[10] We know, for example, that congregations were planted at Lydda and Joppa (see Acts 9:32ff.). Since the apostles must have been active in visiting and supervising these centers of faith, it is not strange that when Paul returned to Jerusalem after his conversion he had contact only with Peter and James the Lord's brother (see Gal. 1:18–19).

No description of the inception of the Gentile mission would be adequate if Stephen were neglected. He is worthy of mention if only because of his connection with Saul of Tarsus. It is possible, even likely, that the two confronted each other in the synagogue (6:9). The debating must have been sharp and determined. When the hellenistic Jews found themselves unable to refute Stephen, they circulated charges against him to the effect that he was claiming that Jesus would destroy the temple and change the customs that Moses had delivered to the nation (6:14).

The question to be raised here is why Luke considered it so important to devote so much space to Stephen. A possible clue is the point in the story at which he is introduced, just ahead of the account of the mission to the Samaritans, which was a stepping-stone to outreach among the Gentiles.

Some scholars have insisted that Stephen's attitude toward the temple is indicative of Samaritan influence upon him (bearing in mind that the Samaritans had their own worship at Mt. Gerizim). But it is far more likely that Stephen's attitude was shaped by Jesus, particularly by the prediction of his death and resurrection in terms of the destruction and raising up again of the temple (John 2:19–21).

In his address, Stephen did not manifest concern for the evangelizing of the Gentiles, so we have no direct evidence that would credit him with inspiring that movement. However, his colleague Philip ministered first to the Samaritans and then to the Ethiopian eunuch, so the circle of witness begins to widen. Moreover, those who made the breakthrough at Antioch by speaking the word directly to the Greeks were Hellenists from the Jerusalem area (see Acts 11:20).

It may be helpful to note that the transition between the Hebrew Christian church and its Gentile counterpart embraces three strands: (1) the evangelizing of Judea and Samaria (8:4–25; 9:32–43); (2) the conversion of Saul, followed by his preaching at Damascus and Jerusalem (9:1–30); and (3) the witness of Peter to the Gentile Cornelius and his friends (10:1–11:18). Once the fanning out from Jerusalem had occurred, the fulfilling of the second and third portions of the Great Commission moved forward.

The somewhat isolated incident of Philip's testimony to the Ethiopian eunuch is mentioned in connection with the first of these developments. As far as one can tell, this incident (8:26–40) created no upheaval in the Jerusalem church. The man was a Gentile, presumably a God-fearer (see Deut. 23:1). But Peter's visit to the home of Cornelius and the turning of a number of Gentiles to the faith brought a reaction at Jerusalem that was little short of consternation (11:2). Whereas the Ethiopian eunuch was a single figure and by this time had left Palestine for Africa, the converts at Caesarea were in the land and their number could easily increase.

Opposition to Peter's mission in Caesarea came from the circumcision party (11:2), a group strong enough to challenge the conduct of the leading

apostle. Clearly the issue of accepting Gentiles into the church was beginning to loom large. The accusation brought against Peter was that he had
broken down the barrier established by the Levitical food laws between
Jews and Gentiles (11:3). If these Gentiles had been circumcised, they could
readily be accepted into the (Jewish Christian) church, for Gentiles had
always been welcomed as proselytes to Judaism. Why should the same
regulations not apply in this case? The idea of a church in which Jew and
Gentile (uncircumcised) would share alike on the basis of faith in the Son
of God had apparently not dawned on the Christian community at Jerusalem. Doubtless they feared that if Gentiles in any great numbers pressed
into the church, not observing the customs of the Jews, such offense would
be created among unsaved Jews that the latter would be unreachable with
the gospel. They might even persecute that portion of the church that had
escaped injury at the time of Stephen's death. There may have been also a
lurking fear that the day would come when Gentiles would outnumber
Jews in the church and the leadership of the movement would pass into
their hands, which at that time was out of the question.

The apprehensive attitude among the Jewish Christians settled into a
passive acceptance after the Jerusalem Council made its pronouncement
about the reception of Gentiles, but it would be going too far to assert that
the Jerusalem church as a whole backed the Gentile mission unreservedly.
After all, even Philip and Peter needed special divine guidance in order to
persuade them to bear witness to Gentiles (see 8:26; 10:9–16, 28). We might
note that in between the records of God's dealings with these two brethren
comes the report of the conversion and commission of Saul of Tarsus
(9:15). In his case, Gentiles were included in the scope of his commission
(Gal. 1:16), but even he needed guidance in realizing this objective (Acts
22:21).

It may be well here, even though it somewhat anticipates later developments, to indicate the measure of support given to the Gentile mission
by the Jerusalem church. (1) It contributed individuals who served actively
in the movement—Peter, Philip, Barnabas, Silas, and Mark in addition to
the unnamed Hellenists noted in 11:19ff. (2) It consented to the principle
of Gentile freedom enunciated at the Jerusalem Council. (3) A fairly strong
Judaizing element in the mother church made a united front impossible
(15:5). (4) No financial support for the Gentile mission is indicated in our
sources, but the necessity for the local church to care for its needy was
probably a factor here. (5) Apparently there was no attempt at official
domination of the Gentile churches—and this despite the precedent of
Judaism's centralized control of its constituents through the Sanhedrin,
temple tax, rabbinic interpretation of the law as definitive for the Jewish
faith, and the like. (6) The majority decision at the Council favoring Gentile
freedom involved sacrifice in the sense that now the leadership of the

universal church would gradually swing over into Gentile hands. Evangelism of the Jewish population would be more difficult.

To continue the story, we note that directly after the account of Peter's ministry at Caesarea and its repercussions at Jerusalem the Hellenists are mentioned again (11:19ff.). Though they are not called Hellenists, the identification is certain because of the mention of Stephen. Now their activities take them into Phoenicia, Cyprus, and Syria (including Antioch). Up to this time the testimony of these men has been borne to Jews only, and this continued to be the case until they reached Antioch. Then, apparently without any special divine guidance, they began to witness to Gentiles. The evident blessing of God on their efforts was sufficient to assure them that they had done the right thing. A turning point in early church history had been reached.

Goppelt suggests that Acts 8–11 was written not simply to recount the progress of the gospel but to indicate "how the earliest Church was led to a recognition of the developing Gentile Christianity."[11] In this connection chapters 10–11 are very instructive. First, Peter was enlightened by the vision on the housetop in Joppa. He could hardly mistake the connection between the threefold presentation of the vision and the arrival of three men from Caesarea. The lesson of the vision, of course, was that clean and unclean animals were mingled together. From the Jewish standpoint that should have made the clean animals unclean, but God insisted to Peter that this was not so. The lesson finally penetrated, as Peter later confessed to his Caesarean audience: "God has shown me that I should not call any *man* common or unclean" (10:28). All this was confirmed when the Spirit fell on his audience, uncircumcised as they were and as yet not even baptized (10:44).

Antioch was a veritable melting pot of humanity, with elements from east and west, north and south. Jews were residents here from the very beginning, when Seleucus I, one of the generals of Alexander the Great, founded the city in 300 B.C. The Jews were brought from Babylonia. In keeping with the cosmopolitan character of the city, they were less exclusive than in most places and thus may have been more open to the gospel. However, as one might expect, even here Gentile converts predominated. It is important to note that in such an atmosphere there was little danger of persecution for the growing church.

Luke does not intimate that the men who founded the work here went on to other places. Some of them were originally from nearby Cyprus (11:20), which doubtless made them feel quite at home. Two factors would have encouraged them to remain—the rapid growth of the church and the relative ease with which they could find employment in this thriving commercial center. It is worth noting that whereas Peter and John moved on from Samaria and Peter moved on from Caesarea, Barnabas, despite having been sent from Jerusalem, did not return to report on developments in the Antioch church but stayed on there as a permanent worker without seeking endorsement from the mother church for what he and others were doing.

Paul was brought into the Antioch situation by Barnabas when the work grew to such an extent that additional help was needed for the instruction of new converts (11:25). For a period of about ten years he had been in and around Tarsus, his native city. Regarding this ministry Luke is silent, an indication that he was not so intent on glorifying his friend as some have supposed. That Paul was active during those hidden years may be regarded as certain. Such a man could not be otherwise. But it appears that the church at large had little contact with him (Gal. 1:21–23). Yet his success during this interval may be certified by the fact that following the Jerusalem Council he and Silas went through Syria and Cilicia strengthening the churches (see 15:40–41). We know of no one else who could have established these churches.

Paul was not destined to become a fixture in the Antioch setting. The same Spirit who directed Philip to leave Samaria to minister to a single Gentile who was on his way from Jerusalem to his native Africa (chap. 8) and who instructed Peter to go from Joppa and preach to Gentiles at Caesarea (chap. 10) now intervened in the affairs of the Antioch church by thrusting forth Barnabas and Saul. Their itinerary took them to Cyprus, Pamphylia, and South Galatia, with satisfying results in place after place. Their report to the home church is significantly worded: they declared all that God had done with them, and *how he had opened a door of faith to the Gentiles* (14:27).

This report, which brought such joy and satisfaction to the saints at Antioch, eventually reached the ears of the Jerusalem church also. To some at least in that church it caused an entirely different reaction. They were concerned—not because of Gentile conversions per se, but because these converts had not been circumcised. Before long a group from Jerusalem appeared in Antioch to protest that without circumcision Gentiles could not be regarded as genuine believers fit for church membership (15:1). The truly remarkable thing is that their complaint was not phrased to apply specifically to the converts made by Paul and Barnabas on their recently completed journey but rather as a direct challenge to Gentile believers in Antioch. Unless *you* are circumcised according to the custom of Moses, *you* cannot be saved (15:1). Several years had passed since the Antioch church had been born, and in those years there had been no such outburst as this.

Obviously the time had come for some decisive action by the church at large regarding the terms on which Gentiles would be accepted into full and regular standing. Barnabas, Paul, and some others were asked to go to Jerusalem to try to settle this issue in conference with the mother church. There had been debate at Antioch; there would be more at Jerusalem.

That circumcision had a biblical base is plain enough (see Gen. 17). That it was required of the strangers residing among the Israelites who desired to observe the Passover is equally plain (see Ex. 12:49). That Judaism had been requiring proselytes to submit to circumcision, be baptized, and assume the yoke of obedience to the Mosaic law is evident also. The Hebrew Christian church considered it only right to insist that these requirements be continued if Gentiles wished to join them. This was the inflexible rule of Judaism out in the Dispersion as well as in Jerusalem, so it was not a matter of geography.

The Judaizers, furthermore, could refer to the fact that Jesus was born under the law and lived in terms of it, having been circumcised as a child, as a basis for assuming that his followers, whether Jews or Gentiles, should follow in his steps. On the other hand, such pronouncements as he made on salvation did not mention these things. His Great Commission did not include any reference to circumcision or observance of the Mosaic law. Moreover, God had revealed to Peter his willingness to seal the acceptance of Gentiles wholly apart from circumcision or assumption of the burden of the law by granting his Holy Spirit to them (chap. 10). Jesus had promised that the Spirit would guide his followers into all truth (John 16:13). Peter's recital of his experience at Caesarea weighed heavily with the Council, probably being more decisive in their estimation than the testimony of Barnabas and Paul regarding their success in evangelizing Gentiles (15:12). It is possible that one of the apostles may have called attention to the fact that in Jesus' contacts with Gentiles no suggestion was made of their need for circumcision if they desired to become his disciples. If so, this could have been a factor in the decision of the Council.

Beyond question the future of the church was at stake here. For Gentiles, especially Greeks, the demand that they be circumcised amounted to a call to renounce their culture. It required them to become Jews, so to speak, in order to become Christians. Modern mission work has repeatedly demonstrated that it is folly to attempt to impose the missionary's culture on those of other cultures who are coming to Christ. Basic to the whole matter is the realization that nothing, no matter how good in itself, can be added to the grace of God as the basis for salvation, which must be received by faith alone. Peter put the matter well when he said, "No! We believe it is through the grace of our Lord Jesus that we must be saved, just as they are" (15:11). The Jew was not on a higher plane than the Gentile. Grace is an effective leveler. Evidently the Spirit brought this home to the Council—to apostles, elders, and others—so that debate came to an end. The cause of Gentile freedom had triumphed. All that remained was to draft a letter to Gentile believers in churches of Syria and Cilicia, asking them to avoid giving offense to Jews by abstaining from what had been sacrificed to idols, from blood, from what had been strangled, and from unchastity. In its letter the Council also disowned the actions of those who had gone to the Gentile churches with a demand for their circumcision (15:24).

The decision of the Council was crucially important. It called for the preservation of the purity of the gospel message, in line with Paul's trenchant presentation in his letter to the Galatians. It also ensured the continuing unity of the church universal, preventing a schism that could have resulted in two churches, one for Jews and the other for Gentiles, in contradiction of Jesus' vision and prophecy of one church (Matt. 16:18).

To be sure, the action of the Council did not silence for all time the Judaizing faction (see Phil. 3:2), but it did free Paul and his fellow workers to carry on their labors among the Gentiles, knowing that they had the backing of the church as well as their own convictions. When Paul went up to Jerusalem for the last time, he took with him several representatives of the Gentile churches (see 20:4), uncircumcised men who bore with them the contributions of their congregations for the relief of poor Christians in Judea. Paul would not have exposed these men to embarrassment and humiliation on that trip. He was confident that the Jerusalem church was continuing to stand behind the decision it had reached at the Council several years earlier.

It will be recalled that F. C. Baur considered the book of Acts unreliable, harmonistic in tendency and late in origin, and nowhere more unreliable than in its account of the Jerusalem Council. An entirely different appraisal is provided by Gregory Dix in his book *Jew and Greek*. He notes that the gospel was proclaimed among the Jews of Palestine for a decade, that for another decade it went to the Jews of the Dispersion, and that in the third decade (A.D. 50–60) it made its great leap into the Gentile world. Something must have taken place just prior to the third phase to make possible this tremendous advance among the Gentiles. Something such as the Jerusalem Council must have occurred and must have occurred where Luke places it. By the time Paul wrote Ephesians (early in the 60s), he could picture Jew and Gentile as sharing on equal terms in the body of Christ. This theology of the church was the expression of what had been taking place for a decade or more in the life of the Christian community.[12]

3. PERSECUTION AND THE BREAK WITH JUDAISM

In following the development of the Gentile mission it was necessary to note the role of persecution in expanding the scope of the church's witness. But this is only a part of a much larger subject—the whole relation of the primitive church to the Jewish establishment.

To grasp the situation we would do well to understand as clearly as possible the nature of Judaism, which is not only a religion but a culture, a way of life. We have some difficulty appreciating this because of our traditional separation of church and state. In the nature of the case, the first adherents of Christianity, being Jews, could not divest themselves of what had been central to their lives, almost the whole of their lives, especially since much of this inheritance was fully in line with the gospel revelation and a preparation for it.

Theologically speaking, it is proper to say that when Jews became Christians, they ceased to be Jews, for in Christ there is neither Jew nor Greek. Consequently, Paul speaks of deliberately becoming a Jew in order to win Jews (1 Cor. 9:20). He was no longer a Jew since he had become a Christian, but he was able to adapt his conduct to the Jew so as to avoid offense. Yet it was equally true that Paul could speak proudly of his Jewish inheritance (see Acts 21:39; 22:3; cf. Phil. 3:4–6). Furthermore, he warned other Jewish Christians against attempting to disavow or repudiate their background (1 Cor. 7:17–24). For a Jew to become a Christian meant not so much conversion from Judaism as conversion to Christ. For a Gentile the need was far greater that he be redeemed from his former environment (see 1 Pet. 1:18).

The primitive Christian community, then, felt no embarrassment about its relation to Judaism. On the day of Pentecost Peter addressed his audience as brethren (see Acts 2:29; cf. Rom. 9:3) even before they made any declaration of faith in Jesus as the Christ. Without apology he made generous use of the Old Testament. Shortly thereafter Peter and John are pictured as ascending to the temple to observe one of the stated hours of prayer (Acts 3:1). On the other hand, the converts at Pentecost could not be advised to take their place once more in the familiar framework of Judaism as though nothing epochal had happened to them. They were warned by Peter to save themselves from the crooked generation that had crucified the Lord (2:40). However, they were not told to separate themselves from it, to form an enclave within the nation that would be virtually isolated from friends and neighbors. They accepted Christian baptism and partook of the Lord's Supper. They became part of a close-knit fellowship that maintained its own worship and religious activity, including systematic instruction, prayers, and table fellowship. These things set them apart from the Judaism around them. After all, the Pharisees had their own cultus and the Essenes their own peculiar practices, both groups being nevertheless units within Judaism.

At this point a few questions come to mind: Did the early church in Jerusalem think of itself as being in opposition to Judaism, as though its own position made it so utterly different as to be alien to the religion of their fathers? Or did they think of themselves as participating in a movement that fulfilled the dreams and hopes of Judaism? National aspirations had a strong hold on the disciples even after the resurrection (see Acts 1:6). A dominant Jewish tinge is observable in the second recorded address of Peter (Acts 3), even though blessing to all the families of the earth is included as the final goal (3:25). The full implication of Jesus' mission in relation to the world at large seems to have been only dimly perceived at the time.

Thus far we have been looking at a church conscious of its own identity within the larger entity of Judaism, yet closely bound up with Judaism in many respects. It remains to be seen whether this tie with Judaism was maintained as a matter of principle and conviction or as a matter of expediency. If adherence to Christianity had been made dependent on the abandonment of everything characteristically Jewish (as summarized, let us say, by the law and the customs), there would have been scant prospect of gaining converts from Judaism. But those who responded at Pentecost had no such demand laid on them, and there was no reason for supposing that they in turn should impose any such demand on those who would become converts in the future. On the other hand, these believers who constituted the original Christian community were apparently quite prepared to endure reproach for the sake of Christ, and we have no ground for thinking that if they had understood their Christian position to entail substantial cleavage from Judaism, they would have been unwilling to make the sacrifice. Everything points to the conclusion that they felt no embarrassment in retaining and emphasizing their Jewish heritage along with their new faith. Conviction united with expediency in leading them to adopt a course that avoided giving needless offense to the Jew. Ample offense was already present in the proclamation of a crucified Messiah. There was no need to compound it.

The fact that persecution soon beset the infant church is not an indication of the futility of this attitude on the part of the Christian community toward Judaism; nor is it an indication of divine disapprobation toward that attitude. After all, Jesus had predicted to the disciples that their countrymen would excommunicate them as a religious duty (John 16:2). The disciples were forewarned that their witness to their Lord could prove costly to themselves. Their fear of the Jews following the trial and crucifixion of Jesus caused them to bar their doors. Who could be sure that those who pursued the Nazarene to his death would not continue the pursuit until his followers were caught in the net? The resurrection did much to remove these fears, causing the disciples to emerge from seclusion. Fifty days passed without any move against them by the authorities. With the advent of the Spirit their fears, already largely subsided, effectually vanished. Even the events of Pentecost left them untouched by harassment. It is reasonable to suppose that in those days the Sanhedrin felt that with Jesus removed from the scene, the movement that centered in him would eventually disintegrate and disappear. To pay it attention might only serve to prolong its life. Meanwhile the apostles and their followers were building good will among the people by their works of healing and by their genuinely joyful demeanor. After all, these believers in Jesus were observing the dietary laws of the Levitical code, were circumcising their children, were fasting and tithing, were observing the stated times of prayer in the temple, and were keeping the Sabbath. Their conduct doubtless played a part in the winning of a large company of priests to the faith (see Acts 6:7). These were not, however, members of the priestly aristocracy but rather ordinary priests such as the father of John the Baptist, so their conversion did not necessarily add prestige to the new movement. But it doubtless disturbed the temple authorities that a breach had been made in the ranks of the priesthood.

It was not long until opposition became open and vocal, originating with the Sadducees (4:1). Luke's statement that the ground of the opposition was the proclamation of the resurrection of Jesus has been questioned. Some have argued that the Sadducees did not take theology seriously enough to raise such an issue, seeing that their real concern was for the preservation of the status quo that found them hand in hand with the Romans who ruled the country. They would naturally resist anything that suggested revolutionary designs, and they had opposed Jesus out of fear that he might lead a popular revolt against Rome. This objection to Luke's account fails to take into consideration the fact that the apostolic preaching included the charge that the Jewish rulers had delivered Jesus over to Pilate and were responsible for his death (4:10; 5:28). "Proclaiming the resurrection of someone condemned by the Sanhedrin struck the priestly nobility as an act of religious fanaticism endangering the existing order and undermining their authority."[13]

According to the apostolic proclamation, the wrong perpetrated by these men had been glaringly revealed by God's action in raising Jesus from the dead. The Sadducees squirmed under such charges, and since they could not deny their part in the death of Jesus, they resorted to forcible means to stop the preaching. Their initial strategy involved imprisonment and a warning to stop this kind of preaching activity (4:18). Refusal to obey the order incensed them, and the situation was not eased by the obstinate attitude of the apostles, who firmly insisted that they must obey God rather than men (5:29). So inflamed were the Sadducees that they were ready to kill Peter and John (5:33). However, they were blocked by the Pharisees in the Council, headed by Gamaliel (5:34ff.; cf. 23:7).

The Pharisees had with some reluctance acceded to the demand of the Sadducees that Jesus be sacrificed for the welfare of the nation (see John 11:49-53), but their principles made them wary of taking human life lest it turn out that a mistake had been made. They were content to let God reveal his will through the passage of time and the outworking of events. Other revolutionary movements had failed, it was argued; this one also would fail if God was not in it. The upshot of the tense situation was that the apostles were simply beaten and released. It may well be that the Pharisees were also influenced by the realization that the inhabitants of

Jerusalem had by and large been favorably impressed by the believers in Jesus, and that any drastic steps taken against the apostles would be unpopular. The Pharisees were in closer touch with the people than the Sadducees were.

A lull in persecution followed, broken by events centering in the person of Stephen. While undoubtedly this servant of the Lord preached the resurrection of Jesus, nothing is said about this in Luke's account. Trouble developed on another front entirely. This fiery preacher, who reminds one of John the Baptist in his bluntness, was accused of speaking out against the temple and the law (6:13) on the ground that the Lord Jesus would set both aside (evidently by his eschatological action). This, of course, implied his resurrection. Stephen's defense was not designed to show that the temple and the law were mistakes, but rather that they were not ends in themselves, that they had a limited place in God's plan. Yahweh had not restricted his self-revelation in the past to the temple or even to the holy land (7:2, 30ff.). As for the law, the fathers no sooner received it than they rebelled (7:39ff.). Their descendants persecuted and killed the prophets, becoming the forerunners of those who put to death the Righteous One (7:51ff.). And all the while these people were living under the law. The indictment was clear and the reaction predictably sudden and sharp. Charged with blasphemy (6:11), Stephen was sentenced to suffer the consequences (7:58). He had dared to attack the bastions of Jewish defense and expose them—and this in the presence of the Council (6:12). If this body were to be called to account by the Roman authorities for permitting the death of this man, they could reply that witnesses had testified against him and that the accused had really convicted himself. Goppelt comments, "The act of violence against Stephen was possible only because Pontius Pilate had to favour the Jews after his protector, the anti-Semitic Sejanus, had been overthrown in Rome in A.D. 31."[14] It has been maintained also that Pilate was no longer on the scene, having been relieved of his position by Vitellius shortly before this time, in the year 36. (Vitellius was the imperial legate over Syria, which administratively included Palestine.) Since the Romans needed Jewish support because of the Parthian menace, they were giving the Jewish authorities a very free hand in their internal affairs.[15]

A fierce persecution against the church broke out immediately after the death of Stephen. No longer do we read of Pharisees holding Sadducees in check, for the law as well as the temple had come under attack. No longer do we read of a favorable attitude on the part of the people toward believers. A new issue had been raised. Judaism itself had been called into question for standing pat on its institutions instead of accepting God's new revelation in Christ. In the face of this new threat, the church began to scatter, but the apostles remained (8:1). It is likely that the brunt of the persecution was borne by the Hellenists, though this is not stated by Luke.

Probably others besides the apostles stayed in the city; otherwise there would have been little point in the decision of the apostles to remain.

Luke's purpose in introducing Saul in connection with the death of Stephen is probably not so much to hint at the significance of the incident in relation to his conversion (cf. 22:20) as to prepare the reader for the role of this young man as the chief persecutor of the church in the following days (8:3). Though he was a Pharisee, he did not hesitate, as Gamaliel had done, to take action. The difference was that now the very foundations of Judaism had come under assault. He felt that it was his religious duty to stamp out this dangerous sect and he went about his task as one who was waging a holy war.

The Lord of the church met this threat by his own direct intervention in the life of Saul, who afterward described his "conversion" as being laid hold of by Christ (Phil. 3:12). Here was a man bent on arresting believers in Jesus, only to be "arrested" himself in the midst of his fiery, headstrong campaign and turned completely around in the whole direction of his life. Christ was defending his church, which experienced a breathing spell when the chief persecutor ceased his threatenings (9:31).

Another stage in the persecution of the church was reached when Herod Agrippa I acted to have James the apostle put to death and to have Peter put in prison pending possible execution (12:1ff.). Herod the Idumean was seeking favor with his Jewish subjects, and he sensed that the sect of the Nazarenes was out of favor with the nation as a whole. Herod was king rather than governor, so his conduct ought not to be construed as necessarily reflecting the attitude of Rome toward the followers of Jesus. Goguel notes the uncertainty among Bible scholars as to why Herod ceased his persecution of the saints. Was it Herod's feeling that he had done enough to establish himself in the good graces of his subjects or was it that he died and Roman rule was reinstituted through procurators?[16] It should be noted that in this persecution, as in that undertaken by Saul, the Lord intervened on behalf of his people. Peter was spared for further usefulness.

To summarize the situation thus far, the following statement will suffice:

> The persecution of Christians by Jews in the thirties, forties and fifties is both a cause of the rupture, and a result of the recognition of the distinctive aspects of Christianity. In this situation it would beg the question to apportion "blame": Christian teaching (rightly) gave offence to orthodox Jews, and the inevitable result was opposition aimed at stamping out Christianity. If Jesus was put to death as a blasphemer (on the Jewish interpretation) and a Zealot (from the Roman side), it was impossible for his followers not to be regarded in much the same light as long as they were vocal about their beliefs. During the first years Christians would have been regarded as a heterodox party still within Judaism, and any punishment might be viewed as necessary internal

correction. This is the atmosphere in Stephen's death and Saul's commission. The persecution is better called "discipline" at this stage, even though it be of the most severe kind. This discipline, as so often is the case, resulted in the hardening of each party's attitude and created a sympathetic hearing for Christians among the populace. But continual discipline slides into persecution, and persecution of one group by another demands separation.[17]

As the new faith spread out into the Greco-Roman world, it met with pressure from the Jews, although they did not dare to launch a campaign of extermination against Christians because they feared Roman reprisals. When Gentile converts increased to the point that they outnumbered their Jewish brethren, however, the Jews perceived the situation as having changed, since only so long as Rome continued to view Christianity as a variety of Judaism would it retain its official protection as a permitted religion. Nevertheless, for some years Rome continued to stand fast in its position of permission and protection. Who can fail to see a wonderful providence in all this—God using the power of Rome to shield the Christian church in the days of its infancy when Jewish hostility might have destroyed it, so that by the time Rome altered its attitude and turned against the Christians they had sufficient strength and maturity to survive all the efforts of the empire to crush them.

Saul the erstwhile persecutor became the leading witness to the Dispersion Jews and to the Gentiles who frequented the synagogues. Above all others he became the target of attack by his countrymen. They felt that he destroyed the very basis of their religion by preaching the gospel of grace that set aside the works of the law as ineffective and useless in attaining salvation, and by preaching that God offered this salvation to all men on the basis of the finished work of his Son.

> The Gentiles who had previously been attracted to the synagogue, and many others besides, now gathered together into a congregation which believed in Jesus as the promised One of Israel. But the broad masses of the synagogue as such rejected this faith and were themselves left behind, isolated in their negation and outlawed as the disobedient, obstinate nation. In encountering Paul's proclamation, the one people who had testified of God's coming salvation to all peoples transformed itself into post-Christian Judaism, isolating itself in its opposition, clinging to the Law instead of the gospel and persecuting the church. With the Gentile church arising in this way, Paul now brought the proclamation which was expelled from the synagogue directly to the Gentiles. Since the synagogue sensed its own condemnation in the existence and proclamation of this church, it tried to suppress them both (I Thess. 2:15f.). It persecuted Paul with bitter hatred to the very end as the man whose proclamation destroyed its previous position among the nations of the world and thus denied its very reason for existence.[18]

So the situation in the Dispersion was completely different from that of the early church in Jerusalem, where the church was a party within Judaism, so to speak, able to carry on its testimony by continuing to observe the law and the customs. Now, in the Dispersion areas, the church and the synagogue were ranged against each other, increasingly competing for the ear of the Gentile who had been prepared by his contact with Judaism for the message that God had fulfilled his promise made to the fathers and had brought salvation in Jesus Christ. The rift between believing and unbelieving Jews was growing wider and deeper with every passing year.

Along with this process went another. Not all Jewish-Christian believers endorsed Paul's law-free gospel. The Judaizing propaganda insisting that one had to become a Jew in order to become a Christian, even though it was rejected by the Jerusalem Council, continued for a time to gain access to Pauline congregations (Phil. 3:2).

The church was also plagued from within by the problem of making adjustment between uncircumcised Gentile believers who did not observe Jewish customs and Jewish Christians who continued to live under the law both as a matter of inheritance and as a means of keeping on good terms with non-Christian Jews. Paul's encounter with Peter at Antioch (see Gal. 2:11ff.) emphasized the sharpness of this issue and also its importance: if it was not settled it could split the entire church. Peter seems to have understood that he had been guilty of wrong conduct in withdrawing from Gentile believers after sharing table fellowship with them. That Paul could write so freely about the situation implies this. So it became understood throughout the church that whereas Jewish believers must be free to observe the customs, circumcise their children, and the like, they were not to withhold fellowship from their Gentile brethren, a practice that would logically compel Gentiles to accept circumcision as the condition for retaining that fellowship.

The other side of the coin was the possibility that Jewish believers would cease to practice the customs and enjoy the freedom that Gentile believers had. In fact, the rumor spread that Paul was advocating this. James was worried enough by this rumor that when Paul came to Jerusalem for the last time this leader of the Jewish wing of the church urged the apostle to put an end to it once for all by joining some Jewish brethren who were being purified in the temple after being for a time under a Nazarite vow (see Acts 21:17ff.). Paul's attitude seems to have been that a Jewish believer should be free to make his own decision about living in terms of the ordinances of the law. Certainly he did not ask any to adopt the position that he must give up the customs.

Paul's situation was exceedingly difficult. He sensed the moving of God's Spirit among the Gentiles and the rapid growth of the faith in their ranks. On the other hand, he sympathized with men like James who felt a responsibility for the Jewish segment of the church, which was in danger of being relegated to a minority status by the growth of Gentile Christianity. His sponsorship of the fund for the poor saints in Judea was an attempt to bridge the gap and maintain cordial relations. The riot that broke out in Jerusalem during his last visit there rendered further efforts along this line impracticable. It also revealed the depth of animosity toward him on the part of both Diaspora and Palestinian Jews.

Luke's report of Paul's arrival in Jerusalem and of subsequent events conveys unmistakably to the reader the atmosphere of tension and disquiet among the Jewish Christians in the city. These people had heard the rumors about Paul and were not sure what to think about him. There is no reason to doubt that the church there knew in advance of Paul's coming and of his purpose in doing so. He had quite a retinue of companions representing the various Gentile congregations, bearing their gifts. In light of this, the existence of the anti-Pauline sentiment is the more remarkable and the more serious. The thousands of Jews who believed and were zealous for the law (Acts 21:20) were residents of Jerusalem and its environs. They were maintaining the customs and they were deeply disturbed by reports that Paul was failing to do so in his work among Diaspora Jews. Paul's attempt to give a report of the tremendous things that God had wrought among the Gentiles apparently went unacknowledged, or at least was not fully appreciated, being overshadowed by the reports that he was alienating Jews (21:19ff.).

Undoubtedly the situation of Jewish Christians in Palestine was difficult. They could not divorce themselves from every phase of Jewish life and still hope to win the Pharisees, with whom they had most in common. On the other hand, they could not minimize their differences lest they sacrifice their Christianity. For example, they could not endorse the Pharisaic doctrine of merit without denying the gospel of grace. Nor could they alter their position regarding the deity of Jesus Christ. What they emphasized, however, was not their dissatisfaction with Judaism (a strategy that could only have promoted further alienation) but the objective fact of God's endorsement of his Son by resurrection.

Presumably Christians in Judea had little to do with either the Sadducees or the Zealots, whose philosophies were diametrically opposed, the one advocating cooperation with Rome and the other fomenting rebellion against the hated foreign power.

So Jewish Christianity was engaged in a holding operation in the years prior to its demise. There were fewer and fewer converts to the faith compared to results in the halcyon days following Pentecost. The minds of Jews were occupied with the political situation above all else as they watched the growing deterioration of Roman-Jewish relations and felt the tug of Zealot propaganda urging their countrymen to seize the opportunity to be free of the hated conqueror, pleading that surely God would intervene to aid their cause and bring deliverance. Some of the Pharisees were caught up in this agitation and became activists contrary to their traditional pacifist stance.

The death of James attests the lawless nature of the times (the 60s) in Judea and the antagonism of some Jews toward the Christians in their midst. Josephus writes that

> upon learning of the death of Festus, Caesar sent Albinus to Judea as procurator. The king removed Joseph from the high priesthood, and bestowed the succession to this office upon the son of Ananus, who was likewise called Ananus. . . . The younger Ananus . . . was rash in his temper and unusually daring. He followed the school of the Sadducees, who are indeed more heartless than any of the other Jews . . . when they sit in judgment. Possessed of such character, Ananus thought that he had a favorable opportunity because Festus was dead and Albinus was still on the way. And so he convened the judges of the Sanhedrin and brought before them a man named James, the brother of Jesus who was called the Christ, and certain others. He accused them of having transgressed the law and delivered them to be stoned. Those of the inhabitants of the city who were considered the most fair-minded and who were strict in the observance of the law were offended at this. They therefore secretly sent to King Agrippa urging him, for Ananus had not even been correct in his first step, to order him to desist from any further such actions. Certain of them even went to meet Albinus, who was on his way from Alexandria, and informed him that Ananus had no authority to convene the Sanhedrin without his consent. Convinced by these words, Albinus angrily wrote to Ananus threatening to take vengeance upon him. King Agrippa, because of Ananus' action, deposed him from the high priesthood which he had held for three months, and replaced him.[19]

Differing in many particulars is the account by Hegesippus, the historian of Jewish Christianity, preserved by Eusebius.[20] The gist of this narrative is that at Passover time the scribes and Pharisees approached James and pressured him to ascend to the eminence of the temple and dissuade the people from turning to Jesus. James took his place but used the opportunity to confess Jesus as the Son of Man who was sitting on the right hand of power. Incensed at this backfiring of their plans, the leaders went up and hurled James to the pavement below. Badly hurt, he continued to pray for his people until a laundryman beat him to death with his club.

Without turning aside to deal with the problem presented by two such divergent accounts, it is of interest to note that in Josephus's story there is the same Sadducaic attitude of hostility as in the early chapters of Acts and the same Pharisaic attitude of hesitation to move against the followers of Jesus. Of great interest also is the way in which the Hegesippus version concludes. After recounting the death and burial of James, he tersely adds, "And at once Vespasian began to besiege them." He apparently saw in the death of James the passing of the last element of restraint. God was now abandoning the city to its doom. Josephus puts the death of James several years earlier and may well have the more accurate report of proceedings. But at the very least it amounted to the martyrdom of the most respected figure in the Jerusalem church. What could the rest of the saints expect?

Another significant aspect of this episode is noted by Goguel: "Josephus actually explains his death as due to the jealousy of the high priest, which presumes that James' influence extended beyond the bounds of the Christian community."[21] One should add that the unpopularity of James's death by murder reflects a considerable influence of this Christian leader on the community as a whole. "Since it was only James who was seized by the high priest, James' personal influence, not the church's, must have alarmed him."[22]

With the mounting of tension between Jews and Romans, induced on the Roman side by poor administration and the rapacity of officials and on the Jewish side by the increase in Zealot pressure on other segments of the population to join them, the Christian Jews were placed in a precarious position by their refusal to adopt the Zealot viewpoint and methodology. What were they to do? They could not conscientiously take up arms against the Romans, nor could they defect to them. According to Eusebius,

> The people of the church in Jerusalem were commanded by an oracle given by revelation before the war to those in the city who were worthy of it to depart and dwell in one of the cities of Perea which they called Pella. To it those who believed in Christ migrated from Jerusalem, that when holy men had altogether deserted the royal capital of the Jews and the whole land of Judea, the judgment of God might at last overtake them for all their crimes against the Christ and his Apostles, and all that generation of the wicked be utterly blotted out from among men.[23]

Pella was one of the cities of the Decapolis. Doubts have been expressed that Jewish Christians would go to a Gentile community and that they could migrate successfully due to the military situation in and around Jerusalem, to say nothing of the physical difficulties involved in such a trek.[24] But Schlatter puts forth the opinion that the Decapolis cities made a distinction between Jews and Christians that would permit these believers to come to the city and even go elsewhere in the area. These Christian Jews may have been welcomed also into Nabataean communities, where the ordinary Jew was thoroughly disliked.

Goguel assays this move as follows: "The exodus of the Christians does not prove that they had detached themselves from the national aspirations of the Jews and that they were indifferent to the fate of Jerusalem; it only proves that they neither shared the sentiments and hopes of the Zealots nor yielded to the tyranny with which they were threatening Jerusalem."[25]

The important fact is that for all practical purposes the Jewish-Christian church came to an end with the Jewish war against Rome. What history knows of the subsequent period concerns the Ebionites, who were heretical in their doctrine of Christ and in their exalted notion of the relation of the law to his followers.

Looking back at the comparatively brief span of the life of the Jewish-Christian church, one cannot avoid a sense of sadness at its demise. External developments played a major role in its eclipse—particularly the loss of James and the war between the Jews and the Romans—but there is a gnawing awareness also that the Jerusalem church grew timid and defensive. So far as our sources indicate, no effort was made to help Paul after he was seized by the mob in the temple area and taken into custody by the Romans. A fear of being identified with him seems to have set in. The Pentecostal boldness of the early days was gone.

4. THE EXTENSION OF THE CHURCH DURING THE FIRST CENTURY

Throughout the Old Testament period, Israel could be called a missionary people only in a limited sense. In the intertestamental period the Macca-bees pressed Judaism on conquered peoples by force. Later on, Philo used the literary method to commend Judaism to the Gentile world. According to Jesus, the Pharisees were prepared to cover sea and land in the hope of making a single proselyte (Matt. 23:15), but this was a display of sectarian zeal more than anything else. In the Diaspora the Jews were active in commending their faith to Gentiles, but even so they were content to let the Gentiles come for instruction rather than go forth to them. The isolated case of disciples of John the Baptist appearing at Ephesus (Acts 19:1-3) suggests the possibility that there were similar groups elsewhere. Even pagan religions, especially those of the mystery cult variety, were beginning to spread abroad in this period. But Christianity, due to the tremendous impact made by Jesus of Nazareth on his followers, accentuated in turn by his death and resurrection and climaxed by the coming of the Spirit, became the missionary faith par excellence. In terms of outreach, the apostolic age was one of its finest hours. Much of the detail is hidden from our view because of the fragmentary nature of our sources, but there is enough to produce amazement and admiration. The early church set a high standard for all succeeding periods to follow.

As noted, there were divine elements that made this development possible. But there were human factors as well—readiness to bear witness to Christ, a noble endurance of suffering for the Lord's sake, and a favorable impression created by Christian character and conduct. One must not overlook also the impetus given to the new faith by the large number of converts gathered in at the very beginning, at Pentecost. Donald McGavran has pointed out that Christianity from the outset was a people movement. The growth was not simply one by one but by groups such as families, associates, and friends. "The fact that a large enough segment of the Jewish people became Christian soon determined the entire course of Christian development. . . . It was because so many had become Christians that ostracism was impossible."[26]

The book of Acts testifies that the church began at Jerusalem. Its first expansion was naturally into its environs, into Judea. Paul mentions the existence of churches there at a period three years after his conversion, perhaps half a dozen years after Pentecost (Gal. 1:22). In another reference to these churches (1 Thess. 2:14) he refers to their sufferings at the hands of unbelieving Jews. Whether he had in mind the persecution at the time of Stephen's death (Acts 8:1) or of later events is not clear, but the use of these believers as an example for the Thessalonians implies that the Judean churches had continued steadfast despite these trials. Luke's statement in Acts 8:1 is simply that believers were scattered by the persecution and went into the regions of Judea and Samaria. It is clear from Acts 9:32ff. that Peter found disciples in communities west of Jerusalem when he made the trip that took him to Joppa and eventually to Caesarea. In one of his summary statements, Luke makes the observation that after the conversion of Saul the persecutor the church as a whole throughout all Judea (cf. the language of 1:8) and Galilee and Samaria had peace, was being edified, and was increasing in numbers (9:31). The inclusion of Galilee is noteworthy because no records have been supplied by Luke concerning the evangelization of this area. Even if the apostles were too occupied in the Jerusalem area to undertake this task, others must have been available to do so—for example, some of the more than five hundred brethren who saw the risen Lord on a certain occasion (1 Cor. 15:6). This may well have occurred in Galilee (see Matt. 28:16–17, in which the doubters referred to could hardly have been the Eleven, since they had already seen the Lord in the Jerusalem area).

Damascus had believers at a very early time, since Saul would not have taken his trip to round up a mere handful of Nazarenes (see Acts 9:1–2). The presence of believers in Damascus gives some warrant for supposing that other cities of the Decapolis had their own groups of disciples.

As for Caesarea, there is a possibility that Philip may have prepared the way for Peter's mission there (8:40). However, he may have been guided to labor mainly in the nearby towns, in view of the divine purpose that Peter should open the door of faith to the Gentiles in this city. He may well have been led to follow up Peter's work by a teaching ministry to Cornelius and his friends. On Paul's last trip to Jerusalem Luke was with him, and he takes note of the presence of disciples at Caesarea (21:16) in addition to the family of Philip. We are also informed of a church at Tyre, farther north on the Phoenician coast (21:3–4). It should be recalled here that the Hellenists who went as far as Antioch passed through Phoenicia and bore testimony to Jews in the region (11:19). We know from Acts 27:3 that Sidon had a group of believers. The same was true of Ptolemais (21:7).

Turning our attention to Antioch, we get the impression of a large and flourishing church there (Luke mentions Antioch thirteen times and Paul refers to it once [Gal. 2:11]). The presence of a group of gifted men engaged in teaching the church would seem to suggest that the city was home to a Christian community of considerable size. Growth continued over the years so that by the time of Chrysostom (toward the end of the fourth century), the church was reputed to have, in round numbers, some 100,000 members![27] Early in the second century Ignatius gave the Antioch church strong leadership prior to his martyrdom.

For some reason Luke has not indicated anything about Paul's activities in Arabia (Gal. 1:17) or in the area around Tarsus prior to his labors in the Antioch church, but it is clear that he saw conversions and established churches, at least in Syria and Cilicia (Gal. 1:22; Acts 15:41).

We have no information in the New Testament regarding expansion eastward from Antioch, but since there was constant travel and commerce over this route, churches must have been planted in this area. In postapostolic times the great center of the Syriac-speaking church was at Edessa, to the east of Antioch. Latourette notes that it was from Edessa that a vigorous extension of the faith reached out to the Tigris-Euphrates valley, Persia, central Asia, and China.[28]

Asia Minor became a major stronghold of Christianity from the first century on. Since people from several parts of this region were present at Pentecost (2:9–10), it is possible that some of them became converted and eventually returned to these places as missionaries. Luke has made us familiar with the labors of Paul and his companions, mainly in the province of Galatia, where he established churches in several of the southern cities (see Acts 13–14). Ramsay and others have noted that where Greco-Roman influence was strong the message took root firmly but in the back country where native languages persisted the progress of the faith was slow. The latter observation seems to fit the northern sections of Galatia where Paul traveled somewhat but where Luke makes no mention of the establishment of churches, referring only to scattered disciples (16:6; 18:23).

The growth of Christianity in the province of Asia owed much to the long and fruitful ministry of Paul in Ephesus. Luke makes the statement that during this period of nearly three years all the inhabitants of Asia heard the word (19:10). Paul probably had many of these people in mind when he wrote the letter to the Ephesians. The letter to the Colossians gives us some light on how the faith grew in this part of the world. Apparently Paul had not founded the church, which was located about a hundred miles east of Ephesus, but Epaphras had proclaimed the word there, probably after being under Paul's instruction. A similar explanation may account for the conversion and spiritual growth of Philemon. There were also groups of believers in the neighboring cities of Laodicea and Hierapolis (see Col 4:13). More complete testimony to the growth of the Christian cause is presented in Revelation 2 and 3, in which the seven churches are addressed. Early in the second century Ignatius wrote letters to some of these (viz. Ephesus, Philadelphia, and Smyrna) and also to believers at Tralles and Magnesia, places not mentioned in the Revelation.

In his first epistle, Peter writes to Christians in areas that cover all the upper part of Asia Minor—Pontus, Galatia, Cappadocia, Asia, and Bithynia. Paul tried to enter Bithynia but was restrained by the Spirit (Acts 16:7). Evidently others penetrated into this area, probably at a later time. The gospel made great progress in this province. Early in the second century, during the reign of Trajan, Pliny the Younger was governor there and he was informed that the sale of sacrificial meat brought from the temples to the markets had fallen off alarmingly due to the great increase in the number of Christians, who refused on principle to buy such meat.

One important factor in the growth of Christianity in Asia Minor was the wide distribution of synagogues, to which Christian missionaries turned their steps just as Paul and Barnabas had done (Acts 13). These tended to be found in urban centers. Some eighty-two synagogues are known to have existed in this area, and doubtless there were others. Asia Minor became the leading stronghold of the faith between the apostolic age and the Council of Nicaea in the fourth century. It was also the chief area of controversy, the church having to contend with both Gnosticism and Montanism.

Harnack emphasizes the importance of the testimony provided by Paul's letter to the Ephesians concerning the unity and peace of the church. What Augustus had done in a somewhat superficial way to draw together diverse elements of the population the gospel of Christ had done more effectively and on a higher plane. The middle wall of partition had been broken down.[29]

Offshore areas were not entirely devoid of gospel testimony. At least the important islands of Cyprus (Acts 13) and Crete (Tit. 1:5) were evangelized.

On his second missionary journey Paul and his companions bore witness to the people of Macedonia and Achaia, touching Philippi, Thessalonica, Berea, Athens, and Corinth. We read of a church at Cenchrea also (in Rom. 16:1). Judging from Paul's mention of "all the saints who are in the whole of Achaia" as potential readers of his second letter to the Corinthians (1:1), other churches must have sprung up, probably evangelized from the groups that he established. This pattern is suggested by the apostle in 1 Thessalonians 1:8, in which he states that the believers in Thessalonica proclaimed the word not only in Macedonia but also in Achaia—which is quite astonishing, since he was writing only a few months after the church had been founded.

Dalmatia, an area lying to the northwest of Macedonia, had the benefit of having received a mission from Titus (see 2 Tim. 4:10). Paul himself must have touched this region as well: he states that he went as far as Illyricum, which included Dalmatia and reached somewhat farther to the northwest along the Adriatic Sea (i.e., Dalmatia constituted the southern part of Illyricum; see Rom. 15:19). It appears that Paul also touched the Epirus region of Greece, for he informed Titus that he planned to spend the winter in Nicopolis (see Tit. 3:12).

On his journey to Rome Paul found brethren at Puteoli, about 150 miles southeast of Rome, where his ship docked after the trip from Malta (see Acts 28:13–14). Outside Rome he was met by brethren from the city (28:15). That the church in Rome was fairly strong in numbers may be judged from Romans 16:5, 14–15, in which mention is made of several house churches. Paul evidently knew of several of these. Church buildings are not referred to in our sources until the third century. The informality of the church in the house undoubtedly aided the process of evangelism as believers shared their faith and experience in Christ with visitors to the services. The Roman church was in existence before the middle of the first century (see Acts 18:2). By the time Paul wrote his letter to that church, its faith had become widely known (see Rom. 1:8). It numbered some of Caesar's household among its adherents (see Phil. 4:22). This does not necessarily mean that any of the imperial family had in the narrow sense become believers; it may well mean simply that certain officials and servants had turned to Christ. At the outbreak of Nero's persecution (A.D. 64) Christians were so numerous in the capital that Tacitus could describe them as "an immense multitude." Harnack estimates that by the middle of the third century there were at least 30,000 Christians in Rome. By the year 300 there were no fewer than forty basilicas in the city.[30]

The beginnings of Christianity in southern Gaul are veiled from view, but a variant reading in 2 Timothy 4:10 (Gaul instead of Galatia), which is accepted by a number of textual critics, may point to the beginnings of evangelization in the time of Paul. If his expectation of going to Spain (see Rom. 15:24, 28) was realized, then contact with southern Gaul en route to Spain becomes a distinct possibility (unless, of course, the journey was made by ship). The whole matter is uncertain for two reasons. For one thing, Paul's captivity letters (which in all probability he wrote from Rome) indicate a change of plans in favor of a return to the east (see Philem. 22). This shift was probably induced by the lack of full cooperation on the part of the Roman church for the Spanish mission (cf. Phil. 1:15–17, written from Rome) and by solicitude for his churches in the east, especially because of the Colossian heresy (cf. Philem. 22 with the Colossian letter). A second reason we are uncertain that Paul made the journey to Spain stems from a statement made by Clement of Rome: "He taught righteousness to all the world, and when he had reached the limits of the West he

gave his testimony before the rulers, and thus passed from the world"
(1 Clement 5:7). The problem is whether the limits of the West meant
Spain or Rome; mention of the rulers seems to favor Rome.

That the gospel did reach Spain, however, is certain. It was one of the
most thoroughly Romanized districts in the empire. Irenaeus and Tertullian
refer to the presence of Christians but give no details. The canons of the
Synod of Elvira, which was held prior to 300, "exhibit in a striking fashion
that contrast between coarse worldliness and fanatical strictness which has
characterized the history of the Spanish church in every age."[31] The
revelations of the sins of both clergy and laity make sorry reading.

Information is similarly scant concerning early Christianity in North
Africa. It is thought that the gospel came first to Carthage, but from what
source in the east is not known. The first documentation has to do with
the martyrdom of twelve Christians, seven men and five women, executed
at Carthage in 180 for refusing to deny the faith. Although the church in
this area prospered for some time, it was plagued by the Donatist schism.
Still later the heavy inroads of Islam all but obliterated it.

The beginnings of the faith in Libya and Cyrene are also somewhat
obscure. The city of Cyrene was founded by Greeks as early as the classical
period. In the first Christian century it was a leading center of the district
of Libya. Ptolemy I of Egypt settled many Jews in this area. According to
Acts 2:10, some people from this region were present at Pentecost. They
were sufficiently numerous to have a synagogue or a share in one at
Jerusalem (6:9). Some of them became Christians and took the lead in
spreading the gospel in Phoenicia and Syria, and later in ministering to
Gentiles at Antioch (11:19). We read of one man, Lucius by name, as a
teacher in that influential church (13:1). Simon of Cyrene bore the cross
of Jesus (Mark 15:21). Doubtless both he and his family were later brought
to Christ, since his sons Alexander and Rufus apparently belonged to the
church at Rome (see Rom. 16:13). To what extent such people carried the
gospel back to their homes in Libya is not known.

Egypt, too, had its representatives at Pentecost (2:10). Alexandrians
were found alongside Cyrenians in their synagogue (6:9). But information
about the planting of the gospel in that country is unfortunately lacking.
One would like to think that the Ethiopian eunuch left a deposit of
testimony there on his way home, but this remains a matter of conjecture.
Apollos was an Alexandrian (18:24). In the following verse the Western text
affirms that he was instructed in the word while still in his fatherland. If
this tradition is accurate, it means that Christianity began at an early time
to make its way into the Nile delta.

Eusebius contributes some traditional material relating to Mark's supposed connection with Egyptian Christianity: "They say that this Mark was
the first to be sent to preach in Egypt the Gospel which he had also put
into writing, and was the first to establish churches in Alexandria itself."[32]

A second statement runs as follows: "In the eighth year of the reign of Nero, Anianus was the first after Mark the Evangelist to receive charge of the diocese of Alexandria."[33] It is difficult to put much credence in these statements, for if the tradition is sound, then we are faced with the difficulty of explaining why Mark would have left such an important work in Alexandria to become involved with Peter and Paul in the latter period of their ministries. Furthermore, the silence of Clement of Alexandria and of Origen regarding such an epoch in Mark's life is damaging to the tradition. These men lived and labored in this very area.

But if the tradition regarding Mark's residence in Egypt is open to doubt, there is more reason for holding that the Gospel which bears his name found its way early to this area, at least by the end of the first century.[34] This clearly points to the presence of believers there at a somewhat earlier time.

In addition, there is the possibility that the epistle to the Hebrews was written from Egypt. This depends largely on the opinion that this book reflects to some extent the work of the Jewish philosopher Philo, who resided in Egypt.

There is general agreement, at any rate, that despite a lack of precise information, in the nature of the case it is virtually impossible that Egypt remained for long deprived of the gospel or the presence of a vigorous church, Alexandria being so accessible from Antioch. One can readily picture the men of Cyprus and Cyrene who brought the word to Antioch turning to this promising field to the south after others assumed the leadership in the Antioch situation. Then, too, there is need to explain Paul's avoidance of Egypt. Why would he fail to include in his travels this great center of population in Alexandria? It seems plausible that he simply did not care to build on another's foundation (see Rom. 15:20).

Claudius became emperor in A.D. 41. Shortly thereafter an embassy from Alexandria waited on him with congratulations and requests. He wrote a letter in reply, a copy of which was discovered in 1921 and was later published along with other papyri finds from Philadelphia in Egypt. The third item taken up in the letter is the disorders that had occurred in Alexandria in the reign of Caligula, when a wave of anti-Semitic sentiment swept over the city and brought destruction of life and property. The Jews protested the disorders through a delegation headed by Philo, but it got nowhere with Caligula. In his letter Claudius finds fault with both the Jewish and the Greek elements in the city for what had happened. The only reason I refer to this letter is that some scholars have surmised that it may have been an introduction of Christian preaching that excited the Jews and made them restless, so that in turn they became the target of Gentile animosity.[35] This is a possibility, but only that.

We are on more solid ground in referring to the existence of early papyri from Egypt containing portions of the New Testament, some of which go back to the second century. Shortly after this the Coptic versions began to appear, reflecting the need of the Egyptian church to have the New Testament in the language of the people.

Brandon is able to point to the undoubted fact that at various times in Israel's history its people resorted to Egypt as a place of refuge. Even the holy family followed this pattern after the birth of Jesus. This observation makes probable the conclusion that the Christian faith was introduced there at a fairly early time, perhaps by refugees fleeing from Jerusalem before the war with Rome.[36] Yet the veil remains. The origin of the church in Egypt is hidden from our sight.

Presumably areas far removed from the eastern Mediterranean sector received the gospel at a time considerably later than the lands already noted did. According to tradition, Thomas went to India; the story of his mission there is recorded in the Apocryphal Acts, but as is typical of this material, the account highlights the miraculous to the point that separation of the historical data from the remainder is difficult indeed.[37]

In post–New Testament times there was a natural tendency to try to relate the apostles as a group and as individuals to the world mission of the church. For example, in a work originating late in the first century or early in the second, we find this statement: "Therefore Peter says that the Lord said to the apostles: If then any of Israel will repent, to believe in God through my name, his sins shall be forgiven him: (and) after twelve years go ye out into the world, lest any say: We did not hear."[38] In the Apocryphal Acts there are traditions concerning the places the various apostles labored and their experiences. It was to be expected that the Gentile church would seek to explain why the participation of the original apostles in the Gentile mission was delayed, thus implying that they took up this task when they had spent a reasonable amount of time seeking to reach the nation Israel. However, Luke has not provided any information to serve as a guide in this area, and the figure of twelve years looks suspicious, as though artificially arrived at to tally with the number of the apostles.

Something should be included about the type of people won to faith in Christ during the apostolic age. Paul gives the impression that for the most part the converts at Corinth were of the lower classes (1 Cor. 1:26). Caird observes, "The long exhortation to slaves and the brief word to masters suggest very strongly that most of the early converts in all the Hellenistic churches were drawn from the lower strata of society."[39] Paul's statement about the Corinthians, however, may have been due, at least in part, to the character of Corinth as a commercial city, a community not known for its intellectual achievements. Since slaves were in a more difficult position than masters, it is natural that Paul (and Peter also, in 1 Pet. 2:18ff.) should have special concern for them.

It is easy to get the impression that Christian society was composed wholly of members of the lower classes in the early days, but this was not the case. People of distinction, of position, of means were numbered among the believers in most places: Nicodemus and Joseph of Arimathea, Barnabas, Mary the mother of John, and Mark in the Jerusalem church, Cornelius of Caesarea, Manaen (brought up with Herod the tetrach) of Antioch, Sergius Paulus of Cyprus, Lydia of Philippi, prominent women of Thessalonica and Berea, Dionysius the Areopagite of Athens, Gaius, Erastus, and Crispus of Corinth, Philemon of Colosse. These are known because they are mentioned. Doubtless there were others who remain unknown because there was no reason to single them out.

How are we to interpret those New Testament statements that seem to indicate a worldwide dissemination of the gospel during the apostolic age? For example, Paul declares that the gospel was bearing fruit throughout the whole world (Col. 1:6) and that it had been preached to every creature under heaven (Col. 1:23). There is obvious and deliberate hyperbole here, designed to pit the widespread acceptance of the gospel over against the local advocacy and limited appeal of the aberrant teaching at Colosse of which he warns. Again, in Luke's account of the evangelization of Ephesus, he throws in the comment that during that period all the Jews and Greeks of Asia (the province, not the continent) heard the word of the Lord (Acts 19:10). This is a general statement, summary in character. The justification for this language may be easier to understand later when we study the Ephesian church. Hyperbole is apparent also in Paul's complimentary statement to the Roman church that their faith is being reported all over the world (Rom. 1:8). He means, of course, that this is occurring among Christians, not unbelievers. His statements fitted in with the eminence and centrality of Rome. As the empire had its base in Rome and spread out across the world, so in a Christian sense the reputation of the Roman church was a part of the awareness of the universal church.

Any statement on the number of Christians at the end of the apostolic age is necessarily only an estimate. Bo Reicke puts the number of believers by the year A.D. 100 at 320,000, including adherents.[40] How is this impressive growth in a few decades to be accounted for? No single explanation will suffice. Diaspora Judaism provided partial preparation, as did the widespread knowledge of the Greek language and the peace and order provided by Rome. Certain other factors, building on these foundational elements, made their contribution, such as the concentration by missionaries on centers of population from which the word could be taken to adjacent areas, the training of new converts to be witnesses, good public relations (the cultivation of friendships with officials), and public exposure occasioned by opposition, as at Athens and Ephesus. To these must be added the still more important factors—love for Christ and obedience to his will, believing prayer, the transformed lives of converts, and the powerful enablement of the Holy Spirit.

5. CHURCH AND STATE

In approaching the subject of the relationship between church and state, a brief glance at the Old Testament background may be helpful. The nation of Israel began as a theocracy. When the kingdom was instituted, God was still recognized as the sovereign, at least by the more devout rulers. There was no concept of a secular state. Disobedience brought divine chastisement in the form of Judah's captivity to Babylon, the northern kingdom having succumbed earlier to Assyria. In the restoration period Judah found life difficult but tolerable as long as freedom of worship was granted. But when Persian rule gave way to Syrian domination, the nation suffered persecution. This served to strengthen the resolve of the people to be free, no matter how great the sacrifice. Under Maccabean leadership Israel gained its religious freedom and, later on, its political independence. It remained an independent state until it came under Roman control, which proved somewhat burdensome but which allowed the institutions and practices of the nation to continue as before. This brief survey reveals that to the people of God religious freedom proved to be more significant than political independence.

The subject of church and state needs to be approached from two sides: the teaching in our sources about the Christian's obligation to the state and the attitude of the state toward adherents of the Christian faith.

The Christian's Obligation to the State

The leading Scripture passages relevant to this discussion are Romans 13:1–7 and 1 Peter 2:13–15. Briefer treatment is provided in Titus 3:1 and 1 Timothy 2:1–4. Scholars formerly attributed the close similarity between Peter and Paul in their handling of this matter to a dependence of one on the writings of the other, but more recent investigation has made probable the conclusion that both men were reflecting the established teaching (*didache*) of the church on this subject.

The book of Acts provides some help in the sense that Christian witness is presented as having been made without any defiance of constituted authority: Roman toleration is apparent. The declaration of Peter about the necessity of giving obedience to God rather than to men (Acts 5:29) was made in reference to the attempted suppression of the Christian witness by an alarmed Sanhedrin rather than by the Roman authorities. Nevertheless, the principle was bound to be applied when pressure began to be exerted by Rome at a later time.

It will be helpful to include with the apostolic teaching on this subject whatever can be gleaned from the attitudes, words, and deeds of Jesus in relation to the Roman state, since it is reasonable to think that the position taken by the early church must in essence have been shaped by his example. This material will follow the presentation of the apostolic teaching.

The following are some observations on the epistolary presentation:

1. *Every* Christian has obligations toward the state (Rom. 13:1). This obligation is part of the will of God for his people (Rom. 12:2).

2. We are probably safe in assuming that the passages in Romans and 1 Peter reflect good relations between Christians and the state, at least in the main, that no official persecution had yet been launched against the church when these passages were written. This assumption has been challenged by some scholars (e.g., C. J. Cadoux and F. W. Beare, who hold that official Roman persecution is reflected in 1 Peter, especially in 4:12-19),[41] but there is no evidence of martyrdom in the passage. The expression "fiery ordeal" might indeed suit martyrdom, but it is not spelled out in any way. Rather, Peter's readers were in danger of being "reproached" for the name of Christ (4:14). This fits in with the indications in 4:1-4 that the nature of the trouble was social pressure on the part of those who were displeased with the unwillingness of converted people to continue their former manner of life. Surprise was mingled with abuse, says Peter. It is risky, then, to suggest that this passage is referring to Roman persecution and on this basis conclude that the epistle was written during the reign of Trajan (early second century), when measures were taken against believers in Bithynia (cf 1:1).

3. Paul insists that obedience to the state is called for because human government has been ordained by God in order to punish evil conduct and to reward what is good. Thus, he urges Christians to subject themselves to political authority not simply as an expedient (i.e., to escape punishment), but as a matter of principle. We should honor what God has established. It may be argued, of course, that the problem remains as to what constitutes a government in the Pauline sense: for instance, if a government fails to punish evil and reward good, does it cease to deserve the respect and submission of Christians? We will return to this question at a later point.

4. An additional element is supplied by 1 Timothy 2:1-4. Here it is presented as a Christian duty to make intercession for rulers, that they may be able to maintain conditions of peace and order in society and thus facilitate the proclamation of the gospel: when there is turmoil caused by war it is difficult to reach people with the message, and even if contact can be made, their minds are apt to be so taken up with the struggle in which they are engaged that they will not be ready to consider the things of God.

5. The Christian attitude toward the state also entails a readiness to pay taxes (Rom. 13:6-7). Jewish resistance to Roman taxation is well-known. It is possible that Paul, aware that the Roman church contained some Jewish believers, may have felt it wise to bear down on this matter of taxation (which is not treated in 1 Pet. 2). He simply throws out the reminder that taxes are necessary if the benefits of the state are to be

extended to the governed in the form of services. It would be highly damaging to the Christian cause if believers at the very heart of the empire were advocating resistance to Rome along these lines.

6. The language of Romans 13 makes plain the fact that believers are not to absolutize the state, and this for at least two reasons. First, the state is twice spoken of here as the servant of God, and its representatives are once referred to as ministers of God. Second, no earthly government is able to bring in the kingdom of God. None can provide an ideal society. The Christian must look beyond the present order to the eschatological kingdom.

7. Careful attention to the language of Romans 13 shows that Paul avoids saying that the Christian is to *obey* the state; instead, he says "Be subject" (13:1, 5). This leaves room for the superior relationship, the ultimate authority, as alone worthy of implicit obedience. In this connection, note Peter's statement that "We must obey God rather than men" (Acts 5:29).

The attitude toward government in general and the Roman state in particular seems to have undergone a change between the time Romans was written and the time Revelation was written. Whereas Romans was composed within a definite historical setting, the Apocalypse goes beyond this with its eschatological thrust, portraying the state finally not as a minister of God for the praise of the good and the punishment of the evil but as an instrument of human rebellion against the authority of heaven and a persecutor of the saints (Rev. 13:6, 7). Of special importance is the introduction of a new factor, the figure of the Evil One as prompting and aiding the state in these activities (13:2). So God is obliged to move against his own ordinance, the state, because it has been vitiated and prostituted by Satan. Consequently the kingdom of the world loses its legitimacy. It must become by conquest and transformation the kingdom of the Lord God and his Christ (11:15). Such a development should not be viewed as strange and improbable, especially in the light of God's dealings with Israel, in which context we can see the divine necessity of imposing chastening by foreign conquerors and by captivity upon the nation chosen of God for his own possession.

It is incumbent on us to trace the connection between the apostolic teaching about the state and our Lord's teaching on the same subject, the more so since the language of Paul in Romans 13:7—"Give everyone what you owe him"—is cast in a form identical to that used by Jesus in his confrontation with the Pharisees and Herodians over the question of paying tribute to Caesar (see Mark 12:17). Cullmann describes the setting well:

> The question is: "Should we pay tribute to Caesar or not?" For themselves the Pharisees would prefer to answer in the negative, although they do not, like the Zealots, draw the extreme consequences. The Herodians,

on the contrary, are the collaborationists who make common cause with the Romans and naturally for themselves return an affirmative answer. It is just the presence of *both* groups which constitutes for Jesus the special temptation. Both want him to compromise himself. If he answers yes, he will be shown up as a collaborationist and will disillusion the majority of the people; for it is precisely in this connection that these have rested such great hope in him. If he answers no, this is an avowal that he himself is a Zealot, and indeed a leader of the Zealots; and we know what that meant to the Romans.[42]

The question posed to Jesus was hardly academic; it was thoroughly existential. To the Jews, the requirement that they pay the poll tax into the imperial treasury was doubly galling: in the first place it kept them impoverished, and in the second place it had to be paid in coinage that bore the image of the current emperor and the writing that contained his titles, proclaiming him worthy of divine honors. Stauffer notes that the Latin inscription, when rendered into Greek for use in Syria, carried the meaning, "Emperor Tiberius august Son of the August God."[43] Jesus had the question addressed to him in Jerusalem at Passover time, the place and the season which found diverse points of view on this subject jostling one another most violently.

Although the motive of the interrogators was wrong—an attempt to embarrass Jesus—his answer was not in the same spirit. It was no mere word play, a bit of flippancy to circumvent a hard question. Rather, literally rendered the twofold question runs as follows: "Is it lawful to give tribute to Caesar or not? Should we give or should we not give?" The word *give* in this context is a euphemism for "pay." In his reply Jesus uses the same root word but in the compound form, meaning to "pay back." This is the sort of language that is suitable for paying a debt, and that is precisely what Jesus means to convey. The very willingness of the people to use the coin has committed them. Stauffer remarks, "He made it clear that His questioners accepted the imperial *denarii* in payment, and that this meant that the people of God had accepted its subjugation to the Roman empire. By accepting imperial money they have profited by the financial, economic and legal order of the empire. . . . They take this money into the temple, although they know that the image and the superscription are polytheistic in character. So they have no right to refuse to pay the tax on theological grounds."[44]

Whereas Jesus acknowledges the right of Rome to collect tribute as conqueror, preserver of the peace, and so on, he refuses to admit that the representative of Rome is deserving of worship. This could have been stated in the form of denial, but Jesus chose to put it positively: "Give . . . to God what is God's" (Mark 12:17). This constitutes a warning not to give Caesar more than is rightfully his. There was another tax that the Jews were bound to pay—the tax for the upkeep of the temple and the maintenance of the sacrifices (see Matt. 17:24–27). "Liturgically, the temple tax signified a contribution to the glory of God in the midst of a world that was filled with the glory of Caesar," says Stauffer; he goes on to summarize his penetrating study of this passage with the following remark on Jesus' dictum: "This messianic proclamation says that the *imperium Caesaris* is the way and the *imperium Dei* the goal of history."[45]

On the basis of this incident it is plain that Jesus did not advocate the attempt to overthrow the established political order. He was no Zealot. Recall how he refused the attempt to draft him as king and revolutionary leader (John 6:15). His counsel to go the extra mile (Matt. 5:41), when properly understood as technical language, is germane also: although he does not mention the Romans, he is referring to their practice of pressing citizens of a country into service to carry the baggage of the soldiers as they moved from place to place. Instead of resisting, says Jesus, one should offer to do more than is demanded. He also taught that God would use the Roman legions to punish his own people who had refused to see in his coming to them a divine visitation (see Luke 21:20–24).

A few scholars, nevertheless, have insisted that Jesus actually was a Zealot or at least had definite Zealot sympathies. Did he not take Simon the Zealot as one of his disciples? Unquestionably he did, but where is the proof that this man continued to hold his former views or that Jesus encouraged him in this? Appeal is made to Judas also, on the ground that Iscariot is a term that may be connected with the Sicarii, the dagger wielders who killed pacifistic Jews because they refused to join their ranks. This is highly questionable. However, did not Jesus himself counsel his chosen followers to take swords in the face of the rapidly growing encirclement that was materially aided by the defection of Judas (Luke 22:35–38)? The passage is notoriously difficult, but at least it is necessary to point out that the Master's word about the adequacy of having two swords among the Eleven argues strongly against taking his words literally. What would two swords amount to among so many? It is safer to understand the reference to swords in a symbolic sense, as indicative that a crisis now faced the disciples and they had better be prepared for opposition. A few moments later Jesus rebuked Peter for attempting to use the sword (see Luke 22:51). He himself made no resistance whatever to his arrest.

S. G. F. Brandon (*Jesus and the Zealots*) has argued that Mark, in writing the earliest of the Gospels and writing it for the Roman church, was embarrassed by the fact that the Romans (through Pilate) had condemned and put to death the founder of the Christian faith, so he subtly and cleverly altered the facts by making the Jews responsible for the death of Jesus, thus covering up rather well the true situation—namely, that Jesus was in the Zealot camp and for this reason had to be put to death by Rome. Brandon proceeds to contend that Matthew and Luke, by virtue of their literary dependence on Mark, took over the same general viewpoint.

More recent critical thinking about the role of the evangelists rejects the idea that they were so slavishly dependent on Mark. Rather the evidence suggests that each writer had his purpose and shaped his Gospel in accordance with that purpose, despite the use of much parallel material. As a matter of fact, the Gospels and the Acts agree that the Romans and the Jews share the guilt for Jesus' death (see Acts 4:27). In preaching to Jerusalem audiences, Peter was blunt in insisting that his compatriots, through their leaders, had murdered God's anointed (Acts 2:23; 3:13; 4:10; cf. 5:28). Stephen brought the same accusation (7:52). Moreover, Paul fixed the responsibility for Jesus' death as belonging to his countrymen (1 Thess. 2:15). One would have to rewrite the New Testament to eliminate this strain. It is arbitrary to set it aside in the interest of a theory that is contradicted by the life of Jesus from beginning to end. He brought division among men, to be sure—even among members of the same household— but this was part of his God-given mission. Politics had no place in that mission.

Returning to our theme of the Christian's obligation toward the state, it is appropriate to inquire what the believer's attitude should be toward it in the area of military service.

1. In Old Testament days the people of God frequently resorted to arms, both for defense and for conquest. The list is long—Abraham, Moses and Joshua, the judges, and many of the kings of Israel and Judah.

2. Messianic prophecy contains warlike language in picturing the confrontation between God's anointed and his enemies (see, for example, Pss. 2, 110).

3. Jesus' teaching and example served to soften this emphasis. He asserted in the presence of Pilate that his kingdom was not of this world; if it were, his servants would have fought to prevent his arrest, and he could see they were not doing so (see John 18:36). Yet in the apocalyptic representations of his return for judgment, the warlike imagery comes into focus again, but in a symbolic fashion. The Lord Jesus will slay with the breath of his mouth and destroy by his coming (2 Thess. 2:8).

4. Warlike language is used to express the sort of conflict that the Christian must wage against the spiritual powers of evil (see, for example, Eph. 6:10–17). The believer is to fight the good fight of faith (1 Tim. 6:12). In his commitment he is to be a good soldier of Jesus Christ (2 Tim. 2:3). Military terminology is sublimated to spiritual use.

5. On the specific point of military service by Christians, there is little information. No record is given of believers going into such service, nor is there any admonition to deter them from it. Paul's principle that one should abide in one's calling (1 Cor. 7:17ff.) has some relevance here. As applied to this situation, it means that those who were soldiers when they came to know the Lord would not be expected to desert their occupation on the ground that they ought no longer to engage in such activity.

Severance would be natural only if military service were intrinsically wrong from the Christian standpoint. Since the state must at times use force if it is to punish evil, the Christian's refusal to participate on principle (as opposed to selective cooperation) would seem to be tantamount to rejection of the position of the state as the servant of God in dispensing justice. The right of protest in the case of what is deemed on good grounds to be an unjust war is not only a Christian right but a Christian duty. It is well to draw a distinction between our attitude toward a personal enemy (covered in such passages as Matt. 5:44 and Rom. 12:20–21) and our responsibility to serve our country in time of war as part of our submission to the state as an authority instituted by God (Rom. 13:1).

Some Christian groups advocate virtual isolation from the state, condemning, for example, suffrage among Christians on the ground that it entails complicity in worldliness. Such an attitude involves a confusion of thought, a failure to distinguish between the state and the world-system in the ethico-spiritual sense, that which is opposed to God and dominated by Satan. Though the Christian is not of the world (see John 17:14; Rom. 12:2), he is very much a part of the state. Voting, for example, is one of his responsibilities in maintaining that relationship.

Additional Notes on Romans 13

1. Barth insists that there is a Christological basis for the teaching at this point. "Paul has no intention of speaking here about an authority based on the 'law of nature,' independent of the authority of Jesus Christ," he says, adding that "because Jesus Christ is the head of his body the Church, he is, according to Col. 1:16f. also the One through whom and in view of whom all things were created: all 'thrones, dominions, principalities and powers.'"[46] Barth's appeal to Colossians 1:16 is not convincing, for in that passage Paul clearly seems to be referring to the celestial powers that were so central to the teaching of the errorists at Colosse. The strength of his case is also diminished by the fact that Christ is not mentioned at all in the text of Romans 13:1–7.

2. Cullmann sees in the term "authorities" (13:1) a dual reference, holding that along with earthly rulers the invisible powers over which Christ triumphed at the cross are being referred to. They are subject to Christ even when they influence earthly rulers.[47] One would think, however, that if Paul intended such a duality, he would have made it clear. Is it likely that the apostle would advocate submission to unseen powers even in such indirect fashion, when he taught in Ephesians 6:12ff. that believers should offer strenuous resistance to such powers?

3. It is not certain that the statement about the state bearing the sword (v. 4) is intended as a reference to capital punishment. Would Christians need a warning against committing crimes of such magnitude as to merit the death penalty? It is more likely that Paul is warning Christians not to

get involved in activities that could be regarded as revolutionary by the Roman state, in which case the use of the word "sword" is readily understandable.

The Attitude of the State toward Christians

The death of Jesus, who bore witness to the truth, was a prophecy of what was in store for many of his followers. He said to his disciples, "No servant is greater than his master. If they persecuted me, they will persecute you also" (John 15:20). As we have seen, persecution began from the Jewish side, but was restrained by Roman protection, as can readily be confirmed in the case of Paul. But Roman pressure on the church came in time. As Pilate was puzzled by Christ, who could have saved himself so easily, many a Roman ruler was likewise mystified and even exasperated by those who stood to be examined. It was so strange to the Roman mode of thinking that a man would not save his own life by being willing to make a pagan sacrifice and swear allegiance to the emperor as lord. They had long before ceased to value truth for truth's sake and were living in terms of expediency. The whole wretched system of worshiping a man as God, a system that people despised even while they went through the forms, had debauched character until the Christian devotion to the Lord was considered to be some sort of madness. It could not even be understood.

The basis on which Rome persecuted Christianity is not totally clear. Perhaps it would be more accurate to speak of bases. To be sure, the issue of emperor worship was sharply defined, but it must be realized that emperor worship was not an end in itself but rather a means for achieving a unified allegiance throughout the length and breadth of the empire. Guterman notes that on occasions Christians were asked to worship before statues of the gods as well as before the statue of the emperor.[48] Religious and civic motifs were combined. By their exclusivism Christians were making themselves enemies of the state. It was enough that they were judged dangerous to the welfare of the empire.

Jesus sought to prepare his followers for the tribulation that lay ahead of them. He told them that they would be dragged before governors and kings for his sake to bear testimony before them and before the Gentiles (Matt. 10:18). On the Jewish side he warned that they would be put out of the synagogues and that those who killed them would think they were offering a service to God (John 16:2). They could expect to be hated by all men for Christ's sake (Mark 13:13). Yet there was comfort to balance the warnings. The wisdom and power of the Holy Spirit would be their portion when they were delivered up and were obliged to answer for their faith (Mark 13:11). The stories of Christian trials and martyrdoms amply bear out the fulfillment of Jesus' promises, as thousands fearlessly confessed their faith and went on to die. Jesus had even said that it is a blessed experience to be persecuted: in it one can rejoice and look forward to reward in heaven (Matt. 5:11–12). The Master also taught that there is great value in tribulation from the standpoint of separating genuine disciples from those who are spurious (Matt. 13:20–21).

Some generations of Christians are spared the ordeal of persecution in its more acute forms. But the readiness to suffer for Christ's sake, whether such suffering proves to be necessary or not, is a mark of the true disciple.

6. CHURCH AND SOCIETY

In approaching the subject of the relationship between church and society it is necessary to bear in mind the gulf that separates the apostolic age from the twentieth century. We tend to read the ancient situation in the light of our own experience in modern America and for this reason are apt to be critical of the early church for dragging its feet in the area of social involvement. Amos Wilder writes,

> Efforts a generation or two ago to describe the social factors in Jesus' setting and mission or to trace the "social origins" of the church are unpersuasive today because the historians in question modernized. To invoke such ideas as "proletariat" or "class struggle," to read in issues of "social justice" in terms of the twentieth century or even of the eighth-century prophets, to interpret the outlook of the Kingdom of God in terms of modern utopianism, to relate the common life of Acts 2 and 4–5 to modern communist ideas, or to see the other-worldly detachment of the Pauline churches in terms of the political and social abstention found in some modern pietism—all this was misleading. If we speak of the social determinations of early Christianity we must recognize that we have to do with social and political realities of an entirely unmodern character.[49]

We need to remember that the very charter of the church was evangelistic in nature: it was the missionary task of the church that was considered all-important. Furthermore, until the church had grown to the point where it had public influence, it would have been vain to attempt to throw its weight around in the social and political arenas. The Roman empire was ready to wield a heavy hand in deterring any movement that would venture to question its laws or its procedures. It was much easier for John the Baptist and Jesus to speak out on social righteousness in Palestine, where they were dealing with their own people, than for the church to do so when scattered over various lands, dealing mainly with pagans who lacked the moral conscience that Jews had acquired through their spiritual heritage.

In pursuing our investigation, it will be helpful to consider the following aspects of the subject individually: (1) the Christian assessment of pagan society, (2) the attitude of that society toward the church, (3) the Christian obligation toward pagan society, and (4) certain problem areas.

The Christian Assessment of Pagan Society

To a great extent the church found itself in agreement with Judaism that idolatry was widespread among the nations, a sin that had wrought havoc in Jewish national life from the time of the divided kingdom until the Babylonian captivity. In its train came a host of sins, especially sexual immorality. "For the devising of idols was the beginning of fornication, and the invention of them the corruption of life" (Wisdom of Solomon 14:12). It is evident that Paul in the first chapter of Romans makes the same general assessment, assigning the basic human failure to the forsaking of the worship of God in favor of the worship of man and his idolatrous creations. These in turn put no restraint on idol worshipers in their pursuit of immorality, to say nothing of a host of other sins that the apostle enumerates toward the close of the chapter, practices that he elsewhere labels as works of the flesh (Gal. 5:19–21).

The indictment in Romans 1 applied not only to the less civilized segments of society in the hellenistic age but also to the sophisticated. Athens still harbored idols in abundance and had become victimized by the dilettantism of the pseudointellectual, not to mention grosser manifestations such as abounded at Corinth. At Rome there was pride and haughtiness engendered by conquest and the growth of wealth and power, with corresponding insensitivity to the condition of the oppressed. Drunkenness seems to have been common in that day (see 1 Cor. 5:11; Rom. 13:13; Gal. 5:21; 1 Pet. 4:3). Christian abhorrence of pagan practices comes to the surface here and there. "For it is shameful even to mention what is done in secret" (Eph. 5:12). It was humiliating to Paul to have to write to the church at Corinth, "It is actually reported that there is sexual immorality among you, and of a kind that does not occur even among pagans" (1 Cor. 5:1). That the apostle should write thus is a reminder that ordinarily Christian conduct was vastly superior to that of unsaved people.

Society is made up of individuals, so the analysis of social evils must begin with the plight of the individual, who is dead (unresponsive to God) by reason of trespasses (Eph. 2:1), without God and without hope (Eph. 2:12), a slave of sin (Rom. 6:20), and on the way to perdition (1 Cor. 1:18), faced with the solemn prospect of being judged for sins committed (2 Thess. 2:12).

But it is natural also to think in terms of the aggregate, and this is often the case in the New Testament. Peter speaks of a "corrupt generation" (Acts 2:40). Paul refers to "the present evil age" (Gal. 1:4). John has much to say about "the world," which has for its components "the cravings of sinful man, the lust of his eyes and his pride in possessions" (1 John 2:16). Those who are in the world in the sense of belonging to this world-system resent having their sins exposed and resent or even hate those who assume this unwelcome task (see John 15:18–25). In uniting with the church,

Gentiles had to overcome the binding influence of their background built up over many generations. Hort's comment on 1 Peter 1:18 is perceptive:

> Hereditary custom was as strong among heathen as among Jews . . . and St. Peter is not here challenging the authority of the heathen *anastrophē* [manner of life], but rather pointing out one of the sources of its tremendous retaining power. The yoke which had to be broken and which for these Asiatic Christians had been broken, was not merely that of personal inclination and indulgence, but that which was built up and sanctioned by the accumulated instincts and habits of past centuries of ancestors.[50]

One may ask at this point whether Jesus shared this rather pessimistic view of human nature gleaned from the epistles or whether his attitude was more favorable. One has to conclude that his assessment was basically the same. Some of his statements have the Jewish nation in view, whereas others are more general and can be universally applied. He referred to his Jewish contemporaries as "a wicked and adulterous generation" (Matt. 12:39; cf. 7:11). He pronounced the human illness to be ethical heart trouble, so to speak, stating that it is from within man that evil thoughts and desires and deeds proceed (see Mark 7:21–23). True, he could speak of men acting out of an honest and good heart (Luke 8:15), but only in the sense of sincerity of purpose rather than complete guilelessness.

Apostolic teaching is similar to that of Christ. It is granted that unbelievers are capable of loving and providing for their families (1 Tim. 5:8). Paul can remind the Philippians that the ethical and moral ideals of Christian life are not greatly different from those that paganism at its best commended—what is true, honorable, just, pure, lovely, and gracious (Phil. 4:8). Consequently, both strains—the negative and the positive—are found in both sources. It is clear, however, that paganism lacked the dynamic to realize the virtues it praised. In fact, all of us know more of good than we practice.

Many terms are used to describe the unsaved. Frequently they are called sinners or ungodly or unbelievers. Of special interest are two expressions that need examining because they are liable to misunderstanding. Paul labels unsaved judges at Corinth as unrighteous or unjust (1 Cor. 6:1). Should this terminology be construed as meaning that Christians were unable to get an impartial verdict from such men? Not at all, for the word occurs again in verse 9 in such a way as to make clear that *unrighteous* is a synonym here for *unsaved*. That it denotes unbelievers is evident from verse 6. The other expression to be examined is "those who are without" (1 Cor. 5:13; Col. 4:5). It is used in contrast to those who are in the church (1 Cor. 5:12), so there is nothing pharisaical or condescending about it, as though Christians were happy to see them outside and wished to keep them there.

Society's Attitude toward the Church

Evidence points to the fact that the conversions of pagans to Christianity stirred considerable resentment at times on the part of former friends and associates because these converts radically changed their life-style. "They think it strange that you do not plunge with them into the same flood of dissipation, and they heap abuse on you" (1 Pet. 4:4). This public attitude of dislike and hostility made government action against Christians that much easier to initiate and carry through.[51]

As time went on, certain prejudices became current, based on rumor and fostered by aloofness of believers from public social life and even more by the privacy of their worship. Charges were made that they were impious (atheistic) because they did not include in their veneration the gods that were honored in the cultus of the various communities where they lived. They were also regarded as unsocial because of their unwillingness to attend public entertainments or to belong to guilds that recognized pagan deities. Jews, of course, faced the same opprobrium. Both groups were viewed as too exclusive, something that was regarded as a serious offense in the cosmopolitan hellenistic age. Christianity was obliged to pay attention to these complaints. They were addressed by the apologists (Aristides, Justin, et al.) in the course of the second century.

Christian Obligation toward Pagan Society

Believers were faced with something of a dilemma. On the one hand they were aliens and exiles in this world (1 Pet. 2:11), whose citizenship was in heaven (Phil. 3:20), who had no lasting abode here but sought for one to come (Heb. 13:14). On the other hand, detachment from the people of the world was unthinkable, for they had an obligation to all men to proclaim to them the gospel (Rom. 1:14). The Lord had told his followers that they were the salt of the earth and the light of the world (Matt. 5:13–14). Both these figures demand contact with people. Furthermore, if the early Christians stood entirely aloof from society, they would only foster the world's dislike and severely limit the possibility of fruitful witness. So they were obliged to walk a rather narrow line: they could not participate in activities that would compromise them in the areas of faith and morals, and yet they were obligated to cultivate contacts that were not per se sinful.

Unquestionably there are passages calling for separation, such as 2 Corinthians 6:14–15: "Do not be yoked together with unbelievers. . . . What does a believer have in common with an unbeliever?" Wider in its frame of reference is the admonition regarding the sons of disobedience: "Do not be partners with them" (Eph. 5:7). Clearly no mere casual contact is being referred to here, for Paul admitted to the Corinthians that when he counseled them not to associate with immoral men he did not have in mind the immoral of this world, since believers would find it necessary to go out of the world entirely to avoid all such contact (1 Cor. 5:9–10). What he had prescribed was denial of fellowship to professed Christians who had turned aside to immorality.

Travel presented a problem. Inns were available in most places, but it seems to have become Christian practice to expect and receive hospitality from brethren. This enabled them to avoid the rowdiness and unsavory conversation typically found in public places. Furthermore, the travelers could frequently be of help to their hosts by extending encouragement and counsel. The impact of such contact on the children of the family could be particularly great. Hospitality was not restricted to mutual friends (Heb. 13:2).

Our sources do not contain any clear-cut information on the matter of Christians seeking public office. Erastus was apparently the city treasurer of Corinth and was still in this position when Paul wrote Romans (see Rom. 16:23). Possibly Christian leaders such as Paul did not consider it wise or necessary to lay down regulations on such matters. Local situations could vary. Probably individuals were encouraged to make their own decisions before the Lord, with the understanding that they would under no conditions compromise the faith.

Turning to the positive side of the church's obligation, we find evidence that believers were instructed to give conscious consideration to the possible effects their life and work might have on unbelievers. Peter stressed what could be called the evangelizing aspect of conduct when he wrote, "Live such good lives among the pagans that, though they accuse you of doing wrong, they may see your good deeds and glorify God on the day he visits us" (1 Pet. 2:12; cf. v. 15). We find no counsel that believers should withdraw from the world—a course taken, for example, by the Qumran community. Jesus provided a powerful example by his manner of life as he went about doing good (Acts 10:38). He maintained a friendly and sympathetic attitude toward sinners and was willing to eat with tax gatherers and other social outcasts, in contrast to the Pharisees. The Lord did this without condoning the sins of those with whom he associated. If believers allowed themselves to get into the habit of thinking that they were somehow superior to the rest of mankind, other Christians were at hand to remind them that by nature they were not different (i.e., not superior), but rather that they owed their deliverance from the old life to the grace of God (see 1 Cor. 6:11; Eph. 2:1ff.).

There were many contexts in which believers might associate with pagans, many means by which they might bridge the gap, including the following:

1. Miracles such as the healing of the lame man mentioned in Acts 3:1ff. (cf. 5:15–16) must have brought gratitude to the individuals involved, to say nothing of their families and friends, inevitably creating a greater receptivity to the message of salvation. P. Gardner-Smith remarks, "In the

Roman empire the sick were dependent on the attentions of their relatives, and when their sickness was known to be contagious they were often deserted and left to die unattended. The Christians not only nursed their own sick folk with tender care, but in many cases they showed scarcely less solicitude for their heathen neighbours."[52] The result of such unexpected concern by Christians was often a surge of genuine gratitude (see Acts 28:7-10).

2. Business contacts could be a fruitful means of testimony. Christians who were employed by unsaved people had a great opportunity to commend the gospel by their industry, cheerfulness, cooperation, honesty, purity of speech, and so on. Paul's words to his Thessalonian converts pertain to this sort of opportunity (see 1 Thess. 4:11-12). His counsel about remaining in the situation that one had when God called him (1 Cor. 7:17ff.) was doubtless meant to substantiate this principle. His warning against being unduly scrupulous has a similar orientation. He seems to suggest that undue sensitivity about whether meat offered for sale in the markets had been offered to an idol could create an unfavorable impression on the merchants, making them harder to reach with the gospel (see 1 Cor. 10:25).

3. Mention should be made of the opportunity presented by mixed marriages (i.e., marriages in which one of the spouses had become a Christian). Counsel on this kind of situation is given in 1 Corinthians 7:12-14 and 1 Peter 3:1-4.

4. Social relationships with pagans were possible as long as they did not lead to compromise. Paul recommended that the saints in Corinth feel free to accept invitations to dinner from unconverted people (Jesus had, after all, pointed the way in such matters by his acceptance of invitations from Pharisees as well as tax collectors), although he puts an entirely different construction on an invitation to a feast in a temple dedicated to an idol (see 1 Cor. 10:20-22).

5. Pagans sometimes found their way into Christian assemblies and were apparently welcomed (1 Cor. 14:23-25). This does not mean, of course, that they were invited to the Lord's table. But apart from this sacred fellowship the meetings were open to such visitors.

6. The daily conduct of believers in all its phases was under the scrutiny of non-Christian people. Paul writes, "Be wise in the way you act toward outsiders; make the most of every opportunity" (Col. 4:5). The apostle admonished the Thessalonians "to lead a quiet life, to mind your own business and to work with your hands, just as we told you, so that your daily life may win the respect of outsiders and so that you will not be dependent on anybody" (1 Thess. 4:11-12). To be careless would be to risk becoming a stumbling block instead of a stepping-stone.

7. It was legitimate to seek opportunities for discussion with unbelievers about the Christian faith. After counseling his readers to deal wisely with

those on the outside, Paul becomes more specific: "Let your conversation be always full of grace, seasoned with salt, so that you may know how to answer everyone" (Col. 4:6). Peter's counsel is similar: "Always be prepared to give an answer to everyone who asks you to give the reason for the hope that you have" (1 Pet. 3:15).

8. Paul set an example for his converts by deliberately becoming all things to all men (1 Cor. 9:19–22). As he explains the principle, it is a matter of adapting oneself to another in all possible ways short of surrendering the truth of the gospel in order to remove prejudice and suspicion as well as to create a spirit of friendliness and openness to the Christian message. This could include the endeavor to arrive at intellectual rapport with others. For example, Paul showed an appreciation for pagan poets by utilizing what he could from them in his Athenian address (see Acts 17).

9. The Christian is expected to maintain peace with all others. Paul puts this rather carefully and explicitly: "If it is possible, as far as it depends on you, live at peace with everyone" (Rom. 12:18). The statement takes account of the fact that we cannot compel others to act peacefully, but we can exercise such self-control as will guarantee absence of conflict as far as we ourselves are concerned.

10. By exemplifying the equality of men and women in Christ, believers possessed a power to challenge and rebuke the inequalities and injustices in the pagan world. As the church increased in size, its potential for influence in this area expanded (see Gal. 3:28; Eph. 2:14; 4:4–6).

11. Both masters and slaves who were Christians had the opportunity to extract much of the poison and bitterness from the institution of slavery by mutual respect and cooperation. Pagans did not think of masters as having any obligation toward their slaves. It was different in a Christian context (Col. 4:1).

Having considered several means by which Christians might reach out to non-Christians, we now ask how inclined they were to do so. What was the church's teaching on how believers ought to relate to unbelievers? In his book *The Early Church and the World*, C. J. Cadoux has suggested that four ethical principles were essential to the teaching: Christians were called to live in love, truthfulness, humility, and wisdom.[53] We will follow Cadoux's argument, considering each of the points separately.

1. *Love*. Cadoux notes that although Christians clearly took it upon themselves to express love in their relationships with other Christians, they do not seem to have been as quick to express it in their relationships with unbelievers—nor were they significantly enjoined to do so in the epistolary literature. This is true, but not really unexpected: relations between Christians as a whole receive far more treatment in the epistles than do relations between Christians and outsiders. And in any case, Cadoux does cite a few verses in which believers are commanded to love nonbelievers—

1 Thessalonians 3:12; Romans 13:8–10; 2 Corinthians 6:6 (and we should probably add Gal. 6:10 and 1 Thess. 5:15, since Paul would hardly prescribe the doing of good apart from the motivation of love).

In noting that love is not as prominent in the epistolary teaching concerning the church's relationship to the world as it is in the ministry of Jesus, Cadoux fails to note that in Jesus' time there was no church set over against the world. Jesus was ministering in a situation in which nearly all the people belonged to the covenant nation Israel. Cadoux seems harsh in his judgment when he says regarding the author of 1 Peter that he "comes dangerously near asserting that God feels no mercy for [the unsaved]." Perhaps he has overlooked 2:12.

Whatever may be said of his followers, the Lord Jesus left a precious legacy with his own by underscoring the need for love between God's children and by stressing that love between believers would have a wholesome effect on the world (John 13:35). J. N. Sanders writes, "If Christians do not love one another, they will neither love, nor prove attractive to, anyone else."[54] He rightly emphasizes that this love is the most effective witness that the church can bear to the world of its faithfulness to its Master.

2. *Truthfulness.* There are two allusions to this principle in 2 Corinthians 6:7–8, the first one referring to speech, the second to character. Both are included in the description of Paul's ministry in the world. "Speaking the truth in love" (Eph. 4:15) can readily be applied to relations with non-Christians, though the primary reference is probably to a Christian context. Most of the references to truth in the epistles pertain to the gospel message as containing the truth of God. One could almost say that the New Testament writers proceed on the assumption that if one's life is transformed through the new birth, the effect in the various areas of human relations can be assumed to be transforming.

3. *Humility.* This principle is inevitably involved in making oneself all things to all men. Paul goes so far as to speak of making himself servant of all (1 Cor. 9:19). After observing that Hillel, in making proselytes to Judaism, owed his success to his humility, David Daube notes that Paul was making use in the 1 Corinthians passage of an established missionary maxim, and that the word *gain* is 'used in a technical sense, namely, to win a convert.[55]

4. *Wisdom*, or *prudence.* On this point Colossians 4:5 is relevant once more. Christians need this quality in dealing with the unsaved. They should learn how to build on what is known in order to proceed to what is new and strange. They need to avoid controversial questions lest they become sidetracked or develop an argumentative reaction that precludes the securing of a favorable hearing for the gospel. They should avoid dwelling on trifles or laying down lists of things individuals must or must not do when they become Christians. Indeed, there is great need for wisdom when

engaging in dialogue with the unsaved. This wisdom, in the last analysis, is the gift of the Holy Spirit (1 Cor. 12:8).

Problem Areas

1. *Marriage.* That a Christian is to marry only in the Lord—that is, marry only a believer—is clearly taught (1 Cor. 7:39). But mixed marriages remained a problem in the case of a spouse who became a Christian while married to a mate who remained a pagan. Paul's counsel was to avoid severing such a connection unless the unbeliever insisted that the marriage be terminated (1 Cor. 7:12-16). Peter suggested that a believing wife should cherish the hope that by her seemly conduct she might win her husband who had heard the gospel but not accepted the offer of salvation (1 Pet. 3:1ff.).

2. *Slavery.* The institution of slavery was practically universal in New Testament times. In earlier periods people had become slaves principally as a result of losing wars, but in the apostolic age most slaves were born to the condition in the households of their masters. Slavery was accepted as essential to the functioning of society. Slaves were not merely manual laborers, but served as secretaries, tutors, managers of business enterprises, and even as doctors. They could look forward to possible manumission, a prospect that gave many hope and inspired them to greater efficiency in their work.[56]

Slavery affected the economic as well as the social fabric of society. Strikes by working men were notoriously rare in those days, and the reason is not difficult to ascertain. A strike could easily be broken by introducing a slave labor force.[57] As a result, workers were at the mercy of employers.

Treatment of slaves was more humane than in the modern period, largely because masters realized that if they abused them, they became less cooperative and did poorer work. As a result they could actually become a drain on the owner's resources.

We may feel disappointed that Christianity did nothing in a public way to break the hold of slavery. But the situation did not permit of direct action. Some solace can be taken, however, from the fact that the church did not descend to the pagan or even to the Jewish attitude. K. H. Rengstorf notes that a Jew could be excommunicated for calling his neighbor a slave. It was one of the worst insults a person could use. In the New Testament a slave "is never spoken of in the disparaging and contemptuous fashion common in the Greek and Hellenistic world."[58]

Actually the New Testament makes a positive contribution by urging Christian masters to treat their slaves with fairness (Col. 4:1) and with love (Philem. 16), and (perhaps) even to consider granting them their freedom (Philem. 21). Converted slaves are admonished to render cheerful and faithful service to their masters, no matter how churlish they might be (1 Pet. 2:18; cf. Eph. 6:5-8). Paul seems to say that the all-important thing for Christian slaves, whether they retain that status or have the opportunity to gain their freedom, is to maintain free spirits, motivated and controlled by obedience to Christ (1 Cor. 7:21). Christian masters are urged to ease the plight of their slaves by equitable, considerate treatment (Eph. 6:9).

It appears that when Paul addresses slaves, he does not address them as a group by themselves, but rather as individuals or groups belonging to individual Christian households. The family structure was important. Furthermore, the whole assembled congregation would hear the apostle's counsel read aloud and would necessarily be affected by the knowledge that individual attitudes and actions would henceforth be judged in the light of what he had written.

3. *Entertainment and occupation.* We have already referred to these matters somewhat, but the following quotation will demonstrate how limited the social contacts of a Christian had to be in relation to the unsaved:

> The Christian could not accept an invitation to dinner because the meat placed before him would almost certainly have been offered to some god, and thus, in his view, dedicated to devils. He could not go to the theatre because the show presented would be both idolatrous and obscene. For the same reason the arena was forbidden. Many trades were connected directly or indirectly with idolatry, and the Christian must avoid or abandon all such occupations. It was difficult for him to serve in the army, because military discipline would require him to participate in various heathen ceremonies.[59]

One good effect of these conditions was that they pulled Christians together into an even closer relationship of dependence, sympathy, and mutual helpfulness.

4.*Asceticism.* To begin with, there is a considerable difference between the Christian piety typical in the New Testament and that which was glorified in the postapostolic age, as seen, for example, in the Apocryphal Acts. In this later period the celibate state was regarded as distinctly superior to marriage. Withdrawal from the world became popular, producing the pillar saints and giving to monasticism the impulse that made it so striking a feature of medieval piety. Asceticism was grounded in a dualism that pitted spirit against matter, which meant that the body was regarded as essentially evil. This was a prominent feature of the thinking of many people in the hellenistic period and it comes out strongly in Gnosticism, but it is foreign to the teaching of Scripture.

If the church had resorted to asceticism on a large scale, it would have given up the possibility of changing society for the better. As Edwyn Bevan notes, "The Christian could never look with the Gnostic's abhorrence upon the earth and all the conditions of bodily life; to pray continually, 'Thy will be done on earth as it is in heaven'—that alone set him on the side of the Hebrew prophets and at variance with a theology for which the earth was incurably bad, and escape from it the vehicle of salvation."[60]

Certainly the church could not derive the ascetic ideal from Jesus. While not married himself, he certainly did not oppose marriage as the normal state for mature persons, and gave his approval by his presence at the wedding in Cana (see John 2). Whereas John the Baptist was to some extent an ascetic because of the Nazarite vow, Jesus came eating and drinking (see Matt. 11:19). Though our Lord fasted at the time of his temptation, he does not seem to have practiced it during his ministry. And although the disciples of John the Baptist fasted (see Luke 5:33), the disciples of Jesus did not, presumably because their Master did not.

Fasting seems to have been a rarity in the early church, making its appearance at times of special urgency when divine guidance was sought in seasons of prayer (see Acts 13:2–3; 14:23). These references are important since they indicate that fasting (and ascetic practices in general) are related to Christian service rather than to personal piety. In fact, when such practices are adopted as a means of cultivating the spiritual life, they all too easily lead to a "merit" complex.

For our purpose it is not necessary to go into all the aspects of personal conduct that fall under the head of self-discipline, since we are examining the relation between the church and society. But the religious philosophy of the times could have rubbed off onto the church were it not for its own established principles of life, which included the honoring of the natural order, so that the body was not regarded as evil. Included also was the ideal of realizing Christ's life, which was holy, in one's own. Sanctification was a positive rather than a negative thing, a matter of aspiration rather than prohibition. The latter course is in fact rebuked (Col. 2:20–21).

It should be obvious that flight from the world in the interest of removing oneself from the temptations of society is largely fruitless, since the world is not the source of temptation but only an accessory to it. One can be as sorely tempted in a monastery as in the midst of a large city— even more so, because of the unnatural conditions under which one lives there. Moreover, direct contact with the unsaved is virtually reduced to nothing. People of the world may reveal their own spiritual poverty and longing for better things by acclaiming the so-called holy men who live apart from the world in apparent self-abnegation, but they derive no help from such men toward the achieving of a better life for themselves.

CHAPTER IV

The Internal Development of the Church

1. THE CONCEPT OF THE CHURCH: ITS ORGANIZATION

THE term *ekklēsia* is perhaps best translated "assembly," although "church" is the common rendering in our Bibles. In ancient times the word was applied to gatherings of various kinds, especially political (see Acts 19:40) and also religious (see Acts 7:38). In the latter case it refers to Israel in the wilderness. This instance is especially instructive, since it indicates that the force of the word is not strictly to designate a called-out body, as distinct from others that are not called: no others were in the area when Israel met as a body in the wilderness. Probably the "out" factor simply goes back to the element of summons, as when the citizens of Athens were called out of their homes to attend the *ekklēsia* of the city-state.

When Jesus spoke prophetically of the New Testament church, he referred to it as "*my* church," which helps us to realize that it is not the idea of *ekklēsia* that is unique, but only the particular assembly of which he spoke. The mere fact that the term is used of Israel in the wilderness does not warrant the conclusion that *the* church was already in existence in Old Testament times. This observation is in no way meant to challenge the concept of the essential unity of the people of God throughout redemption history (on which see Heb. 11:40; 12:23); rather, it is meant to underscore the newness of what began at Pentecost. Paul described the church as he knew it in terms of a mystery hid from ages past (Eph. 3:1–6).

Certainly nothing like the New Testament church is found in the Old Testament as an institution; it is not even formally predicted. Rather, the raw materials are there in the prophecies concerning the work of the Servant of the Lord and in the repeated declarations of a divine purpose toward the Gentiles as well as toward the covenant nation Israel.

A certain parallelism is recognizable also between the church and Israel, particularly in the separated, holy character of the people of God, distinct from the nations of the world. Yet there is also a difference, for in the older dispensation the accent is more heavily on lack of contact with surrounding peoples so as to avoid contamination, whereas the church must maintain a positive contact with the world in order to reach it with the gospel. We can see the appropriateness of each emphasis for its own time. Israel was charged chiefly with custodianship of the oracles of God and the preparation for the coming of the Messiah, whereas the church from its very inception was outgoing, missionary, propagandist in nature.

As far as the Gospels are concerned, the word *church* is found in only two passages, both in Matthew. To these we will turn after observing how the word is used in Acts and in the epistles. In these sources a notable feature is the occurrence of the word in both singular and plural forms— the church and the churches, the universal and the particular. In the very early days of the Jerusalem church the distinction was not yet apparent, for the two elements were coextensive. The local or distributive sense occurs, for example, in Acts 15:41, where it is stated that Paul went through Syria and Cilicia, strengthening the churches. His letters furnish additional examples, such as those written to the church at Thessalonica. Acts 9:31 contains a slight textual problem, but the singular is the better attested reading, as follows: "So the church throughout all Judea and Galilee and Samaria had peace and was built up . . . and was multiplied." Bultmann is probably correct in his claim that the local use of the term *ekklēsia* springs from the conviction that the individual church (congregation) manifests the one church, of which it is representative.[1] This is rather different from the idea that it is necessary to add up all the various local churches in order to have the church. Such an approach ignores the fact that wherever Christ is, even in the midst of only two or three gathered together, there is the church.

As a matter of interest, our English word "church" is from the Greek adjectival term *kyriakos,* meaning "of or pertaining to the Lord." In the biblical text this term is used to describe the Lord's Supper (1 Cor. 11:20) and the Lord's Day (Rev. 1:10). In contemporary usage, the word is evident in the etymological background of the German *Kirche* and the Scottish *kirk.*

Before turning to the crucial passage in Matthew 16, we would do well to consider the several factors that point to the emergence of something new from Jesus' ministry rather than merely a rejuvenated Judaism:

1. The choice and training of the Twelve can best be understood as being in line with his purpose to prepare these men for their leadership in what actually developed—namely, the church.

2. It was to the immediate followers of Jesus rather than to the nation or its representatives that he extended the promise of the kingdom. "Do not be afraid, little flock, for your Father has been pleased to give you the kingdom" (Luke 12:32). On the other hand, Jesus said to the nation, "Therefore I tell you that the kingdom of God will be taken away from you and given to a people who will produce its fruit" (Matt. 21:43).

3. The statement of Jesus regarding the temple of his body in John 2:19—"Destroy this temple, and I will raise it again in three days"—seems to have been intended both in a personal and in a corporate sense. John

2:21 states that he spoke of the temple of his body. While it is true that nothing in this setting necessarily demands more than a personal reference, we must reckon with Mark 14:58, in which we learn that witnesses appeared at the trial of Jesus claiming, "We heard him say, 'I will destroy this man-made temple and in three days will build another, not made by man.'" It is hard to account for this addition—"not made by man"—unless it rests on something Jesus said. The alternative is to presume it to be an editorial addition. Even if the latter be allowed, it shows how the church at a fairly early time interpreted the saying of Jesus—namely, as involving the introduction of a new order to supersede the old, of which the temple was a symbol. Stephen seems to have had this understanding (see Acts 7:47-48).

The authenticity of the dominical saying in Matthew 16:17-19 must be established before we attempt any interpretation. The saying has been discounted on the ground that it occurs only in this Gospel. Such a criterion is arbitrary. If it were rigorously applied, we would have to give up the incomparable parables of Luke 15 as well as many other sayings of Jesus that are self-authenticating. The textual critic cannot take exception to the passage on the ground of omission from the manuscripts. Its firm position in the text has to be granted. In addition, there are positive factors pointing to authenticity. Newton Flew makes the following observations: "The Semitic colouring of these verses is unmistakable. The opening beatitude, the designation of Simon by his father's name, the Rabbinic expression of 'binding and loosing,' the eschatological struggle with the powers of the underworld—all these are indications of a primitive origin for the whole paragraph."[2] Other items could be added to this list. The expression "flesh and blood" is typically Semitic. The same can be said respecting the term "rock": it is at home in a metaphorical sense in the Old Testament and in Rabbinic literature (Abraham, for example, is called "Rock of the world").

With reference to the overall interpretation of the passage, when Jesus speaks of "*my* church" it seems that he is thinking in terms of the godly remnant in contrast to the bulk of the nation that had become either legalistic or revolutionary minded, restless under Roman rule. At the same time the word *build* suggests that his language does not indicate some sort of renovation of existing Judaism, but rather a new edifice.

The history of the interpretation of the passage is too extensive to reproduce here. Suffice it to say that the Reformation view, in contrast to that of the Roman Catholic Church (which has traditionally seen in it the preeminence of Peter and his successors in the church), understood the rock to mean Peter's faith or confession or both. It is difficult, however, to resist the conclusion that there is a personal reference to Peter here, in light of his prominence in Acts and in the Epistles. Ephesians 2:20 is especially important, since it informs us that the church is built on the foundation of the apostles and prophets as well as on Christ Jesus as the cornerstone. We ought not to sacrifice the human truth to accentuate the divine. The Roman Catholic view has an element of truth in it, but it is wrong to extend the prediction of Jesus to include Peter's successors.[3]

Matthew 18:15–17 contains a second saying of Jesus concerning the church. K. L. Schmidt takes the position that this passage does not refer to the church at all but to the synagogue.[4] There is no hint of futurity here, as in Matthew 16, and current conditions are pictured: "If he refuses to listen even to the church, let him be to you as a Gentile and a tax collector." These arguments are hardly decisive, for the element of futurity could readily be intended to carry over from the previous utterance in chapter 16 and the contrast between those addressed and the Gentile may simply be intended to reflect the Jewish character of the early church at the beginning. One wonders, too, whether Jesus would be inclined to legislate for the synagogue.

Schmidt's contribution to the study of *ekklēsia* lies mainly in the realm of the linguistic approach. He raises a question as to what word Jesus was likely to have used in the Aramaic when speaking about the church. If we could know that, it would assist in the interpretation of the concept behind the word. Schmidt searches for an Aramaic equivalent for *ekklēsia* and finds that the most common is *kᵉnishta*. The Syriac, which is closely related to the Aramaic, uses *kᵉnushta*, and the Sinaitic Syriac (a manuscript of the Syriac version) uses it to render both *ekklēsia* and *synagōgē*. He therefore sees the strong possibility that Jesus used *kᵉnishta*. This word, like *synagōgē*, could denote a fellowship in the local sense. From the Jewish standpoint early Christianity could well be looked upon as a small, recalcitrant sect within Judaism. But from the standpoint of Jesus the word could readily convey the essential idea of the remnant, with the implication that he was tacitly judging the rest of the Jews as being out of line with the divine purpose. Schmidt has captured for us something of the probable force of the word as Jesus used it and as it was understood by those who heard him speak.

In English, as in German, two words are in fairly common use— *congregation* and *church*. The difficulty is that *church* can be used to denote a building or property, a congregation, and even a denomination, as well as the church universal. This puts a heavy strain on one word.

The term *ekklēsia* has a somewhat similar sort of versatility. For Luke it had the significant advantage of calling forth associations with the people of God in Old Testament times while at the same time being applicable to the Gentiles. (The Gentiles would themselves have been able to understand the term in part, though they would have had to be educated about its uniquely Christian connotations.) It is somewhat surprising, then, that *ekklēsia* appears only once in the book of Acts prior to the account of Stephen (in 5:11). One reason Luke used the term so sparingly would seem to be that he had a number of other descriptive terms to use in its place. These alternatives include the following:

1. *Disciples* (Acts 6:1; 9:1, 36; 11:26). This word has a background of use in the Gospels, where it sometimes denotes the followers of Jesus in general (e.g., in Luke 6:13) and at other times is used more restrictively of the Twelve (e.g., in Luke 9:18). The expression "*his* disciples" (as distinct from those of Moses or of the Pharisees or of John the Baptist) reflects the newness of the relationship, whereas in Acts "*the* disciples" is sufficient identification. In the Gospels the word *disciple* is sometimes also used to denote one whose life is characterized by dedication and sacrifice (see Luke 14:25–33). In Acts it simply denotes a believer in Jesus. The epistles lack the word entirely. In Acts the term may be said to reflect the self-consciousness of the church in perceiving itself as linked to Jesus through the tradition and through the individuals who had known and served him.

2. *Brethren* (Acts 6:3; 11:1). The Old Testament used this term to designate one who was a member of the same family, or a neighbor, or a member of the nation Israel. In the New Testament these familiar meanings are retained, but they are supplemented by an additional meaning—namely, "fellow Christian," a member of the family of God through Christ. It was destined to denote those who were Gentiles as well as those who were Jews, though this extension did not emerge immediately. The specifically national connotations of the term persisted as Christian Jews addressed other Jews who were not believers (see Acts 2:29; Rom. 9:3).

3. *Saints.* This term is found often in the address of Paul's letters. In the Old Testament it signified those who were separated to God and on this account ideally had a godly walk in the fear of the Lord. In the New Testament the set-apart quality is the primary emphasis, lending itself to an appeal to a life of godliness: "Let us be in fact what God tells us we are."

4. *Christians.* This term is not found in the Jerusalem setting of the early church. The first notice appears in Acts 11:26. There is little doubt that it originated with outsiders who needed a handle by which to identify these people who gave Jesus Christ such a large place in their proclamation and in their lives. In time the label became popular within the church and has continued in general use ever since.

5. *The Fellowship* (Acts 2:42). I touch on this term because some understand it as a synonym for the church, the society of believers, whereas it is not entirely clear that this is the case. J. A. Fitzmeyer translates *koinōnia* in this passage as "community-spirit." Certainly it is more than a feeling, for it seems to have included participation in the things that bound the group together—a common faith, the Lord's Supper, a community of goods, and a common witness. The community of goods was a tangible expression of the spirit of love and unity that prevailed among these early believers.

The Leadership and Organization of the Church

Ever and again during the course of his ministry Jesus spoke to the Twelve about the days when he would no longer be with them in person. In Acts we find these men giving witness to the unsaved and providing direction for the church. They were fulfilling their appointed role as apostles. The word *apostle* occurs only once in the Septuagint (1 Kings 14:6), where the Hebrew term is *shaluach*, meaning "one sent." In Jewish literature this term came to be used of those who belonged to deputations from the Sanhedrin to people in the Dispersion and vice versa. This function does not really correspond to the missionary role of Christ's apostles. As Goppelt notes,

> Jesus sent his disciples out as his personal representatives, and in so doing he created an office which was unique to his environment. All of the special Jewish groups maintained the Old Testament Jewish offices of prophets, priests and scribes, which represented the Torah, whereas the office of Jesus' disciples could only represent him personally. The form of this new office was already given in the legal institution of the *shaliach*, "the one who is sent"; such a one was the authorized representative of his employer.[5]

During the period covered by the Gospels, the Twelve are designated usually as disciples, with the word *apostle* appearing only rarely, and principally in connection with being sent forth by Jesus on a mission calculated to prepare them for their future work (see Mark 6:7, 30). The use of the word in the report of the Last Supper (see Luke 22:14) provides the transition to the permanent mission that would unfold following the ascension. John has something parallel, although he uses the verb *send* instead of *apostle* (see John 17:18; 20:21).

It is a question how Ephesians 4:11 should be related to this background. There we read that the risen Lord gave the apostles as gifts to his church. Are these the original apostles, now confirmed for their permanent role in the church? This may well be the case. It is helpful to note that the *shaliach* in Judaism did not have a permanent office. His standing pertained only to the specific mission in which he was engaged. The status of the Twelve during Jesus' ministry, when they were rarely called apostles, seems to have basically resembled this standing: permanence awaited action by the risen Lord (see John 20:21-23).

It should be noted that the word *apostle* is used of others than the Twelve. Paul traced his apostleship to the risen Lord (Gal. 1:1). This rank seems to be asserted for James, the brother of the Lord (Gal. 1:19). Barnabas is so designated (Acts 14:4, 14), which may have its explanation in his having been sent forth by the Antioch church along with Paul (see Acts 13:1-4). We read of "all the apostles" in a setting that makes it likely that the term is not being restricted to the Twelve (see 1 Cor. 15:5, 7). In Romans 16:7 two men are named and described as being "of note among the apostles." Other references can be found in 1 Thessalonians 2:6 and 1 Corinthians 9:5.

All the persons mentioned as apostles are evidently associated with mission for Christ, but it is doubtful that all of them had the same authority as the Twelve, or Paul, or James. Paul and James were called by the risen Lord (see 1 Cor. 15:7–8). Such information is lacking in the case of others. At least two items support the observation that *apostle* had a broad as well as a restricted meaning in the first century. One is the claim of some at Corinth, probably interlopers, that they were apostles. At least Paul uses the term "false apostles" to label them, speaking of those who were "masquerading as apostles of Christ" (2 Cor. 11:13). The other item is the claim of some at Ephesus to be apostles (Rev. 2:2). Neither of these groups could have hoped for any acceptance whatever if apostleship was recognized as confined to the Twelve or even simply to include in addition Paul and James.

Apostolic succession cannot be grounded in the New Testament data. Mattathias, as successor to Judas, was a special case. When James, the brother of John, was killed, no provision was made for a successor (Acts 12:2). The first account of apostolic succession as ordained by the apostles appears in 1 Clement 44:2. A few years later, early in the second century, the term *apostle* occurs in the sense of "missionary" (see Didache 11:3).

Goppelt makes the helpful observation that although the apostles are included with Christ as the foundation of the church (Eph. 2:20), they are not listed as elements constituting the unity of the church—one body, one Spirit, and so on (see Eph. 4:4–6). The situation is different in the postapostolic age, in which the bishop and other officers are seen as humanly expressing the unity of the church which exists spiritually in God, Christ, and the apostles.[6]

As the church grew, offices other than the apostolic were added. The Seven who are mentioned in Acts 6, for instance, were set aside to attend to the daily distribution of food. Luke does not specifically refer to these men as deacons (to have done so in this context would have been virtually redundant: the word *deacon* comes from the same root word as *distribution*), but the term *deacon* is used in Philippians 1:1 to refer to a similar group in that church. It would seem that this office was soon expanded to include women, although the term used to describe Phoebe in Romans 16:1 is alternately translated as "deaconess" and "servant." The extension of the office to women would have been a natural enough development, however, since it would have been problematical for men to minister to women except in a public, collective fashion. Women afflicted with sickness would have needed other women to assist them in their distress. The official involvement of some women would not have precluded the unofficial involvement of others (see Acts 9:36–39).

Luke does not say whether the Seven became a permanent part of the organization of the Jerusalem church. The question arises not only because they are not mentioned again but also because of the fact that when financial relief was sent from the Antioch church to Jerusalem it was delivered to the elders rather than to the Seven (11:30). Perhaps we are to conclude that by the time this relief came the daily ministration was no longer a feature of the life of the Jerusalem church. The very fact that Philip, one of the Seven, left Jerusalem to minister at Samaria (see Acts 8:5) may well be a further indication of a still earlier breakdown. The qualifications of the Seven were eminently spiritual (6:3, 8), so it is not surprising that these men did not content themselves with their mundane duties on behalf of the congregation but in some cases took a prominent part in the proclamation of the word, a proclamation that was supported by miracles (see Acts 6:8, 10; 8:5–6).

The situation is further complicated by the fact that Paul does not mention elders when writing to his various churches, although he may have been making references to individuals serving in this office when he used such terms as "those who are over you in the Lord" (1 Thess. 5:12; cf. Rom. 12:8); and "bishops"—literally "overseers" (Phil. 1:1). Elders are referred to as such in 1 Timothy 5:17; Titus 1:5; James 5:14; and 1 Peter 5:1.

Closely allied to the term *elder* is *overseer.* This word was rather widely used in the hellenistic age in reference to general superintendence. It appears several times in the Septuagint and four times in the New Testament (Acts 20:28; Phil. 1:1; 1 Tim. 3:2; Tit. 1:7) in this general sense; additionally, it is used once in reference to Christ (1 Pet. 2:25). Its appearance in Acts 20:28 is of special interest because the same men who are designated as overseers there have already been described as elders (in v. 17), suggesting that the terms could probably be used interchangeably. Presbyterian polity holds that the two functions ascribed to such men in 1 Timothy 5:17—namely, ruling and teaching—serve to designate the equality of these leadership roles in the congregation. Apparently there was only one group in the early church charged with leadership, but of that group one or more individuals had the gift of teaching, while others had the gift of ruling. Both functions are listed as spiritual gifts (1 Cor. 12:28; Acts 20:28). Anglicans tend to hold that although all bishops (overseers) in the New Testament were elders, not all elders were bishops. Yet in Acts 20 both terms are applied to all the men who met with Paul.

With reference to the Jerusalem church, it is evident that Peter retained the leadership among the apostles (in keeping with his prominence among the Twelve during the Gospel period), but that it was moral rather than ecclesiastical leadership, based on personal qualities and the special role assigned to him by the Lord (see Matt. 16:18–19; John 21:15–17). When he began his superintending work in Judea and Samaria, James took over the leadership of the Jerusalem congregation (see Acts 12:17; 15:13ff.; 21:18), aided by the elders. Paul mentions him before he mentions Peter and John (see Gal. 2:9). Some regard him as the prototype (and warrant for) the later monarchian bishop who begins to appear early in the second century. However, the New Testament does not assign to James the title *episcopos* or anything similar. F. F. Bruce notes that

When Eusebius says that James was "the first to be allotted the bishop's throne in Jerusalem after our Saviour's assumption," the language he uses is that of his own day (for it is most improbable that James was called *episkopos* during his lifetime), but the tradition expressed in that language antedates Eusebius's day by several generations. Antioch and Rome might invoke the primacy of Peter, but the Jerusalem tradition had no doubt where the primacy originally rested, and none could deny that the church of Jerusalem was the mother-church of Christendom.[7]

In any case, all discussion of polity should rest on the basic fact that the Lord Jesus Christ is the head of the church and all human agents are subordinate to his direction.

In the unfolding of the story of the Jerusalem church, elders are mentioned next (11:30). This is close to the time when persecution struck the church again, bringing death to James and necessitating Peter's flight. There was need for another type of leadership to supplement that of the apostles, who were not always available because of their task of superintending Christian communities in Judea. Luke has no account of the selection of elders. Lindsay holds that the elders are to be identified with the Seven,[8] but this is by no means certain. Influenced by the organization of the synagogue, the church could quite naturally have taken over this form of leadership for itself. Luke's failure to mention elders in the early part of his account may simply indicate that their importance was overshadowed by the prominence of the apostles. Or it might be that in view of the long history of eldership in Israel he felt no need to mention their presence. It was something that could be taken for granted.

We do know that Barnabas and Paul appointed elders in the churches they founded on the first missionary journey (see Acts 14:23). Nothing is said about such men in connection with the founding of the church at Ephesus, but they are mentioned at a later point, in the account of Paul's journey to Jerusalem, when he summoned them to meet him at Miletus (see Acts 20:17). One must conclude either that Luke assumed their presence at the time the church was established but for some reason did not mention them or that they were appointed at a later time, perhaps just prior to the apostle's departure from the city en route to Macedonia and Achaia.

It should be noted also that in the apostolic age there was ample room for voluntary, spontaneous leadership on the part of those who saw a need and moved to meet it. Instead of rebuking this sort of thing as dangerous to the structure of the church, Paul commended it. He rejoiced in such spiritual leadership, even when it was devoid of any official status (see 1 Cor. 16:15–16).

Qumran Influence

Jerusalem was only a short distance from the Dead Sea area where the Qumran settlement was located, and the community there was active at the very time the early church began. Consequently the Dead Sea Scrolls have been studied with great interest to discover whether there is any relationship between Qumran and the early church. In terms of organization rather than doctrinal concepts, two items are especially pertinent. First, the ruling assembly at Qumran, made up of all "mature members of the covenanted community" is called *Rabbim*—"the many." This compares rather strikingly with Luke's use of the word *plēthos*, "multitude" (see Acts 6:2, 5; 15:12, 30), to designate those who responded to the suggestion of the leaders in any important matter. Second, Qumran had a council of twelve, plus a group of three priests, as leaders of the community. Some have suggested that James, Cephas, and John—who are called "pillars" in Galatians 2:9—may correspond to the three. However, the difficulty is that the latter were not priests. As to the twelve, the precedent doubtless was that of the Old Testament (the twelve tribes of Israel).

Qumran influence need not be ruled out completely, but it was probably less significant than some have alleged. Both groups used the phrases "new covenant" and "the way" in reference to their movement, but whether or not Qumran is responsible for the parallel remains an open question. When one moves from terminology to content, differences begin to appear at once.

2. THEOLOGY
(Gleaned Mainly from the Preaching)

What follows is an intentionally limited survey of theology apparent in the speeches in Acts. We might have extended the scope of inquiry to include material from the narrative portions of Acts, in which more information is available, especially with reference to the Spirit. Or we might have gone further still to include the epistles, which contain a good deal of additional data, but the survey would then have become unmanageable.

In approaching the speeches as our source material, we should observe that most of them are addressed to unbelievers, so the content is largely limited to what one should know in order to make an intelligent decision for Christ. We will study the material inductively, examining the data in various categories: the doctrine of God, Christology, the Holy Spirit, Scripture, and salvation.

The Doctrine of God

1. God is Spirit (7:48; 17:24. Neither of these verses constitutes a definition, and both are less precise than John 4:24, but they do emphasize that God cannot be confined to a building erected by man. Cf. 1 Kings 8:27).

2. God is living, in contrast to idols (14:15; 17:29; cf. 1 Thess. 1:9).

3. God is Creator (14:15; 17:25–26). He is no demiurge. It was unnecessary to state this truth to a Jewish audience.

4. God has not left himself without witness; the regularity of the seasons and the supply of human needs attest to his existence (14:17).

5. God is the source of Old Testament prophecy—concerning the suffering of the Christ (3:18), concerning the sending of the Spirit (2:17), and concerning the consummation through Christ (3:21).

6. God made a covenant with Abraham (3:25; 7:2–8).

7. God promised Moses that he would raise up a prophet like him (7:37; cf. 3:22).

8. God promised to David a continuing seed and throne (2:30).

9. God brought Jesus into the arena of history (3:26; 13:33).

10. God anointed Jesus with the Holy Spirit and power (10:38).

11. God attested Jesus through signs and wonders (2:22; cf. 10:38).

12. God purposed through Jesus to turn Israel from iniquity (3:26; 5:31).

13. God foreknew the death of Jesus (2:23; cf. 4:28).

14. God raised Jesus from the dead (2:24, 32; 3:15; 4:10; 5:30; 10:40 [on the third day]; 13:30, 37; 17:18, 31).

15. God exalted Jesus as Lord and Christ (2:36); prince and Savior (5:31).

The Doctrine of Christ

1. His historicity (2:22).

2. His humanity (2:22; cf. 1:14; 17:31).

3. His lineage—of the seed of David (2:30; cf. 13:34).

4. His anointment with the Spirit and power (10:38).

5. His attestation by God through miracles (2:22; 10:38; cf. 3:16; 4:10).

6. His death.

   a. According to the Scriptures (3:18; 26:22–23).

   b. According to the purpose of God (2:23).

   c. Accomplished by wicked men (2:23).

7. His resurrection.

   a. A fact of history (2:24).

   b. Anticipated by prophecy (2:25–31).

   c. Attested by witnesses to whom he appeared (3:15; 10:40–41).

   d. Assurance created thereby concerning the reality of future judgment (17:31).

8. His exaltation (ascension and session).

   a. Announced in Scripture (2:34).

   b. Part of his glorification (3:13).

   c. Attested by his outpouring of the Spirit (2:33).

   d. Enables him to save his people (5:31).

   e. Prepares the way for the consummation (3:21).

9. His return (3:20).

10. His work as judge (10:42–43; 17:31).

11. Belief in him essential for receiving forgiveness of sins (13:38–39; 10:43).

12. His titles.

a. Lord (2:36; 10:36; cf. Rom. 10:9–10). The affirmation that Jesus is Lord became the church's fundamental article of faith concerning the Savior. It helped to remove the stumbling block of the cross for Jews, who could now see that the unexpected humiliation was a necessary but temporary phase that led to the exaltation.

b. Christ (2:36). That we speak of "Christ" rather than "*the* Christ" calls for some explanation. We might take a representative passage in which the definite article occurs in connection with this title—Luke 24:46, for instance. In the course of teaching his disciples after the resurrection, Jesus made the pronouncement that "This is what is written: the Christ will suffer and rise from the dead on the third day." Here "the Christ" is a title rather than a name. He is the anointed one. In his Pentecost sermon Peter used the article (see Acts 2:31), which helps to determine the sense in 2:36, where the article does not appear. In this verse "Lord" and "Christ" are correlative, neither one having the article. The force of the statement is on this order: Jesus is now affirmed by resurrection and exaltation to be truly Lord and Christ. The inclusion of an article with Christ would have been awkward when it was not used with Lord. The article reappears in 3:18 and 20, however, so the meaning Peter gives to the term is consistent throughout.

A problem remains concerning these two titles. Are we to understand that it was only after his exaltation that Jesus could properly be designated by these terms and that all previous uses are essentially anachronistic, a matter of the church reading his later glory back into the events recorded in the Gospels? A close parallel to the situation presented by Acts 2:36 is found in Romans 1:3–4: in v. 4 it is stated that Jesus was declared with power to be the Son of God by his resurrection from the dead, but v. 3 makes it plain that he was the Son of God to begin with. In the same way, the titles in Acts 2:36 must be considered in light of 3:18, which makes it plain that Jesus was the Christ before he suffered (cf. Luke 24:26, 46; Acts 17:3).

C. F. D. Moule has made an important study of the Christology of Acts.[9] His main thrust is to combat the idea that the Gospels cannot be taken as sober history because they are written from the standpoint of faith and have a theological axe to grind. He points out that Luke-Acts presents a real opportunity to test such a theory because both books are written by the same man. Among other titles he examines *kyrios* (Lord) and notes that it appears only in very limited fashion in the Gospel. His conclusion is that Luke is not guilty of reading back into the Gospel period a title that takes its real significance from the resurrection. Further, "the use of *kyrios* in the Gospel and Acts suggests that Luke at least was deliberately making a distinction; and that its associations in Acts are decidedly transcendental."[10] What Moule's survey brings out is the decisive effect of the resurrection as certifying what may indeed have been true before but not demonstrably true.

Another point about the church's testimony concerning the Lord and Savior is raised by Otto Betz: "The church adorned the risen Lord with a multitude of titles and designations of sovereignty. Who gave it the right to do this if the historical Jesus did not claim any of these titles for himself or did not hold them to be in accordance with his mission? And how can our message then be made credible?"[11]

    c. Prince (or author) of life (3:15; cf. 5:31).

    d. Servant (3:13; 3:26; 4:27, 30). The word is *pais*.

    e. Savior (5:31; 13:23).

    f. Holy and just one (3:14; 7:52; cf. 22:14).

    g. Prophet (3:22; cf. 7:37).

    h. Judge (10:42; cf. 17:31).

    i. Seed of David (2:30).

    j. Seed of Abraham (indirect reference in 3:25).

    k. Son of Man (7:56). Just before his death, Stephen looked heavenward and was given a glimpse of the exalted Lord. "Look," he said, "I see heaven open and the Son of Man standing at the right hand of God." In the Gospels, only Jesus uses this title of himself. Others avoid it. How is this solitary instance in Acts to be explained? As Jesus uses it in the Gospels, it refers either to the current situation, his state of self-humbling, or to the future, when the Son of Man will be glorified. In Acts, that time has now come, though the glory is not yet publicly displayed. Moule comments, "The term is used to denote Christ's already achieved glory and his championship of the first martyr. It has been subtly and convincingly adapted to a distinctively post-resurrection martyr-situation."[12]

    l. Son of God (13:33; cf. 9:20).

The Doctrine of the Holy Spirit

1. Recognized as having inspired the prophets (4:24; cf. 2:29–30).
2. Promised by the prophets (2:16ff.).
3. Came upon Jesus prior to his ministry (10:38).
4. Sent by the ascended Lord to his church (2:33).
5. His coming marked by signs (2:3–4).
6. Described as filling the apostles and others (2:4).
7. Bestowed on all who receive Jesus as the Christ (2:38; 5:32).
8. A witness along with the apostles (5:32; cf. John 15:26–27).
9. Able to convict sinners (10:44; cf. 2:37). This particular ministry was bound to confirm the confidence of the apostles in Jesus, for he had

declared in advance that the Spirit would convict of sin, righteousness, and judgment (see John 16:7).

10. Can be resisted (7:51).

The Doctrine of Scripture

1. The combined testimony of the prophets points to the messianic age which has now dawned (3:24).

2. Opposition to the Lord's anointed by peoples and rulers was declared in advance (4:25–26).

3. The sufferings of the Servant were announced beforehand (8:32–35).

4. The resurrection of God's holy one was foreseen (2:25–31; 13:33–35).

5. The exaltation of the Lord was foretold (2:34–36).

6. The downfall and supplanting of Judas were foretold (1:20).

7. The advent of the Spirit was predicted (2:17–21).

8. The pressing of Gentiles into the church was foretold (15:15–18).

9. The unresponsiveness of Israel was seen from of old (28:25–27).

10. The consummation (or restoration) of all things was foretold by the prophets (3:21).

It was a tremendous help to preachers of the word in the early days of the church to be able to do as Peter had done on the day of Pentecost, saying "this is what was spoken by the prophet Joel." It was especially helpful in reaching their own countrymen who reverenced the Old Testament as God's word. Judging by the fact that even the disciples had to be enlightened concerning the prophetic Scriptures, especially in the area of messianic predictions (see Luke 24), many Jews must have been amazed and blessed as they read their Scriptures over again in the light of recent fulfillment. God had spoken and then acted to fulfill his word in the person of the Messiah.

This flood of new light on the Old Testament must have been shared by the apostles with other believers in the early days of the church. It is significant that when Philip dealt with the Ethiopian eunuch he was able to expound Isaiah 53 as a prophecy fulfilled in Jesus of Nazareth. It may seem strange that Peter did not quote this portion in his Pentecost sermon, but he was obliged to deal with two basic items on that occasion: the explanation of the phenomena that marked the coming of the Spirit and the resurrection of Jesus as God's answer to what the nation Israel had done to its rightful king.

The Doctrine of Salvation

1. It is available only in Christ (4:12).

2. It is by grace alone (15:11).

3. It requires faith on the part of the recipient (2:38, 40; 3:19).

4. It was proclaimed first to Israel (13:26; cf. 13:46; 3:26).
5. It is intended also for Gentiles everywhere (13:46–47).
6. It involves repentance (3:19ff.).
7. It includes forgiveness of sins (2:38; 10:43; 13:38).
8. It has present and future aspects (3:19–21).

It should not be thought that the various topics listed above represent a complete conspectus of the material relating to the theology of the sermons. For example, one could include the resurrection of both saved and unsaved (24:15). However, the purpose has been to provide coverage of the principal topics in their more important aspects.

Some Concluding Observations

1. Certain titles used of Christ in Peter's Pentecost preaching—"servant" (*pais,* not *doulos*), "author of life," "the just one," "the prophet"—are non-Pauline. F. F. Bruce notes that what we find here is "Christian preaching of an obviously primitive character, against the background of Jewish Messianic expectation. That this should be so in a report written by a Gentile, and by one who came so much under Paul's influence as Luke did, is a compelling token of the genuineness of these speeches."[13]

2. There is a virtual absence of theological elaboration on aspects of the death of Christ such as its substitutionary and reconciling character or its effect on cosmic powers or its importance for the sanctification of Christian life such as Paul develops in Romans 6, for example. The death is viewed rather from the standpoint of human guilt and divine foreknowledge, and little attention is given to its saving efficacy (although 2:38 and 20:28 are notable exceptions). Forgiveness of sins is viewed mostly as part of the whole mission of Christ (3:26) or as the result of his exaltation (5:31). Even Paul in proclaiming justification (13:39) does not connect it with the death of Christ as he does in his letters (in 26:18 it is included in his commission from the Lord).

3. A perceptible difference between the handling of Christology by Luke and by Paul is that whereas the presentation of the exalted Christ in Acts is primarily spatial (i.e., it is suggested that he is with the Father rather than with us), in Paul the gap is effectively bridged by the doctrine of the Spirit's presence in the child of God whereby Christ's risen life actuates the believer. Acts does provide a considerable amount of teaching about the Spirit, but it is mainly of a descriptive nature, indicating what the Spirit does in various aspects of his ministry. It is true that Luke can speak of the Spirit of Jesus (a term for the Holy Spirit), but not in such a way as to convey the truth that the Spirit is within, witnessing with the redeemed human spirit.

4. The resurrection of the Lord Jesus, the most constantly stressed theme in the sermons of Acts, is treated from the standpoint of apologetics (God has reversed the human verdict on Jesus) rather than from the standpoint of its theological implications (e.g., the assurance that the pen-

alty for sins was actually borne by the Savior) or the standpoint of the relation of Jesus' resurrection to the present spiritual resurrection of believers or their future bodily resurrection. On the other hand, the significance of the event for an unbelieving world is stated in its ominous reality by Paul (17:31).

5. The type of audience has much to do with the content of the sermon. The preacher does not need to speak of God as the Creator when addressing Jews or God-fearers, but this subject is strongly featured in messages to Gentiles (see Acts 14, 17). God is the central issue when Gentiles are being addressed, Christ when Jews are being addressed. Likewise, the audience determines whether or not appeals to Scripture are made; obviously this approach would be valid in speaking to Jews but largely meaningless when dealing with Gentiles.

6. The fact that Paul's presentation of the gospel to Jews (Acts 13) bears such marked similarity to Peter's presentation in its general outline warrants the conclusion that there was a basic content for the proclamation (*kērygma*) that could be expected no matter who was speaking. It included the appeal to fulfilled prophecy, mention of the person of Jesus in terms of his Davidic lineage (important for the realization of the Davidic covenant), and discussion of his death, burial, resurrection (little if any attention is given to the events preceding the Passion), exaltation, and return as consummator and judge.

7. The speeches do not provide a complete Christology; there is, for example, no affirmation of his preexistence or his relation to the Father in terms of being his only son (cf. John 1:14). The reason for such omissions is simple: they were items of importance for the saints to know and to treasure but were hardly essential to evangelistic proclamation. What we notice in these sermons of Acts is their plain and factual nature. They were intended to impart a knowledge of God's unspeakable gift that was adequate as a basis for making a decision to put faith in him for salvation.

3. INCIPIENT CREEDS

As we have seen, among the basic elements in the theology of the early church the most prominent was Christology, which is wholly natural in view of the unique and epochal character of Jesus' person and ministry, a ministry that culminated in death and resurrection. It was not necessary that apostolic preaching dwell on elements that the followers of Jesus shared with their Jewish compatriots. Their view of God and the world was basically the same as that of their fellow Jews. What came into prominence in their preaching was the new element introduced through the incarnation.

It is one thing to have a theology, another to give it expression in the form of a creed. In the apostolic age the church was not concerned with formal creeds of the kind produced in the following centuries, yet ever and again the New Testament yields statements that are creed-like in character, though often brief and seldom wrought into a schema that covers several aspects of theology. We are to examine an area, then, that lies between the sermonic material of Acts and the ecumenical creeds of the church. The book of Acts provides little help, but the epistles are quite rich in nascent formulations of Christian truth, for they reflect a church situation rather than evangelistic proclamation.

A Brief Survey of Critical Opinion about the Formation of the Creeds

From the latter half of the second century on, it was believed and maintained that the teaching of the church along theological lines was the deposit handed down from the apostles as the rule of faith for believers. There is testimony that at about A.D. 400 the opinion of church leaders was that the apostles had actually handed down a creed for later generations. Arnold Ehrhardt traces this position to Ambrose, bishop of Milan.[14] Rufinus, a contemporary of Jerome, said in reference to the apostles that

> As they were therefore on the point of taking leave of each other, they first settled an agreed norm for their future preaching, so that they might not find themselves, widely separated as they would be, giving out different doctrines to the people they invited to believe in Christ. So they met together in one spot and, being filled with the Holy Spirit, compiled this brief token, as I have said, of their future preaching, each making the contribution he thought fit; and they decreed that it should be handed out as standard teaching to believers.[15]

Rufinus is referring to the Apostles' Creed. He hints at something that was declared more specifically at a later time—namely, the individual contributions of the various apostles to the statement, each item being attributed to the illumination of the Holy Spirit. This tradition became current in the Western church, but the Greek church did not endorse the theory.[16] Through the medieval period the Latin church continued to espouse the tradition, but about the time of the Reformation Lorenzo Valla exposed the groundlessness of this view, showing that it lacked support from ancient sources. For an account of the gradual development of the Apostles' Creed, one should consult the work of Philip Schaff, who supports the Valla position.[17]

As the critical spirit developed in modern times, it tended to sweep away every suggestion of the presence of creedal elements in the apostolic age. Superficially this verdict appeared to be sustained by the fact that nowhere in the New Testament is the Apostles' Creed referred to, or anything similar to it. This negative viewpoint was supported also on the ground that creeds take shape as the result of a rather long development, so could hardly be expected to emerge in New Testament times. At the beginning of the twentieth century, Harnack drew a contrast between the Old Catholic Church, with its interest in institutional Christianity (including creedal formulation), and the church of the apostolic age, which was guided by those who possessed the gift of prophecy. This neat contrast was overdrawn, however, especially in that it failed to recognize the dominance of the apostles in the early church, which meant that prophets had a secondary role (Eph. 2:20).

Today the critical consensus is a position between that of the Latin Fathers and the modern negative approach of Harnack and others. It is recognized that we cannot rule out all creedal elements from the church of the apostolic age, for the New Testament itself bears witness to the beginnings of creedal emphasis. The apostles and their colleagues based their preaching and teaching on certain convictions that could be expressed in propositional terms. It is evident from the epistles that those who wrote them were for the most part dealing with theological truths shared by their readers. Indeed, the New Testament writings are frankly theological from beginning to end.

Terms That Suggest Creedal Ingredients

It should be evident that the term *gospel*, when it is accompanied by the definite article, presupposes a precise content, for it denotes not good news in general or good news of a local and temporary kind, but the good news of salvation in Christ. In the Septuagint only the plural form *euaggelia* occurs—denoting various items of good news. The supreme message of good news was not yet available, for redemption had not yet been wrought. Conversely, the New Testament does not use the plural: no other items of good news are allowed to compete with the gospel. Since this message calls for acceptance in order to be efficacious, it must be definite and it must be understandable. This precise character is what Paul affirmed when he anathematized those who proclaimed another, that is to say, a different gospel—which is thus no gospel at all (Gal. 1:6–7). So the Christian gospel has a fixed content (cf. 1 Cor. 15:1, 3–4). This should not be understood as meaning, however, that every statement of the content of the gospel in the New Testament is obliged to contain a complete list of all the ingredients that constitute this message. What has been noted about the term *gospel* is essentially true also of the term *kērygma* accompanied by the article—"the proclamation" (Rom. 16:25; 1 Cor. 1:21). It concerns Christ and what he accomplished by his saving mission.

To move to another term, *the faith* can mean the content of what is believed by Christians as distinct from the exercise of faith in Christ (see Jude 3). While the presence of the definite article is not an infallible indication that the word is being used in this objective sense (e.g., as in

Rom. 3:31), often this is a clue indicating the objective force (unless the article has possessive force, as in Eph. 3:12).

The Way is a term that occurs several times in Acts (e.g., in 9:2; 19:23) concerning the Christian movement, denoting a distinctive way of believing and living. This is especially evident from Acts 24:14, 22, where "the Way" is identified as a sect that held unique positions in the face of opposition from other groups.

Several expressions used in the pastoral epistles deserve to be included here. We read of "the *pattern* of sound words" in 2 Timothy 1:13. Some understand this word *hypotypōsis* in the sense of "outline" or "sketch," but the other meaning seems more likely in this passage: it is something to be maintained and followed. Paul goes on to exhort Timothy to guard the good *deposit* through the Holy Spirit (2 Tim. 1:14). The truth is a sacred trust, something left with another for safekeeping, a *parathēkē,* that must not be lost or misused. Another expression is "the good teaching" (1 Tim. 4:6), in which the word denotes what is taught—namely, Christian doctrine, upon which Timothy must continue to be nourished. On several occasions in the pastorals Paul uses the term "sound doctrine" to indicate its ability (in contrast to false teaching) to promote spiritual health.

Sometimes *the word* is used as a synonym for the gospel, as in 1 Peter 1:25, in which the word of the Lord is identified with the proclaimed message (cf. v. 23). For other examples, see Acts 6:2; 8:4; 13:49; and 2 Thessalonians 3:1.

In writing to the Corinthians about the gospel and its transmission (1 Cor. 15:1ff.), the apostle says that he *delivered* to them what he had *received.* In the Greek, both words are compounded with the preposition *para,* which suggests transmission without any loss in what is passed on. The gospel was too precious to allow addition or subtraction or alteration in connection with its conveyance.

To accept the gospel and thereby receive Christ into one's heart and life leads to another step—confession of one's faith. Confession is a familiar concept with reference to sins (see 1 John 1:9), a procedure in which we say the same thing that God says about our transgressions; we concur with his verdict that we have done wrong and we deplore our failure. But confession in a creedal context has a somewhat different nuance. It means that we say the same thing that other believers say about the items that constitute our faith. The creedal statement in 1 Timothy 3:16 is introduced by the adverb *confessedly* or *by common confession* (NASB), which seems to mean that the following articles of faith about the Lord Jesus Christ are held to be true by believers everywhere. In a worship setting this calls for united declaration.

Confession is also an appropriate term for personal witness to the unsaved. Jesus made a confession before Pilate (see 1 Tim. 6:13). He gave an impetus to confession as witness by declaring, "Whoever acknowledges me before men, I will also acknowledge him before my Father in heaven" (Matt. 10:32). Confession is usually bound up with one's affirmation of the person of Jesus Christ and one's relationship to him. It presupposes faith and it gives expression to that faith (Rom. 10:9–10 makes specific mention of both heart and mouth). Confession stands over against denial, which involves rejection or forsaking of Christ (Acts 3:13). An Old Testament background for the practice of confession is found in the Shema, the verbalization of Israel's faith in the one true and living God (Deut. 6:4), which was an integral part of Jewish worship in New Testament times.

There were several contexts in which public confession of faith was practiced: (1) baptism, when the candidate affirmed his or her faith in Christ as the condition for reception into the church; (2) worship, when the living Lord was acclaimed by the congregation; (3) a service of ordination or dedication, when a Christian worker was set apart for special ministry (see 1 Tim. 4:14; 6:12); (4) a court trial or a hearing (see 2 Tim. 4:16); and (5) discussions with unsaved persons (1 Pet. 3:15).

Confession and *witness* are somewhat synonymous, but confession has a more solemn and at times a more intellectualized content. It usually connotes a more public situation—"before men"—whether in Christian assembly or under interrogation.

Criteria for Identifying Creedal Statements

In his *New Testament Theology,* E. Stauffer presents a full list of the characteristics of creedal statements in Scripture.[18] The following are the most obvious of the points he notes:

1. Creedal formulas are often introduced by such terms as *deliver, believe,* or *confess.* (See 1 Cor. 15:3; 1 John 5:1, 5; 1 John 4:2. Note should be taken also of Rom. 10:9–10 and 1 Tim. 3:16.)

2. Sometimes they exhibit a different linguistic medium than the writer himself is using (e.g., 1 Cor. 16:22 at the end), or a different vocabulary or style than he is accustomed to use.

3. They tend to avoid particles, conjunctions, and complicated constructions. Their statements are more in the nature of theses or propositions than a discussion or argument (e.g., Acts 4:10).

4. They are sometimes phrased in antithetic style (as in 1 Tim. 3:16) and also in rhythmic style.

5. They frequently make use of a noun predicate, such as "Jesus (is) Lord."

6. They often involve statements about elementary Christian truths centered in events of redemption history (e.g., in 1 Cor. 15:3ff.).

Christological Statements

1. Jesus is Lord. The *Sitz im Leben* for this item seems to be the preaching of the early church (Acts 2:36; 10:36). The affirmation of lord-

ship was closely connected with the resurrection and ascension of Jesus Christ.

In 1 Corinthians 12:3 this declaration is contrasted with "Jesus is anathema," suggesting that at times this brief affirmation was used in a polemical context. In Romans 10:9 the setting appears to be the declaration of a candidate about to be received into the church, presumably in connection with a baptismal service (note the reference to evangelistic preaching at the end of verse 8 and the promise of salvation at the end of verse 9 to the one who believes and confesses). In Philippians 2:11 the setting appears to be worship in the sense that the congregation that bows the knee now and confesses Jesus Christ as Lord also anticipates the day when the number of those who acknowledge him will be vastly augmented.

Goppelt observes that this brief creedal statement had a limitation: "The early confession of the Hellenistic church, Jesus is Lord (1 Cor. 12:3; Rom. 10:9; Phil. 2:11), did not suffice against docetism. To counter this, one needed to confess according to 1 John 4:2, 'Jesus Christ has come in the flesh.'"[19]

2. Jesus is the Christ (1 John 2:22). This affirmation roots itself in the confession of Simon Peter (see Mark 8:29), and it appears consistently in apostolic preaching to the Jews (see Acts 2:36; 17:3). It presupposes the national expectation of a Messiah.

3. Jesus is the Son of God (see 1 John 4:15, where it is said to be *confessed* or *acknowledged;* cf. 1 John 5:5). In certain passages with a synagogue setting, the statement has an evangelistic thrust (see Acts 9:20; 13:33). Its occurrence in Matthew 14:33 anticipates its use in Matthew 16:16. Some Christological statements contain more than a single affirmation, such as Romans 1:3–4, in which the basic truth about our Lord's sonship is amplified to express the incarnate and glorified aspects.

Note should be taken of those passages that deal with the work of our Lord in distinction from his person or dignity. Outstanding in this category is Paul's word about the kernel of the gospel: "that Christ died for our sins according to the Scriptures, that he was buried, that he was raised on the third day according to the Scriptures, and that he appeared . . . " (1 Cor. 15:3–5). Romans 8:34 includes the death, the resurrection, the present position at the right hand of God, and the intercession of Christ. Quite elaborate is the statement in 1 Peter 3:18–22, which includes Christ's substitutionary death, the righteous for the unrighteous, his quickening and preaching to the spirits in prison, his resurrection, ascension, session, and preeminence over angelic powers. Sometimes there is an accent on contrast, as in 2 Corinthians 13:4, where it is stated that Christ was crucified in weakness but lives by the power of God. There is contrast also between the descent involved in the incarnation and the ascent to heaven that followed the earthly sojourn. Examples of this type are Philippians 2:6–11 and Ephesians 4:8–10. Notable for its hymnic character is 1 Timothy 3:16, which has some unique statements presented in three pairs, each containing a contrast: flesh/spirit, angels/nations, and world/glory.

In an article dealing with the creedal statements in 1 Corinthians 15 and 1 Timothy 3, Eduard Schweizer has observed that with the exception of one item, namely, "Christ died," all the other statements in both passages are couched in the passive voice. He suggests that this indicates an interest "in what God let happen to him."[20]

Confession of Christ in Hebrews has some distinctives. The content embraces not only the Son of God (1:2–3) but recognition of him as high priest and apostle (3:1; 4:14). There is also an emphasis on exhortation to hold fast the confession (4:14).

Statements That Include Father and Son

In this category is Paul's word that "for us there is but one God, the Father, from whom all things came and for whom we live, and there is but one Lord, Jesus Christ, through whom all things came and through whom we live" (1 Cor. 8:6). The first half reflects Old Testament truth as well as New, and the second half notes both the person and work of Christ in its overarching character. Observe that the distinctive roles of God the Father and of Christ are recognized (*from* whom and *for* whom in the case of the Father; *through* whom in the case of the Lord Jesus Christ).

Another passage is 1 Timothy 2:5–6: "For there is one God and one mediator between God and men, the man Christ Jesus, who gave himself as a ransom for all men—the testimony given in its proper time." In this instance only the Christological portion of the statement is elaborated.

Somewhat related to such affirmations are the opening statements in many of Paul's letters, which could be regarded as indirect creedal statements. For example, "Grace and peace to you from God our Father and the Lord Jesus Christ, who gave himself for our sins to rescue us from the present evil age, according to the will of our God and Father" (Gal. 1:3–4).

Trinitarian Statements

The Great Commission contained in Matthew 28:19–20 has a command to baptize in the name of the Father, Son, and Holy Spirit. Again, this is only indirectly a creedal statement, but it reflects the New Testament doctrine of God in full expression. Somewhat closer to a creedal formulation is the so-called apostolic benediction of 2 Corinthians 13:14: "May the grace of the Lord Jesus Christ and the love of God, and the fellowship of the Holy Spirit be with all of you." The grace of Christ is affirmed again in 2 Corinthians 8:9; God is called the God of love in 2 Corinthians 13:11; and the Spirit's fellowship is mentioned in Philippians 2:1.

Concluding Observations

From this brief survey it is evident that statements of a creedal nature at this early period in the history of the church are fairly numerous and show considerable variety, a testimony to the newness and vigor of the Christian movement. Underlying the element of variety as a solid base is the core of the *kērygma*, the rule of faith, which has much more uniformity. There is something of a parallel in the history of the canon in that the principle of canonicity was firmly held despite the fact that the lists of accepted books in the early period of the church do not always fully agree with one another.

As a footnote to our discussion it should be stated that several scholars have contended that some passages of a creedal nature in Paul bear marks of a non-Pauline origin and should therefore be regarded as having been taken over by him from existing usage in the church. A good case can be made for this in connection with 1 Corinthians 15:3ff.[21] The situation is not as convincing with regard to Romans 1:3-4, Philippians 2:6-11, and Colossians 1:15-20.[22]

The element of affirmation or confession is related to belief, centering on what God has done for sinful mankind. It is not centered on human conduct, important though this is. The lesson to be grasped here is the basic importance of conviction in relation to manner of life. The former leads to the latter, but the latter cannot stand alone. From time to time emphasis on social action is needed as a corrective for indifference, but it should not be kept always in the forefront lest the church lose sight of its basic nature and purpose.

New Testament creedal statements are largely confined to Acts and the epistles, especially the latter. Consequently, those who are inclined to find the essence of the gospel in the teaching of Jesus tend to take lightly the importance of the creedal element in Christianity, whether in the New Testament itself or in the creeds of the church. There are others who cordially embrace the Scriptures, including their doctrinal teaching, but who refuse to be bound by creedal statements drawn up by churchmen. Perhaps those who take this position are unaware that by taking the New Testament in this normative sense they are thereby embracing incipient creedal statements despite their avowed dislike for creeds. There is something of a parallel in the case of speakers who claim they have no theology to present but who proceed to make a great many theological assertions.

4. BAPTISM

In Acts and in the epistles baptism is presented as the rite by which those who have put their faith in Christ are inducted into the church. No doubt it was considered to be a fulfillment of the requirement of confessing him before men—not in an exhaustive sense of course, but rather as a first step.

Background

Obviously we would not expect to find references to Christian baptism as such in the Old Testament. Water as a cleansing agent is often referred to there, particularly in the rituals of purification for those who were ceremonially unclean, but also in reference to cleansing from moral and spiritual defilement (see Ezek. 36:25; cf. Zech. 13:1). Paul uses the term *baptized* with reference to Israel in connection with the Red Sea experience and seems to say that thereby the people were put into a special relationship with Moses that might be described as one of loyalty and obedience (see 1 Cor. 10:1–2). The construction in the Greek is the same as that which the apostle uses in referring to baptism into/unto Christ (see, for example, Rom. 6:3).

This reference by Paul in 1 Corinthians 10 raises the question of whether he was influenced at all by the practice of proselyte baptism in Judaism. It is likely that this institution was part of Judaism by New Testament times.[23] W. F. Flemington agrees with W. L. Knox that

> in much of his teaching about baptism St. Paul was adapting for Christian purposes a well-known method of Jewish *kerygma*. The story of the Exodus became a regular "form" under which the message of Judaism was preached to the Gentile world. So it was taught that through circumcision and the *tebilah* the proselyte came out of "Egypt" and passed through the "Red Sea" into the "Promised Land."[24]

David Daube notes the importance of "going up" or "coming up" as the decisive moment in proselyte baptism. The candidate thereby emerged as a true Israelite. Daube thinks this might be associated with the going up into the land of Israel under Joshua.[25] As it stands, there is no certain explanation of the origin of proselyte baptism, although it could have developed in connection with the Pharisaic missionary propaganda of which our Lord speaks in Matthew 23:15.

But whatever similarity there may be between proselyte baptism and Christian baptism, it is outweighed by the differences. Proselytes were non-Jews won over to Judaism, whereas Christian baptism, according to Acts, was practiced on Jews before it was extended to Gentiles. A weightier distinction is the fact that whereas the proselyte was brought under the regimen of the Mosaic law, the convert to Christianity was put into relationship to Jesus Christ and his finished work. Consequently, if proselyte baptism exercised any influence on Christian baptism it was only in a formal, external sense.

We are on more solid ground when we come to John's baptism, in that it was performed on Jews and was endorsed by Jesus—and that in the most striking way possible, when he presented himself to John for baptism. John's rite differed from Jewish proselyte baptism in that it was not self-administered and had eschatological overtones, being a preparation for the coming messianic age, in view of which the candidate had to repent of his sins.

Several items establish a relationship between the baptism of Jesus at the Jordan and Christian baptism: (1) attestation of sonship, in the one case by the Father on behalf of Jesus, and in the other by the Spirit on behalf of the believer (see Rom. 8:14–16); (2) the parallel between Jesus' waiting on God in prayer and then experiencing the descent of the Spirit on the one hand, and the early church's waiting for the baptism of the Spirit prior to Pentecost on the other; and (3) Jesus' act of identification with the people by submitting to baptism (see Luke 3:21), which is paralleled in Christian baptism in that converts are thereby incorporated into the body of Christ and thus identified with the people of God.

It is important to note that apart from a reference in John 4:1–2 to some baptizing activity by the disciples of Jesus, there is neither any indication that believers were gathered together and inducted into a fellowship by baptism nor any indication of the Spirit's presence among the disciples; there is only a promise that he would come after the departure of Jesus (see John 16:7). Why are baptism and the gift of the Spirit delayed? Because Jesus' baptism in water had not yet been completed by his baptism in blood (see Luke 12:50). Only after the cross and resurrection could Christian baptism be administered. Paul made it plain that to be baptized into Christ is to be baptized into his death (see Rom. 6:3). The values of Christ's redemption, then, are expressed and appropriated in Christian baptism, when the convert is sealed by the Spirit and placed into the body of Christ with other believers.

A comparison between John's baptism and that which was practiced by the church yields certain differences:

1. As noted, John's baptism anticipated the coming of the messianic age. It looked forward. On the other hand, Christian baptism looks backward to the finished work of Christ.

2. Whereas both John and Jesus had disciples, for the most part the people who received John's baptism returned to their former situations without forming a new sect within Judaism. On the other hand, those who received Christian baptism formed a distinct community, the society of the redeemed.

3. John's candidates for baptism confessed a variety of sins, whereas those who confessed Jesus as the Christ at Pentecost acknowledged above all other sins the very specific sin of concurring in the national rejection of Israel's Messiah.

Though Jesus received baptism at the hands of John, it seems that he did not refer people to him for baptism when he commenced his own ministry. For a brief period, according to John 4:1–2, the disciples of Jesus baptized, probably on the analogy of John's baptism. But as the ministry progressed and Jesus dealt with many repentant sinners, apparently he did not baptize. In fact, as far as the record goes, he did not even require baptism. Personal contact with him gave far more assurance of forgiveness than submission to baptism. When he was no longer personally available, when the mediation of his apostles and others became necessary, the appropriateness of the rite of baptism was evident once more.

There is a strong probability that the disciples, some of whom were John's followers before they came to Jesus, received baptism from John. We have no record that they received Christian baptism. This may seem strange in light of the fact that certain men at Ephesus who acknowledged having received John's baptism were rebaptized in the name of Christ (see Acts 19:1–5). But again, the factor of contact with Jesus in the days of his flesh gave the apostles, in contrast to others, all they needed. The ritual of baptism would not be as meaningful for them as for those who had not been privileged to associate with the Master.

A direct connection between Christian baptism and the Lord's person and work is provided by the postresurrection command contained in Matthew 28:19. Some scholars have questioned the authenticity of this saying. Though the passage cannot be rejected on the basis of omission in the manuscript testimony, the attempt has been made, particularly by Kirsopp Lake,[26] to show that Eusebius must have known of texts in which the reference to baptism was lacking, since he sometimes quoted the passage this way. But this apparent inconsistency is easily explained on the ground that on those occasions when he used the shorter form he quoted only as much of the passage as was needful for his immediate purpose.

The authenticity of verse 19 as the word of Jesus has also been questioned on the ground that it contains the trinitarian formula—baptism in the name of the Father, Son, and Spirit. This is a much more serious objection, since nowhere in the book of Acts or in the remainder of the New Testament is baptism described in these terms. It is easy to conclude, therefore, that the Matthean passage must be a reflection of later church usage. However, the Didache, which belongs to the early postapostolic period and which speaks of administering baptism with the trinitarian formula in chapter 7 also speaks of baptism in the name of the Lord in chapter 9. Since the New Testament does not describe a baptismal service with a reproduction of what was spoken, it is quite possible that the triune formula was actually used but that the shorter expression "in the name of Christ" was regularly used in the sacred text because it set forth the significance of the rite. From the time of baptism onward the baptized person belonged to Christ.

Some have concluded that the tension in Acts 1:5 between the water baptism of John and the baptism with the Spirit predicted by Jesus represents a tacit denial by the Lord of the relevance of water baptism for his church, but this involves reading something into the passage. The magnifying of the greater baptism does not necessitate the omission of the lesser.

All the evidence we have points to the practice of water baptism from the very beginning of the life of the church. Hebrews 6:2 speaks of "instruction about baptisms" as belonging to the first principles of Christ (elementary Christian teaching). When Paul wrote to the church at Rome, which he did not personally establish, he was able to assume that his readers had been baptized (see Rom. 6:3) and that they were informed as to its meaning ("do you not know?"). Moreover, the apostle evidently attached great importance to his own experience of being baptized (see Acts 22:16).

With this in mind, it is surely a mistake to appeal to 1 Corinthians 1:14–17 as a disparagement of baptism. Paul grants that the rite does not constitute an element of the gospel. It lacks the power to save or make a contribution to salvation. Neither here nor elsewhere does he designate the saints as "baptized ones," though he frequently refers to them as believers. Through the gospel Paul was the spiritual father of most of the Corinthians (4:15). Since he baptized virtually none of them (1:14, 16) he would not have been able to claim them as his spiritual children if baptism had been part of the gospel. The reason for his remarks about baptism in the opening chapter of the letter can readily be seen from the context, which deals with the spirit of competition and the practice of setting one human leader over another, exalting one to the detriment of others (1:14ff.). Paul tells his readers that he deliberately avoided baptizing his converts at Corinth personally, lest they claim to have been baptized in his name. It was their relationship to Christ that counted, and no human participant in a baptismal service could afford to becloud the candidate's obedience to Christ by emphasizing any claim on the candidate. Jesus had allowed his disciples to baptize rather than do it himself (see John 4:2). Paul followed essentially the same pattern at Corinth, it seems, probably requesting his helpers to baptize the converts (cf. 2 Cor. 1:19). He would have been appalled had they imagined that through his personal participation in their baptism he had effected some sort of union with himself, when union with Christ was the truth to be grasped.

The Relation between Water Baptism and Spirit Baptism

The problematic relationship between water baptism and Spirit baptism arises at the very inception of the church, when Peter tells his hearers to repent and be baptized in the name of Jesus Christ for the forgiveness of their sins, then in almost the same breath tells them that they will receive the gift of the Holy Spirit (Acts 2:38). The acceptance of baptism seems to guarantee the reception of the Spirit. But the idea that baptism is a quasi-magical formula for acquiring the Spirit is contradicted by the passage itself, for if that were the case the Spirit would no longer be a gift. Furthermore, it is apparent from the whole range of New Testament teaching on baptism that this requirement is something that follows faith, and this is implied in the passage before us as well (cf. 2:44).

That baptism in itself has no power to bestow the Spirit is also made plain by the account of Philip's ministry in Samaria. People believed and were baptized, yet the Spirit was not given to them on that occasion, but only later, when the apostles Peter and John came from Jerusalem (8:12, 14–17). Admittedly this was an unusual situation, but it demonstrates that baptism did not automatically entail the bestowal of the Spirit. Normally, as at Pentecost, water baptism (on the basis of faith) resulted in the gift of the Spirit (cf. Eph. 1:13). The case of Cornelius and his company is of great interest because the usual order of these two things was reversed. The Spirit fell on the people as Peter spoke, and after this he called for their baptism. Knowing that water baptism and the gift of the Spirit went together, Peter reasoned that the coming of the Spirit implied faith on the part of the hearers and he concluded that faith, now evidenced by the Spirit's presence, should be declared in the usual way—that is, by baptism.

We might call 1 Corinthians 12:13 a problem passage because of some uncertainty concerning the meaning of the last clause and the relation of that clause to the rest of the sentence that speaks of baptism with the Spirit. The verse reads as follows: "For we were all baptized by one Spirit into one body—whether Jews or Greeks, slave or free—and we were all given the one Spirit to drink." G. W. H. Lampe states that "Pauline thought affords no ground whatever for the modern theories which seek to effect a separation in the one action and to distinguish a 'Spirit-Baptism' and a 'water-Baptism,' not as the inward and outward parts of one sacrament, but as independent entities."[27] Lampe also calls attention to the conjunction of the two elements at the baptism of Jesus:

> Whereas the multitudes were baptized by John as a remnant elected to wait the dawning of the age to come, Jesus received the promised descent of the Spirit, and the association of water and Spirit which had been prefigured in the metaphorical language of the Prophets became translated into reality. Hence, when the death and resurrection of the Christ had established the New Covenant, and the Spirit could be bestowed on all those who responded in faith to His saving work, the union of water and Spirit as the outward sign and the inner reality of the sacramental rite became normative for the baptismal theology of the early church.[28]

It could be questioned, however, whether Paul is including water baptism in this passage (1 Cor. 12:13). The word *baptize* occurs here only in connection with the Spirit. Although it is true, as Lampe points out, that the descent of the Spirit on Jesus at his baptism suggests a connection between water and Spirit baptism we need evidence from the New Testament itself that mention of the one type of baptism carries with it the other. James Dunn points out that exclusive of 1 Corinthians 12:13 there are six passages that speak of Spirit baptism (Matt. 3:11; Mark 1:8; Luke 3:16; John 1:33; and Acts 1:5 and 11:16), and in all of them the Spirit is referred to as characterizing the element of the Messiah's baptism in contrast to water as the element of John's baptism.[29]

There are other considerations also. The setting for the statement in 1 Corinthians 12:13 is a long passage dealing with spiritual gifts. Since he begins verse 13 with the word *for,* Paul is clearly establishing a close relationship in that verse with the preceding material. Moreover, it would be strange for the apostle to make a reference to water baptism at all in this context. When he refers to water baptism at earlier points in the letter, the allusions are clear and the meaning unmistakable. If there is any reference to water baptism here, he would be mentioning it without explanation. Also he would be referring to the rite after dealing with the Spirit's work of putting believers into the body of Christ and equipping them for spiritual service. This amounts to a strange reversal of order— strange for the epistles at any rate.

We ought to look at one other problem passage before moving on. In Ephesians 4:5 the apostle speaks of "one Lord, one faith, one baptism." Is this Spirit baptism or water baptism? The Spirit has been mentioned in the preceding verse—"there is one body and one Spirit"—but the fact that the mention of baptism does not come at this point but after "faith" points rather clearly to the answer: it is water baptism that is being referred to here, for that is the prescribed method of giving expression to faith. We may take it as a rule of thumb that unless the Spirit is mentioned in conjunction with an allusion to baptism, it is probably water baptism rather than Spirit baptism that is being discussed.

Baptism in the Name of Christ

We have already observed how Paul shrank from even the possibility that those whom he baptized would think that they had been baptized in his name (see 1 Cor. 1:15). The book of Acts states repeatedly that converts were baptized in the name of Christ (2:38; 8:16; 10:48; 19:5). This is more than a formula, just as the use of the Lord's name in prayer (see John 14:13–14) is more than a conventional device for closing one's address to God. The name of Christ was used also in the performance of miracles (see Acts 3:6) and especially in the exorcism of demons (see Acts 16:18). We must connect the "name" with the person, which is exactly what Peter does when he affirms that there is no other name under heaven, given among men, whereby we must be saved, than the name of Jesus (4:12). To the person we may add the element of authority, as is evident in the question of the Sanhedrin to Peter and John, "By what power or by what name did you do this?" (4:7), in the matter of the healing of the lame man.

Matthew 28:19 contains the command of Jesus to the disciples that they baptize in the name of the Father, Son, and Spirit. There is no tritheism here, as the singular form "name" reminds us. "Baptism into the name means that the subject of baptism, through fellowship with the Son who is one with God, receives forgiveness of sins and comes under the operation of the Holy Spirit."³⁰

Though Paul does not speak of baptism in or into *the name of* Christ, he undoubtedly provides the ultimate meaning of the phrase when he speaks of baptism into Christ (Gal. 3:27; Rom. 6:3). Since he uses the same idiom in speaking of what happened at the Red Sea—stating that the children of Israel were baptized into/unto Moses—there is the implication that in the same way Israel thereby accepted Moses without question as the one through whom God had wrought their deliverance and signaled their confidence in his leadership and submission to his authority, so in Christian baptism converts to Christ acknowledge their gratitude and obedience to the Lord Jesus.

Summary of the Significance of Baptism in the Early Church

1. The forgiveness of sins is mediated through the rite (see Acts 2:38). Sometimes the emphasis is placed on the cleansing from the stain of sin. This is true not only for the licentious Corinthians (1 Cor. 6:11) but for the morally upright Saul of Tarsus (Acts 22:16).

2. Those candidates who accept baptism acknowledge that they now belong to Christ and are subject to him. In a number of crucial passages Paul affirms the basic Christian confession, "Jesus is Lord." Of these passages the one most clearly connected with baptism is Romans 10:9—"if you confess with your mouth, 'Jesus is Lord,' and believe in your hearts that God raised him from the dead, you will be saved." E. F. Scott writes,

> It may be regarded as practically certain, in view of the whole sequence of ideas, that Paul is here thinking of a declaration of faith that accompanied the saving act of baptism. But if the confession "Jesus is Lord" was thus inseparable from the ordinance we have a clew to the meaning of the vexed phrase "baptised in the name of Jesus." The "name" was not the personal name, employed by way of incantation, but the sovereign title of *kurios*. It is this which Paul had in mind when he speaks of Jesus as bearing "the name that is above every name," and we may well suppose that in ordinary Christian language Jesus' "name" had the accepted meaning of the supreme title which was now his. Of such a usage we seem to discern not a few indications in different books of the New Testament. Baptism "in the name of Jesus" consisted, therefore, in the acknowledgment of Jesus as the Lord.³¹

3. Baptism carries with it the promise of the gift of the Holy Spirit (Acts 2:38). The Spirit then becomes the seal unto the day of redemption that marks the completion of the saving process (Eph. 4:30) and the means of sanctification (Rom. 8:2; Gal. 5:16) and fruitful service (Acts 1:8).

4. Baptism gives expression to the believer's union with Christ and with fellow believers in his body, the church (Gal. 3:26-27).

5. Baptism into Christ means baptism into his death (Rom. 6:4) and

therefore contains a reminder to Christians that they have died to sin and should be alive to God and his righteousness. The background for this lies in the Savior's recognition that his baptism in the Jordan was preliminary to another baptism at Calvary (see Luke 12:50). Implicit in a believer's baptism is the obligation to join Paul in seeking to be conformed to Christ's death (see Phil. 3:10).

6. Baptism does not promise regeneration apart from faith, which is always the underlying presupposition for submission to the rite. If one quotes Acts 2:38 as teaching baptismal regeneration, one should consider equally another statement by Peter, namely, "Everyone who believes in him receives forgiveness of sins through his name" (Acts 10:43). As James Denney has noted, "Baptism and faith are but the outside and the inside of the same thing."[32]

7. The once-for-all character of baptism is intended to symbolize a decisive repudiation of one's sins and on the positive side a lifelong commitment to Jesus Christ as one's Savior and Lord.

Note on Hebrews 6:4

Beginning with Justin Martyr around the middle of the second century, it became common practice to speak of baptism as enlightenment. Probably the term was applied first to the instruction that preceded baptism, but eventually it was applied to the rite itself, so that one who had been baptized could be described as one who had been enlightened. It is not clear that "the once enlightened" of Hebrews 6:4 are "the baptized." (Bauer's Greek lexicon does not list the verb *photizo* as having this meaning in the New Testament or in early Christian literature.) But once the word began to be used in this sense it was natural that the church would seek biblical basis for the usage, so Hebrews 6:4 and 10:32 may well have been cited as background. Lampe is of the opinion that the incident of the granting of sight to the man born blind, involving as it did the washing in the pool of Siloam (see John 9:7), could hardly have been overlooked by the church as it moved to the use of *enlighten* in this technical sense. But in the New Testament the prevailing meaning is "to give spiritual illumination" (see, for example, Eph. 1:18).

5. WORSHIP (INCLUDING THE LORD'S SUPPER)

The Biblical Concept

Since Scripture as a whole is involved in this theme, it is fitting to begin with the background provided by the Old Testament. There are two basic Hebrew terms, one meaning "to prostrate oneself," the other referring to cultic service. Corresponding to these in the New Testament are *proskuneo*, "to bow down" (always as a verb, never used in the noun form) and *latreia* "service" (which appears five times in the noun form and twenty-one times in the verb form). The priestly service of the Old Testament sanctuary is described as *latreia* in Romans 9:4. The strong accent on the verbal use (*latreuō*) in the New Testament suggests that worship was treated not so much as a concept but rather as an activity.

The Decalogue contains a prohibition of false worship (Ex. 20:5), and the first four commandments all involve worship in one way or another. It has priority over all else, being at once the most demanding duty laid upon God's people and the highest privilege. In its purest and most exalted sense it refers to the soul's preoccupation with the Almighty in the attitude of adoration. By extension the word can be used of various activities in the cultus, carried out by the people who make their offerings and pray as well as those acts performed by ministering priests. The call to worship is a call to bow down in reverence before God's majesty. This in turn should lead to service in loyal and obedient performance of his will.

Translators and interpreters vary somewhat in their understanding and treatment of *latreia* in Romans 12:1. Some prefer to render it "worship," while others favor "service." There is an advantage to choosing the latter option, since the term in this context seems to be intended as a kind of caption for the areas Paul will be treating in the remaining chapters of the book—the relations of Christians to each other, to society, to the state, and so on— which is to say that its impact appears to be horizontal rather than vertical in this instance. It is unfortunate that worship is sometimes treated so broadly as to include the whole of Christian activity. Granted this activity should be carried on with an eye to glorifying God, but this broad application of the term tends to detract from the uniqueness of worship as something directed to God himself. To be sure, though, this activity of worship in the narrow sense should find expression in the entire life pattern of the believer as a result.

A third word, *leitourgeo* (noun *leitourgia*) is used occasionally. As a rule it has sacerdotal associations (see Luke 1:23), but it can also be used to include prayer (see Phil. 2:17) and even such a ministration as an offering for needy saints (see 2 Cor. 9:12). At its core, the word contains the idea of something public; our word *liturgy* is derived from it.

The Example of Jesus

Jesus' first visit to the temple at the age of twelve was prescribed for him (see Luke 2:41ff.), but his attendance was far from being a routine matter. It was the first of many such pilgrimages, not only to observe the Passover but other festivals also. On the Sabbath he made his way to the synagogue, as was his custom (see Luke 4:16ff.). There he saw and heard things that must have been distasteful to him—scribes claiming the best seats (Matt. 23:6), hypocrites boasting of their generosity and parading their piety instead of engaging in true prayer (Matt. 6:2, 5)—but he did not cease to attend because of these blemishes. During his ministry he made use of the synagogues throughout Galilee (see Mark 1:39), teaching and healing in them.

Although Jesus loved the temple, seeing it was his Father's house (see Luke 2:49), he knew that this focal point for all of Jewry would not remain standing for long; he even went so far as to predict its fall (Mark 13:2). In its place he envisioned a new temple, his own body in its risen state (see John 2:19–21). He himself was to become the means of access to God. The same idea lies just beneath the surface in John 4:23–24. Nor is this realization confined to the Johannine account; it is also evident in the Synoptic tradition: "I tell you that one greater than the temple is here" (Matt. 12:6). Jesus seems to have anticipated Christian worship in its simplest form: "For where two or three come together in my name, there am I with them" (Matt. 18:20). Though he ascended to the Father, he was able by the Spirit to be present among his gathered people. In fact, to use Paul's metaphor, they constitute his body and are individually the members through whom he expresses himself and makes his impact on the world.

The Contribution of Judaism to the Church's Worship

For at least three decades Jewish Christians continued to make use of the temple as a place of prayer and also frequented it during the national festivals (see Acts 20:16). They observed the stated hours of prayer (see Acts 3:1) and made use of the temple courts for preaching and teaching (see Acts 5:42). Synagogues were also accessible to them both in Jerusalem (Acts 6:9–10; cf. 9:29) and in various places in the Dispersion (Acts 13:14–15), although persecution and expulsion sometimes followed, as Jesus predicted (see John 16:2). But it is notable that this rejection did not produce so strong a revulsion against the synagogue as to keep the early church from modeling its own worship substantially after the Jewish pattern, having the same basic ingredients of prayer, confession of faith, reading of Scripture, an exposition or homily, and the blessing of the congregation at the close. The word *synagogue* could even be used to refer to a Christian gathering (see James 2:2).

Elements of the Service

1. *Prayer.* Immediately after the ingathering at Pentecost the new believers were introduced to a pattern of life that included several things. In Acts 2:42 each of these aspects of worship appears with the definite article appended. The word *prayer* is plural, suggesting a reference to the stated hours of prayer prescribed for the temple. This is the one item of the four that would most likely be observed in this public fashion, and the note about the participation by Peter and John in one of these seasons of prayer (3:1) furnishes sufficient substantiation. Even so, it would be hazardous to rule out times of prayer when Christians only were present (cf. 4:24).

One wonders whether they used the Lord's prayer on such occasions. We know it was used in the early part of the second century (see Didache chapter 8), so it could well have been a part of the worship in the apostolic period. After all, the Lord had given it out for the guidance of his disciples, though not necessarily as a ritualistic medium (not pray "this," but pray "thus").

If the prayers found in the epistles are any indication of the nature of extemporaneous prayers in the Christian assemblies, they were rich expressions of thanksgiving and petition (see Acts 4:24–30). Paul's mention of the "amen" in 1 Corinthians 14:16 suggests that it was customary for the congregation to follow and then to unite in the "amen" at the close. The setting of this passage makes it fairly clear that prayer could be offered by any member of the congregation, in line with the freedom enjoyed in the synagogue. Confession of sin would have been a natural part of the prayer pattern, and there may have been petition for rulers (see 1 Tim. 2:1–2).

2. *The reading of Scripture.* This aspect of worship was also borrowed from the synagogue. As Schlatter remarks, "To listen to the word of God from the books inspired by him—that was divine service; for the first service which man must render to God is to listen to him."[33] But whereas Judaism was in danger of becoming static through the exaltation of the Mosaic law as virtually a substitute for God, the Christian use of Scripture was dynamic because of the realization that God had already made good his promise regarding salvation through his anointed one.

Two passages bear clear testimony to the practice of reading the word in the services: Paul writes to Timothy, "Until I come, devote yourself to the public reading of Scripture, to preaching and to teaching" (1 Tim. 4:13); and at the beginning of the Apocalypse John writes, "Blessed is the one who reads the words of this prophecy, and blessed are those who hear it" (Rev. 1:3). In all probability a substantial portion of the worship time was devoted to this public reading. Writing at the middle of the second century, Justin Martyr gives a glimpse of worship in his time, saying that "the memoirs of the apostles or the writings of the prophets are read as long as time permits."[34]

It would be wrong to give the impression that believers were exposed to the written word only on occasions of public worship. Paul indicates that Timothy had known the Scriptures from his childhood and by this means had learned his "letters" (see 2 Tim. 3:15). We cannot be sure, however, that this was true of the children of Gentile believers.

Little information is available about how early the Gospels came to be read publicly. We have noted Justin's testimony. Perhaps the prologue of Luke's Gospel gives warrant for the view that from the time of publication they were pressed into service in this way. Schlatter makes the interesting surmise that the custom of exchanging the kiss of peace was an outgrowth of the public reading of letters from the apostles, for it is enjoined at the close of several of them (Rom. 16:16; 1 Cor. 16:20; 2 Cor. 13:12; 1 Thess. 5:26; 1 Pet. 5:14). This was a symbol of the unity and brotherly love that the reading of Scripture promoted, whether the reading was from the Old Testament or from something written by an apostle to meet the needs of the local congregation. The presumption is that the kiss was shared by the men with one another and by the women with their own group. This understanding of the situation is favored by the division of men and women in the services and by the apostolic insistence that everything be done decently and in order (1 Cor. 14:40). Later, however, the kiss was shared between the sexes, which created some offense; pagan husbands whose wives attended the services were naturally upset when they learned of this practice. Ultimately the church found it necessary to revert to the apostolic custom.

3. *Exhortation.* In Acts 13:15 the "word of exhortation" designates the homily that followed the reading of the Scripture. In that situation the message doubtless included information about the gospel as the basis for evangelistic appeal. In the case of a gathering of believers, it would serve to designate the application of Scripture to the lives of the people in the congregation. This same term *paraklēsis* is used in Hebrews 13:22 as a description of the entire epistle, and quite aptly so, since the hortatory element is so strong throughout the book. Basically, exhortation is an appeal to apply the gospel.

4. *Singing.* Psalmody was a part of the synagogue service that naturally passed over into the life of the church, although other categories of praise soon came to be included. For this reason it is better to speak of singing than of psalmody. (The word *psalmos* is used in Acts 4:25–26 and 1 Cor. 14:26, though in the latter passage it may mean "hymn," perhaps one of Christian origin.)

At crucial moments in redemption history the people of God have characteristically broken forth into spontaneous song, as in the song of Moses at the Exodus, the song of Deborah over the defeat of Sisera, and the Magnificat of Mary. It is inconceivable that expressions of a poetic nature could fail to arise from the bosom of the church in response to the great work of salvation wrought by Christ and attested by the Spirit. After admonishing his readers to be continually (or "ever and again") filled with the Spirit, Paul goes on to say, "Speak to one another with psalms, hymns and spiritual songs. Sing and make music in your heart to the Lord" (Eph. 5:19). C. F. D. Moule takes note of the mention of the heart both in Ephesians 5:19 and in Colossians 3:16, and on this basis thinks that "the direct reference is thus conceivably not to audible, corporate worship but to the constant secret recollection of corporate praise which the Christians are to cherish—all unknown to their heathen masters or companions—as they go about their work."[35] This is an interesting suggestion, but it seems to overlook the fact that the singing is said to be directed to one another (more clearly so in Ephesians, to be sure, than in Colossians).

Singing has continued to be an important part of Christian gatherings from the first days of the church to our own time. Early in the second century, Pliny the governor of Bithynia wrote to Trajan the emperor about the Christian practice of which he had been informed—namely, that on their day of gathering together, at an early hour, they sang a hymn to Christ as God. This clearly entailed going beyond the bounds of the Psalter.

5. *Prophetic utterances and speaking in tongues.* Paul reveals a remarkable diversity and richness in congregational participation when he writes, "When you come together, everyone has a hymn, or a word of instruction, a revelation, a tongue, or an interpretation" (1 Cor. 14:26; cf. 1:5). Evidently the services, at least at Corinth, were anything but stereotyped. Likely there was a "free" time when general participation was encouraged. Certainly prophetic utterance and glossalalia would not be expected in the course of the *paraklēsis*. Cullmann suggests that "Speaking with tongues is perhaps explained as arising from the enthusiasm roused by the experience of Christ's coming in worship in the common meal, by the fulfillment of the *Maranatha.*"[36] He holds that *Maranatha* is supremely a eucharistic prayer. If his suggestion is sound, the "free" time would have come after the observance of the Lord's Supper.

6. *Confessional statements.* We have already taken a look at some of these statements. For the most part they focused on the person and work of our Lord. In the context of worship they would have helped to underscore the lively sense of the presence of the risen Lord in the midst of his people.

7. *Doxology.* This accents the element of praise and would most naturally have come at the conclusion of prayer (see Eph. 3:20–21, following as it does the prayer in 3:14–19). The fairly frequent occurrence of doxologies in the epistles suggests that they may have been used similarly in the services of the church. Their variety in the epistles attests the vigor and spontaneity of the faith of these early believers.

Doxology is often confused with benediction but the two are distinct elements in the service. Doxology is something voiced to God on behalf of the congregation as an item of praise and adoration; benediction is God's word of parting blessing on his people, spoken through the leader of the service. On the basis of this distinction, some argue that benedictions appear only twice in Scripture: the Aaronic benediction of Numbers 6:24–26 and the apostolic benediction of 2 Corinthians 13:14.

The word that perhaps best describes early Christian worship is *vitality.* Formalism had not yet laid its restraining, deadening hand upon the service. The Spirit was active in making the presence and preciousness of Christ a reality to his people. It was the high point of the day and of the week rather than merely a break in the routine of daily life and work.

Cullmann discusses the question of diversity in the services, (i.e., whether there was one service for the proclamation of the word and another for the observance of the Lord's Supper) and concludes that there was only one kind of worship service, which included the ministry of the word and the observance of the Supper.[37] The only exception is the baptismal service, which was a distinctly different type. It is well to bear in mind that the earliest Christians did not meet in church buildings, so there was little opportunity for reaching unbelievers in their gatherings, which for the most part were small. On the other hand, it appears from 1 Corinthians 14:23 that unbelievers were not excluded, although naturally they would have been barred from partaking of the Lord's Supper. Evangelistic preaching was engaged in when Christian Jews were able to speak in the synagogues. We see this pattern in Paul's missionary journeys. In reaching pagans directly, a hired hall was useful (see Acts 19:9) as well as the agora of a Greek city (see Acts 17:17). Much evangelistic work was carried on by individual witness.

Possibly Cullmann has overlooked the likelihood of gatherings for catechetical instruction (Acts 2:42). It might be argued on the basis of 1 Timothy 4:13 that teaching was as much a part of the service as reading and exhortation. Surely this could be granted regarding teaching in the broad sense, but the possibility remains that there were special meetings for the training of converts, on the pattern of Acts 2:42.

Thomas Lindsay opts for three types of services in the early Christian communities: a meeting for edification (the worship service); a meeting for thanksgiving (for the observance of the Lord's Supper); and the congregational business meeting.[38] There may have been an occasional meeting for business (cf. 1 Cor. 5:5–6), but it is not certain that such gatherings were held at regular intervals.

The Lord's Supper

This distinctive observance of the church is likewise bound up with the history of the people of God from the Exodus onward, for it was established by our Lord at Passover time in conjunction with the celebration of that festival (see 1 Cor. 5:7).

For our purpose it is advantageous to begin with the early church rather than with the information provided by the Gospels concerning the institution of the Supper, since the Gospel material is meager and raises some difficult questions. For instance, the Synoptics contain nothing to indicate that the Supper was to be repeated apart from the statement in Luke 22:19—"do this in remembrance of me" (and indeed, this statement is part of the so-called longer reading which has material—vv. 19b–20—not found in a few manuscripts). Likewise, apart from this disputed passage in Luke there is no indication in the Gospel accounts that the Supper was to be a memorial for the Savior. However, these two items, the repetition of the observance and the memorial character of the Supper are clearly presented in Paul's account in 1 Corinthians 11:23–26.

No doubt partly with the textual problem in mind, Goguel has noted that "There is a sharp contrast between the importance of worship for primitive Christianity, and the scanty and sporadic character of the surviving evidence for it."[39] We may perhaps conclude that the early church simply was not self-conscious, that it did not seek to impress the world by advertising its conduct of worship. Several scholars, notably Joachim Jeremias, have suggested that even in the apostolic age the church tried to protect its worship, especially the Supper, from outside curiosity, and that consequently little is said about it in the New Testament.[40] In later times even catechumens were kept from participation in this sacred mystery of the Supper. Paul's discussion in 1 Corinthians 11 is part of his effort to correct abuses in the local church rather than a theologically elaborated exposition.

In Acts 1:4 the term *synalizomenos* may mean "to eat with others"; if so, it reflects the usage in Luke 24:43, though it does not necessarily refer to the same occasion. The two passages are not fully parallel, since in Luke the Lord is represented as eating *in the presence* of his disciples rather than *with* them. However, Acts 10:41 gives a clear parallel, for Peter says that he and others ate and drank with Christ after he rose from the dead. But there is no interpretation of these actions or any attempt to relate them to the Lord's Supper.

After the ascension, references are made to the breaking of bread (Acts 2:42, 46). Do these point to ordinary meals at which Christian fellowship was emphasized or should they be understood as sacramental in character? Since all the other items mentioned in verse 42 are distinctly spiritual in nature, it is probable that the breaking of bread is intended to denote the Lord's Supper, even though this would involve a daily rather than a weekly service of observance. Enthusiasm for the new faith and life may well have made this frequency seem both natural and desirable. The problem with this viewpoint, however, is the fact that there is no mention of the cup such as we find in Paul's account in 1 Corinthians 11. It is helpful to approach the problem by way of Acts 20, which contains a report of Paul's meeting with the church at Troas to break bread, to preach, and to converse with the saints. The narrative contains no mention of the cup despite the fact that this meeting took place after Paul had written 1 Corinthians 11. We cannot imagine him limiting the observance to the use of bread only on this occasion, so it is likely that the term "the breaking of bread" was used as a kind of shorthand expression for the partaking of both bread and wine.

We are left, however, with the problem of trying to explain the background for such a usage. Cullmann has given helpful guidance here. The breaking of bread reported in Luke 24:35, which involved the two disciples at Emmaus, was a joyful return to fellowship with the risen Lord after the devastating disappointment occasioned by his death. These two recognized the Lord when he broke the bread at their table. This element of fellowship on resurrection ground, when bread only was used, both in the case of the Emmaus disciples and in the case of the Eleven later the same evening, tended to color the terminology for the observance of the Lord's Supper in the early church. In other words, fellowship with the risen Lord overshadowed the realization that this fellowship was made possible only by the fact of his sacrificial death on their behalf. Gradually, however, mention of the cup came back into its own and became a part of the tradition as it appears in Paul's account (which depends in turn on the tradition and practice of the Jerusalem church).

Hans Lietzmann has attempted to explain the divergent terminology (the breaking of bread in some sources and the inclusion of the cup by Paul) as having devolved from two traditions. Starting from the liturgies of the third and fourth centuries, he sought to find in the Egyptian liturgy of Serapion (fourth century) a descendant of the tradition found in the Didache, in which there is no mention of the blood of Christ in connection with the cup as an explanation of its significance, even though both bread and cup are mentioned in chapters 9 and 10. Turning to the Roman liturgy of Hippolytus (third century), the parent of a number of later liturgies, he found a tradition that he felt could be traced back to Paul because of its emphasis on a true Eucharist (as distinct from the meal of the Jerusalem church, which he concluded was simply one of fellowship).

In view of what we have already noted about "breaking of bread," Lietzmann's view is neither necessary nor particularly plausible. The great argument against it is that Paul was apparently as dependent on the Jerusalem church for information concerning the institution of the Lord's Supper (see 1 Cor. 11:23) as he was for his statement of the content of the gospel (see 1 Cor. 15:3ff.). It is true that in 1 Corinthians 11:23 Paul indicates that he received his information about the Supper from the Lord, but the preposition *from* (*apo*) suggests that he was the ultimate rather than the intermediate source. Lietzmann contends for a special revelation to Paul at this point. Jeremias answers by showing that there are un-Pauline elements in the language of the passage that suggest that the apostle is simply passing on traditional material to the Corinthian church. These un-Pauline elements include the words *received* and *passed on* (cf. 15:3), which are the Greek equivalents of two rabbinic technical terms. Thus, "1 Cor. 11:23 says nothing other than that the chain of tradition goes back unbroken to the words of Jesus himself."[41]

It appears from Paul's account in 1 Corinthians 11 that the *Agape,* or love feast, was held prior to the observance of the Lord's Supper. He notes that because of the failure of the wealthier members to share their food, the poor had little, and so when the congregation partook of the Supper some of them were stuffed and even inebriated while others were hungry and in no mood to celebrate the sacrifice of Christ properly. From the tenor of the apostle's counsel ("if anyone is hungry, he should eat at home") some have concluded that he is abolishing the *Agape* because some had abused it. If such a separation was made between the *Agape* and the Supper, it was doubtless a step toward the more definite formalizing of the Eucharist in the practice of the church as a whole. However, it is by no means clear that Paul's language should be understood as abolishing the love feast.

In the Eastern Church (but not in the West), the use of the *epiklēsis* became a part of the celebration of the Eucharist—that being an invocation in which

> the Church asks God to send down the Holy Spirit on the congregation and on the eucharistic elements so that they may be consecrated to become the body and blood of Christ and that the congregation may be formed into the one Church and delivered from condemnation at the Last Judgment. . . . It challenges the idea that the mere recitation of the words which marked the institution of the Supper constitutes the Supper without there being any need to beseech the Holy Spirit Himself to complete what is then taking place.[42]

Summary of the Significance of the Supper

1. It is a distinctly Christian observance, exclusive in the sense that only believers should participate.

2. As differentiated from baptism, which is individualistic, the Supper emphasizes corporate observance and thereby underscores the unity of the body of Christ. It would be rather incongruous for a believer to partake of the Supper alone, unless the circumstances were extraordinary.

3. Its observance involves a combination of word and act. The words spoken or voiced in prayer keep the act from being merely cultic and ritualistic.

4. It preserves a sense of the centrality of the cross. It should be noted, however, that instead of observing it on Friday, the saints came together on the Lord's Day, because the death of the Savior derived its full meaning and comfort for the believer from the resurrection (see Rom. 4:25). This emphasis on the expiatory nature of the death of Christ is also central to baptism, since the baptism of Jesus by John was completed and fulfilled in the baptism of blood at the cross. There was no Christian baptism until after the death, resurrection, and ascension of Jesus. Thus, even though baptism and the Lord's Supper differ in that baptism is once-for-all and the Supper is a repeated feature, there is an underlying unity between them in that both focus on the finished work of Christ.

5. It involves an appreciation of the divine love and grace, well

expressed in the designation commonly given to it—the Eucharist, meaning "thanksgiving."

6. In the early church there was no magical concept connected with the elements such as came to be attributed to the observance by some people in later times.

7. It brought a great awareness of the presence of Christ among the redeemed. The first observance in the Upper Room was unthinkable apart from the Lord who instituted it and joined the disciples in it. The consciousness of the Lord's presence in a special sense may well be reflected in the language of Revelation 3:20—"I will . . . eat with him, and he with me."

8. It is intended to be a memorial of Christ, a means of bringing him to active remembrance (see 1 Cor. 11:25). This is not quite the same thing as an ordinary memorial service, which can be quite perfunctory. Rather, as the people of Israel in their Passover observance sought to recapture and recapitulate the experience of the nation at the Exodus and enter into it for themselves as though they had been there, so believers are to renew their contact with the historic Savior in his death and resurrection, making it a real communion. The death of Christ can be called an "exodus" (see Luke 9:31): like the Exodus from Egypt, it marked a deliverance, and a greater one by far.

9. The concept of covenant is central to a proper understanding of the Lord's Supper. In this way it is linked to the former dispensation. The old covenant made at Sinai was sealed by the sprinkling of blood on the altar (representing God) and also on the people (see Ex. 24). In Paul's account of the Supper it is noted that Jesus explained the cup to his disciples as the new covenant in his blood (1 Cor. 11:26; cf. Mark 14:24). The epistle to the Hebrews presents Christ as a mediator of the new covenant (Heb. 9:15) that is based on his shed blood and secures eternal redemption (Heb. 9:12). Paul makes the observation that whereas the old covenant was a ministration of death in its practical outworking, the new covenant in Christ brings righteousness. Implemented by the Spirit, it also produces in the believer increasing likeness to the Savior (see 2 Cor. 3:7–18).

10. The eschatological significance should not be overlooked. Just as Jesus spoke of eating the feast anew with his disciples in the kingdom, so in Paul's words of institution there is reference to the coming again of the Lord (1 Cor. 11:26). The Supper in the present age holds the promise and expectancy of the messianic feast in the coming kingdom (see Mark 14:25 and parallels).

6. CHRISTIAN LIFE

For the purposes of this discussion we will distinguish Christian life from spiritual life. We will understand the latter as pertaining to the somewhat limited sphere of personal, individual communion with God and the resultant deepening and strengthening of the redeemed personality. On the other hand, we will understand Christian life as embracing both personal and corporate elements and emphasizing the factor of interaction in a way that spiritual life does not.

Christian life can be viewed in three broad categories: (1) the spiritual life, (2) the ethical life, and (3) the social life. A perusal of our sources reveals the presence of all three, though not in equal measure. Concerning the first, it is obvious that early Christianity was nothing if it was not the experience of God in Christ as mediated and ministered by the Spirit. Believers were individually regenerated, given the mind of Christ and a wholly new outlook on the meaning of human existence. But just as surely they were also baptized into the larger organism of the body of Christ, the church (1 Cor. 12:13) and made aware of the demands and values of Christian fellowship and a common service in the name of Christ.

We should ask ourselves what effect these spiritual realities had upon the character of the early Christians. The danger of preoccupation with the spiritual is exposed early in the life of the church by the Ananias and Sapphira incident—a jolting episode for the infant church and a reminder that the Spirit not only reveals spiritual truth but also inculcates righteousness of a practical sort (see Rom. 14:17). The writers of the epistles evidently had a burden to impress on their readers the command to lead transformed lives as witnesses to light in the midst of the darkness of a corrupt and degenerate society.

The social aspect of Christian experience receives testimony both from the book of Acts and from the epistles. A key word for setting forth the interdependence and mutual upbuilding of the saints is *koinōnia* ("fellowship," "participation"). Again and again the people of God are admonished to love one another, to pray for one another, to submit to one another, to honor one another, to help one another. Paul effectively uses the figure of the human body with its various members to underscore the need for mutual concern and cooperation.

To be sure, in adopting this threefold analysis we do in one sense omit any substantive consideration of Christian service, especially the verbal witness to Christ's saving power. We have already briefly reviewed the gospel witness and its outreach as such, however. The Christian life itself constitutes a distinct, complementary sort of witness: we should not lose sight of the fact that transformed lives are in themselves a necessary and potent endorsement of the gospel to those who are in a position to observe the change that conversion has brought.

Spiritual Life

We need some background here. A study of the word *life* in the Synoptic Gospels discloses that the prevailing association of the term is eschatological: life is something to be entered into (Mark 9:43), to be received in the coming age (Luke 18:30). In John, on the other hand, the emphasis falls on the present possession of life by the believer in the Son of God (see John 3:36). Moreover, inasmuch as we read that life is *in* the Son (John 5:26; 14:6), we can conclude that it is the gift that comes to one who is related to Jesus Christ by faith, not as something detached from the Son but as a participation in the very life of the Son, which is in turn the very life of the Father (see John 14:20).

The future-oriented emphasis on life in the Synoptics is congruent with the emphasis they give to the theme of discipleship. People are summoned to follow Jesus, which suggests present incompleteness and progress toward a goal. The consummation lies ahead. Parenthetically, in the very nature of the case discipleship involves a protest against any doctrine of sinless perfection in the present life: we will continue to be followers.

Though the word *disciple* means "learner," its genius does not lie in the intellectual realm but in the area of devotion and sacrifice. Jesus declared that no one who came to him and did not "hate" father and mother and spouse and children and brothers and sisters and even his or her own life could be his disciple (Luke 14:26). Our Lord concluded this severe statement with another that was even more drastic: "anyone who does not carry his cross and follow me cannot be my disciple" (v. 27). The initial call to discipleship that seemed to offer training accompanied by happy association with a fascinating person now turned out to be the ultimate demand that could be made of any person. William Manson quite properly sees this as the second stage on the path of discipleship.[43] To follow this leader is not as simple as it seemed to be at the beginning.

It comes to this, then: the Christian life entails a willingness to renounce life in the natural, normal, accepted sense insofar as it stands in the way of participation in the life of Jesus Christ, whose passion was to do the will of God even to the point of death—and especially at the point of death. This is not nihilism. It is the path to life in the largest possible sense, life that is sublime and glorious.

The Gospel according to John is in full accord with the Synoptic accounts in this emphasis. Our Lord taught his disciples that as surely as the world hated him and persecuted him, it would treat them in the same way (John 15:18–20). He was not predicting a wave of anti-Semitism, since he hastened to explain: "They will treat you this way because of my name" (v. 21). Their relationship to him would prove costly. The more faithfully they reflected him, the more they would incur the hatred and opposition of their countrymen. Already during the Savior's earthly life discipleship was no pastime but something deadly serious. The very terms in which it was stated loudly proclaimed that the believer in Jesus must share in the life of the Son of God, in its bitterness as well as in its sweetness.

For those on our side of the cross, a certain amount of restatement is necessary. The prospect of death for Christ's sake hung over the disciples during the last months of his earthly life (see Mark 8:34; 9:31; 10:33–34; John 11:16) and became a reality for some of them later on as it also did for Stephen, Paul, and a host of others. But the church learned, especially through the teaching of Paul, that all believers have in fact died together with Christ in his crucifixion (Gal. 2:20). This co-crucifixion is the God-appointed way for his people to realize what Jesus called for—namely, death to sin and self. All that remains in order to make it a working principle of life is the appropriation of its power. As Paul put the matter in Romans 6, we must first of all *know* that we died and rose again with Christ, then thoughtfully *reckon* on this as a fact of utmost importance, and finally, *present* ourselves and all our redeemed powers to God for his use.

This does not mean that appeal to the example of Christ as a sufferer is outmoded. To Christian servants who experienced suffering, Peter gave the reminder that "Christ suffered for you, leaving you an example, that you should follow in his steps" (1 Pet. 2:21). Paul affirmed to the Thessalonian believers that "You became imitators of us and of the Lord; in spite of severe suffering, you welcomed the message with the joy given by the Holy Spirit" (1 Thess. 1:6).

In the *kērygma* the complement of death is resurrection life, so as surely as the believer has shared in the death of the Savior he has also participated in his risen life. Paul's passionate desire was not only to know Christ by way of fellowship in his sufferings but also in the power of his resurrection, which means life on the highest plane, new creation life (Phil. 3:10; 2 Cor. 5:17).

One may conclude that despite Paul's lack of association with Jesus in the days of his flesh, nevertheless by his teaching and by his example he wonderfully possessed the mind of Christ in the matter of discipleship, even though the word *disciple* does not appear in his writings.

What are we to say about the book of Acts, where the word *disciple* abounds but is not associated in any precise way with the teaching of Jesus on the subject? The word may seem to be simply a way of distinguishing Christians from those who are not (see, for example Acts 21:16). However, allowance should be made for the possibility that in the eyes of the early church, led as it was by men who had companied with Jesus, the identification of a person as a disciple carried with it the implication that he or she had embraced the costs as well as the benefits of being a follower of the Lord Jesus.

The picture given to us of the apostles in the book of Acts is quite different from that which is contained in the Gospels. In the earlier period these men are pictured as hesitant, confused, and faltering—so much so that they forsook their Master and fled when he was apprehended in Gethsemane. As they come to lead the church, however, they are new men, bold and determined. They have found themselves. A casual observer of this contrast might conclude that it is advantageous for a believer not to have the immediate presence of the Lord. To reason thus would be to misapprehend somewhat the actual state of the case. When the Son of God returned to the Father, he continued to be with the disciples as they represented him in the world, just as he had promised before he left them (Matt. 28:20). Furthermore, they were "in" him as their very life and he was in them, as he had said they would be (John 14:20). The dynamism of that life was mediated by the Holy Spirit, who now directed and empowered them. To be sure, they had also the example of Jesus as a treasured memory, but they needed more than that to be his fruitful and effective servants. Karl Barth has a choice observation that reminds us of what God rightfully expects of us in view of the divine indwelling and working: "He will not have, He will not suffer the anomaly of His living for us and in us, and our living a different kind of life altogether."[44] The new creation is indeed new, different, infinitely superior to the old. It is the very life of God lived out in a human context by the indwelling Christ. If the Lord Jesus is not seen in his people, it is because they have failed to appropriate him and make him their Lord.

We should pursue the discipleship matter a bit further. Recall that the word *disciple* does not occur in the epistles, yet its essence is there. The idea of following—of having a pattern to look at and appropriate, of being in a process of becoming, of having not yet fully arrived—is sufficiently apparent. It is deeply woven into the texture of the epistle to the Hebrews, for example. The recipients of the letter are addressed as those who "share in the heavenly calling" (3:1), meaning those who share "in a call to the possession of the heavenly world to come."[45] Again we read, "Let us, therefore, make every effort to enter that rest" (4:11). Further, "We want each of you to show this same diligence to the very end, in order to make your hope sure" (6:11; cf. 6:19). Jesus has gone on ahead as our forerunner (6:20). The life of faith and hope is represented as a race to be run with perseverance and by the inspiration stemming from the fact that Jesus, who endured the cross and despised the shame, is the Pioneer and Perfecter of our faith (12:1–2). Finally, we note a passage that combines acknowledgment of the present stress with the assurance of the blessed state that awaits the faithful: "Let us, then, go to him outside the camp, bearing the disgrace he bore. For here we do not have an enduring city, but we are looking for the city that is to come" (13:13–14).

This tension between the present with its conflicts and sufferings and the future as the goal and culmination of the Christian's course appears also in 1 Peter. As he delves into the body of his communication, the apostle sounds a note of praise to God, who has given us new birth into a living hope through the resurrection of Jesus Christ from the dead, into an inheritance that can never perish, spoil, or fade—kept in heaven for his people (1:3–4). Having read this, it is instructive to turn back to the address of the letter and be reminded that the recipients are described as "strangers in the world," scattered over five areas of Asia Minor (1:1). Their real home is in heaven, where their inheritance is being kept for them even as they are being preserved so that they can ultimately enjoy it. For the present they are strangers in the earthly setting just because they are citizens of heaven.

This pilgrim aspect of the Christian life, most keenly felt when believers are in a minority and subject to misunderstanding and persecution, became something of an embarrassment in the postapostolic period, when Christians came into more public notice and were roundly criticized for their detachment and exclusiveness. Yet to fraternize with the world and condone its life-style would not only constitute a denial of the church's charter but would actually make it ineffective in reaching society for Christ.

Before concluding our examination of the spiritual life, it is well to ask how the early church sustained it. Not much information is available for our guidance, but we can safely assume that the use of Scripture in a devotional pattern, the resort to prayer, and the cultivation of obedience to the will of God (which both Scripture reading and prayer are designed to promote) were characteristic. Mutual encouragement and the sharing of spiritual experience must also have played a part.

The use of the written word was made difficult by its relative unavailability. In the apostolic age the Old Testament was of course completed and occupied a place of honor in every synagogue. Doubtless copies were possessed by some individuals, whether portions or the whole text (see Acts 8:30; 2 Tim. 3:15; cf. 1 Macc. 1:56–57). In the case of the Jews of Berea it is uncertain whether their daily consultation of Scripture indicates personal possession or resort to the local synagogue. But whatever the situation among Jewish Christians was, it is highly unlikely that many Gentile believers had personal copies of the Old Testament. If they had been God-fearers prior to conversion, they had been able to acquire some knowledge through hearing the word read during the synagogue services. Paul nowhere implies the personal use of the Old Testament on the part of his converts from paganism. As for the New Testament, this was not available either except on a gradual basis as churches allowed copying and distributing of letters written to them, and as the Gospels were written, used locally, and gradually copied for wider use.

No such limitation, however, applied in the case of prayer. Every believer was encouraged to participate by way of private exercise. Prayer was a vital feature of the life of the Jerusalem church, though the record is naturally concerned to emphasize corporate rather than private prayer (see Acts 2:42; 4:24ff.; 12:5; but see also James 5:13, 16). Paul's fidelity in praying for churches (see, for example, Col. 1:9) must have stimulated the prayer life of these believers in turn. We get glimpses of his own activity—following his conversion (Acts 9:11), in the temple after returning to Jerusalem (22:17), in prison (16:25), parting from the Ephesian elders (20:36), with believers at Tyre (21:5), and on behalf of the father of Publius (28:8). Peter prayed before raising Dorcas (9:40) and on the housetop at Joppa (10:9). Cornelius prayed even before he became a Christian (10:2) and must have continued the practice.

While private concerns were unquestionably brought before the Lord, one gets the impression that the chief emphasis was on intercessory prayer for other believers (see Acts 13:3; Eph. 1:15ff.; 3:14ff.; 6:18ff.; Heb. 13:18). Prayer was the believer's weapon in combatting the pressure exerted by the powers of darkness on God's people (see Eph. 6:18ff.).

Ethical Life

The ethical aspect of the Christian faith is most definitely set forth in the apostolic teaching, with isolated incidents serving to show that teaching in action, such as Stephen praying for those who were stoning him to death and Paul expressing a desire that Agrippa and all the others who listened to his defense might be such as he himself was—"except for these chains" (Acts 26:29). Such practical testimonies as these reflect the spirit of the Master (see Luke 23:34). It is the teaching and the life of Jesus, then, to which we should turn to discover the foundations of the Christian ethic. From his teaching we can isolate certain distinctives:

1. It has a lofty ideal, perhaps best expressed in these terms: "Be perfect, therefore, as your heavenly Father is perfect" (Matt. 5:48). There is no compromise with halfway measures. The manner of statement leaves one no alternative but to depend on the mercy and grace of God in order to realize the fulfillment of his will.

2. Thought and motive are as important as action. In the kingdom of God, righteousness plumbs the very depths of the human heart. There is no place for pretense or superficiality. Adultery can be committed in the heart (Matt. 5:28). To kill makes one liable to judgment, but to be angry with another makes one liable to judgment also (Matt. 5:21–22).

3. Love is central. Here, too, the coverage is wide. The law had enjoined love for one's neighbor, but Jesus added, "Love your enemies" (Matt. 5:44). This puts God's people in his company, for God loves the world (John 3:16).

4. We will be called to give an account for all we think and do. Repeatedly our Lord taught that judgment is an inescapable factor in human existence. It belongs to the order of things since the fall. It is agreeable to God's righteous character and government. The consequences of disobedience that are experienced in this life are simply pointers toward the great day of reckoning that the future holds. Parenthetically, the fact that believers also must give account of their life and service (see 2 Cor.

5:10) demonstrates how deeply ingrained in the texture of the moral universe is this factor of judgment.

Did these features of the Lord's ethical teaching become normative in the church? Since Paul is the chief figure to be considered, we shall limit the investigation to him.

1. Unquestionably he felt and taught the demand for completeness, for maturity, while acknowledging that he himself had not yet fully attained it (Phil. 3:12; cf. Rom. 12:2).

2. The importance of the inner life is reflected in the Pauline teaching. He presents saving faith as a matter of the heart (Rom. 10:9) and suggests that conduct is truly Christian only when it can be said to be doing the will of God from the heart (Eph. 6:5–6; Col. 3:22). He also points out that judgment will probe the purposes of the heart as well as outward acts (1 Cor. 4:5).

3. Paul's teaching on love also coincides with that of Jesus. He states that love is the fulfilling of the law (Rom. 13:10). He urges believers who have enemies to deal with them in kindness rather than in a spirit of retaliation (Rom 12:19–21).

4. Paul also maintains that God's judgment proceeds according to truth and reality and that it is inescapable (Rom. 2:2–3) as well as that judgment in the sense of chastening is a fact of Christian experience (1 Cor. 11:29–30).

Paul does not present an ethical system, a carefully worked out code of conduct. Rather, he treats the active side of Christian life as closely allied to theology, as the expected output of the divine input of salvation. Its motivation is gratitude for God's gift, its enablement is the Holy Spirit (Rom. 8:4). One is expected to live a life of obedience and fruitfulness under the lordship of Christ. It is helpful in this connection to utilize terminology that has become fairly common, borrowed from the field of language study. The *indicative* of the Christian ethic includes all that God in Christ has done for us in the area of soteriology, including what he has pledged to do in the future. As the complement to the indicative, there is also the *imperative*. The believer is exhorted to give fitting expression to the new life God has bestowed: "I urge you, brothers, in view of God's mercy . . . " (Rom. 12:1). Equally explicit is Paul's word "Continue to work out your salvation with fear and trembling, for it is God who works in you to will and do what pleases him" (Phil. 2:12–13). The salvation is now possessed as God's gift; the outworking of it, providing avenues for its manifestation, is the task of Christians in terms of conduct, but it is not their unaided effort, for God is at work in them and through them to accomplish the desired result.

Social Life

At an earlier point we examined the relation of Christians to pagan society, but here we are thinking of the relation between believers, and not so much in the context of worship as in everyday contacts.

In the Old Testament the basic unit of society is the family, followed by the clan, the tribe, and the nation. Since the Christian movement began in a Jewish setting, it was inevitable that when converts were gathered the church was composed in the main of families rather than separate individuals. It should not disturb us that the word *family* occurs only once in the New Testament (Eph. 3:15), for there is another term—"house," or "household"—that is fairly common. It is not always possible to pin down the precise meaning intended, for the word can be a substitute for *family* or it can have the force of *establishment,* as in the case of Caesar's household (see Phil. 4:22), where in addition to the imperial family there must have been literally thousands—officials, clerks, guards, servants, and so on. Lydia's household probably was not large, but nevertheless probably numbered several people (Acts 16:14–15). Since some families included slaves as well as husband, wife, and children, we should not be surprised to find Paul addressing this group when giving counsel to households (Eph. 6:5–8; Col. 3:22–25). The very fact that he gives them counsel presupposes that they will hear the message when it is read. They attended the meetings of the church in the house. Just to be thought of and noticed by the apostle must have been heartwarming to these people. On the other side, for the masters to fail to show fairness and kindness toward their slaves could be counted a failure to apprehend the equality in and unity of the body of Christ.

The Jerusalem church had two foci—the temple, where preaching and teaching were carried on, and the homes of the saints, where communal meals were enjoyed (see Acts 2:46). We read that they partook of their food with glad and sincere hearts. They shared what they had with those who were in need, which made both giver and recipient happy. The conversation around the board must have been on an exalted level. When there was a call for a larger group to assemble, someone with a commodious house was ready to volunteer (see Acts 12:12; cf. 1:13–14).

In Paul's letter to the Romans we find what appear to be references to several house churches in that city (see chap. 16). It is fortunate that in most communities there were believers who had dwellings large enough to accommodate a goodly number of people, as in the case of the Colossian church (see Philem. 2). A home, as opposed to a public place, would naturally foster a close relationship and encourage the formation of friendships, and impressionable children in the household must have been profoundly influenced as well.

Another aspect of the Christian home that needs to be considered is hospitality. In writing to the Roman church Paul passes on the greeting of Gaius, "whose hospitality I and the whole church here enjoy" (Rom. 16:23). This house in Corinth was a center for meetings and for hospitality as well. Peter, we recall, was a guest of Simon the tanner at Joppa (Acts 9:43) and then of Cornelius (10:23, 48). The practice of hospitality was a boon to traveling servants of the Lord and doubtless proved to be a mutual blessing.

We have a record of at least one instance in which Christians were brought together under one roof by reason of having the same occupation. When Paul came alone to Corinth, he found living and working quarters with Aquila and Priscilla (see Acts 18:3). No doubt much of the effectiveness of this couple in the Lord's work was attributable to this close, sustained contact with the apostle (see 18:26). We know their association bound them firmly to Paul in a lasting friendship, for they were ready to lay down their lives for him when a crisis developed at Ephesus (see Rom. 16:4).

As far as we know, Paul remained single during his life, which in itself could have fostered loneliness. Furthermore, it seems that his family did not become Christians, unless his sister in Jerusalem was an exception (Acts 23:16), although her manifestation of concern may have been caused simply by the blood tie. Paul tells us that he suffered the loss of all things by following Christ (Phil. 3:8), and there is no basis for excluding kith and kin from the "all things," but the Lord gave him many close friends who were like brothers and sisters to him. He goes so far as to speak of a Christian woman at Rome as his mother (see Rom. 16:13; cf. Mark 10:29–30).

The very terminology used in the New Testament for believers and for the church includes language that inevitably suggests a family relationship. Believers are sons of God, children of the heavenly Father, brothers of Christ (Rom. 8:29; Heb. 2:11, 17), and together they constitute a brotherhood (1 Pet. 2:17; 5:9). This is not at all the same as "the brotherhood of man" in modern parlance, which many have tried to baptize into a Christian setting. It is true that all are the offspring of God (Acts 17:29), but this speaks only of the bestowal of human life. To become a son of God one must receive God's Son (see John 1:12). The very fact that first-century Christians could not find fellowship with the unbelieving world made their association with fellow believers the more precious.

Scripture is not written to satisfy our curiosity, so we are not told much about what believers did in common apart from their times of worship, but we can be sure that their daily activities were sanctified and lifted to a higher plane because they lived wholly "in the Lord" and to please him.

7. MINISTRY

Despite the fact that the noun *ministry* or *service* occurs only once in the Gospels (in the case of Martha's effort to prepare a meal), we find ourselves using this word more than any other as the most appropriate label for the public career of our Lord. The verb form *diakoneo* occurs fairly often in references to Jesus and others. Even when the word does not appear, the concept is often present. For example, when Jesus described his mission in terms of Isaiah 61 as he read the Scripture in the synagogue at Nazareth, he was indicating with perfect clarity that his calling was in terms of ministry to people and their needs.

This magnifying of the servant role was quite contrary to the Greek ideal expressed in the complaint "How can a man be happy when he has to serve someone?" The Hebrew attitude was different in that servanthood was not held to be dishonorable. However, in the period covered by the earthly life of Jesus and in the years immediately preceding, a spirit had crept in that proved harmful, even vitiating. Hermann Beyer puts it this way: "Service was less and less understood as sacrifice for others and more and more as a work of merit before God."[46]

The contemporaries of Jesus were prone to think of Messiah in terms of a dominating figure, the warrior-king who would restore to Israel her lost inheritance in the world. But Jesus assigned to Messiahship quite a different content, retaining the role of Messiah but giving to it above all else the character of ministry by identifying it with the mission of the Servant: "For even the Son of Man did not come to be served, but to serve, and to give his life a ransom for many" (Mark 10:45).

T. W. Manson points out that in the Israelitish kingdom each subject was the servant of the reigning monarch, even though they were free men and not slaves in the technical sense. Jesus is not demeaned, then, in taking the title "Servant of the Lord." He deliberately chose to do the Father's will (Heb. 10:5–7). Having settled the issue of his relationship to the Father, he adopted servanthood as the keynote of his relationship to men as well: "I am among you as one who serves" (Luke 22:27). The washing of the disciples' feet was but a parable of his consistent attitude. What made it so telling was the fact that he was Lord and Master of these men.

Manson notes that Jesus made a point of contrasting the society he came to form with the two existing societies with which his followers were familiar, the Gentile and the Jewish. In the former, as was strikingly evident in the period of Roman occupation and control, the established practice was for rulers to lord it over their subjects. But greatness in Christ's economy would come through being a servant (see Mark 10:42ff.; Luke 22:24–27). In the Jewish society the scribes and Pharisees loved to get recognition from the rank and file of the people, deeming it only suitable and right, whether in public or in the place of worship. But again, by means of contrast, Jesus indicated that in his order the greatest one is the servant (see Matt. 23:6–11).

It is most important that we understand the overarching consideration that the ministry of the men whom Jesus chose and called and equipped is to be the ministry of Christ their Lord; that is to say, in the last analysis there is only one ministry, and it is his. This means that his ministry is continued through the church (Acts 1:1). The risen Lord continues to work (see Rom. 15:18–19), laboring through believers in the same categories of his own earthly ministry—preaching, teaching, healing, and helping—while he ministers personally on behalf of the saints by his heavenly intercession (see Heb. 4:14–16; 7:25). When we firmly grasp the concept of a single ongoing ministry, then the idea of ministry in Christ's name becomes truly significant: it is not so much something carried on *for* him as *by* him, as he uses the human instrument. It is not enough to take the earthly ministry of the Savior as the presupposition and basis for our own, seeking to make our own accord with his as we are influenced by what he did and the way he did it. Rather, there ought to be a consciousness of our need to fulfill his commission by remaining faithfully and consistently dependent on his Spirit, who was provided for the very purpose of glorifying him. Jesus insisted that "whoever serves me must follow me" (John 12:26). The same holds true of anyone who seeks to serve others in his name.

The Ministry Committed to Jesus' Followers

We will be discussing the idea of ministry primarily in terms of Jesus' commission of the Twelve, though the principles involved carry over to others in large part. Rengstorf's article on *apostolos* in the *Theological Dictionary of the New Testament* provides a helpful background.[47]

In classical Greek the idea of ministry is mainly one of mission. It appears sometimes in a philosophical setting—mission in the realm of thought. The Cynic and Stoic philosophers conceived of themselves as sent by Zeus for the good of mankind. But along with their sense of mission went a certain consciousness of superiority that marred the concept of calling. They were also hindered by an uncertainty or lack of conviction about what they taught, cut off as they were from special revelation.

As we have already noted, the meaning of *apostolos* in the New Testament is wrapped up with the use of the Hebrew word *shaluach* (*shaliach* in late Hebrew), meaning "one sent." The etymology of the words prepares one to expect a greater similarity of meaning than is in fact the case. Rengstorf notes that Jewish missionaries in the time of our Lord were not designated by the term apostolos. In fact, missionary activity, such as it was, could be classed as meritorious in nature. All the functions of the *shaliach* were carried on within the Jewish community. A bearer of the half-shekel tax or one who represented the congregation in some aspect of the synagogue service could be called a *shaliach*. Out of the usage of the term certain conclusions can be drawn. A *shaliach* had a definite mission, had authority vested in him by the person or agency who sent him, and had a responsibility to render an account of his mission. He could not transfer his commission to another. Finally, the genius of the term is not to denote status but function.

With regard to the matter of status versus function, we might note the rarity with which *apostleship* occurs in the New Testament (Acts 1:25; Rom. 1:5; 1 Cor. 9:2; Gal. 2:8). In Acts 1:25 the word is preceded by *ministry* as though to give emphasis to the fact that apostleship was not primarily a matter of rank but of service. No doubt this ought to be viewed as a carry-over from the example of our Lord and from his teaching: the disciple was not above his Master. "As the Father has sent me, I am sending you" (John 20:21). Manson remarks that "Jesus has given to Apostleship the same content that He had given to Messiahship, thus making it inevitable that those who would represent Him must represent Him in *His* way."[48]

It is clear from our records that the Twelve were equals. No one was appointed as their superintendent (see Matt. 19:28; 23:8). That sons of Zebedee could ask for places of prominence (see Mark 10:37) indicates that at that time no one held such a place of eminence. Though Peter was the usual spokesman for the group, he stood on the same level as the rest; Paul could challenge him when he was in the wrong (see Gal. 2:11ff.).

Apostolic succession is a theory designed to give validity to ministry by connecting it with the Lord himself through his apostles. It rests on the idea that to be an apostle one must be appointed by one who has the rank of apostle. There are several reasons for rejecting the theory.

1. A *shaliach* could not appoint another person as his *shaliach*. It would therefore not be expected that an apostle would dream of appointing a successor.

2. The argument that the appointment of Matthias involved human mediation and therefore can be viewed as the pattern for the church to follow is offset by the fact that when James the brother of John was killed, no provision was made for replacing him. At least, nothing is indicated to this effect. Similarly, Paul did not name Timothy as his successor, despite the close relationship between the two.

3. It is obvious that Paul was an apostle, yet the Twelve had nothing to do with his appointment. All they could do was to recognize it (Gal. 2:1–10). It was Paul, rather than the Twelve, who took the lead in fostering the mission to the Gentiles.

4. If the qualifications advanced at the time of the selection of Matthias are to be regarded as normative, then it is clear that men of succeeding generations were ruled out, for they could not have been witnesses of the resurrection of Jesus, much less of his ministry since the days of John the Baptist (Acts 1:22).

5. The theory of apostolic succession did not originate in the apostolic age. Not until late in the second century did lists of succession begin to be compiled. At that point it was useful to the church to make such a claim in order to combat heresy. Bishops came to be regarded as the custodians of the apostolic teaching and practice.

Ministry in the Christian sense needs no more authentication than the example of Jesus and the permission he gave to all his followers to minister in his name. Geoffrey Bromiley is surely justified in asserting that

> This serving of Jesus and fellowmen is not restricted in the New Testament to any one group, for example, the twelve disciples within the first community of believers. All Christians may not be called to minister in the same way, so that we need not be surprised if a special commission and task of ministry are assigned to particular men. Yet all those who are associated with Jesus are equally called to serve Him and therefore their fellows according to their differing opportunities and capacities.[49]

A splendid example of this freedom of action in the service of Christ is provided by the words of Paul: "You know that the household of Stephanas were the first converts in Achaia, and they have devoted themselves to the service of the saints. I urge you, brothers, to submit to such as these and to everyone who joins in the work and labors at it" (1 Cor. 16:15–16). This *diakonia* was undertaken without any authorization (it did not need any), and it gave to those who performed the service a certain spiritual leadership, since the apostle urges *subjection* to such men, no doubt in the sense of willingness to follow their example and learn from their success.

How far the church moved away from this autonomy in the area of ministry after the interval of two generations may be seen in the word Ignatius of Antioch wrote to the Trallians: "He who is within the sanctuary is pure, but he who is without the sanctuary is not pure; that is to say, whoever does anything apart from the bishop and the presbytery and the deacons it is not pure in his conscience."[50]

It would indeed seem that God's word approves general participation by the saints in ministry. In Ephesians 4:11–13, Paul pictures the ascended Christ as having bestowed on the church certain gifted people—apostles, prophets, evangelists, pastors, and teachers. Then he goes on to give the purpose of this arrangement, apparently suggesting that these gifted persons are raised up to equip the saints for their work of ministry, to build up the body of Christ. The meaning depends on how the passage is punctuated. If the RSV is followed ("for the equipment of the saints, for the work of ministry, for the building up of the body of Christ"), these three items represent the responsibility of the gifted people noted earlier in the passage. This would tend to restrict ministry to a few. "To prepare God's people for works of service" (NIV) is preferable. A possible objection to this construction of the verse is that if the gifted people are bestowed on the church for the strengthening of the saints for their work of ministry, then the same group that is being built up is identified with the ministering group—that is, the church as a whole. But this picture of mutual involvement and mutual benefit is the way God intended it to be. In ministry, one not only gives but also receives. The humblest saint may be used of God to bless the preacher, just as the preacher brings blessing to the other through his ministry.

Paul's figure of the body looks in the same direction. No member of the body is without its contribution to the growth and activity of the body as a whole. The service is rendered to other members of the body and also beyond, since the body as a whole has its sphere of activity in the world. A distinction between clergy and laity may be necessary as a matter of convenience, of ease of identification, but it tends to obscure the equality of saints in the body and the common possession of the commission to exercise ministry in Christ's name. The struggling pastor, trying to do almost everything by himself, should be the first to recognize this basic equality and capitalize on it by channeling the energies of the congregation into ministry inside the church and without.

Ministry may be said to involve three aspects, for there is a ministry of word, of act, and of rule or leadership. The distinction between the first two is brought out well by the situation pictured in Acts 6. Evidently the apostles had been preaching the word and also superintending the daily ministration of aid to the poor of the congregation. When difficulties arose that led to the selection of men who would attend to this latter sphere of service, the apostles handed over the responsibility to the Seven and were greatly relieved that they could now give themselves to prayer and the ministry of the word (see Acts 6:4). There is no reason to think that the apostles discontinued all service of act, such as the working of miracles. The third area, that of ruling, involved discipline such as was invoked in the case of Ananias and Sapphira. This sphere fell increasingly to the lot of the elders, the men who were set apart to oversee the flock, not only to feed the sheep but to watch over their souls and protect them from harmful influences (see Acts 20:28-31).

The Charismata as Means of Ministry

Ernst Käsemann has addressed the subject of *charismata* in relation to ministry in his article, "Ministry and Community in the New Testament."[51] Noting that the New Testament avoids the technical concept of office, he goes on to point out that is does employ the concept of *charisma* to cover both ministry and function. Käsemann's contribution lies in his exposition of the breadth of usage enjoyed by this term. It is used of eternal life (Rom. 6:23) and of certain specific divine enablements intended to serve the body of Christ (here belong the various lists of *charismata* found in 1 Corinthians 12, Romans 12, and Ephesians 4), but also of one's whole position as a Christian, with the various relationships involved. For example, Paul can speak of the gift (*charisma*) of celibacy as well as the gift of marriage (1 Cor. 7:7)—contrasting items, but both *charismata*.

> The intention is to embrace the total reality of our life, and this is clearly a polemic against an Enthusiasm which contents itself with segments of this reality or with some illusory inwardness. . . . The true measure of this gift is the way in which, in and for the Lord, an existing set of

circumstances is transformed; that is, it is the obedience of the Christian man.[52]

While it may be true that a given *charisma* can be of great value in the spiritual development of the individual to whom it is given, nevertheless the central purpose behind the granting of the gifts is edification, the building up of the body of Christ for its more effective service. Paul rings the changes on this word edification in 1 Corinthians 14. The idea is directly in line with what we discovered in Ephesians 4:11ff.

It is not possible here to treat each gift individually; instead we propose to set out a series of questions suggested by Paul's presentation.

Q: *What is the relation between the divine and human factors?*

A: One aspect of this problem is the matter of congruence between the *charisma* and a previously possessed natural gift. For example, would we expect the gift of tongues to be given to one who lacks the power of ordinary speech? If this were done, the result would be double miracle, so to speak. We would assume that ordinarily the spiritual gift is built on the natural gift to which it corresponds in some measure. Another aspect is the tension between the sovereign bestowal of the gift (see 1 Cor. 12:11) and human desire for the gift (see 1 Cor. 14:1): to what extent does the latter element enter into the divine bestowal? Further, is the gift a quantitative thing that remains static indefinitely, or can it be increased by devout use or diminished by neglect? The answer to this appears to be fairly plain from 1 Timothy 4:14 and 2 Timothy 1:6–7. Again, is it possible for a person to misconstrue the divine intent expressed through a charismatic message because of one's own attitude or desire? A case in point is the Spirit's disclosure of bonds and imprisonment awaiting Paul in Jerusalem (see Acts 20:22–23; 21:4; 21:11). It looks as though the believers at Tyre added to the information provided by the Spirit the conclusion that Paul was being forbidden to go to Jerusalem. He himself did not so understand the matter, receiving from the Spirit only information, not prohibition (Acts 20:22–23). No rebuke was given him when he went on (Acts 23:11).

Q: *Were gifts distributed to all the saints?*

A: Such seems to be the meaning of 1 Corinthians 12:11, and the matter is put even more clearly in 1 Peter 4:10: "Each one should use whatever spiritual gift he has received to serve others, faithfully administering God's grace in its various forms." It is obvious that some had several gifts, as in the case of the apostle Paul. His language in 1 Corinthians 14:1, 23–24 implies the same thing so far as others are concerned. Perhaps some had only the gift of being "helpers" (1 Cor. 12:28), but this gift could result in untold good to the household of faith.

Q: *Was the Spirit active in bestowing* charismata *in all the local congregations during the apostolic age?*

A: As already noted, Paul has lists of gifts in three letters and Peter touches the subject briefly (1 Pet. 4:10). Paul also warns the Thessalonian believers against quenching the Spirit (1 Thess. 5:19). This is not to be understood as raising the possibility of extinguishing the Spirit, driving him from one's life, but should be interpreted in light of the command: "Do not treat prophecies with contempt." Apparently these Christians were less enamored of the gifts than the believers at Corinth. This incidental reference should serve as a warning against coming to the conclusion that some of the Pauline churches had no experience of the *charismata*. The argument from silence needs to be applied with care.

Q: *What safeguards were provided against misuse of the gifts?*

A: One danger was disorder and confusion arising from the desire of several persons to participate by making their individual contribution at the same time. Paul laid down directions for regulating participation (see 1 Cor. 14:26–33). Another danger was deception through apparent disclosure of God's message on the part of one who was actually making himself the vehicle of untruth (1 Cor. 12:10). The gift of prophecy was especially vulnerable to this danger (see 1 John 4:1). A congregation needed familiarity with the apostolic rule of faith in order to detect error, especially in the area of Christology, where deviation would be most damaging.

Q: *How is it possible to distinguish closely related gifts?*

A: An example of this problem is the need for clarifying the areas included in prophecy and teaching. To be sure, in the sphere of prediction, prophecy would not be confused with teaching, but since it seems to have involved instruction as well (see 1 Cor. 14:31), the two gifts come close to intersecting (see Eph. 3:4–5). But whereas instruction through prophecy partook of the nature of revelation (see 1 Cor. 14:30), this was not true of the instruction given by the teacher. Presumably the latter was well informed about the meaning of the Old Testament, was familiar with the tradition of the church regarding the ministry of Jesus, and was able to instruct people in a rather orderly fashion concerning the rudiments of the faith and something of the ramifications of Christian doctrine. It is noteworthy that the strong church at Antioch had a corps of teachers as well as a group of prophets. The work of each group must have complemented that of the other.

Q: *Does the fact that Paul dealt so largely with tongues and prophecy indicate that these were the most important of the gifts?*

A: This conclusion does not necessarily follow, since the letter in which this issue looms so prominently (1 Cor.) is of a decidedly occasional character, being taken up with questions put to him by the church or raised by him for the church. When he wrote to the church at Rome, the apostle did not discuss tongues at all and included prophecy without any of the sort of elaboration that occurs in 1 Corinthians. His list in Romans is broader in character, including such items as liberality and the doing of acts of mercy (see Rom. 12:6–8). Even in 1 Corinthians he puts in the foreground such unspectacular items as wisdom, knowledge, and faith (12:8–9). These were the things that stood out in the ministry of our Lord, to whom the Spirit was given without measure (see John 3:34; cf. Isa. 11:1–2).

The key to ministry in terms of the *charismata* is the realization that the ministry of Christ must shine through these gifts when they are exercised. The gifts are not intended to call attention to the person who exercises them but rather should point to him who is the minister par excellence, who made no ostentatious display of his powers but used them unsparingly for the realization of the kingdom of God in the hearts of men, and all to the glory of God the Father.

It is no accident, then, that the point is made that love is essential to any charismatic ministry. Love has first place in the listing of the fruit of the Spirit (Gal. 5:22) and it is the indispensable ingredient for the proper operation of the gifts throughout the church (1 Cor. 13).

A Spirit-filled and Spirit-led ministry has as its true objective not *ecstasy* (a spiritual "trip")—which pertains to the emotions, the least important and least stable aspect of the human constitution—but rather *dynamic*, the action of the Holy Spirit in laying hold of the will, making ministry positively effective in its outreach.

8. TEACHING

The Old Testament Background

We tend to think of the prophets as teachers, but this is true only to a limited degree. They could better be described as patriots, revivalists, and reformers. Their task was to call the nation back to God when it had fallen away and to make known what the future held by way of judgment or blessing. We do not ordinarily think of the priests as teachers, yet this was a part of their ministry. When serving at the altar they were representing their fellows before God; when engaged in teaching they were representing God before the people (see 2 Chron. 15:3; 17:7–9; Mal. 2:7).

John the Baptist as Teacher

Although the mission of the forerunner called for preaching as his major task, the Baptist was consulted by the people for counsel along lines of practical living (see Luke 3:10–14), a request to which he gladly responded.

It is recorded that he also taught his disciples, especially in the area of prayer (see Luke 11:1).

The Teaching Ministry of Jesus

We can view Jesus' teaching as a foil to the rabbinic practice of the time. The rabbinic tradition emphasized the necessity for a long process of learning both in the content of Scripture and in the traditions of the elders. This bore its inevitable fruit: before the middle of the second century A.D. some rabbis were promulgating the notion that studying the Mosaic law was more necessary than practicing it.

The Gospels clearly indicate that teaching was a prominent part of our Lord's ministry. Again and again he is represented as teaching in the synagogue and also in the open air, where he could reach larger numbers of people. The synagogue was known as the house of instruction, so Jesus would be expected to teach there. From our standpoint it is unfortunate that the writers of the Gospels were usually content simply to note the fact that Jesus taught in this setting without going on to describe or report the teaching. A notable exception is found in Luke 4:16–30, a passage that stands out all the more because it is flanked by references to his teaching activity in other places (Luke 4:15, 31), where nothing is indicated as to the content of his instruction. After reading the Scripture, he sat down, which was the normal posture for teaching (see Matt. 5:1).

Out of this episode in the synagogue at Nazareth two things emerge that have a bearing on the teaching activity of the church. One is the importance of the prior revelation in the Old Testament; the other is the fact that Jesus related Scripture to himself and his mission. What he did publicly on this occasion was continued, especially after the resurrection, in his instruction of the Eleven (see Luke 24:44–47). It was inevitable that this instruction became the focal point of the apostles' teaching in the early church.

Of equal importance is the provision Jesus made for the future, when he would no longer be personally present. In the upper room he declared to the disciples that he had many things to teach them but that they were unable to receive them due to their distraught condition. He promised to send another Counselor, the Spirit of truth, who would take over the ministry of teaching. The Lord made three important statements about the Spirit's teaching activity: (1) he would recall to their minds what Jesus had taught them (John 14:26), (2) he would teach them all things (John 14:26), and (3) he would declare to them the things that were to come (John 16:13). A glance at these three items shows that they involve the past, the present, and the future. The promise of the Spirit was the assurance by the master teacher that this ministry would not fade with his departure but would be amply cared for by the Spirit of truth. In a very real sense the departure of the risen Lord did not involve his abdication of the office of teacher, as Luke makes clear in the opening lines of the book of Acts, wherein he refers to his Gospel as containing "all that Jesus began to do and teach." The implication is plain: the ascended Lord is still active in these areas of ministry, but now by means of the Spirit acting upon the church.

Matching the provision of the Spirit as teacher is the human obligation laid upon the church in the persons of the apostles, as set forth in the Great Commission—"teaching them to observe all that I have commanded you" (Matt. 28:20). Some critics doubt that Jesus actually spoke these words, as we noted in our discussion of baptism. And yet, how strange that the church would have elected to make Jesus say that the disciples were to teach Gentile as well as Jewish converts all that he had taught them if in fact the church did not possess and cherish his teaching! On the other hand, the scarcity of references to our Lord's teaching in the epistles would be understandable if we were to presume that new converts had already been schooled in this corpus of teaching. That the church sought to be faithful to the charge of the Savior is indicated by the fact that as soon as converts were made at Pentecost they were placed under apostolic instruction (see Acts 2:42).

Teaching in the Early Church

The activity noted in Acts 2:42 may have been the first attempt at teaching undertaken by the apostles, even as Peter's sermon on the day of Pentecost was the first attempt at preaching the gospel. No doubt the success registered in the evangelistic witness gave encouragement to the group to address themselves to the task of instruction. Some of them, as followers of the Baptist, must have heard him give counsel to those who sought his help, but that was of a very limited nature. They had also listened frequently to Jesus as he taught the multitudes for hours at a time and then engaged his chosen band in serious conversation in private. All this was good preparation. These men must have been encouraged also by the Master's assurance that the Spirit would be with them in the future to enlighten them and to give them utterance.

The three thousand Pentecost converts presented a staggering challenge to the apostles, if only because of the number. Conceivably they divided the multitude into smaller groups and assigned an apostle to each group. If so, a practical problem had to be faced: How could divergence in the teaching be avoided? It would hardly be realistic to suppose that the apostles had busied themselves preparing a teaching manual for their common use. Apparently they were otherwise engaged during the ten days prior to Pentecost (see Acts 1:14). However, if the gospel involved virtually the same presentation no matter who voiced it (see Acts 2; 13; 1 Cor. 15:11), the teaching could also be expected to follow a fairly well-defined pattern. The necessity of maintaining this instruction on a daily basis (see Acts 2:46–47) must have required conference and planning so that all the converts would move at approximately the same pace through the material that was presented to them.

It is natural to wonder about the content of the instruction. Although Luke has included several accounts of apostolic preaching, he has not done likewise for the teaching. Even in the account of Paul's meeting with the Ephesian elders in Acts 20, there is virtually no report of teaching in the accepted sense, but rather counsel. Likewise, in Luke's report of activities in the Antioch church teaching is noted (see Acts 11:26) but nothing is indicated as to the nature of the instruction. However, the apostles were rich in available resources. Their experience with Jesus—what they had seen and heard—gave them ample material. They had been instructed by him to pass on to others all that he had commanded them (see Matt. 28:20), and the highlights of his life could have served as a framework for the teaching. In addition, there was the new light that came to them on the messianic teaching of the Old Testament as Jesus had unfolded it to them after the resurrection. And finally, they could hardly omit all reference to things that were to come (see John 16:13; cf. Acts 3:19–20). It is safe to say that the longer such teaching continued to be given out the more it must have tended to crystallize in both thought and expression. So the foundation was laid for catechetical instruction.

As at Jerusalem, so at Antioch, teaching was carried on by a group of men (13:1) covering an extended period of time (11:26; 15:35). Since this was basically a Gentile church, it is reasonable to conclude that some elements of teaching were introduced that were not necessary in the Jewish-Christian congregations, such as the doctrine of God, warnings against idolatry and its attendant evils based on a survey of God's dealings with Israel, and a presentation of the difficulties and challenges facing a Christian who must live in a pagan society. F. F. Bruce has advanced the suggestion that

> As the number of converts increased, especially in the course of the Gentile mission, "schools" for the training of instructors would have become almost a necessity, and digests of the teaching of Jesus would have inevitably been drawn up, orally if not in writing. We may envisage such a life-setting for the "sayings collection" on which Matthew and Luke drew, and at a later date the Matthean Gospel itself has been viewed as taking shape in such a school.[53]

At this point it may be well to inquire if the teaching function of the church was restricted to those who possessed a spiritual gift that qualified them. While their leadership in this area would be recognized, it is reasonably clear from Scripture that the saints in general had some responsibility. Perhaps the clearest indication of a larger circle of teachers comes from the pen of Paul: "Let the word of Christ dwell in you richly as you teach and counsel one another with all wisdom" (Col. 3:16). A certain danger lurks in this situation, well expressed by James—the possibility that some people will not be content to teach in this limited, nonofficial role that gives them no status, but will aspire to recognition as teachers. To such James addresses his words, "Not many of you should act as teachers, my brothers, because you know that we who teach will be judged more strictly" (James 3:1).

Returning to the Colossians passage, we note that two terms are used there: *teaching* and *counseling* (or *admonishing*). The former term implies instruction in Christian character and deportment, affording us a bridge to our next study, that of discipline. Paul has already used both terms in describing his own ministry (Col. 1:28).

It is pertinent to include Paul's counsel to Timothy: "And the things you have heard me say in the presence of many witnesses entrust to reliable men who will also be qualified to teach others" (2 Tim. 2:2). As time went on, the need for teachers to train others as teachers would naturally have increased.

Teaching in relation to the Gospel Message

In recent years a notable contribution to New Testament study has been made by C. H. Dodd through his distinction between the *kērygma* (i.e., gospel proclamation of the church intended for unbelievers) and the *didache* (i.e., instruction directed toward believers), the latter being doctrinal to some extent but chiefly practical. Fairly wide agreement has been reached that Dodd somewhat too rigidly distinguished the two genres. The *kērygma* must often have been taught to the church with greater depth than in its proclamation to the unsaved, if only to give believers a better understanding of it as preparation for their own witness to those outside the fold. Furthermore, it is clear that the most basic ingredients of the *kērygma*, the death and resurrection of the Savior, formed the basis for instruction on sanctification, at least as Paul expounded the message in a passage such as Romans 6. This was church truth.

As Filson points out, it is possible to make room for a third category which at times must have involved both preaching and teaching, namely, discussion or disputation, such as Paul carried on in the synagogue, marketplace, or rented hall where he met with people who were willing to hear what he had to say.[54] Luke notes that Stephen also had considerable disputation with the Hellenists (see Acts 6:9).

Terminology

Several words are used to express the imparting of Christian truth to the church. *Didache* can mean "teaching" (the activity) or "doctrine" (the content). In 2 John 9–10 a particular doctrine, that of the person of Christ, is in view. In 1 Corinthians 14:6, 26 an unnamed item of Christian truth is intended. In Romans 6:17 Paul reminds his readers that from the time of their conversion they were committed to a certain standard of teaching;

the very fact that he could write thus is an indication that wherever Christians were found, whether converts of Paul or of some other person, they had been placed under teaching that was basically uniform throughout the church. From the context of Romans 6:17 it is apparent that this standard pertained to a righteous life to be lived out in terms of deliverance from the power of sin, a deliverance grounded on the believer's identification with Christ. In the sight of God, the Savior's death involved the death of all who belong to him. And just as believers died thereby to sin, so they rose with Christ to walk with him in newness of life. The apostle assumes that his readers are familiar with this line of teaching (see Rom. 6:3, 6, 9). It must have been diffused throughout the church, an indication of close communication and common concern.

Paradosis ("tradition") comes from a verb meaning "to hand down," "to transmit faithfully." Luke uses this verb in the prologue of his Gospel concerning the service performed by eye witnesses and ministers of the word in communicating what they had seen and heard of Jesus and his ministry to people such as Luke who had not enjoyed a firsthand knowledge of that ministry. Paul employs the verb in describing his communication of the gospel to the Corinthians (1 Cor. 15:3) and also in connection with passing on certain traditions (see 1 Cor. 11:2, in which both verb and noun are used). In the latter passage it is apparently not the gospel under consideration but directions for the guidance of Christian living and for the regulation of worship. During the brief period of Paul's first visit to Thessalonica he had occasion to stress the importance of work. Later, when writing to the church, he reminds his readers of the teaching given at that earlier time and refers to it in terms of tradition (see 2 Thess. 3:6). In this case the tradition was reinforced by the apostle's example of labor and toil while he was with them. Here, then, such a practical matter as daily work is dignified as a part of the program of life set forth in the tradition.

Katēcheō (the verb from which *catechesis* is formed) means literally "to sound down" (the teacher delivered the lesson to students sitting at his feet). The verb has two meanings—"to inform" (possibly intended in Luke 1:3, certainly so in Acts 21:21) and "to instruct" (as in Acts 18:25; Gal. 6:6; 1 Cor. 14:19), especially relating to the content of the Christian faith. The Galatians passage, with its mention of both the instructor and the one taught, is particularly pertinent to our theme. As H. W. Beyer indicates, it "establishes the claim of the teacher to support, and therewith confirms the validity and neccessity of a professional teaching ministry in the congregation."[55] One should compare with this what Paul says in 1 Timothy 5:17-18. It would be going beyond the evidence to assert that the catechumenate in the technical sense of later church usage is already found in the New Testament. Rather, the basis is being laid for the development of this later feature.

At first sight Paul's expression, "my ways in Christ" (1 Cor. 4:17) may seem to be a reference to his personal life as a Christian, but when he goes on to say that in accordance with these ways he teaches everywhere in every church, it is clear that he is referring to something normative for believers. Undoubtedly "ways" have to do with conduct. It may be that in the background is the rabbinic idea of *halachah*, the principles regulating conduct that are applicable to all members of the Jewish community. Paul is fond of mentioning the "walk" of believers, which has a certain prescriptive character rather that being a matter of the discretion of the individual. Paul's ways, then, are not his in some individualistic sense but are his in the sense that he gives them prominence in his instruction of the churches. Yet he is conscious of being faithful in practice to what he teaches others and for this reason can urge on his readers that they be imitators of him (v. 16). As he is their spiritual father, responsible for their birth into the kingdom of God, he also accepts responsibility to lead his spiritual children by word and example. This legitimately includes discipline if that should be needed (see v. 21).

As Paul writes to the churches he has established he is able to build on the foundational teaching he has left with his converts; in some cases he has only to remind them of its nature—for example, "Finally, brothers, we instructed you how to live [literally "walk"] in order to please God, as in fact you are living. Now we ask you and urge you in the Lord Jesus to do this more and more" (1 Thess. 4:1).

Modern Research on the Didache

The pioneer in research on the *didache* was Alfred Seeberg (in *Der Katechismus der Urchristenheit* [1903]). He discerned the great importance of the oral period during which Christian teaching was achieving more and more of a fixed form. Although he went too far in the direction of positing a definite catechism for the early church, he demonstrated the existence in the New Testament of the materials for such a catechism. Starting with Paul's statement about his ways, Seeberg concluded that these ways involved avoidance of certain sins as well as the pursuit of certain virtues. By comparing the various lists contained in Paul's letters he was able to isolate several items that recurred more than others—proscriptions of fornication, covetousness, malice, abusive speech or slander, uncleanness, strife, jealousy or envy, anger, and self-seeking—and was able to conclude that these must have been part of a pattern of instruction. In many cases the pattern seemed to hold when early patristic writings were consulted. Similarly, certain virtues such as compassion, kindness, humility, meekness, longsuffering, love, peace, faithfulness, and steadfastness seemed to stand out as more or less constant ingredients. It could be concluded, therefore, that such items formed the common basis for moral and ethical instruction in the early church, varied here and there and added to in accordance with specific local needs. Seeberg was encouraged by his discovery that the great bulk of terms that dominate the New Testament reappear in the postapostolic period as the Fathers discuss "the way."

Philip Carrington's *The Primitive Christian Catechism* (1940) is a study of the hortatory sections in Colossians, Ephesians, 1 Peter, and James in which Carrington notes that the commands tended to focus on four lines of thought: put off all evil, submit yourself (to God and one another), watch and pray, and resist the devil. What impressed him in this comparative study was the fact that these ingredients were not only present in all these epistles but that they tended to appear in this order (1 Peter presents a slight variation in that the second and third items reappear in the closing chapter). Carrington advances the opinion that the first of the series (putting off evil) is associated with instruction connected with baptism and rests on the requirements of the Levitical Code for proselytes to Judaism (see Lev. 17–19), which calls for abstention from idols, fornication, and blood (cf. Acts 15:29).

In *The First Epistle of St. Peter* (1946) E. G. Selwyn notes elements common to 1 Thessalonians, 1 Peter, and the Apostolic Decree (Acts 15) and suggests that since Silas apparently had a hand in the drafting of all three documents, his influence should be reckoned with, although it is not the whole explanation for the similarity. Selwyn, like Carrington, would emphasize that something in the nature of a Christian holiness code (influenced by Leviticus) is reflected here, associated with the baptism of converts and the summons addressed to them to put off the old life and walk as children of light. But he goes on to suggest that somewhat altered forms of *didache* developed as the church became more largely Gentile and depended less on Old Testament backgrounds, giving more attention, among other things, to the means by which worship should be carried on.

One notable result of the isolation of forms of *didache* is the likelihood that close agreements in the paraenetic sections of certain epistles do not point to literary dependence by one writer on another but can be more readily explained on the ground that the writers involved were drawing on the common store of teaching materials found throughout the church. A case in point is the similarity between Paul (in Rom. 13:1–7) and Peter (in 1 Pet. 2:13–17) in dealing with the Christian's obligation to the state.

C. H. Dodd, having the work of previous investigators to stimulate him, chose the following methodology: "To examine the ethical portions of a number of epistles, and see whether the material common to them all betrays any signs of originating at a stage antedating the particular writing." He discovered that writers as diverse in style as Paul, Peter and the writer of the Epistle to the Hebrews nevertheless shared much the same style in their hortatory sections, which are concisely worded and rhythmic. It is not likely that all three dropped into this pattern accidentally and independently. Dodd also made use of an observation by David Daube to the effect that a feature of these sections is the use of a participle where an imperative would be expected. He remarks, "This is entirely unGreek, and appears to be an imitation of a Hebrew idiom which is not infrequent in certain types of Jewish ethical instruction. It is not found in the epistles outside of these characteristic passages of ethical teaching, but in such passages it is employed by Paul in Romans and Colossians, by Paul or an imitator in Ephesians, and by other writers in Hebrews and I Peter. This seems to be conclusive evidence that all are following some common model."[56]

The Content of the Didache

We have already touched on the content of the *didache* to some extent, but it may be helpful to cite the more complete statement of the matter supplied by Dodd, especially since it is arranged in logical order. He lists the following as content:

1. A reminder of the readers' conversion and call, together with the change demanded in their manner of life. Here belongs the "put off"/"put on" motif.

2. A statement of the virtues to be personally cultivated, such as purity, gentleness, hospitality, patience, and the like.

3. The Christian ordering of family relationships, with the duties of husband, wife, children, masters, and servants delineated.

4. Teaching concerning the concept of believers as one body, involving matters of worship, one's relationship to one's leaders, and the employment of gifts.

5. Admonition respecting the conduct of Christians in their contacts with pagan society so as to avoid giving offense and to gain a hearing for the truth.

6. Orientation to the stringent nature of the times, to the imminent end hovering over the world, demanding watchfulness and self-discipline.[57]

As various writers have pointed out, two important sources used to substantiate the *didache* were the *testimonia* (groupings of Scripture passages supporting a Christian teaching, such as the combination of texts used by Paul in Romans 3:10–18) and the *verba Christi* (which occur most notably in 1 Peter; James also has a number of them, although his are not quotations but attempts to catch the gist of the Master's utterances).

The general conclusion to which one is led is that although the *didache* is much more diffuse than the *kērygma* and therefore not so readily reducible to a few simple propositions, its presence in the church is suggested by the book of Acts and illustrated by the practical sections of the epistles. Its rough outlines are discernible even though its language may vary from one writer to another.

The Purpose of the Didache

Paul's inclusion of the role of pastor/teacher among the gifts of the ascended Lord to his church (Eph. 4:11) is highly suggestive. It seems to point to the fact that teachers were not expected to itinerate in the same manner as prophets, but would live among the people and learn of their needs, so that in spite of the standardization of the *didache* they would be able to treat it with sufficient flexibility to meet the special needs of those for whom they were responsible. Paul has succinctly set forth the goal of the Christian teacher: referring to Christ, he says, "We proclaim him, counseling and teaching everyone with all wisdom, so that we may present everyone perfect in Christ" (Col. 1:28). We see this passion displayed in Paul's earliest letter, as he commends his readers for their faith and love but goes on to urge them to more and more of the same (1 Thess. 4:1, 10). A similar thrust is evident in the epistle to the Hebrews (5:12; 6:1).

Multifarious injunctions may seem like so much bird shot. The maze of duties set before the convert to the faith may appear to minister to discouragement. If so, it is a matter of appearance only, for there is a unifying factor. Paul puts it sublimely when, after reminding his readers of the sins that characterize the Gentile world, he goes on to say, "You, however, did not come to know Christ that way. Surely you heard of him and were taught in him in accordance with the truth that is in Jesus" (Eph. 4:20–21). As the evangelist must preach Christ, so the teacher must teach Christ "until we all reach unity in the faith and in the knowledge of the Son of God and become mature, attaining the full measure of perfection found in Christ" (Eph. 4:13). To achieve such a magnificent result the teacher himself must be taught by the Spirit of God, who is intent on glorifying the Son of God.

In the teaching ministry of the church lies the promise of its very continuance: "the things you have heard me say in the presence of many witnesses entrust to reliable men who will also be qualified to teach others" (2 Tim. 2:2). It has been observed that four generations are included here: Paul, Timothy (his son in the faith), those whom Timothy will teach, and those whom these individuals will teach. This is true Christian *paradosis.*

9. DISCIPLINE

The Latin term *disciplina* (cf. disciple) means "instruction" and carries with it the idea of training, which serves to bring into the concept all the influences that have a part in one's education. Consequently, the subject is closely related to teaching.

The basic Greek word is *paideia* (literally, "child training"), which occurs half a dozen times in the New Testament (the verb form is used more frequently). In classical Greek usage the term can be rendered as "education," "training," "nurture," or even "culture." In the Hebrew tradition, however, education was less distinctly intellectual in its orientation than among the Greeks. Consequently in the Septuagint the word becomes the vehicle oftentimes for the idea of chastisement and correction, since the concept is ethico-spiritual more than intellectual. The book of Proverbs is strongly colored by this emphasis.

In the New Testament the old Greek idea of education can still be expressed by the verb *paideuō* (used of Moses in Acts 7:22 and of Paul in Acts 22:3). Paul's description of the Mosaic law as a *paidagōgos* designed to lead one to Christ (Gal. 3:24) is probably intended to convey the combined ideas of instruction and discipline.

On a logical basis two broad types of discipline can be distinguished. One is preventive, the other is purifying. The divide between the two is the actual commission of an offense. But preventive discipline can be analyzed into self-discipline (e.g., as in 1 Cor. 9:24–27) and discipline imposed by the control of others through counsel, admonition, and so on. The former is part of personal character development. The latter is associated with the catechetical instruction given by the church.

There would be no need for ecclesiastical discipline if believers availed themselves fully of the divine provision for the overcoming life. But the very fact that self-control is a part of the fruit of the Spirit (see Gal. 5:23) is a clear indication that it is to be understood as control of the self by the aid of the Spirit rather than by one's own determination alone.

Discipline of the corrective or purifying type recognizes that an offense has been committed (and possibly has become habitual) and that it has to be dealt with. Both the good of the offender and the spiritual health of the church have to be considered in connection with the measures adopted to deal with the situation. Indeed, the possible effect on the outside world requires attention also. The goal is to restore the offender and at the same time protect the congregation from being contaminated by the same offense.

Two areas are embraced in discipline. One is Christian doctrine, an area in which deviation from the rule of faith in important matters calls for action to forestall the possible spread of false teaching. The other area is deportment; wrong conduct can distress the Christian body and bring disrepute on the gospel.

There is a sphere in which the church is unable to operate, for it is limited in its jurisdiction to what has been committed and has become known. Believers may be failing terribly in their inner life and yet may not be living in open sin so as to invite discipline by the church. Or they may be guilty of persistent sin that they are able to hide successfully from the gaze of fellow-believers. Only God's chastening can reach a person in such circumstances. It is conceivable that a congregation as a whole could become so lax, so carnal, that action against individuals in the group could not be successfully undertaken. Something of this sort appears to have been the condition of the church of Laodicea (see Rev. 3:14–18). The Lord himself must deal with such a situation, promising reproof and chastening unless the church bestirs itself to repentance (v. 19). His discipline is prompted by love, no matter how severe it may be (see Heb. 12:6). Paul's reminder that if Christians would exercise true self-judgment they would render unnecessary the chastening judgment of the Lord is presumably applicable both to individuals and to groups (1 Cor. 11:31). In chastening his people, the Lord is not treating them as he will treat the unbelieving world in the day of judgment (see 1 Cor. 11:32–33).

The Teaching of Jesus relative to Discipline

The chief passage concerning Jesus' teaching on discipline is Matthew 18:15–18, which follows naturally the parable of the shepherd and the lost sheep (vv. 12–14). As Plummer notes, "The way in which God deals with his erring sheep leads on to the way in which a man should deal with his erring brother."[58]

1. The offended individual is to seek out the offender and make known to him privately what he has done. The initiative lies with the injured party. Presumably, however, there is no intention to rule out the possibility that the offender may take the initiative by confessing his wrong.

2. If the offending brother acknowledges his wrong, the breach can be repaired then and there, so that right relations are restored. On the other hand, if he will not acknowledge his fault, the offended individual is to take one or more witnesses with him (not witnesses of the original offense but of the attempt to establish reconciliation). They must be able to testify to the earnest effort of the offended party in his second attempt to gain his brother.

3. In the event that this procedure does not move the offender to confess his wrong, the injured party, together with the witnesses, is to lay the matter before the church. If the sinning party heeds the overtures of the church, the affair is closed, for fellowship has been restored.

4. If the offender does not accede to the church's decision, the church is to take formal disciplinary action consisting of excommunication from the fellowship. The very fact that these directions are so explicit indicates a concern on the part of Jesus for the maintenance of spiritual unity among those who belong to him.

Appropriately, these directions are followed by a statement of the authority vested in the apostles to exercise discipline: "I tell you the truth, whatever you bind on earth will be bound in heaven, and whatever you loose on earth will be loosed in heaven" (Matt. 18:18). The similarity to the authority vested in Peter (see Matt. 16:19) is obvious. It is possible that in both passages the sense is better conveyed by the rendering "shall have been bound" and "shall have been loosed."[59] The meaning of the passage seems to be akin to that in John 20:23, where the sense is more easily grasped because nontechnical language is used. Binding is the enforcement of excommunication; loosing is the reinstatement of the offender, which implies forgiveness of the offense.

Discipline in the Book of Acts

A certain amount of risk was involved in the practice of the immediate reception of new converts into the church based on a profession of faith in the Lord Jesus, with no period of instruction and probation prior to baptism. The church may have felt the abnormality of any considerable interval between professed belief and baptism (see Acts 2:38; 8:36, 38). Actually, the power of the Spirit was so manifest and the conviction of sin so searching that the danger involved in immediate baptism was more theoretical than real. The masses did not dare to identify with believers apart from the experience of conversion based on conviction of sin (see Acts 2:43).

It is tempting, no doubt, to try to explain the Ananias and Sapphira incident on the ground that this couple could not have been true believers, but there seems to be no proof of this. Believers are capable of deception as of other sins. Peter's charge that Ananias had lied to the Holy Spirit suggests that the Spirit was indeed dwelling in this man. The infliction of the death penalty does not alter the situation, since this was imposed on other occasions (see 1 Cor. 11:30). Peter's prediction of death for Sapphira was not an arrogation of authority. He knew that God had smitten her husband and could readily conclude that the same sentence would be imposed on his wife, seeing that she was equally guilty (v. 9). To understand the severity of the judgment one has only to reflect on the fact that the church was just beginning to make an impact on the community. God could not bless his people if selfishness and deception were permitted to mar their common life. In the body of Christ, what one does has an effect on all. If action had not been taken speedily, the Spirit would have been grieved and the testimony of the church severely limited. Sometimes the church must have subtractions before it can have additions. In the history of Israel, the case of Achan presents a somewhat parallel situation, for the sin of one man meant the withholding of God's blessing from the nation and defeat on the field of battle (see Josh. 7). Both the speed and the drastic nature of the discipline in the case of Ananias and Sapphira kept the church from suffering powerlessness. Motives were sifted, hearts were searched, and any temptation on the part of the multitude to slip into the church and share the benefits of its *koinōnia* was nipped in the bud (Acts 5:11). The most impressive thing about the whole incident is not the use of stern measures but rather the high level of spiritual life and sensitivity that permitted detection and removal of a cancer that threatened the corporate soundness of the people of God.

The case of Simon Magus was quite different, though the Holy Spirit was involved there as well. That Simon was not a genuine believer seems reasonably certain, despite the statement that he "believed" (Acts 8:13; cf. John 2:23–25). Therefore he was not subject to discipline in the Christian sense. The words Peter addressed to him may well serve as a guide for those who are obliged to deal with people who for wrong motives make a profession of faith in Jesus Christ. Unless they repent and truly believe in him (Simon was given this opportunity—see v. 22), they will perish in their sins.

Other accounts in Acts of confrontations between Christian missionaries and those addicted to magic and the occult are likewise not pertinent to the sphere of church discipline, but they serve to underscore the assertion of Jesus that the gates of Hades would not prevail against the church. When the enemy comes in like a flood, the Spirit of the Lord raises a standard against him. Instances of this sort include the dealings of Paul with Elymas (Acts 13:8–12), with the damsel possessed by a spirit of divination (16:16–18), and with Sceva and his sons (19:11–20).

Discipline in the Letters of Paul

In his correspondence with the Thessalonian church the apostle had occasion to warn against sexual immorality, as he had done when his readers became Christians (1 Thess. 4:6). There is no indication as to the measures that could be expected in dealing with the problem, but the implication is that God could be counted on to intervene (cf. Acts 5). The second item that provoked concern was a tendency on the part of some to be idle (1 Thess. 5:14; 2 Thess. 3:6ff.) What made this situation galling to the apostle was that this conduct persisted in spite of his initial warning. It was grossly unfair to expect industrious believers to maintain those who were shiftless. Indeed, this was a form of stealing. Continued admonition may not be sufficient. If the condition persists, with the offenders challenging the apostle's authority by their disobedience, then the church must refuse fellowship to such persons until there is true repentance (2 Thess. 3:14–15). Paul felt the wrong of this situation keenly because he had personally set an example of diligent labor during his stay in Thessalonica (2 Thess. 3:7–9).

In writing to the Galatians the apostle pronounces anathema on anyone who proclaims a false gospel (Gal. 1:8–9). This was not strictly a matter for church discipline, but rather the delivering over of such an offender to the righteous wrath of God (cf. 1 Cor. 16:22). Closely related is the warning statement that he who is chiefly responsible for troubling the Galatian churches will bear his judgment (Gal. 5:10).

Paul's altercation with Peter at Antioch did not involve appeal to any church authority to settle their difference. Peter stood condemned by the very truth of the gospel that he had confessed (Gal. 2:7–9) but later clouded by his conduct (Gal. 2:11–14)

The dealings of Paul with the Corinthian church were delicate and highly involved, frequently requiring the application of discipline or the threat of its use. Disorders at the Lord's table had already brought sickness to some and death to others (1 Cor. 11:30). Presumably the God-sent sickness was intended to produce repentance. In those cases where repentance was not forthcoming, death ensued. God had acted directly in this situation in order to safeguard the sanctity of the Supper. How much more, then, could he be expected to destroy anyone who sought to ruin the church (1 Cor. 3:17). The factions in the church and the arrogant spirit manifested in connection with them led the apostle to threaten to use the rod of judgment during his next visit unless a different spirit prevailed (1 Cor. 4:21). The rod was symbolic of his apostolic authority. No indication is given of the precise nature of the steps to be taken.

In the following chapter (1 Cor. 5) two items of discipline come to the fore. A previous letter from Paul, no longer extant, had indicated that the church should withdraw its fellowship from any who were guilty of patently wrong conduct—immorality and other sins such as idolatry, drunkenness, and the like. It seems that the church had not taken action, pleading that Paul's letter had not made it clear that he had in mind brethren rather than sinners in general. Probably the meaning was clear enough but the church was unwilling to bear down on offenders in its ranks. We can understand this if they were somewhat numerous. In response Paul reiterates his command and makes it still more explicit (1 Cor. 5:11). Evidently it was his hope that vigorous exclusion from fellowship would effect a change of heart and conduct.

Of special interest is the case treated at the beginning of this chapter, involving a man who was cohabiting with his stepmother. Paul objects to the lack of concern on the part of the church over this outrageous condition, a festering sore in the spiritual body. He seems to suggest that the church should have taken action to exclude this person from its fellowship. Since it has not done so, he must take the initiative. The decision has already been made. The congregation must carry it out. He wants the Corinthians to realize that this church of his founding is so dear to him that when the meeting is held to deal with the matter, he will be there in spirit, even though absent in body. Moreover, the Lord will be there too (v. 4).

It appears that partly because the church has defaulted its responsibility, Paul has passed sentence as Christ's representative, no doubt after much prayer. The congregation must meet in solemn conclave to put the verdict into effect. This means that the offender is to be turned over to Satan for the destruction of the flesh in order that the spirit may be saved in the day of the Lord Jesus (v. 5). But what is meant by the destruction of the flesh?

With Paul the usual meaning of flesh is the sinful nature of mankind, but occasionally it is used as the equivalent of the body. G. W. H. Lampe points out that "it is unthinkable that victory over 'flesh,' in the ethical sense of the term, could be brought about by the agency of Satan,"[60] so we should assume that physical affliction is meant here, as it is in 1 Corinthians 11:30. Perhaps the expected repentance will come soon, but if not, then on the offender's deathbed. His spirit will be saved in the day of the Lord Jesus (cf. 3:15). That Satan would gladly bring affliction to God's people if permitted to do so is apparent from the case of Job and from Paul's own experience (2 Cor. 12:7). The apostle is concerned for the spiritual welfare of the guilty brother and also for the reputation of the church in the community.

Another case comes to light in 2 Corinthians 2:5-11. Interpreters are not agreed as to whether the reference is to the forgiveness and restoration of the man mentioned in 1 Corinthians 5. Some regard it as a different case entirely, one that involved some offense against Paul personally, hence his eagerness to forgive. But this is not absolutely clear since Paul, as we have noted, speaks of his spirit as present when the congregation acts (5:4). In both passages Satan is mentioned. One item of interest is the indication that when the congregation acted, a majority voted for the punishment (2 Cor. 2:6). This seems to indicate that total agreement was not demanded in dealing with disciplinary cases. Paul asks the church to receive the offender back into fellowship, now that he repented in sorrow, forgiving him and confirming their love to him.

Some others in the church may be due for disciplinary action when the apostle makes his next visit (2 Cor. 13:1-3). He is hopeful that by mentioning it, nothing beyond his warning will be needed. He is allowing time for the situation to be cleared up before his arrival.

The epistle to the Romans has an item bearing on discipline, a warning against false teachers, couched in language suggesting that they were not active in the church at that time but that they might come to disturb it. The one recommendation given is to avoid such people (Rom. 16:17-18).

The pastoral epistles reflect conditions that called for disciplinary action. Apparently Paul had already acted in the case of two so-called Christian teachers, Hymenaeus and Alexander, whom he had excluded and turned over to Satan in the hope that they would repent of their wrong (1 Tim. 1:20; cf. 2 Tim. 2:17-18).

A charge against an elder is not to be entertained, Paul counsels, unless it is backed up by two or three witnesses. Thus, good men will be encouraged in their work and be relieved of the fear of groundless attacks. On the other hand, Paul says that if an elder is guilty of wrongdoing he must be rebuked openly before the congregation. Only in this way can the purity of the people of God be safeguarded (1 Tim. 5:19-20). Incidentally, it is worth noting that in his discussion of the value of Scripture, Paul includes its usefulness for reproof and correction (2 Tim. 3:16). In writing to Titus he charges him to be ready to confute false teaching and to rebuke sharply those who engage in this acitvity (Tit. 1:9, 13). If a man gives evidence of sectarian tendencies, he is to be warned once or twice; if he persists, he is to be dropped from further consideration, for he stands self-condemned (Tit. 3:10). This instruction from the apostle may indicate that the warnings to be given will not be simply from Titus but from the elders or even from the church as a body, making it fully evident that the individual in question is out of step with the Christian community.

Discipline in the Remainder of the New Testament

Hebrews 12:5–11 contains some valuable teaching on discipline. The word itself occurs here repeatedly (see the RSV). However, it is put forward not in the context of congregational action but rather of the personal relationship between the heavenly Father and his child, whom he is bringing to a place of strength and maturity by his wise dealings.

The epistles of John are concerned with the inroads of false teaching. Teachers who promote heretical views are labeled antichrists if they go so far as to actually deny the Son of God his divine status (1 John 2:22–23). Some have left the fellowship, to which they never really belonged, thus obviating the necessity of dealing with them by church action (1 John 2:18–19). No hospitality is to be extended to a heretic, lest one become implicated, however indirectly, in the doctrinal error espoused by the other (2 John 10–11). In 3 John we find the elder much distressed that his friend Gaius, to whom he is writing, has to contend with a man who has arrogated to himself autocratic leadership in the local church. This Diotrephes will not acknowledge the authority of the elder who writes. Yet the latter anticipates making a visit to the church, at which time there will have to be a showdown. Apparently he is confident that the congregation will come to his support. In Diotrephes one may perhaps see a budding tendency toward the monarchical bishop of the sort we encounter by the time of Ignatius.

In the Revelation, discipline is viewed from the standpoint of the Head of the church, who keeps his eye on the individual congregations and knows the conditions in each one. Repeatedly in the letters to the churches (chaps. 2–3) the Lord threatens to come and chasten the local church in one way or another unless there is repentance. The strongest language is addressed to the Laodiceans, whom he threatens to spew out of his mouth (3:16).

Summary

1. The imposition of discipline is irrational without the existence of a standard to which believers are expected to adhere, whether in doctrinal

belief or in ethical conduct. This standard was doubtless provided in the catechesis of the church. Education, then, served a preventive function in addition to providing a basis on which to deal with offenders.

2. God's direct, supernatural action on certain occasions (Acts 5; 1 Cor. 11) may have made the attitude of the church tentative and tardy about developing formal discipline, lest this be regarded as usurping a divine prerogative.

3. The whole area of discipline is difficult, calling as it does for forming judgment and developing action respecting one's peers by those who are themselves fallible and sinful. Even when the guidelines are reasonably clear and the offense readily identified, the fear that motives have not been fully assessed or other factors evaluated correctly makes for some hesitation on the part of those who must formulate the decision.

4. Apostolic authority was an important factor in discipline. While the authority was real, it could encounter opposition such as that which Paul experienced in Galatia and at Corinth. He referred to the signs of an apostle (2 Cor. 12:12), but these were displayed in connection with the founding of the church and do not seem to have operated in the area of discipline. If God did not intervene on his behalf in a supernatural way, he would be rather helpless unless the majority of the local church concurred with him and supported him. One wonders if he had definite measures in mind when he threatened to use his authority in the Corinthian situation (1 Cor. 4:21; 2 Cor. 13:10).

5. There is a place for private, personal ministry by Christians who observe that a brother has erred from the truth or strayed from the path of rectitude. If this ministry is carried out faithfully and discreetly, it may forestall the necessity for ecclesiastical action by achieving restoration without the knowledge of others (Gal. 6:1; James 5:19–20).

6. In writing to churches he had not personally founded, Paul was either silent on the subject of discipline (e.g., in the case of Colossians) or was content simply to give general guidance about a situation that might arise in the future (Rom. 16:17).

7. In the pastorals, although elders are noted and their functions indicated (including the ruling of the congregation), in the main the responsibility for initiating discipline seems to have rested with Timothy and Titus because of their position as representatives of the apostle Paul.

8. On occasion, Paul makes reference to the participation of Satan in the disciplinary process (1 Cor. 5:5; 1 Tim. 1:20). To the denial of human fellowship is added the terror of becoming the pawn of the Evil One. But the purpose is remedial rather than merely punitive. The God-given permission that enabled Satan to afflict Job seems to be at least roughly parallel.

9. Although we have no detailed description in the New Testament of what exclusion from fellowship would mean to a person (2 Cor. 2:7

provides only a hint), it is clear that the penalty was severe. "Expulsion from the Church in one place meant loss of Christian privileges everywhere, because it was impossible to be recognized without the recommendation of the Church of which one was a member."[61] The same writer notes how great the personal loss would be to a person thus excluded—a loss so great as to give pause to any who challenged the authority of the church:

> The brethren cared for one another in sickness and poverty, the aged were provided for, employment was found for those who had abandoned their callings from religious scruples. The days of persecution drew the faithful very close together. Thus apart from the great spiritual benefits offered by the Church, there were other inducements to remain within the pale. To be driven out of a society so affectionate, so tenderly compassionate, was dreaded by all who appreciated its benefits. Therefore the Christian body preserved a power of discipline.[62]

10. We have observed that in the Corinthian situation the whole church was brought into the exercise of discipline. This procedure changed with the passing of time. In the second century the locus of authority shifted to the bishop, partly due to the pressure of persecution. The church found it necessary to close ranks and maintain a tight-knit structure. Since the bishop was its spokesman, he naturally came to exercise discipline for the church.

11. The success of the Christian community in the area of discipline is attested by its survival under persecution. Having learned to apply discipline in deference to the demands of revelation, the church was strong enough to withstand the external pressure imposed by man.

CHAPTER V

The Individual Churches

ONE of the most notable features of the hellenistic age was the establishment and growth of cities. These became the nerve centers of civilization. They fostered commerce and culture in addition to providing opportunities for the religious expression of their inhabitants. One could argue that the city is characteristically evil if not actually anti-God—the world has after all had its Babels, nor have we seen the last of them—but that is not to say that the city is necessarily and inevitably stained with corruption. In fact, the final abode of the redeemed in glory is pictured as a city (Rev. 21:10), and for good reason, since the city speaks of the human desire for association and for mutual stimulation and encouragement.

It is not surprising, therefore, that the churches of which we read in the New Testament are without exception located in cities. The gospel was taken to where people were found in community rather than in isolation. This did not mean that the country areas were totally neglected, but the city was clearly given the priority and with it the obligation to carry the message to the surrounding territory (see 1 Thess. 1:8). No doubt the church kept in mind the fact that Jesus not only visited the population centers but also the hamlets and the countryside.

1. JERUSALEM

We have already considered the church at Jerusalem from the standpoint of the coming of the Spirit and the inception of the Christian movement. We will now proceed to take a closer look at the believing community in terms of its life and activity.

Evangelism

Evangelism is the lifeblood of the church at any place and in any period. Luke's account gives it primary attention. In the background is the Lord's choice and training of the Twelve as well as his commission (Acts 1:8) and the promise of the Spirit. The human agents are Peter and the rest of the apostles (2:14; 3:12; 4:33; 5:42), aided no doubt by the more than one hundred persons who spent ten days with the apostles in an upper room prior to Pentecost (1:15). Probably this company included some, if not all, of the seventy who were sent forth by Jesus to prepare the way for him in connection with his final visit to Jerusalem (Luke 10:1). In addition, the text notes the presence of his family and the faithful women who accompanied him from Galilee (1:14).

The impact of the spoken word was aided by the manifestations of divine power in miracles (3:1; 4:10; 5:12; 6:8). In at least one passage (5:12–14) these beneficent ministries seem to have had an important influence in effecting or aiding conversions. The same could be said of the healing of the cripple (3:1–4:4).

Jerusalem is the one place where the size of the church is indicated by figures. These figures are stated in round numbers and show increase as the narrative unfolds. This was a *growing* church. First we read of three thousand who responded on the Day of Pentecost (2:41). Next we read of five thousand *men* (4:4), although these are not all new converts. The figure represents the sum of male converts at this point in the narrative; when the families of these men are included, we can think of a group of at least 10,000 (cf. the situation described in John 6:10). Beyond this point Luke makes only general statements to the effect that converts were continuing to increase in number (5:14; 6:1, 7). At a much later time James could point to the fact that believing Jews (apparently those in Jerusalem and environs) could be reckoned in terms of myriads (21:20). This is a general and doubtless hyperbolic statement, but it seems to signify a steady growth over the years, despite persecution.

This church was literally born in a day. The ingathering of so many converts at one time must have created a strong sense of assurance among them that they had not been deluded in making their decision to trust in Jesus of Nazareth as Savior. Doubtless there was also a feeling of excitement at being privileged to be part of a mighty spiritual movement at its very beginning, one that was destined to be epochal for the nation Israel and the world.

In making their decision they were reminded by Peter that there was a price to pay—namely, separation from the sinful and unbelieving community around them. They were no longer to share the views and attitudes of the nation's leaders regarding Jesus of Nazareth (2:40).

By their repentance and faith, expressed in submission to baptism, they were able to receive the gift of the Holy Spirit whereby they gained assurance of their salvation and the ability to understand and embrace the teaching of the apostles (2:38, 42).

There seems to be no intimation of any attempt to screen applicants for church membership, nor any indication of disdain for any stratum of society. The example of Jesus in his attitude toward tax gatherers and notorious sinners must have been a factor. At one point (6:7) we read of the acceptance of a large body of priests. They were not rejected on the ground that they belonged to an order whose leaders, the chief priests, had taken an active role in the arrest and execution of Jesus. These were ordinary priests, men who resented the worldliness of their superiors. No information is supplied in the narrative as to the influences that operated to bring them into the church. The healing of the cripple in the temple probably had an effect on them. In addition, they must have observed the followers of the Lord Jesus, since these people frequented the temple courts, especially during the hours of prayer; they could hardly have failed to see the joy written on their faces, a token of their inner peace.

We do not read of evangelistic teams moving out into Judea during these early days of the church's life; nevertheless, the new movement became known by word of mouth so that people came into the city bringing their sick with them for healing (5:16). No doubt there were many conversions under these circumstances. As these folk returned to their homes they became forerunners of those who fanned out into the countryside under the pressure of persecution after Stephen's death (8:1, 4).

The most distinguished resident of Jerusalem to become a brother in Christ was Saul of Tarsus, but he was hand-picked by the risen Lord on Syrian soil (chap. 9) and was not destined to be a worker in the Jerusalem church (22:18–21), though he kept in touch with it during his ministry in other lands.

So far as the record goes, no Sadducee became a convert, which is not surprising in view of this group's rejection of the doctrine of resurrection (Matt. 22:23). The resurrection of Jesus was central to the apostolic proclamation. On the other hand, some Pharisees accepted the gospel, as we learn from Luke's account of the Jerusalem Council (15:5).

Probably the church had many people who can be classified as belonging to the *'Am ha-'aretz* ("people of the land"). They did not belong to any of the various Jewish parties of that period and tended to be despised because they were not students of Mosaic law and did not conscientiously observe the customs.

Thus from the very beginning Christianity was able to demonstrate both its leveling and its elevating power. It was able to unify in the bonds of Christ and the Gospel the most diverse elements in society. In addition, it was able to handle the linguistic barrier presented by the presence of both Aramaic- and Greek-speaking people in the congregation (6:1).

Teaching

In his Great Commission the risen Lord indicated that evangelism, sealed by baptism, was to be followed by a program of teaching (Matt. 28:19–20). This sequence was observed at Pentecost and in subsequent days. In baptizing converts the apostles may have had help from some of the 120, but the teaching ministry fell to them alone (2:42). So far as we know, these men were without teaching experience, although they had sat under the instruction of the master teacher, whose work was now being continued through them (1:1) under the guidance of the Spirit of truth (John 14:25–26).

Prophecy in the sense of revealed knowledge, as distinct from prediction, belongs roughly to the sphere of teaching and has as its goal the edification of those who receive it from the prophets. Peter's quotation from Joel's prophecy prepares the reader of Acts for the introduction of prophets in the life of the early church at Jerusalem (2:17–18), yet the chapters immediately following are silent about such a ministry. Later notices make it evident that this church did indeed have prophets in its membership, however, not only for purposes of prediction (11:27–28; 21:10–11), but for exhortation (15:32). Barnabas seems to be called a prophet as well as a teacher (13:1), and he must have ministered in the Jerusalem church before being sent to Antioch to aid the church there. So, despite Luke's silence in the earlier chapters, it is reasonably certain that the Jerusalem church enjoyed a prophetic ministry capable of being classed as teaching.

The apostles carried on their ministry of teaching both in the temple and from house to house (5:42), and did so on a daily basis. Remarkable indeed is the notice of this full-time nature of their work, indicating both the thirst for learning on the part of the converts and the ample store of information possessed by the apostles. Important here is the promise of the Master that the Spirit would call to their remembrance all that he had taught them (John 14:26). Between preaching in the temple and teaching believers in homes the apostles must have had little time for anything else. Yet it seems virtually certain that in addition they had another instructional task, that of discipling the men, or some of them, who were designated to take charge of the distribution of help to the widows (6:5). Since two of these seven men soon became active in public ministry, namely Stephen and Philip, and had not been under the Lord as far as one can tell, it is probable that these two at least and perhaps others were especially schooled by the apostles and groomed for leadership prior to their selection for service in the temporal affairs of the congregation. Stephen showed a comprehensive grasp of the Old Testament (chap. 7) and Philip was able to use the prophecy of Isaiah effectively in preaching Christ to an inquiring stranger (chap. 8).

Fellowship

The term *koinōnia* ("fellowship") appears in Acts 2:42 along with teaching. However, the order of words makes it reasonably clear that the reference is not to the apostles' fellowship as something that was now opened up to the new converts. Nor is it a synonym for the church. Rather, it seems to denote the common life shared by believers. In keeping with this, the verb that is used here ("they devoted themselves") suggests participation in an active way rather than merely a feeling of oneness. C. Anderson Scott writes, "If, as seems probable, the group of followers whom Jesus gathered most closely round Himself, took or had given to it some distinguishing name, that name would naturally be 'the *Chabūra* of Jesus'; and the name *koinōnia* or Fellowship under which it first presents itself in the Acts is simply the Greek for *Chabūra*."[1]

Fellowship in this biblical, apostolic sense implies being together frequently with other believers, and this is clearly stated (2:46). Faith in the living Lord drew people together, eager to learn and to grow. Homes were made available, including that of John Mark's mother (12:12). The church in the house was a great boon. The people who gathered in this way had the promise of the Master that where two or three were gathered in his name, there he would be in the midst of them (Matt. 18:20). It is possible that in each such home group there were people who could pass on to the others many recollections of the Savior due to personal contact with him. These memories were still green and they meant much to those who had not been his followers. One can envision Mary and her children visiting such gatherings and giving their recollections of the boy Jesus and then of the great change that came over them when the resurrection confirmed all his claims that had seemed so visionary at the time. Others who must have taken an active part in these gatherings were Lazarus and his sisters, Nicodemus, Joseph of Arimathea, and the two Emmaus disciples. Nor should we forget also the owner of the house with the upper room. What a thrill awaited those who came to his quarters to meet with others in the very place where the Lord had instituted his memorial feast with the disciples.

Community of Goods

The fact that the believers held their property in common is mentioned after the allusion to the fellowship (2:44) so as to make it clear that the *koinōnia* of verse 42 is not the same as the sharing in material things. It is tempting to try to find a precedent for this feature in the practice of the Qumran community, but the practices are not equivalent: in the Dead Sea community the sharing of possessions was obligatory, whereas in the Jerusalem church it was voluntary.

The explanation for the emergence of this practice seems to be twofold. For one thing, the teaching of Jesus furnished a powerful motivation for it. Not only did he teach that one should not be anxious about material things (Matt. 6:25, 28) but he also made it plain that one should be prepared to part with one's possessions for the sake of the needy (Luke 12:33; 18:22). The one who had left the glory of heaven and then the security of the carpenter shop called on his followers to leave all and follow him (Luke 14:33). He was content to subsist on what was given to him and his followers for their daily sustenance (Luke 8:1–3). The likelihood is that the women who shared with him were now residing in the Jerusalem area. If so, their presence must have been an inspiration to other believers, leading them to give generously to meet the needs of the poorer brethren. The other factor that helped to develop the practice of sharing was the familiarity these people had with almsgiving as a part of their experience in Judaism. Jeremias notes that there was a weekly dole to the poor of Jerusalem consisting of food and clothing as well as a daily distribution of food.[2]

However, even the double precedent furnished by Jesus and by Judaism might not have sufficed by way of example had it not been for the dynamism of the new life in Christ fostered by the indwelling Spirit. The joy of salvation yoked to love for the brethren brought an outpouring of gifts sufficient to meet the need. Some, like Barnabas (4:37), sold their property and gave the proceeds to the common fund.

As time passed, the resources of the local church were unable to cope with the situation. When a famine compounded the problem, the church at Antioch graciously sent relief (11:28–30). Later, under the sponsorship and superintendence of Paul, the Gentile churches that he and his companions had founded sent a substantial contribution to the Jerusalem saints (Rom. 15:25–27). James the brother of our Lord and head of the Jerusalem church had a great concern for the poor who were under his care (Gal. 2:10), and beyond this his church reached out to embrace Jewish Christians dispersed in other lands (James 1:27; 2:5, 15–16). Possibly the trip of Paul to Jerusalem reported in Acts 18:22 was for the purpose of discussing with James and the elders the acceptability of his plan to raise among the Gentile churches the fund of which he writes in some of his letters (1 Cor. 16:2–4; 2 Cor. 8–9; Rom. 15:25–28). The acuteness of the need of the Jerusalem church is attested by the fact that even as early as the sending of famine relief by the Antioch church there is no mention of the Seven as receiving and distributing the contribution. It was accepted by the elders (11:30). Apparently the regular distribution referred to in the early days of the church had to be discontinued.

According to some scholars the generosity of the saints in the Jerusalem church toward their poor was heightened by their confidence that the Lord would soon return, in which case they would have no use for their possessions anyway. This may have been a factor, but it was certainly not the principal motivation.

The burden of distribution fell on the apostles at the beginning (4:37; 5:2). This, in addition to their preaching and teaching, largely accounts for a certain amount of neglect of the poor, particularly of widows in the Greek-speaking portion of the church (6:1). Conscious that they were unequal to the total responsibility, the apostles called for the selection of qualified men who would assume the oversight of the distribution, thus freeing themselves for prayer and the ministry of the word. Some students are prepared to see here a definite cleavage between the Hebraists and the Hellenists, with a virtual separation of the two groups. This goes beyond the evidence. The apostles had been trying to provide for the whole church in the daily distribution. Now the Seven, mostly if not altogether Hellenists, took over the task of caring for the needy, not simply for the Greek-speaking people but for all the needy in the church.

The Temple

Several allusions to the temple are scattered over the first few chapters of Acts, indicating that this sacred place continued to be used by believers both for worship (2:46; 3:1) and for testimony in its spacious courts (3:11ff.; 5:21). No doubt the brethren were encouraged to use the temple because Jesus had taught there and had purged its outer court of commercialism despite his awareness that thereby he would bring upon himself the wrath of the Jewish leaders. Furthermore, the apostles had easier access to crowds of people at that spot than anywhere in the city.

The apostles and their helpers probably pursued this course of action with mixed feelings. They knew that Jesus regarded it as his Father's house but they knew also that he had predicted its destruction (Mark 13:2). The latter consideration may have acted as a spur, causing them to conclude that they should make use of these precincts while they were available.

Before long the temple itself became an issue between the church and the Jewish authorities, coming to a head during the public ministry of Stephen. He was accustomed to debate with Greek-speaking Jews in the synagogue and it soon became evident that his views on the temple were a great affront not only to these opponents in debate but also to the Aramaic-speaking Jews and their representatives in the Sanhedrin. It is probable that he understood more clearly than the other leaders in the church what the Lord's attitude toward the temple involved.

Jesus and his mission represented something greater than the temple (Matt. 12:6). He was the divinely ordained focus of worship directed through him to the Father (John 4:23). His bodily resurrection signaled the fact that he was replacing the earthly sanctuary as the means of approach to God (John 2:19-21). By virtue of being joined to Christ the church becomes a spiritual house and its members priests unto God (1 Pet. 2:4-5). In clinging to its cherished temple as the way to God, Judaism was rejecting God's provision in his Son. It would be going too far, however, to claim that in Acts 7:47-50 Stephen was arguing that Solomon had erred in constructing the first temple; he was merely suggesting that when the Jews clung to the temple as the way to God in preference to the revelation in his Son their attachment became a sin.

It is possible that the apostles were not prepared to go as far as Stephen regarding the temple question. The fact that they were able to stay in the city even after persecution broke out following Stephen's martyrdom (8:1) may suggest that they were not identified with Stephen's position regarding the temple, at least in a public way. Possibly their hesitation, if that is the proper term to use, was due to their fear that an open break with Jewry over the temple issue would virtually close the door to further opportunities to bear witness to their nation. They seem to have been willing to treasure their knowledge of the new temple in Christ as their spiritual heritage without flaunting it before their countrymen. As it turned out, their ministry was less acceptable to the Jewish people after the Stephen episode. Though they were able to remain in the city, they did not enjoy the same favor with the populace that was previously accorded them.

The fact that Stephen's associates led the way in taking the gospel directly to the Gentiles (11:20) must have made the situation of the Jerusalem church more difficult. A movement sponsored by Jews that did not honor the medium of proselytism as practiced by Judaism could only provoke resentment. The virtual elimination of the hellenistic element in the Jerusalem congregation, especially by the zeal of Saul, helps one to understand the rather detached attitude taken toward him when he came to Jerusalem for the last time (21:18ff.).

2. ANTIOCH

Seleucus, one of the generals of Alexander the Great, founded Antioch in 300 B.C., naming it after his father Antiochus (or possibly his son of the same name). The site, strategic both militarily and commercially, provided access to Asia Minor on the north and west as well as to Palestine and Egypt on the south and southwest. In addition, it was on the most important trade route between the East and the West. The region around it was well watered. Lying along the Orontes river, it had ready access to the sea by way of Seleucia, its port city a few miles downstream (see Acts 13:4). The geographer Strabo noted that "Antiocheia is . . . a Tetrapolis, since it consists of four parts; and each of the four settlements is fortified both by a common wall and by a wall of its own." The famous grove known as Daphne, a few miles away, contained a temple of Apollo and was a magnet for pleasure seekers, rivaling Corinth in this respect. Like Corinth, Antioch failed to develop into an intellectual center. The temper of its citizens was a combination of lightheartedness and buffoonery.

In size and importance Antioch during the first Christian century yielded the palm only to Rome and Alexandria. Its population during this period may have reached the half-million mark. Here Greeks and Orientals lived side by side, joined later by the Romans. Jews were well represented also. Josephus writes,

The Jewish race, densely interspersed among the native populations of every portion of the world, is particularly numerous in Syria, where intermingling is due to the proximity of the two countries. But it was at Antioch that they specially congregated, partly owing to the greatness of that city, but mainly because the successors of King Antiochus had enabled them to live there in security.[3]

He goes on to state that in the second century B.C. the successors of Antiochus Epiphanes granted to the Jews the right of citizenship on an equal basis with the Greeks. He affirms also such a strong influence by the Jews on the pagan population that great numbers of them, attracted by the Jewish religious ceremonies, were "in some measure incorporated with themselves." This seems to suggest that these people became God-fearers. As a result of the war between the Jews and the Romans (A.D. 66–70) the Jews were in mortal danger at Antioch and some lost their lives by mob action. However, Titus befriended them, decreeing that their status should remain the same as before the war.

The Founding of the Church

As early in his account as Acts 6:7 Luke drops a hint regarding things to come when he identifies Nicolas, one of the Seven in the Jerusalem church, as being from Antioch and a convert to Judaism. Originally a Gentile, he had apparently been won over to the Jewish faith in his native city and had subsequently moved to Jerusalem. At this point, it seems Luke is telling his readers that Antioch is going to play an important role in the progress of the gospel (see 6:58; 8:3 for the historian's methodology of anticipating events by introducing persons who have some relation to later developments). The outbreak of persecution at the time of Stephen's death figured largely in the spread of the faith to areas outside Palestine. Persecution is often a blessing in disguise. Some Hellenists who made their way along the Phoenician coast, preaching to Jews as they went, came at length to Antioch. Whether Nicolas was a member of this company or not remains uncertain, since Luke does not name any of the persons involved. At first the new arrivals witnessed to Jews only, as they had been doing, but some of them were constrained to proclaim the word to Greeks also (11:20). These became the predominant element in the church.

Since Luke does not trace any further travels on the part of these Hellenists, the presumption is that they remained in the city, at least for some time. In the plan of God others were to build up the congregation until it would in turn become a leading source of fresh missionary advance. Even so, the original witnesses continued to have a place in the leadership (see 11:20; 13:1).

It is important to notice the point at which Luke introduces his account of the establishing of the Antioch congregation—namely, immediately after the experience of Peter at Caesarea and the report he gave of the matter

to the Jerusalem church. There is no sure way to establish the chronological relationship between the events at Caesarea and Antioch, but the order
of narration is suggestive. Gentiles are becoming more prominent, whereas
the Caesarea incident was an innovation (see 11:18).

The Jerusalem church was obliged to come to terms with the new
Gentile surge. It showed its interest by sending Barnabas to investigate the
situation at Antioch (11:22). This was a good choice, for a native of Cyprus
(4:36) would have been more familiar with Antioch than most of the
brethren. That he was pleased with what he found there is apparent, for
instead of returning to Jerusalem to report he continued in the northern
city, identifying himself with the church and ministering to its people with
notable success (11:23–24). His only return trips to Jerusalem were as a
representative of the Antioch congregation (11:30; 15:2).

It is a virtual certainty that Peter's experience at Caesarea, once it was
approved by the leaders at Jerusalem (11:18), prepared the mother church
to accept the developments at Antioch. No criticism seems to have been
voiced, although later on a faction within the church became unhappy
because Gentiles were received without circumcision (15:1, 24). Peter himself visited the church at Antioch (Gal. 2:11), apparently after the Jerusalem
Council (reported in chapter 15). His visit may testify to his hunger to
witness again the work of grace in a Gentile setting such as he had seen in
Caesarea.

Luke may have been a resident of Antioch and a member of the
congregation, for Codex Bezae (D) has a statement that the prophecy of
Agabus was uttered "when we were gathered together" (11:28). If this is a
sound tradition (Eusebius supports it) then we can assume that Luke knew
this church firsthand and must have had a special interest in presenting its
contribution to the development of the church universal.

The Growth of the Church

This is attested by the fact that before long, apparently shortly after Barnabas came to share in the work, "a great number of people were brought to
the Lord" (11:24). That this is no exaggeration is indicated by the fact that
Barnabas had to seek out help, taking the time and trouble to go to Tarsus
in search of Saul. Several years earlier he had shown appreciation for him
and for his service at Damascus following his conversion (9:27). Whether
he had kept in touch with him since his departure from Jerusalem to
Tarsus is not known, but Luke's statement that Barnabas went to Tarsus "to
look for Saul" hints that he had not. Evidently Saul was impressed with the
need and the opportunity at Antioch and was willing to change his sphere
of labor. The two men had a fruitful ministry for a year in teaching the
converts, who by this time could be described as constituting "great numbers of people" (11:26).

We ought not to suppose that this was Saul's first experience of ministering to Gentiles. Years before this the Lord had made clear to him that he was being sent far from Jerusalem to the Gentiles (Acts 22:21). At this point he went directly to Tarsus. At the close of the Jerusalem Council that body authorized the sending of a letter to "the Gentile believers in Antioch, Syria, and Cilicia" explaining the decision of the conclave. Under what circumstances were Syria and Cilicia evangelized? The most likely answer is by the labors of Saul of Tarsus the apostle to the Gentiles during a period of approximately a decade. It is reasonably certain that during this time he ministered in synagogues, where he contacted both Jews and God-fearers. The evidence for this is contained in a passage describing his sufferings (2 Cor. 11:24ff.), which included five instances in which he was beaten by the Jews. Luke is silent about these events in reporting the experiences of the apostle during his missionary journeys emanating from Antioch, so they must have occurred during the decade of witness in northern Syria and Cilicia. Saul, then, was well prepared to labor in the Antioch situation.

One wonders if he and Barnabas carried the total responsibility of leadership in the ministry there at this juncture. Other teachers and prophets are mentioned before long (13:1), but possibly their gifts had not become evident at the time Barnabas enlisted the help of Saul.

No mention is made of contact with the synagogues of the city, but this is implied in Luke's statement that at first the Hellenists brought the message only to Jews (11:19). However, the gospel had its larger response among the Gentiles, as is intimated by the fact that the issue of requiring circumcision for Gentile converts was not raised here as it was in the Jerusalem church.

Luke says nothing about the meeting places of the believers. It is likely that several groups met in homes throughout the city, though we should not rule out the possibility that some public meetings for evangelistic purposes were held in halls.

Features of the Antioch Church

1. It was in Antioch that believers were first called "Christians." There is no hint that the name was given by revelation from the Lord. The word *Christ*, from which *Christian* is derived, does not appear at all in this paragraph of the text (11:19–26). Clearly this label could not have originated with the Jews, for they refused to acknowledge that Jesus was their Messiah (the Hebrew equivalent of Christ). Furthermore, they had a different term than *Christian* for Jewish disciples of Jesus. They called them "the sect of the Nazarenes" (24:5).

It is widely held that the origin of the term *Christian* should be sought in the fun-loving, ridicule-prone Gentile population of the city. They needed a tag of identification for this group in their midst, and since they heard them speaking of the Christ they made this term the basis of the epithet they chose. The word *called* that appears here (11:26) is not the ordinary term for giving a name such as is used in Matthew 1:21 in connection with Jesus, but a term that designates a person with respect to business or special interest (see, for example, Rom. 7:3). The other appearances of the term *Christian* in the New Testament (Acts 26:28; 1 Pet. 4:16) tend to support the position that the name had a non-Christian origin and was intended to convey a measure of reproach.

2. The title *Lord* is prominent in Luke's account, appearing five times (11:20–24), apparently as a designation for Christ (13:2 may be a reference to God). W. Bousset has investigated Paul's use of this title in his letters and its connotations in the context of the Antioch church.[4] In his judgment the Jerusalem church did not think of Jesus in these terms, but rather as the Son of Man who was expected to return in glory. But at Antioch, mystery religions made use of the Greek term *Kyrios* for the deity honored in the cultus, and Bousset postulates that early Christianity adopted the title and applied it to Jesus, thereby promoting a mystical element that made religion more personally satisfying as the Spirit mediated the Lord Jesus to the believing heart.

This reconstruction, however widely heralded, has weaknesses. It is obliged to make light of the close ties between the Jerusalem church and the Antioch church. It also ignores the biblical evidence contained in Acts 2:36 and Galatians 1:19, as well as the use of *Maranatha* (1 Cor. 16:22), an Aramaic term that can mean "Our Lord, come" or "Our Lord comes." This term must have originated in the Palestinian church and then become a part of the cultic terminology of Gentile churches.

3. The church at Antioch was probably the first to realize and express the actual unity of Jew and Gentile in one group (see Eph. 2:11–22, which may well reflect Paul's experience in Antioch). Luke's report is confirmed by the testimony of Paul, who indicates that at Antioch Jews and Gentiles sat down together at their meals (Gal. 2:11–14). This was an innovation (Acts 11:2–3). This table fellowship at Antioch was disrupted only when people from the Jerusalem church arrived and let their disapproval be known. This unity between the two groups meant that when Paul and Barnabas were called on to fight the battle for Gentile freedom from the law, a freedom that gave the Gentile believer an equal place with the Jewish believer in the body of Christ, they could point to the workability of this principle. It had proved itself in the Antioch church under the blessing of God (Gal. 2:12).

4. Luke's account emphasizes the large place teaching assumed in the life of the church. It was for the purpose of having help in this area that Barnabas went to find Saul (11:25–26). Gentiles needed more guidance than Jews because of their ignorance of the Old Testament and because their environment did not provide them with adequate ethical and moral standards. As one reads the so-called practical portions of Paul's letters to

his young churches, it is possible to conclude fairly accurately that much of the teaching had already been forged in the Antioch setting.

5. The church was blessed with a wealth of diversified ministry. Several prophets and teachers are noted by name (13:1). If we grant that the raising up of these gifted individuals was for the purpose of stimulating the rank and file of the congregation to take up their own ministry (as laid down in Eph. 4:12), we can conclude that a very large company of people received encouragement to witness and serve in accordance with the gifts for ministry they had received.

6. Whereas this church had the same pattern as the church in Jerusalem in matters of preaching, teaching, and giving, the third element took a somewhat different turn here. In Jerusalem the beneficence of the congregation had its own poor in view, whereas there is no mention of the poor in the Antioch situation. It was a prosperous city, and this prosperity seems to have been reflected to some extent in the constituency of the church. Luke says that each gave according to his ability (11:29). When prediction was made of an impending famine, there was a generous outpouring of assistance for the mother church in Jerusalem to alleviate additional problems in the already burdened congregation (11:27–30). It would be a mistake to suppose that this gift involved no sacrifice, for shortage of crops was felt in Syria as well as Judea.[5]

7. The Antioch church was a missionary church par excellence. An overview of the apostolic age enables one to sense a divine providence in the creation of a strong Christian community at Antioch just at this time. As the Jerusalem church for various reasons became less and less significant for the evangelization of the Greco-Roman world (we have already noted its lack of zeal as a group for evangelizing Gentiles), its sister church in this leading center of the hellenistic world was ready to step forward and sponsor a great missionary outreach, becoming thereby the catalyst for the tremendous growth of the Gentile congregations in Asia Minor and Greece (including Macedonia).

Antioch differed from Jerusalem, which became missionary largely as a result of persecution. Antioch was a missionary church in the twofold sense that is was founded by missionaries and in turn became a missionary base for sending out the gospel to regions beyond. So far as is known, it was the first church to undertake the fulfilling of the last portion of Christ's commission to be witnesses to the ends of the earth (1:8). The decision of the Jerusalem Council concerning the reception of Gentiles gave fresh impetus to this missionary outreach. It is to the credit of the believers at Antioch that when the Spirit called for its leading men to go forth as its representatives, there was no hesitation but rather complete obedience. The whole incident was marked by deep earnestness, attested by fasting and prayer (13:2–3).

8. The continuing relationship between Paul and the Antioch church

may have become somewhat clouded by the confrontation he had with Peter (Gal. 2:11ff.), especially since Barnabas sided with Peter and may therefore have been censured by Paul. It is sad to have a rupture of this sort that mars fellowship, but Paul was clear in his own mind that Peter's actions endangered future relations between Jews and Gentiles in the church. Some scholars maintain that this episode marked the end of satisfactory relations between Paul and the Antioch congregation, but this may be reading too much into the incident. Prior to settling down at Ephesus for an extended ministry Paul visited the Jerusalem church and on the way back to Ephesus stopped for "some time" at Antioch (18:22–23). This suggests that he still had a good relationship with the church.

9. It is probable that the pattern of self-help followed by Barnabas and Paul in later days (1 Cor. 9:6) was developed during the period when these men labored together in the Antioch church. If so, the example probably stimulated believers to do all they could for themselves and their dependents rather than look to the brethren for help. This would mean that more assistance would have been made available to answer the cry of need in other places. One would like to know just what was involved in the statement that the church sent the two missionaries off on their journey (13:3). Was this sending a matter of prayer and good wishes or did it also involve the taking up of an offering for their travel needs? The latter is probable, but beyond such provision the two men could be trusted to support themselves (see 1 Cor. 4:12).

Relations with the Jerusalem Church

Since the founders of the mission to Antioch had been associated with the mother church, it was natural for the latter group to keep in touch with it in various ways. It was, in fact, "a sort of colony of Jerusalem."[6] Barnabas came next, then a group of prophets headed by Agabus (11:27), followed by Judas and Silas (15:22), Peter (Gal. 2:11), the men who came from James (Gal. 2:12), and John Mark (15:37). Others came (15:1), but it is doubtful that they were deputed by the church; they seem to have come on their own responsibility (15:24).

The two churches were alike in that they experienced the ministry of the Holy Spirit as the one who honored the preaching that centered in the Lord Jesus, blessed the teaching of the word by illuminating it for the hearers, granted gifts for ministry, and summoned the church to obedience to its mission as a sending body. It is apparent, too, that both groups magnified prayer.

On the other hand, certain differences emerge. Whereas the Jerusalem believers saw the power of God released in terms of miracles and signs, nothing of this nature is reported in the Antioch setting, although this does not of itself prove that miracles did not occur. Nothing is said of fasting in the Jerusalem setting, whereas it is rather prominent at one juncture in the life of the Antioch church (13:3). This remained a feature of Paul's life on occasion (14:23; 27:9). Whereas the mother church was called on to face severe persecution resulting in missionary outreach, the Antioch church undertook its missionary role out of a deep sense of obligation, wrought by the Spirit, to reach the pagan world with the gospel. Moreover, its interest was sustained over the years, no doubt because of continued prayer and contact with its missionaries, who were able to report victories for the gospel that prompted great rejoicing.

3. PHILIPPI

Named for Philip, the father of Alexander the Great, Philippi was about ten miles inland from the Aegean Sea. First settled in the fourth century B.C., its prominence dates from the time of Philip, who worked the gold mines in the vicinity in order to build up his army. With these forces he was able to subdue the cities of Greece. Later, Alexander took the troops into Asia for an extensive campaign of subjugation. Philippi was on the Egnatian Road, the military highway constructed by the Romans across Macedonia for a distance of nearly four hundred miles. A crucial battle near the city in 42 B.C. brought Brutus and Cassius on the one side (the conspirators who assassinated Julius Caesar) up against Octavian and Antony on the other, with the result that the Roman republic came to an end and was replaced by the empire with Octavian (Augustus Caesar) as its first head.

Luke makes two statements about the city. He calls it the leading city of the district of Macedonia and a Roman colony (16:12). Amphipolis was actually the administrative center of this area, so Luke must be referring to Philippi's reputation, its outstanding importance. Since, as we shall see, he became a resident of the place, his evaluation probably reflects his feeling of pride. His observation that Philippi was a Roman colony is of interest because there were other places visited by Paul that had this status (e.g., Pisidian Antioch), but Luke does not state the fact except in the case of Philippi.

The population of the city was largely Roman at this time. Octavian settled many of his veterans there after the battle of Philippi. Luke refers to the rulers of the city as *stratēgoi*, which usually means "generals," but the word occurs elsewhere as a popular designation for *praetors*, the official Latin term. Luke's account makes it evident that the inhabitants were fond of citing the Roman character of the community, especially in contrast to Jewish intrusion (16:20-21).

H. J. Cadbury has noted that "of all the environments which encircle the book of Acts the most universal though in some ways the most superficial is the Roman."[7] The Roman atmosphere comes out most decidedly in the report of the mission to Philippi.

The Founding of the Church

On the second missionary journey Paul and his companions were somewhat frustrated because after revisiting the churches that had been established on the first journey, they found no field of work that was open to them. Apparently Paul wished to push on to Ephesus but felt divine restraint (16:6). A similar obstacle beset the desire to set out for Bithynia to the north (16:7). Turning westward, the party came down to the coast at Troas and waited for guidance. This came in the form of a vision. A man of Macedonia appeared and appealed to Paul, "Come over to Macedonia and help us" (16:9). It is unlikely that this vision was intended to convey to Paul the impression that there were believers in Macedonia who needed his help in their task of witnessing to the unsaved. He found it to be virgin territory for the gospel. After being checkmated in attempts to reach the province of Asia and then of Bithynia, Paul must have felt assured that God was now giving the needed positive guidance.

This venturing onto European soil was a new departure, even though it lay nearby. There is something fascinating for the Christian historian in this situation, and Luke may well have felt it also. Centuries before, Alexander the Great had moved from Macedonia across the Hellespon into Asia Minor and had inaugurated a wide-ranging military thrust into Asia and a bit of Africa (Egypt) bent on bringing Hellenism to the Levant. Now a redeemed Jew in the service of the Lord Jesus, unarmed and with a tiny retinue, makes the reverse journey into Europe to conquer it for Christ. In the long run this unpretentious invasion was to be more influential in world history than Alexander's conquest. Paul may have sensed the potential of this new venture. Philippi would be a testing ground for the gospel in Europe. This important juncture in the apostle's life, marked by special guidance, recalls an earlier time in Jerusalem when he was seeking to minister to that city, only to be deterred by an appearance of the Lord with the information that he was to go far away to the Gentiles (22:17–18).

The language of Acts 16:10 is important, for it indicates that Luke was now a member of the missionary team (*"we* got ready at once to leave for Macedonia"). No hint is given of the background for Luke's joining the group. Perhaps Paul needed medical help (cf. an earlier situation cited in Gal. 4:13). Ramsay's idea that the man of Macedonia was Luke and that he joined the others in Troas is intriguing but not compelling.[8]

The sea journey to Neapolis seems to have taken two days, in contrast to a later one in the opposite direction that required five (20:6). This was likely taken as a propitious token. No attempt was made to evangelize Neapolis. From the start Philippi was apparently set as the first objective. The journey from the seaport required less than a day.

It appears that several days were spent in getting adjusted to the surroundings (16:12). Resting, planning, and praying were in order. Learning that there was a place of prayer by the river outside the city, they waited till the Sabbath and joined the worshipers there. Though the word *proseuchē* can be used for synagogue, it is not likely that this meaning was intended here, for the gospel team found only a company of women when they reached the spot. If it had been a synagogue, some men would surely have been present: Jewish law required a minimum of ten men in order to have a synagogue in a given area.

One of the women present that day was Lydia (16:14). She had the name of the region from which she had come, and the city of her residence was Thyatira. She was a God-fearer, a status that is probably related to those earlier days, since Philippi had no synagogue. Her prominence in the story suggests that she may have had a leading part in the establishing of the place of prayer outside the city. One can conjecture further that her success as a businesswoman ("a dealer in purple cloth") enabled her to have a considerable share in the erection of the *proseuchē* or at least in its upkeep. Her success is attested by the fact that she had a household (16:15) consisting of several persons, whether children (in which case she was a widow), or staff people who were helpers in the business, or both. Members of her household followed her in the decision to receive Christ (16:14–15) and thus the Philippian church was born. Paul and his group continued to visit the place of prayer (16:16), having in the meantime been taken as guests into Lydia's house (16:15). This quiet beginning did not last, for the Christian witness was about to get wide public notice that brought opposition but also additional converts.

The Exorcism and Its Consequences

On their way to the *proseuchē* the little group was intercepted by a slave girl who had a spirit that enabled her to foretell (16:16). People were glad to pay money to her owners in order to learn what was going to happen to them. Her statement about the missionaries and their message (v.17) was true enough (cf. the testimony of demon-possessed people to Jesus, as in Mark 1:24) but unwelcome, the more so since it continued for several days. Eventually Paul felt it necessary to deal with the situation by invoking the name of Jesus Christ and commanding the spirit to depart from the girl.

As at Ephesus later on (19:23ff.), the loss of revenue provoked hostile action by the owners of the girl. In both situations the leverage for persecution was not personal financial loss, which would hardly excite much sympathy, but rather an appeal to local pride and the status of the city as a Roman municipality. Knowing that Jews were not particularly welcome in the community, the owners were quick to note that the new arrivals were Jews. It is not clear how they could expect to support their claim that the visitors were disturbing the peace (beyond the episode of the exorcism) or advocating customs unlawful for Romans to accept. Probably they hoped that their outcries would have such an effect that it would not be necessary to prove their allegations. They quickly gained the support of the populace and of the magistrates (16:22), with the result that the missionaries were beaten on the spot with rods (see 2 Cor. 11:25).

Two things deserve special notice here. One is the appeal to anti-Semitic prejudice that apparently touched a responsive chord in Philippi. It may be possible to explain this as partly induced by the action of Claudius about this time to banish Jews from Rome (18:2). The second item is the failure of Paul and Silas to declare their Roman citizenship at this point in the story. Ramsay may have been right in suggesting that to have done so would have availed nothing, since the people and the officials were in no mood to heed them, stirred as they were by the inflammatory charges raised against the visitors. Ramsay also grants that an attempt may have been made to assert Roman citizenship but it could not be heard amid the clamor of the mob.[9]

It is not necessary to follow the remaining events of the stay in Philippi, but it should be noted that even in the time of incarceration the servants of God continued to bear a witness by their joy at being privileged to suffer for Christ's sake (16:25). The timing of the earthquake would not escape the notice of their fellow prisoners, coming as it did in apparent response to the singing of Paul and Silas. Luke does not indicate that any of these responded in faith, since he concentrates on the jailer and his family. The question, "What must I do to be saved?" presupposes at the very least that this man had heard of the demon-possessed girl, and it may imply that he had heard God's servants preach in the city. Having received the Lord, where would the jailer and his family go for Christian instruction and fellowship? It is quite possible that most of the women at the *proseuche* rejected the gospel and continued their loyalty to Judaism. In such a case it is almost certain that Lydia opened her home as a meeting place for believers. It had the advantage of being more conveniently located than the place of prayer outside the city.

Paul's insistence that he would not leave Philippi at the request of the police, demanding instead that the magistrates come in person with an apology for beating Roman citizens (which was against the law) was not to show his pique but was done for the sake of believers. He wanted to insure that the authorities would not treat them in an unlawful or highhanded manner after his departure.

Following a brief time of refreshment at the home of Lydia, the missionaries said their farewells and left the city. At this point the use of "we" in the narrative is discontinued, suggesting that Luke remained. Doubtless he assumed a measure of leadership in the Christian group. It is just possible that he is the one referred to by Paul as "the brother who is praised by all the churches for his service to the gospel" (2 Cor. 8:17). He probably wrote this from Philippi in connection with a later visit to the city (20:1; cf. 2 Cor. 2:12-13). Luke was evidently more than a physician and a man of letters. Probably his modesty kept him from detailing his contribution to the development of the Christian community at Philippi.

The Church as Reflected in Paul's Letter

1. It is possible that when Paul asserted "But our citizenship is in heaven" (3:20) he was thinking by way of contrast that Philippi as a political entity, a colony of Rome, was preoccupied with earthly things. Believers who lived in Philippi had a heavenly home and even then were living under its constitution (cf. 1:27, in which the same root word used in 3:20 denotes one's manner of life). Roman affiliation comes to the surface also in 4:22, in which Paul sends the greetings of Christians in Rome who belonged to Caesar's household.

2. Opposition to the gospel and its emissaries, given prominence in Luke's account of the founding of the church, is hinted at in the letter as a continuing phenomenon (1:27–30).

3. Paul is grateful for the church's partnership with him in the extension of the gospel from the time of his initial visit (1:5). This recalls the kindness of Lydia (Acts 16:15, 40) and the gifts sent to him in the days that followed (4:16). The most recent gift, to which the letter is a thankful response, is treated first of all as a token of the desire of the church to support gospel proclamation through the apostle (1:5). Only later is it treated as something to be personally used (4:10ff.). This revived concern (4:10) recalls to the mind of God's servant their original kindness (Acts 16:15, 33).

4. The prominence of women in the church, so evident in Luke's account (Acts 16:13ff.) and elsewhere in Macedonia (17:4, 12) is also apparent in Phil. 4:2–3.

5. The appeal to honor Paul's authority is coupled with a reminder that it was accepted when he was with his readers in person (2:12).

6. Paul recalls how he was an example to the Philippian believers. That example is still relevant and calls for emulation (4:9).

7. The apostle makes reference to Timothy's proven worth as evidenced by his valuable service as a coworker when the church was founded. Timothy's contribution was known to the congregation, though Luke does not mention it in his account which deals only with the highlights (see 2:22).

8. An appeal to someone in Philippi to give help to two women so that they will be reconciled may be intended to refer to Luke (4:3), who, as noted above, apparently remained in the city to shepherd the Christian group. Some have taken *yokefellow* as a proper name (Syzygus), but this seems unnatural when prefixed by the word *loyal*.

In addition to these allusions to the Philippian church in Acts, there are references to Paul himself that he may have included in his letter to the church because of some connection with his experience in Philippi.

His reference to the prison in Rome, from which he writes (Phil. 1:7, 17) may have been meant to serve as a reminder to his readers of his detention in the Philippian jail. His allusion to the praetorian guard (1:13) would have special meaning for his readers, since Philippi was settled largely by retired army personnel. As he had been delivered from prison, a fact known to believers at Philippi, he hopes for a similar divine intervention on his behalf, though not in the same manner (1:19, 26). As he was able to have a witness in the Philippian jail, so in his Roman situation he is letting those who guard him know that he is a servant of Christ the Savior (1:13). Further, the note of joy that resounds in the letter as Paul's response to the Lord and as his encouragement to his readers is in full agreement with the praise that ascended from his lips the night he was jailed in Philippi.

It is widely recognized that the Philippian church held a special place in the heart of the apostle. "I thank my God every time I remember you" (Phil. 1:3). They were bound together by a common experience of suffering for Christ's sake and of joy that such suffering brings. As a group they were not wealthy, yet they gave liberally (2 Cor. 8:2), and this touched the heart of Paul, a man whose life was continually poured out in sacrificial service.

4. THESSALONICA

Originally known as Therme (due to its hot springs), Thessalonica was located at the northern end of the Thermaic Gulf. In 315 B.C. Cassander, one of Alexander's generals, undertook to reestablish the city, giving it the name Thessalonica after his wife, who was Alexander's half sister. The modern name is Salonika. In connection with the battle of Philippi, the city favored the cause of Octavian and Antony and was rewarded when they were victorious, being made a free city (which meant that it had its own local officials and was not required to accept a Roman garrison). It was strongly fortified with walls extending for six miles around the city, interspersed by towers. The famous Roman military road, the Egnatian Way, bisected the community.

Though Luke apparently remained at Philippi, he knew the situation at Thessalonica well. From him we learn how the city government was constituted. There was a popular assembly ("the people" of Acts 17:5) and the city authorities, known as *politarchs* (17:6), a group of five or six men who formed the city council.

Thessalonica was basically a commercial city. Around it on the north side lay a fertile valley of considerable extent. To the south stretched the waters of the Aegean Sea offering transport to points near and far. Its population approached the 200,000 figure, presenting a challenge to the heralds of the gospel.

Due to the size and situation of the city, it is not surprising that it contained a fairly large community of Jews. This is substantiated by mention of the synagogue (17:1) and by the fact that Jewish-inspired agitation against Paul and his companions was taken seriously by the authorities.

The Founding of the Church

Journeying from Philippi, the missionary party probably made overnight stops at Amphipolis and Apollonia but apparently attempted no witness in these places (see 16:11). Clearly their objective was Thessalonica. According to custom, Paul used the synagogue as the base of operations (17:2), ministering there on three Sabbaths—or perhaps, as the RSV has it, for three weeks, a rendering that implies the synagogue was utilized on a daily basis. We know that similar ministry took place on a daily basis at Berea (17:11) and at Ephesus (19:9), although in the latter place the scene was a public hall rather than the synagogue.

Uncertainty exists as to whether the missionaries stayed in the city longer than three weeks. Lightfoot argues for a more extensive ministry, in which case it must have been carried on apart from the synagogue because of growing Jewish opposition. He advanced the following reasons: (1) the large number of Gentile converts; (2) Paul's resort to manual labor both day and night, as though he had settled in for a longer stay than three weeks (1 Thess. 2:9); and (3) the contributions from the Philippian church, made more than once, while he was at Thessalonica (Phil. 4:16).[10] In his letters to the Thessalonian church the apostle says nothing to indicate the length of his stay, so the problem remains unresolved. It does seem likely that there was a period of ministry apart from the synagogue, but it need not be thought of as lasting for long, since effective opposition developed rather quickly.

As to the method used in the synagogue presentation, it is evident from the terms employed to describe it that there was lively participation. Discussion and even disputation took place as Paul opened the Scriptures that called for the death and resurrection of the (promised) Christ. Probably the disagreement between him and the Jews grew most violent when he went on to the next step, declaring that Jesus of Nazareth was indeed this promised Messiah (17:3). Silas was present also, ready to affirm what Paul was asserting (17:4). Nothing is said of Timothy. Apparently he kept himself in the background, conscious of his youth and relative inexperience.

As a result of the presentation of the gospel on these occasions, "some of the Jews were persuaded" (17:4), though their number was smaller than those of the two groups that are mentioned next—"a large number of God-fearing Greeks and not a few prominent women." Regarding Macedonian women, Lightfoot makes the following comment: "The extant Macedonian inscriptions seem to assign to the sex a higher social influence than is common among the civilized nations of antiquity. In not a few instances a metronymic takes the place of the usual patronymic, and in other cases a prominence is given to women which can hardly be accidental."[11]

The Jews who did not respond to the gospel refused to be passive. Resentful over the loss of some of their number to the new doctrine and jealous of the success gained in the winning over of so many Gentiles whom they had hoped to make proselytes to Judaism, these Jews devised an effective way of dealing with the new arrivals. A commercial center such as Thessalonica would have plenty of people who could be labeled "rabble." Such men were ready for excitement, and it must have amused them to see Jews egging them on against other Jews. Soon the city was in an uproar. The crowd, swelled by the curious, headed for the house of Jason, where Paul and his companions were being entertained. It is likely that Jason was a Jew who responded early to Paul's preaching (many hellenistic Jews used this name). Fortunately, Paul and his companions were not at the house, but the mob, frustrated at not being able to lay hands on the missionaries, grabbed Jason and some other believers, dragged them before the politarch, and lodged their complaint.

The account is highly compressed here, which makes it difficult to determine whether there was an intermediate step in the proceedings—namely, an attempt to bring the suspects before the popular assembly (v. 5). Luke's term (*dēmos*) fits the assembly, but it could be used also of a crowd. However, for the latter, a more appropriate term would be *ochlos*, which Luke uses later on (v. 8). At any rate, the historian focuses our attention on what transpired in the presence of the politarchs.

Here the allegation was made that the visitors, all of them, were opposing the decrees of Caesar by maintaining that another king should be recognized: Jesus. Words are carefully chosen here. Note the absence of *Christ*, which has been prominent in the report of the synagogue preaching (17:3), since that term would have been strange if not altogether meaningless to the authorities. But the significance of *king* was unmistakable. The missionaries were being charged with treason.

The Jews knew better than to claim that the visitors were guilty of political subversion, but they counted on their statement to be taken in that light. Since the decree of Claudius had recently expelled the Jews from Rome (18:2), it is possible that a wave of anti-Semitic sentiment may have swept through the provinces. Since the accusers were themselves Jews, it was not expedient to bring this up, but they probably counted on the popular mood to add weight to their allegation. The mob settled down sufficiently to hear the accusation made in the presence of the politarchs, and when they heard it they and their rulers were troubled. Theirs was a free city, but it might not retain that status for long if disloyal agitators were permitted to spread such propaganda in their midst.

The most expedient way to handle the problem from the standpoint of the authorities was to "take security" from Jason and his Christian friends, which probably means that these men gave a pledge that the missionaries would leave town. This action effectively terminated Paul's ministry, though it did not preclude the possibility of sending a messenger to find out how the church was getting along (1 Thess. 3:2). But Paul may have felt that the pledge prevented his personal appearance, much as he longed to see his friends in the city and be of further help to them. The best he could do was to write to them, which he did on two occasions, probably with only a short interval between the two letters.

Light from the Letters on the Ministry at Thessalonica

Since little information is provided in Luke's account, it is helpful to be able to glean some items from 1 and 2 Thessalonians. Though Paul wrote the letters, he included his companions in the address (1 Thess. 1:1; 2 Thess. 1:1). At this point we will consider the work done by the missionaries, turning later to Paul's characterization of his readers.

1. There is evidence of an extensive teaching ministry (1 Thess. 4:1–2; 2 Thess. 2:15) in which the following points were made:

a. Suffering and affliction are to be expected as ingredients of Christian experience (1 Thess. 3:4). Others have suffered for the faith. Why not they (1 Thess. 2:14)?

b. A holy life is called for on the part of believers (1 Thess. 2:10; 4:11ff.).

c. A Christian has an obligation to be industrious, avoiding idleness (1 Thess. 4:11; 2 Thess. 3:6). Reasons were given for such conduct—namely, to gain the respect of non-Christians and to avoid being a burden to others (1 Thess. 4:12).

d. The Day of the Lord and its significance is explained (1 Thess. 5:1ff.), and the events that will transpire at that time are discussed (2 Thess. 2:3–6).

2. This teaching ministry was undergirded by a truly Christian example in the life and conduct of the missionaries: "You know how we lived among you for your sake" (1 Thess. 1:5). To this general statement is added a somewhat detailed account of how the ministry was carried on (1 Thess. 2:3–8). This section was drafted, it seems, in answer to the allegations of the Jewish opponents of Paul that he had acted improperly and had been guided by wrong motives. On the positive side, the apostle recalls for his readers the kind of example he and his friends had provided, suffering for Christ's sake (1 Thess. 1:6; 2:2), toiling at his trade so as not to be a financial burden to others (1 Thess. 2:9; 2 Thess. 3:7–8), demonstrating an outgoing love and concern for the converts (1 Thess. 2:8).

3. To provide leadership for the church, the missionaries supervised the election of elders (though the word elder itself is not used). The duties mentioned here (1 Thess. 5:12) correspond to those assumed by elders in other places.

Paul's Evaluation of the Thessalonian Christians

Paul makes a number of statements about the Thessalonian church throughout the letters, making the following points:

1. They readily accepted the message spoken to them, receiving it as God's word (1 Thess. 2:13; 2 Thess. 3:1), and on this basis renouncing idolatry and turning to the true and living God (1 Thess. 1:9–10).

2. They are commended for their faith (1 Thess. 1:3; 3:7), their love (1 Thess. 1:3; 4:10) and their hope (1 Thess. 1:3; 4:13; 5:8). They excel in the cardinal virtues.

3. Their zeal in bearing witness to the Lord and his salvation is recognized (1 Thess. 1:8). It is not clear whether this has been done through travel to other places or by testifying to visitors who have come to their city.

4. They have suffered reproach and persecution for Christ's sake (1 Thess. 1:6; 2:14; 3:3–4; 2 Thess. 1:6).

5. In the midst of this suffering they have experienced the joy of the Lord (1 Thess. 1:6). They, in turn, are a source of joy to the apostle (1 Thess. 2:19–20; 3:9).

6. Their initial eager expectation of the Lord's return (1 Thess. 1:10), now somewhat shaken by his apparent delay, needs strengthening by means of further teaching and by the comfort this explanation will provide (1 Thess. 4:13–18). They must remain alert and expectant (1 Thess. 5:4–11).

7. The believers must not be content with their performance to date. A notable feature of Paul's counsel is that he commends the church in every way possible but couples this with a charge to improve. They are to live so as to please God more and more (1 Thess. 4:1), their love for one another should keep increasing (1 Thess. 3:12; 4:10), and they are to keep on encouraging one another and building one another up (1 Thess. 5:11).

8. Since they are called to holiness (1 Thess. 4:7) and this is clearly God's will, they have a responsibility to abstain from immorality (1 Thess. 4:3). God's Holy Spirit will enable them to do so (1 Thess. 4:8).

9. Though they have leaders (1 Thess. 5:12), they themselves must accept responsibility for admonishing the idle, encouraging the faint-hearted, helping the weak, and being patient toward all (1 Thess. 5:14).

10. Just because they are a young church, privileged to have only a brief period of apostolic instruction, they need a considerable variety of explicit exhortations so that they cannot complain about lack of direction (e.g., 1 Thess. 5:13–22).

5. CORINTH

Our interest is not so much in the old Corinth, destroyed by the Romans in 146 B.C., as in the new Corinth, restored by the Romans a century later.

It grew rapidly because of its strategic position on the isthmus of Corinth, with port cities both to the east and to the west. Not inaptly it has been compared with Houston, Texas, in respect to commercial importance and resulting population growth. People of all kinds found their way to this center, enticed by work opportunities and by the free and easy life-style of the city. In these respects the resemblance to Antioch is worth noting. Though the city was founded by Romans, it had a large Greek population and in addition opened its arms to people from many lands. It presented a striking contrast to Athens, a contrast exemplified by their patron deities. Athens had Athena, the goddess of the mind, representing the wisdom for which the Athenians were famous. Corinth had Aphrodite, the goddess of the body, the goddess of love. Athens was associated with culture, Corinth with commerce. Athens had its idolatry, Corinth its immorality; Paul knew that the former led to the latter (Rom. 1:22–24).

The economic opportunities at Corinth attracted Jews. Luke makes reference to a synagogue (18:4), which could mean one among several or the only one in the community. It was, at any rate, the synagogue into which Paul made his way.

The Founding of the Church

The apostle was fortunate in being able to find living quarters with a couple who had recently come from Italy (18:2). Since Luke says nothing about their conversion, it is likely they were already believers. Though they shared the same trade, this in itself would not bring them close together. They became Paul's fellow workers in the gospel.

In attending the synagogue Paul gained recognition as a Jewish scholar and was given permission to speak, an opportunity for declaring the good news that he eagerly embraced. His audience was composed of Jews and God-fearing Greeks (18:4). This continued for some weeks. Though Luke says nothing about a ministry during the week, it is probable that inquirers were encouraged to come to the quarters Paul shared with Aquila and Priscilla. Before long Silas and Timothy arrived from Macedonia, bringing with them financial help, it seems, so that Paul was set free to devote himself to gospel witness (18:5; cf. 2 Cor. 11:8–9; Phil. 4:15). At this point the new arrivals joined in the ministry, making five workers in all (2 Cor. 1:19).

Before long the expected break with the synagogue took place, brought on by Paul's insistence that the promised Messiah of Israel should be identified with Jesus of Nazareth (18:5). Perceiving that the minds of his Jewish auditors were for the most part closed to this line of proclamation, he left with this parting salvo, "From now on I will go to the Gentiles." (He said this in reference to the local situation, however, not his entire future ministry.)

At this point it is important to return to Luke's statement that in the synagogue he had been addressing Jews and Greeks (v. 4). These Greeks became a bridge to the next phase of ministry. Doubtless some of them had been saved under Paul's preaching in the synagogue. Now that he was forced to leave, they no doubt left with him. A God-fearer whose house adjoined the synagogue, one who must have been won to the faith shortly before, Titius Justus by name, opened his quarters for the apostle's use. So the testimony continued with God's blessing, and many of the Corinthians responded (18:8).

We can be sure that Jewish opposition continued, intensified by the proximity to the synagogue of Paul's preaching post. He may have considered leaving, but was deterred by a night vision in which the Lord appeared and encouraged him by saying that many people in the city belonged to him. This is best taken as meaning future believers. Thus he continued for a year and a half (18:11), the amount of time he spent there being significant in contrast with the length of stay in other places he had visited in that it reflects the potential for evangelism there as well as the actual growth in the number of believers. The extended stay also gave him the opportunity to teach the converts the implications of their new faith in terms of Christian life and service.

Jewish opposition was held in check by the size of the city and its cosmopolitan character (cf. Antioch), but it finally flared into the open, only to be rebuffed by Gallio's refusal to give consideration to charges brought against the apostle. He sized up the case as an internal squabble between those who professed the faith of Judaism (18:15).

When Paul finally departed, accompanied by Aquila and Priscilla, the church may have been left with only local leadership, though it is possible that Silas and Timothy continued for a time. The latter joined Paul later on at Ephesus (1 Cor. 16:10).

Paul's Additional Contacts with the Corinthian Church

Sosthenes (1 Cor. 1:1) was a member of the church who joined Paul at Ephesus. He may be the same individual who succeeded Crispus as ruler of the synagogue. If so, the example of Crispus (18:8) may have influenced him. His failure to prosecute successfully the case against Paul before Galio led to his being beaten by disgruntled Jews (18:17). This may have caused Sosthenes to rethink his position and to follow "the way" of the Nazarenes. His visit to Ephesus meant that Paul gained up-to-date information about the state of things at Corinth.

Apollos, a Jew from Alexandria who was helped by Priscilla and Aquila at Ephesus while Paul was on a trip to Jerusalem (18:21–23), went on to minister at Corinth. By the time Paul wrote 1 Corinthians, Apollos was back in Ephesus and was doubtless another source of information for the apostle concerning recent developments (1 Cor. 16:12).

Members of Chloe's household came also, conveying some rather unwelcome news (1 Cor. 1:11). Information about Chloe is lacking, but these people provided Paul with word about the Corinthian situation.

Three other brethren are mentioned by name as having come to see him (1 Cor. 16:17), but nothing is said of their mission. It is possible that they brought with them a letter from the congregation (1 Cor. 7:1). These several contacts are important because they assure us that when Paul replied (1 Cor.) he was not writing in ignorance of conditions in the church. An even earlier letter of a rather limited character (1 Cor. 5:9) has not been preserved.

The reception given 1 Corinthians was somewhat less than cordial. In fact it became necessary for Paul to interrupt his work in Ephesus and return to Corinth for what he described as a "painful visit" (2 Cor. 2:1). This was followed in turn by a severe letter to the congregation after his return to Ephesus (2 Cor. 2:4). Unable to bear the suspense of not knowing how the letter affected the church, he sent Titus to find out. Failing to hear from him after a reasonable time, he himself set out to meet Titus. Unable to find him at Troas, his agitation prevented him from accepting a preaching opportunity there (2 Cor. 2:12–13). Pressing on to Macedonia, he located him and was relieved to find out that although there was some continuing opposition to him, the situation had cleared up considerably.

The Composition of the Church

We have noted that Gentiles predominated among the believers in Corinth. Judging from the apostle's description, most of the converts were from the lower classes (1 Cor. 1:26–28), but he did not hold this against them. Rather, divine sovereignty was evident in their calling. On the other hand, notice is taken of a few people of rank, including Tertius, Gaius, Erastus (Rom. 16:22–23), and possibly Sosthenes (1 Cor. 1:1). More important than social status is the influence of the pagan environment, which continued to be a factor in their lives to a greater or lesser degree. The apostle recognized this influence and gave it due attention in his treatment of their problems.

We tend to think of Paul primarily as an apostle, an able preacher, and a missionary statesman. We do not usually think of him as a pastor. Yet he did have this task thrust upon him, especially in the Corinthian situation. When the troubles that erupted there came to his attention, he was heavily involved in a demanding ministry at Ephesus. No wonder he had to confess that a climactic factor in his sufferings was his daily concern for all the churches (2 Cor. 11:28). High on the list was the congregation at Corinth.

The Problems in the Church

To a great extent the church's problems emerged after Paul's departure from Corinth; otherwise he would have dealt with them in person rather than handle them by correspondence. The pagan environment encouraged their development, as did the commercial life and wealth of the city.

It was easy to be drawn into habits of "fast" living and to develop a false evaluation of material things. More innocuous, but still diversionary, was the fact that Corinth was a sports center. But the most devastating element was the immorality of the city that reached out a beckoning hand. Paul notes the following difficulties:

1. *Factions in the church.* The very fact that Paul addresses himself to this first of all is indicative of the seriousness of this development from his standpoint (1:10–4:21). The most illuminating approach to the factions is to see them in the light of traditional Greek preoccupation with various schools of philosophy. In contrast to Athens, Corinth had no famous teacher of philosophy, but it was well acquainted with the tradition. There was a natural inclination to view Christianity as a system of thought that might be given varied interpretation and expression. The church split into various groups, each of which attributed its particular interpretation to an individual, some choosing Paul, some Apollos, some Cephas.

Paul fought this factionalism by pointing out that he and the other leaders all belonged to Christ as well as to the whole church, and not to individual coteries (1 Cor. 3:21–23). Furthermore, the apostle injects into his treatment of the problem a discussion of wisdom, contrasting the wisdom of the world with that of God (1:18ff.). He sets revealed truth, centering in Christ and him crucified, over against knowledge arrived at simply by human wisdom (2:6–16). Moreover, he denounces the factious spirit as a mark of carnality that was keeping the Corinthians in a state of spiritual babyhood (3:1–3). They were acting like the unsaved around them—mere men. Paul makes it clear that the Christian leaders named at the beginning were only servants of Christ (4:1). They may have been pillars in the church, but Christ was the foundation (3:10).

2. *Lawsuits.* The Greek temperament was tremendously individualistic. This trait not only led to creation of factions but also led to the problem of lawsuits as individuals all insisted on having their own way, refusing to look at things from the standpoint of those with whom they were contending. The apostle complains, "Brother goes to law against brother, and that before unbelievers" (6:6). Again, they were acting like mere men—that is, unsaved men. They should at least have looked to one or more among the believers to adjudicate their differences. But the root of the trouble reached deeper. If they had in fact had the mind and the grace of Christ they would not have permitted these cases to arise in the first place, much less been inclined to pursue them in pagan courts. It would have been better to suffer injury than to have darkened the cause of the Lord Jesus.

3. *Immorality.* We have already noted a flagrant case of immorality in our discussion of discipline, but Paul broadens his treatment to remind the church that sexual immorality has no place among sons of the kingdom: it belongs to the old life, not to the new (6:9ff.). Some in the congregation had adopted a haughty, independent attitude on this. Paul appears to be

quoting them when he writes, "All things are lawful for me" (6:12). He reminds them of a few things they have overlooked: to be joined to a prostitute is to enter into union with her, to become one flesh with her (6:16)—a clear contradiction of one's union with Christ. Moreover, such a thing is a grievous affront to the Holy Spirit, who has made their bodies his temple (6:19). Finally, these believers are not their own, for they were bought at the price of the body and blood of the Savior. They are no longer free to give themselves to sin.

4. *Marriage (1 Cor. 7)*. Paul relates his discussion of marriage to that of immorality by noting that marriage can serve as a deterrent to keep one from immorality (7:2), but he also treats it as a *charisma*. On the other hand, he treats the ability to remain unmarried as a *charisma*, too, putting himself in this category. Each one has his gift, whichever it is, from God. Marriage is honorable and permissible, but it should be entered into only with another believer.

It would seem that in writing this section, Paul is dealing with a point of view that questioned marriage, an ascetic attitude. When he says, "It is good for a man not to marry" (7:1), he may be reproducing a sentiment that has been passed on to him by some in the church. The ascetic attitude is clearly the opposite of an immoral attitude, but both approaches can derive from a common source—namely, a dualism that makes a sharp disjunction between the spirit and the body. The immoral individuals who had cast their lot with Christ might claim that by that act they had become so purified that in their inner life they were impervious to any merely physical contamination. On the other hand, the ascetics claimed that the spirit should be separated entirely from the flesh and ruled out marriage on that ground. Paul's position is that living as a single person is feasible when that status is a gift from God, but otherwise it can be a tragic mistake. He was himself set free from family obligations by his single status and was thereby enabled to do more in the cause of Christ than he could otherwise have done. Each must get his guidance from God and act accordingly.

5. *Eating meat offered to idols (chaps. 8–10)*. The matter of purchasing sacrificial meat was a practical matter for many in the church, especially the poor, since they could likely save money by doing so. Doubtless these were those to whom it seemed a mark of punctiliousness to differentiate between meat that had and had not been placed before an idol. On the other hand, people with a tender conscience found it hard to view the practice of eating meat of this sort as anything but complicity in idolatry. Paul took his stand with the former group, which argued that no change had taken place in the meat by reason of its exposure to an idol. The apostle points out, however, that while one should have liberty to partake, all should be governed by love, and if one's conduct would cause a "weak" brother to eat and by so doing violate his conscience, then "strength" would merely be a stumbling block (8:9). The argument is threefold: One

should have liberty to partake, but if this example leads others to partake, and thus violate their conscience, love should bring willingness to forgo the exercise of liberty. The highest principle of all is to do everything to the glory of God (10:31).

In dealing with this problem the apostle mentions freedom of action. He goes on to apply this principle in other areas. He himself is free to marry, for instance, as other Christian leaders have done (9:5), but he has chosen not to use this right. Again, he is free to claim financial support as a Christian worker (9:6–7), but here also he has not used his right. He notes in reference to his former association with Barnabas that they have worked with their hands to provide their basic needs (cf. 1 Thess. 2:9). So Christian liberty is a great truth that must be upheld, but we are not compelled to insist on our rights; we can forgo them for the sake of the gospel.

6. *The resurrection of the body.* Paul devotes a whole chapter (15) to the subject of bodily resurrection. His readers had embraced the gospel as he presented it to them (15:1), a gospel that included the resurrection of Christ, but their Greek background had made it hard for them to accept this teaching. They had inherited the idea that the body is the prisonhouse of the soul and that death brings welcome freedom from this confinement. Paul's thrust is to emphasize along with the truth of Christ's resurrection the companion truth that he shares our humanity. If one does not hold that the Christian dead are raised, he argues, then one cannot hold that Christ rose from the dead, and if that is so, then we are without hope, being still in our sins. Christ is in fact the last Adam, the head of a new humanity. The resurrection attests this; whereas the first Adam gave us sin and death, only the last Adam provides a life that is impervious to the ravages of these two enemies.

7. *The* charismata *(chaps. 12–14).* There are many angles to this subject, but space does not permit our entering into them all. We will touch only on the main points.

The Spirit is the source of the *charismata,* granting to each one a gift or gifts according to his good pleasure. These gifts are for the edification of the body as a whole; they are given for the benefit of all believers. The gifts are not to be exercised selfishly, as a matter of display. Recipients cannot plead that they are carried away, for we are told that they are able to control the manifestation of the gift at least sufficiently to permit others to have their turn in the assembly (14:30, 32). This can be related to the teaching in chapter 13, where love is exalted not merely as the manner in which gifts are to be exercised, but also as greater than the gifts, for love partakes of the essential nature of God himself.

The Corinthians were difficult people to work with. Though Paul had begotten them through the gospel and was therefore their spiritual father, they were problem children. Some of them were prone to question his apostleship (1 Cor. 9:1), probably as an excuse for ignoring his teaching when it pleased them to do so. He had to threaten to use his authority as a rod of punishment (4:21). They could be petulant, accusing him of fickleness because he changed his visitation plans (2 Cor. 1:15ff.). He himself, on the other hand, was conscious of being led in triumph by virtue of his relationship to Christ (2:14).

We find that his apostleship is also denied in 2 Corinthians, where it seems to be connected with the complaint that, unlike other Christian workers, he refuses to accept financial support (11:7-15; 12:11-18). This complaint was apparently planted in the minds of his converts by men who came to Corinth with letters of recommendation (3:1), perhaps from the mother church in Jerusalem but more probably from an element in that church (cf. Acts 15:24). They likely demanded financial support and cited Paul's refusal to do the same as evidence of his awareness of inferiority to the Twelve and other Christian workers.

This pressure from outsiders casts its shadow over much of 2 Corinthians, differentiating it from the first letter which deals largely with problems that had arisen within the local church. Paul is obliged to defend himself against these interlopers and in so doing to retaliate. He calls them false apostles, deceitful workmen, and servants of Satan (2 Cor. 11:13-15). The apostle admits that he is indulging in foolishness even to try to defend himself (11:21; 12:11), but he feels obliged to do so because the Corinthians have not themselves countered the charges made against him. He feels isolated. The best he can do is to turn the tables on his opponents by resorting to boasting (11:21ff.). He notes that his Hebraic origin is as authentic as theirs. If they are servants of Christ, he is a better one. Can they match his record in the area of suffering (11:23-28)? These experiences have taught him to be thankful for his weakness and the necessity of depending on Christ. They seem to get along without a thorn in the flesh such as he has, but he would not care to exchange places with them.

It was a hard situation for Paul. The more his heart is enlarged toward his children in the faith and the more he yearns over them, the more they seem to close their hearts against him (2 Cor. 7:2).

Before writing 2 Corinthians, while still in Ephesus, he had spoken of a plan to go to Rome and the West (Acts 18:21). But as long as the Corinthian situation remained troubled, he felt compelled to stay in the East. His pastoral concern would not permit him to leave (2 Cor. 10:15-16).

By the time he reached Corinth, his letter (2 Cor.) had effected a real change in the attitude of the church. Even before he wrote, the congregation had moved to restore good relations with the apostle by dealing with one person who had wronged him (2 Cor. 2:5-11).

From Corinth he wrote to the Roman church a letter that is free of any overtones of continuing turmoil in his environment. Evidently peace and good will had been restored.

Summary

Church life, whether ancient or modern, is beset by potential hazards. The danger of being adversely influenced by a pagan environment, by the spirit of the age, is very real. Further, a church should beware of an undiscerning acceptance of the ministry of those who profess to know Christ but do not build on the firm foundation of the gospel an appropriate superstructure— a life molded by grace and filled with divine love. Nor should we overlook the importance of remaining receptive to the influence of the Holy Spirit, for the alternative is stunted growth and disunity in the body of Christ.

Paul's ministry exalted Christ and him crucified. "And he died for all that those who live should no longer live for themselves, but for him who died for them and was raised again" (2 Cor. 5:15). Self-seeking was a basic problem for the Corinthians. For example, they were able to do far more than they were doing in the area of giving. They had made a promising start in pledging toward the fund for the poor saints at Jerusalem (2 Cor. 9:2), but their zeal had slackened. Paul was not content merely to nudge them by pointing to the example of the Macedonian believers who had given out of their poverty (8:2), but went on to cite the example of Christ, who, though rich, for our sake became poor with a view to enriching us (8:9). This is Paul's typical appeal to Christ. It is overwhelming and final.

The apostle also dares to use his own example for the help of young believers. "Be imitators of me, as I am of Christ" (1 Cor. 11:1). The second clause is the justification for the first. The Corinthian correspondence is filled with allusions to Paul's manner of life, his way of doing things, his conduct, his motives. His readers were immature Christians. They needed this flesh and blood example (cf. 4:6; 7:7; 9:1–6, 24–27). How magnificently did this man meet the situation, faced as he was with belligerence without and fears within. And he did so in love, even when it seemed that his beloved children had ceased to love him (2 Cor. 6:11; 12:14–15).

We get the impression that the Corinthians were so mired in their problems that they had little time or inclination for missionary outreach. Such a judgment may well be mistaken. A few miles away a church was started at Cenchreae (Rom. 16:1). By the time Paul wrote 2 Corinthians he included in his greeting "all the saints throughout Achaia" (1:1). We cannot be sure that the Corinthians were responsible for all this evangelism, but neither can we rule out their participation. The apostle could rest in the assurance that he had not labored in vain.

6. EPHESUS

Ephesus was located at the mouth of the Cayster River in western Asia Minor, a site on which there had been a settlement for hundreds of years before New Testament times. When the Romans organized the province of

Asia in 133 B.C., Ephesus was its chief city. The situation was favorable for the development of commerce, so population and wealth there increased. It was somewhat behind Antioch in these respects, but it was a notable center during the Roman period. Urban rivalry was keen in Asia, with various cities claiming the first rank, to the annoyance of their Roman overlords. The era of peace brought about by Augustus made possible the construction of many public buildings, including the theater in which the rioters congregated during Paul's ministry in the city. This structure, visible today, had an estimated capacity of nearly 25,000 persons.

The other prominent edifice mentioned by Luke, the temple of Artemis, was unearthed by J. T. Wood after six years of searching for the site. He found it northeast of the city proper. This famous building was one of the seven wonders of the ancient world. Its 100 columns, 60 feet high, made it an imposing sight. The temple itself covered an area 340 by 160 feet, resting on a platform considerably larger. It was filled with paintings and sculpture. Though somewhat detached from the city, the extent to which it was the real center of the life of Ephesus is indicated by the fact that it was an asylum for fugitives and even runaway slaves, as well as being a repository of treasure and containing a bank.

Ephesus was the center for the worship of Artemis. She represented a fusion of the Asiatic earth-mother worship with the Greek veneration for the goddess of the hunt. To show their devotion, worshipers brought to her miniature replicas of the temple (in distinction from statuettes of the goddess that people had at home). It is to these shrines that Luke's account draws attention. Many of them, made of terra cotta or marble, have been found, but so far none made of silver. Sir William Ramsay explained this on the ground that the offerings made of silver, being gifts of the wealthier classes, would in time have been melted down by the priests rather than be allowed to accumulate. People came from far and near to honor the goddess. Her worship was "big business" for the city.

It was to be expected that Jews would flock to a city of this sort, drawn not by pagan worship, to be sure, but by the economic advantages of the place. Asia Minor as a whole had one of the heaviest concentrations of the Dispersion. Juster lists eighty-two places where Jews are known to have congregated.[12] They are prominent in Luke's account (19:8–9, 13–17, 33; cf. 20:19). A degree of tension between the Jewish and pagan elements of the population is hinted at in 19:34.

The Importance of Ephesus in Paul's Ministry

It is clear that the apostle had his eye on Ephesus when he envisioned the itinerary of the second missionary journey. As soon as he and his companions had revisited the Galatian churches he was ready to make a move in this direction, but it was not the will of God at that time (Acts 16:6). However, we may be sure that he continued to want to pursue a ministry in this city as he attended to the campaign in Macedonia and Achaia. When he did settle in Ephesus, it proved to be for his longest stay apart from his unrecorded labors in and around Tarsus (9:30; 11:25). In contrast to a few weeks in Philippi and in Thessalonica, probably less time in Athens, and a year and a half in Corinth, he remained for the greater part of three years in Ephesus (20:31). In turn, this sphere of labor was a stage in preparation for the final move to the capital of the empire (19:21).

Arriving at Ephesus, Paul found the area still unevangelized, so God allowed him to fulfill his earlier desire to reach this region for Christ. With this city as his base of operations, the apostle had the opportunity to develop a witness to the entire province of Asia (19:10). At the same time he was close enough to Corinth to keep in touch with that troubled congregation by letter, by personal representatives, and by his own visits on two occasions.

Realizing the strategic importance of the Ephesian ministry for the future of the church in the East, Luke provided a fuller account of it than of any other situation involving the apostle. In addition to his contribution we are fortunate in having other portions of the New Testament that in one way or another reflect this period of Paul's work, especially the report of the apostle's meeting with the elders of the Ephesian church (chap. 20) and to a lesser extent the letters to the Corinthians, Colossians, and Ephesians. For later developments in Asia we have the letters to the seven churches (Rev. 2 and 3). The priority given in these passages to the church in Ephesus testifies to the prominence of this congregation in the historic development of the faith in the province of Asia.

Paul's Contacts with Ephesus

Paul's first contact with the Ephesians came in a brief visit following the conclusion of the ministry in Corinth (Acts 18:18–21). Luke informs us that at the time Paul was headed for Syria, a journey that proved to be a circuitous one (18:21–22). A glance at the map assures us that a stop at Ephesus was not out of the way for the first stage, since Ephesus was due east of Corinth. The purpose of the trip to Syria is not stated, but since Antioch is mentioned (v. 22) the likelihood is that Paul wanted to report on his missionary activities, for Antioch was his base (15:40). Silas may have remained for a time in Corinth. Timothy was with Paul for at least part of his sojourn in Ephesus (19:22; cf. 1 Cor. 4:17; 16:10). Paul landed at Caesarea and proceeded to Jerusalem ("he went up and greeted the church"). Luke does not pause to give the purpose of this visit to Jerusalem beyond mentioning the greeting aspect. It may be that this was the main objective, just to keep in touch with the mother church. But it is also possible that the apostle wished to discuss with its leaders his plan to raise a fund among the Gentile churches for the benefit of the poor in the

Jerusalem church. He probably wanted to ascertain the degree of the need and the acceptability of his plan.

Looking back for a moment to the brief stop at Ephesus, we observe two items pointing to Paul's purpose to conduct his next campaign in this metropolitan center. One is the fact that he left Priscilla and Aquila there, probably to find living quarters (see 18:2–3). The other item relates to his own activity. He made contact with the synagogue, as he regularly did. His presentation provoked discussion and perhaps some argument (the Greek term used will allow such a reading), but his message was probably stated in such a way as not to elicit too much resistance, for he was looking forward to the time of his return, when he hoped to find the door of the synagogue still open to him. The seed thoughts he planted were sufficient to create a demand for more—hence the invitation to return, rare enough in Paul's experience. He readily agreed to rejoin them if it proved to be the will of God (18:20–21).

After the brief stop at Jerusalem, Paul journeyed north to Antioch and made his report to the church of what had happened in the furtherance of the gospel since he left them for his second campaign. We may be sure that he also took them into his confidence about the prospects at Ephesus. No doubt there were sessions devoted to prayer and planning before he ventured forth again.

During Paul's absence from Ephesus, Priscilla and Aquila performed a service by instructing Apollos in the fullness of the Christian message, so that he was able to proceed to Corinth and conduct a ministry there (18:24–28). Problems haunt this passage, including the matter of the identity of the brethren mentioned in 18:27. Do they reflect a Christian testimony at Ephesus prior to the initial visit of Paul, or were they won to the Lord through the ministry of Priscilla and Aquila? Then there is the problem of possible connection between Apollos and the little company of disciples that Paul encountered when he returned to the city (19:1–7). They, like Apollos, connected baptism simply with the ministry of John the Baptist. The oddity of the situation is that in case these men had been instructed and baptized by Apollos before he was helped by Priscilla and Aquila, it is almost incredible that he would have gone off to Corinth without leading them to higher ground. The puzzle is not easily unraveled.

However, Luke must have regarded the incident as important to give it a place in his narrative. There was a theological reason for including it—namely, to highlight the truth that John the Baptist had indeed decreased and that Christ had increased. John was content with the privilege of being forerunner. Some of his disciples were not. But the incident before us points to the proper course for those in the movement that still centered itself in John. There was also a practical reason for including this item in the Ephesus story. For Paul this initial victory in the campaign meant that the situation was solidifying. With possible rivalry from the Baptist movement now precluded, he could give himself to the synagogue and the city without distraction. The absorption of this little band into his own company, in case they were Jews, would help his cause as he resumed his contact with the synagogue.

This understanding of 19:1–7 must face an objection, however, inasmuch as Luke indicates that the men involved were disciples, a term regularly used in Acts to designate believers in Jesus; furthermore, it is explicitly indicated that they believed (v. 2). On the other hand, the fact that they had not received Christian baptism seems to point to ignorance of the finished work of Christ and the coming of the Spirit. So there is a problem either way.

Paul's Ministry in the City

The incident involving the twelve disciples is palpably introductory to the principal labors of the apostle, which began with a return to the synagogue (Acts 19:8; cf. 18:20–21). Three months may not seem to be a long period, yet it represents a readier reception than Paul experienced in most of his synagogue contacts. His methodology is described as arguing and pleading. His message is summarized as the kingdom of God (see 20:25). Clearly this expression is intended to denote more than the rule of God in this instance and more than the eschatological aspect of that rule. It seems designed to include the gospel, as in other passages (8:12; 28:23, 31). Some time passed before opposition hardened and expressed itself, and when this happened there was no violence, but the public resistance was a signal to Paul that his usefulness in the synagogue had ended. Some fruit was realized, for in withdrawing he took "the disciples" with him (19:9). There is no obvious intention to identify these with the twelve men described in the previous paragraph, so they were apparently converts from the three-month ministry in the synagogue.

It will be recalled that at Corinth the apostle left the synagogue in order to carry on at the house of a God-fearing convert nearby (18:7). At Ephesus he sought and found more commodious quarters in the hall of Tyrannus, which was really a school, a place where lectures were given and students were gathered together. Whether Tyrannus was the owner or the lecturer is not known. Conceivably he could have been both. Here Paul was safe from Jewish pressure and was able to continue for a period of two years, setting forth the gospel and training converts in the implications of their new faith. The Western text of 19:9 mentions a detail of the arrangement that casts some light on Paul's ability to rent these quarters: here we read that he had the use of the building from the fifth to the tenth hour of the day (i.e. from 11 A.M. to 4 P.M.). For business people this was siesta time, the heat of the day. Shops reopened as the cool of the afternoon came on. The situation was a test of the apostle's ability to draw people in. His dedicated converts probably did their utmost to advertise the sessions, with the result that many came and found the Lord.

That this was an exceedingly fruitful period of gospel testimony is indicated by the assertion of Luke that "all the Jews and Greeks who lived in the province of Asia heard the word of the Lord" (19:10; cf. 19:20; Col. 1:23; 4:13). The statement is intentionally hyperbolic (cf. Matt. 3:5; John 21:25) but nevertheless impressive. Clearly this was a time of great advance for the gospel throughout the province. It was made possible by the collaboration of many helpers. At a later point in the narrative Luke refers to two of the colaborers, Timothy and Erastus (19:22). That he had others is clearly implied. We can picture Paul as discipling converts who in turn bore their witness in place after place, wherever they went. As a result, people were drawn into the city to attend the meetings. Returning home, in many cases they founded churches in their home communities (1 Cor. 16:19). One thinks here of the situation at Colosse, where Epaphras ministered on Paul's behalf in establishing a church (Col. 1:7). Churches were established also at Laodicea and Hierapolis (Col. 4:13). It seems that Philemon, likewise a resident of Colosse, who had a church in his house, must have had contact with Paul at Ephesus (Philem. 1; cf. v. 23). At least some of the churches mentioned in Revelation 2 and 3 were probably established during this period. All this outreach could well have reacted on the church at Ephesus, spurring it to renewed dedication to the task of witnessing. Seldom has the word of God spread so rapidly over so large a territory in such a limited time. Even Paul's enemies were obliged to acknowledge his success (19:26).

For the apostle it was a time of strenuous activity. He worked with his hands to supply his temporal needs and those of his associates (20:34). In addition to his public ministry at the school of Tyrannus he sought to shepherd the flock, teaching them from house to house (20:20) and admonishing everyone with tears (20:31). He sought to declare the whole counsel of God (20:27, cf. Col. 1:28). As though all this were not enough to tax his strength and patience, he had opposition to face, such as plots of the Jews (20:19). The opposition was due to the fact that Paul had siphoned off many God-fearers whom the Jews had hoped to win to proselyte status in Judaism. Any move against him had to be of a somewhat subtle character because of the cosmopolitan nature of Ephesus, where the Jews were a minority. Only when he reached Jerusalem on his last visit were the Ephesian Jews in a position to make a public charge against him (21:27–29). Writing from Ephesus to the Corinthian church, the apostle summed up his situation by saying, "A great door for effective work has opened to me, and there are many who oppose me" (1 Cor. 16:9).

An incident involving Jews but probably not related to the local Jewish body is reported by Luke in connection with his observation that God did "extraordinary miracles" through Paul at this time, including exorcisms.

Some wandering Jewish exorcists sought to capitalize on the situation by way of imitation (19:13–14). However, when an evil spirit, adjured to depart by the use of the name of "the Jesus whom Paul preaches," refused to recognize the authenticity of the command and instead enabled the possessed man to overpower the seven sons of Sceva, the whole community was shaken with fear. Paul recognized that lying behind the human factors one must face in proclaiming the gospel was the presence and power of the supernatural world of spiritual darkness (Eph. 6:12ff.). Human opponents were bad enough. Paul seems to liken those at Ephesus to wild beasts (1 Cor. 15:32). On both levels he knew that he had with him the supreme power, that of God himself, working on his behalf. The result of the Sceva incident was that everybody was able to see that *Jesus* was not a name to conjure with, as though it were simply a magical formula, but was rather the key to the power of the true and living God, a key given only to those who truly knew and served him.

The effect of this event on believers was actually more startling than its effect on unbelievers. "They now came and openly confessed their evil deeds" (19:18). Many of them had retained their books of magic, their formulas and their trinkets, after becoming believers. Now all these things were tossed into a huge fire and were consumed. What is truly astonishing is the fact that so many believers allowed these reminders of their pagan life-style to have a place in their affections after turning to Christ. To Paul the pastor this must have been a great concern. But he could thank God for the fire of purification and the fresh start that many were able to make in the Christian life. He could thank God also that as a result of this affair "the word of the Lord spread widely and grew in power" (19:20).

Though deeply engrossed in his various labors at Ephesus, Paul was looking ahead, as usual, seeking the mind of the Lord and the guidance of the Spirit concerning his future movements. At this juncture plans began to take shape in his mind for a final visit to Macedonia and Greece, to be followed by a trip to Jerusalem and then a major shift in his sphere of operations from the eastern Mediterranean area to Rome (19:21). It seems that he was content to lay the groundwork in any situation, nurture it for a time, then entrust it to others that he might be free to proceed to the regions beyond. Success, no matter how great, did not blind his vision for continuing outreach.

The decision to move on was soon confirmed by his encounter with the silversmiths who made shrines for the devotees of the goddess Artemis (19:23ff.). Their revenue was drying up because the demand for their product had fallen off (a situation paralleled somewhat in Bithynia in the early part of the second century: Pliny complained to Trajan that due to the spread of Christianity the temples had become almost deserted and the demand for sacrificial animals had diminished drastically). The leader of the silversmiths, Demetrius by name, had only to point to the drop in their business to rouse their passions, especially when he linked the decline with the disfavor that Paul's preaching had created toward Artemis and her worship. When the religious motive was added to the economic, a huge demonstration was in the making. The cry "Great is Artemis of the Ephesians" rang through the city streets as the milling crowd advanced toward the theater, there to continue their rhythmic chant and in the process incite a large assemblage of people who had no clear idea of what caused the outburst of feeling.

Paul was ready to intervene in order to quiet the people, as in the case of his later defense in the temple area at Jerusalem (21:40), but this would only have inflamed the crowd even more. As it turned out, believers surrounded him and succeeded in dissuading him from making an appearance in the theater. To their pleas was added the urging of the Asiarchs, the sponsors of the cult of emperor worship in the province. Did they intervene because Paul was a Roman citizen? Or had they become his friends because his work had reduced public interest in Artemis worship, with which they were in competition as sponsors of emperor worship? It is hard to say. However, it is worth noting that Paul accepted their friendship, which seems to indicate that he did not go out of his way to attack emperor worship (though he could not of course have subscribed to it) any more than he had directly assailed the Artemis worship, even though his teaching must have included the necessity of making a choice between idolatry and the worship of the living God. One gathers that his public ministry had struck a positive note, pointing to Christ as the way to God (see 19:23).

There is a point to be made here regarding missionary strategy. It is reported that in the early days of modern missions some went to people who worshiped idols with the words of Psalm 115 on their lips to deride these creations of men—"they have mouths but cannot speak, eyes, but they cannot see, they have ears but they cannot hear." It should be observed that in Scripture this taunt is directed to a nation that had a revelation of the true God. This is not the case with the so-called heathen world. Their idols are all they have. It is better to supplant than to rob. It is better to preach Christ and let him take away desire for gods made by human hands.

When the town clerk, the leading official in Ephesus, dismissed the assembly, it seems that the leaders of the riot were still so inflamed against Paul that they sought him out at his living quarters. Very likely it was then that Aquila and Priscilla were prepared to lay down their lives for the Lord's servant (Rom. 16:3–4). Paul was able to make his escape and leave the city. A few days later, writing from Macedonia, he could say, "We were under great pressure, far beyond our ability to endure, so that we despaired even of life" (2 Cor. 1:8). But he could also note that God had delivered them from this deadly peril (v. 10). In departing from Asia, he left behind him a strong work blessed with able leaders and a host of willing workers.

Characteristics of the Ephesian Church

1. The church at Ephesus was strategically located, having a great opportunity for outreach into the province of Asia. There are indications that the opportunity was grasped and that many went forth for the sake of the name to spread the gospel. These accomplishments were inspired by love for the Lord (Rev. 2:2, 4). This Christian body compares well with that at Thessalonica in the matter of outreach. Instead of being content to minister only to a large city, it sought to fulfill its obligation to a whole province.

2. It was a church that was aided by the labors of many servants of God, in line with Ephesians 4:11ff. Primarily these were Paul and (later) John the apostle. Because of the fairly long time he spent in the city, Paul was able to have an extensive sowing of the seed of the word, more so than in other places he had visited, and was able to raise up many helpers.

3. It was a church that achieved success in the face of considerable opposition (1 Cor. 16:9). Speaking of Paul, A. Schlatter comments, "The vehemence of the opposition he encountered is a sure sign of his success. The passionate hostility of his Jewish adversaries proved that Judaism was shaken to its foundations."[13] The opposition was not only strong but varied. He was obliged to face the inroads of the occult, as in connection with the incident involving the sons of Sceva, and experienced strong pressure from the business community allied with pagan worship. The church he left behind him had to learn to carry on spiritual warfare against the powers of darkness (Eph. 6:10–20).

4. It was a church directed by a group of godly elders who in addition to their own call to service as shepherds of the flock had the example and counsel of Paul, who had so conscientiously cared for the people of God during his sojourn among them (Acts 20:17ff.).

5. It was a church that apparently enjoyed some charismatic manifestations of the Spirit. This can be deduced from the narrative in Acts 19:1–7, and in a general way it is supported by the letter to the Ephesians (3:5; 4:11–13; 6:18).

6. It was a church in which the unity of Jew and Gentile in the body of Christ was emphasized and seems to have been realized in a notable way (cf. Eph. 2:11–22). This agrees with the clear indications that both groups were evangelized (Acts 19:10, 17; 20:21). In view of the encyclical nature of the letter to the Ephesians, we can think of its message as adapted to and influential in the entire area of which Ephesus was the hub. What Augustus had tried to do by political and cultural means, Christianity accomplished at a deeper and more significant level.

7. COLOSSE

Colosse was located somewhat less that one hundred miles east of Ephesus in the Lycus valley. In pre-Christian times it was a city of considerable size and prominence, but its importance was greatly reduced by the time the gospel reached the area. Luke makes no mention of a visit by Paul to the region. In fact, he indicates that the apostle was supernaturally guided to avoid it (Acts 16:6). However, during Paul's stay at Ephesus, a resident of Colosse, Epaphras by name, came under his influence and apparently returned to his native place to herald the gospel. Paul looked on this man as his personal representative, ministering in his stead (Col. 1:7). Epaphras may also have established the neighboring churches at Laodicea and Hierapolis (4:13).

The apostle had another contact with the church through Philemon and his family, who resided in Colosse. He referred to Philemon as a dear friend and fellow worker (Philem. 1). In addition he greeted Archippus, probably the son of Philemon, and acknowledged his valuable service for the cause of Christ (v. 2). He also had a word for him in writing to the Colossian church (4:17). Perhaps the entire church met in the home of Philemon (Philem. 2), although it is possible that there were other house groups, since the address in the Colossian letter is to "the holy and faithful brothers in Christ at Colosse."

In writing to Philemon, the apostle included a request that his friend prepare a guest room for him, thereby indicating his purpose to visit Colosse (Philem. 22). Since he was still a prisoner at the time (v. 1), it is evident that he anticipated a speedy release. The situation of Onesimus, a slave of Philemon who had escaped from his master and sought out Paul for his help, provides the main theme of this brief letter, which belongs to the same time frame as the letter to the Colossians (Philem. 23–24; Col. 4:12, 14).

Paul's contemplated visit to Colosse raises the question of where he was located at the time he wrote to Philemon. It has been customary to assume that his imprisonment at Rome is the setting for the captivity letters. This is quite clearly the case for Philippians (see 4:22), but not so obviously for Colossians, Ephesians, or Philemon. We know that when Paul wrote Romans from Corinth, he was anticipating a trip to Rome and a missionary journey beyond, including Spain (Rom. 15:23–24). If the apostle wrote Philemon from Rome, it seems strange that in this letter he would express a purpose to visit Colosse in the near future, since that would constitute a change of plans, exchanging a contemplated trip to the West for a trip back to the East. But if he wrote Philemon from Ephesus during his stay of nearly three years, the difficulty would be resolved. This would also be the case if he had written from Caesarea, but there was no real prospect of release during the period he was there.

There is some question as to whether Paul was imprisoned at Ephesus. Although Luke reports that he met with considerable opposition there, he makes no mention of an imprisonment (whereas in Acts 16 he does include that sort of information about Paul's ministry in Philippi). Some critics contend that Paul's statement that he fought strong beasts at Ephesus (1 Cor. 15:32) constitutes evidence that he was jailed there, since it was not uncommon for prisoners to be thrown to wild animals. This argument is weak for a number of reasons, however. In the first place, it is entirely possible that Paul's statement about wild beasts was figurative, that he was in fact referring to human opposition. Additionally, Paul's friendship with the Asiarchs (Acts 19:31) and his Roman citizenship (see Acts 16:35–39) would have made imprisonment unlikely. These facts, together with Luke's failure to mention any imprisonment, suggest that such action may well not have been taken against him in Ephesus.

To conclude, even though an Ephesian imprisonment would readily account for the action of Onesimus in seeking Paul's help and for Paul's plan to visit Philemon when he has been released, we have no real evidence for such a detention. The difficulty raised for a Roman imprisonment by the apparent reversal of the apostle's plan to go to Spain in favor of a visit to Colosse may be cleared away by his own indication that the united cooperation for his plan that he anticipated on the part of the Roman church did not materialize (Phil. 1:15–18).

Whether Paul was at Ephesus or Rome when Epaphras reported to him on conditions in the Colossian church is relatively unimportant. What is important is the fact that Epaphras was evidently so disturbed over conditions that had developed in the local church that he sensed the need for Paul's help, so he sought him out and explained the situation (Col. 4:12). Incidentally, it seems unlikely that the troubles besetting the church could have reached the peak indicated in Paul's letter to the congregation during the brief period between the initial ministry of Epaphras to his own community and his return to the apostle if the latter was still at Ephesus.

In writing to the Colossians Paul avoids mentioning the source of his information about conditions in the assembly, lest some of the readers might take offense at Epaphras and resist his further efforts at ministry in their midst. The apostle is equally careful to commend Epaphras, noting his prayerful concern for his converts (4:12) and his reporting of their love in the Spirit (1:7). It is possible that Timothy was also a source of some information, provided, of course, that he had visited Colosse (see 1:1).

Problems in the Church

Paul makes a point of assuring the Colossians that he delights in them because of their firm faith and their orderliness (2:5). This is his way of letting them know that he has not written them off as apostates, even though he is aware of dangerous ideas that have been dangled before them by those who have allowed themselves to be captivated by tendencies alien to the gospel.

He gives them something to reflect on when he deliberately resorts to hyperbole to underscore the fact that the gospel that is being preached and received throughout the rest of the world does not have the dangerous frills that have enticed some believers in Colosse (1:6, 23).

It is much easier to grasp the positive counsel given by Paul than to decipher the nature of the ideas that were being promoted at Colosse. Scholars differ as to whether the heresy was pagan or Jewish in its character (although 2:16 clearly enough points to Jewish influence). Nevertheless, we will put aside any discussion of this problem until after we have considered the main lines of Paul's presentation.

Paul describes the prevailing intellectual system in Colosse as "hollow and deceptive philosophy, which depends on human tradition and the basic principles of this world" (2:8). Regarding the last portion of this statement, it is doubtful that the alternative rendering "the elemental spirits of the universe" really fits the Colossian situation, though this understanding of the phrase would adequately represent the usage of the second century A.D. The system involved the worship of angels (2:18)—meaning, almost certainly, that people were worshiping the angels rather than that worship was being carried on by angels: Paul would hardly object to the latter provided the object was God in Christ (cf. the argument in Heb. 1). In any case, this sort of concern about the meaning of specific terms Paul is using will not be as worthwhile as developing a general overview of the situation facing the church at this juncture. In that regard, R. N. Longe-necker's comments are helpful:

> It is plausible to view the basic problem in the Colossian church as that of the harmonization of a primarily religious conviction with an interest that is dominantly cosmological. It was the problem of reconciling the Christian conviction of the primacy and priority of Jesus—which hitherto had been considered mainly in religious and historical terms, but without any real thought given to questions of cosmology—with a Grecian un-derstanding of gradations and relative orders of primacy in the uni-verse.[14]

Over against faulty notions of the necessity of angelic mediation Paul puts the uniqueness and sufficiency of Christ. In his being he is the image of the invisible God (1:15). In his work, he is responsible for creation (1:16) and redemption (1:20). He is all-sufficient for the believer. He is head not only of the church but of every power and authority (2:10). In him is all the fullness of the Deity (2:9). What reason then can there be to fear or adore heavenly beings who were created by him and remain subject to him even if some are antagonistic?

In addition to its speculative aspect, the Colossian heresy called for certain cultic observances and the regulation of diet (2:16), with a definitely ascetic emphasis (2:20–21).

Though it may be necessary to posit an ultimate pagan source for some of the elements being urged on the Colossians, it is nevertheless true that for the most part they had already made inroads into Judaism, so that it is unnecessary to posit a direct impact from Gentile sources. The intertestamental literature of an apocalyptic character has ample place for angelic mediation. Further, the Qumran scrolls testify to the great importance attached to an ascetic life-style. These observations are important in view of the fact that Jews were relatively numerous in and around Colosse. Because of their veneration for the Old Testament it is understandable that Christians would be more receptive to their ideas than to direct pagan propaganda.

Somewhat puzzling is the relatively mild tone of Paul's corrective teaching addressed to the church at Colosse. His refutation of the Galatian error is much more intense and cutting. Perhaps his moderation in dealing with the Colossians stemmed from the fact that he had not brought the gospel to these people; they were not his spiritual children. Furthermore, he indicates that the church had not completely succumbed to this deviant position (2:4, 8, 18). If he censured them too severely, he might alienate them and even drive some of them out of the church. In addition, whereas the heart of the gospel (the message of grace unaided by human works) was the issue in the Galatian situation, the Colossian problem was more subtle and required a tactful approach.

Since Paul apparently installed Timothy as the overseer of the work at Ephesus during the interval between his first and second Roman imprisonments (1 Tim. 1:3), it is possible that Timothy had some contact with the Colossians after Paul's death. Little is known about the subsequent history of the congregation. It is not included among the seven churches addressed in Revelation 2 and 3.

8. ROME

Known as the eternal city, built on seven hills, Rome was founded in the eighth century B.C. In the beginning it had had to struggle to survive, but in the early days of the Christian era, when wars near and far had practically ceased, it was at the height of its magnificence. People from many lands came to visit. Some remained as permanent residents, giving the city an international character. Its educated citizens were usually capable of handling Greek as well as Latin. The wealth of many lands flowed into it by way of trade and taxation. This opulence was reflected in handsome public buildings and in the homes of the wealthy. Slaves were more numerous than free men in this metropolis of over a million people.

Slums marred the beauty of the city and the tenants became a public burden. A large body of officials was needed to govern the far-flung empire and to make conquered lands feel the firm hand of Roman control and the equity of its administration. Travel was relatively easy and safe at this time, aiding the communication of ideas and, providentially, the spread of the gospel.

The Founding of the Church

Luke, to whom we are indebted for information about the establishment of churches in the East, says nothing about the origin of the Christian movement in the imperial city. He does note that among those present in Jerusalem on the day of Pentecost were "visitors from Rome" (Acts 2:10). Conceivably some of these could have returned to Italy with the message of the gospel. Not necessarily opposed to this possibility is the tradition emanating from Ambrosiaster in the fourth century and stated in the introduction to his commentary on Romans, as follows:

> It is established that there were Jews living in Rome in the times of the apostles, and that those Jews who had believed passed on to the Romans the tradition that they ought to profess Christ but keep the law. . . . One ought not to condemn the Romans, but to praise their faith; because without seeing any signs or miracles and without seeing any of the apostles, they nevertheless accepted faith in Christ, although according to a Jewish rite.[15]

What is of special interest here is the fact that Ambrosiaster's commentaries on Paul's letters date from a period when there was a tradition that both Peter and Paul had established the church at Rome. This is found, for example, in Irenaeus's *Against Heresies* (3.3.2). But since Irenaeus must have known that in composing Romans Paul was writing to a church he had not personally established, it follows that he must have meant that these apostles nurtured the church and built it up by their presence and teaching when they came into contact with it. That Ambrosiaster could write as he did at a time when Peter's role as founder was widely accepted in the West is significant. He may well have passed on a faithfully preserved tradition concerning the circumstances surrounding the beginning of the faith in the capital of the empire.

Paul's interest in the Roman church was either begun or quickened by his contact with Aquila and Priscilla, who came to Corinth from Rome after Claudius had issued his order expelling the Jews from the city (Acts 18:2). Priscilla was evidently a woman of considerable distinction, but whether Jewish or Roman is not known. If she and her husband were believers when Paul met them, which is probable, then we can assume that a church existed in Rome before the middle of the first century. There may be evidence to support this supposition in what Suetonius indicates as the occasion for the order of expulsion: "Since the Jews constantly made disturbances at the instigation of Chrestus, he expelled them from Rome."[16] If Chrestus is intended to indicate Christus (this confusion in rendering the Greek form into Latin is sufficiently attested), this tantalizing reference could mean that converted Jews were keeping the Jewish community in a state of commotion by their testimony to Jesus as the promised Messiah, so Claudius determined to end this state of affairs by ordering the Jews out of the city. This is the usual understanding of the matter, and if it is correct, we can conclude that Christianity had been in Rome at least by the late 40s and possibly before. In his closing chapter Luke indicates that there was a group of believers at Puteoli (28:13–14) as well as another at Rome (28:14–15).

Luke is strangely silent about Paul's contact with the church once he was established within the city in his own hired quarters. What he emphasizes is the apostle's attempt to reach the Jews who came to hear him. In the closing verse, however, he mentions that Paul conducted a preaching and a teaching ministry free from any restrictions (Acts 28:31). There may be a hint here that members of the Roman church did visit the apostle from time to time for instruction.

In writing his letter to the Romans from Corinth Paul makes clear his own understanding that the church in the capital had existed for some time. He tells his readers that he had often intended to come to them, but was always prevented (Rom. 1:13). Again, he states that for many years he had had a longing to come to them (15:23). Such statements remove any lingering doubt about the existence of a Christian community in Rome by the middle of the first century or somewhat earlier.

The Composition of the Church

Was the Roman church mainly Jewish or Gentile, or did it have a fairly equal number of the two? The data do not permit a precise answer. To be sure, the apostle mentions Abraham as "our forefather" (4:1), but since he used similar language in writing to the Corinthians (1 Cor. 10:1), who were predominantly Gentile, it is hazardous to regard this passage as deciding the matter. Jew and Greek are mentioned together in 1:16 and 2:10. The need of salvation for both groups is spelled out in the opening chapters. It is a reasonable assumption that when Paul discusses the problem of the weak and the strong in chapters 14 and 15 he has in mind the Jewish and the Gentile wings of the church, respectively. As he concludes this discussion he speaks of Christ as a servant to the circumcised to confirm the promises given to the patriarchs and in order that the Gentiles might glorify God for his mercy (15:8–9). The same duality of approach characterizes chapters 9–11, in which the question regarding Israel's past, present, and future is under review. This would be of special interest to the Jewish wing of the church, but it is clear that Paul has his eye on the Gentile contingent as well. He digresses to say "Now I am speaking to you Gentiles" and then goes on to warn them not to boast over their position, since God who cut off the natural branches to graft in the wild olive shoot can just as easily cut off the grafted branches (11:13–24).

With regard to chapters 9–11 Johannes Weiss observes that "The whole section is remarkable for the profound agitation with which Paul protests his sympathy with the destiny of his people . . . as if he had a reason for defending himself against the charge of disloyal apostasy."[17] During his last visit to Jerusalem, when he had to defend himself against the allegations of the Jewish community, he allowed his Jewishness to come out strongly (Acts 22:3ff.; 24:11ff.; 26:4ff.). This is all of a piece with what we find in Romans 9–11.

This much is clear, that both Jews and Gentiles were substantially represented in the church at Rome. One gets the impression that the Gentiles were somewhat in the majority (see 1:13 again).

> The Jewish and the Gentile converts may have formed distinct communities, or rather two sections of one Christian community.
>
> Paul and Peter, if they met together in Rome (after 63), would naturally, in accordance with the Jerusalem compact, divide the field of supervision between them as far as practicable, and at the same time promote union and harmony. This may be the truth which underlies the early and general tradition that they were the joint founders of the Roman church. No doubt their presence and martyrdom cemented the Jewish and Gentile sections. But the final consolidation into one organic corporation was probably not effected till after the destruction of Jerusalem.[18]

At this point consideration of the epistle to the Hebrews is useful. J. A. T. Robinson writes,

> The most natural supposition to be drawn from the message, that the letter was sent to Rome, is the one, I believe, that yields the most fruitful results. When it is made, a good deal else falls into place. All that we can expect here is not a conclusive demonstration but a hypothesis that gives the most reasonable explanation for the largest amount of the data. I am persuaded that the one that does this is that which postulates that the epistle was written to a group or synagogue of Jewish Christians within the church of Rome in the late 60s.[19]

Even though the Jewish Christian community must have suffered virtual depletion for a time because of the order of Claudius, at his death in A.D. 54, at any rate, the way was open for these people to return to the city. This occurred in the case of Aquila and Priscilla (Rom. 16:3). A slight problem presents itself here. Among those whom Paul greets in chapter 16 almost none have Semitic names (Mary in v. 6 is an exception). However, it is well known that Jews in the Dispersion took Greek, Latin, and Egyptian names. Aquila is a Latin name, but we know he was a Jew (Acts 18:2).

The Organization of the Church

It is noteworthy that Paul does not address the believers in Rome as a church. Rather, he writes to "all in Rome who are loved by God" (1:7). The single occurrence of the word *church* as applied to Roman believers (16:5) relates to those who gathered in the home of Priscilla and Aquila. This is a curious situation. It is clarified, however, by evidence from chapter 16 that several groups of believers had been formed, probably in various sections of the city. One is associated with the name of Aristobulus (v. 10). He himself is not included, so either he was dead at this time or else was not a believer. A similar group affiliated with Narcissus is also mentioned (v. 11). There was a freedman by that name, prominent at Rome, who died before this time. If he is the one mentioned here, the Christians were either members of his family in the narrow sense, or (what is perhaps more likely) they were his retainers and slaves. A somewhat different situation presents itself in connection with the two remaining house groups. Five individuals are greeted in v. 14 in addition to "the brethren who are with them." The same is true of the last group. In these two instances especially the indication of a church in the house is quite clear.

Elders are not mentioned in this chapter or anywhere else in Romans except possibly in 12:8, which has two possible renderings. RSV renders, "he who gives aid," but most versions have "he who leads" or its equivalent. The latter is the more usual meaning in the rest of the New Testament and probably should be preferred here.

Paul assumes that spiritual gifts are being exercised in the Roman church (12:3ff.). His concern is that they be employed in the right way and to that end he gives counsel.

The Social Status of the Church's Members

By way of introduction to the topic of social standings in the church, the words of James Orr are worth noting:

> The flow of rank and wealth into the Church, far from proving a source of blessing to it, has proved often a cause of backsliding and corruption. But it may fairly be contended that just in proportion to the obstacles which lay in the way of persons of rank and wealth becoming members of an obscure and uninfluential sect, the more signally was the power of the gospel magnified in overcoming these obstacles, and bringing them to the feet of the Crucified.[20]

This is a general observation, but it can well be applied to the Roman church because in the capital city it was especially difficult for a person in the government or in high society to escape observation as to his or her Christian commitment.

Intriguing is the brief word of Paul written, it seems, from Rome: "All the saints send you greetings, especially those who belong to Caesar's

household" (Phil. 4:22). At the time of writing there were believers in the
imperial establishment. No doubt some were slaves, but one should not
exclude the likelihood that others were freedmen. It is even possible that
some of the Roman nobility, officials in the government, may have belonged to the church at this early period. Citing Tacitus's *Annals* 13.32 as
source, C. E. B. Cranfield concludes that

> There would seem to be a distinct possibility that Pomponia Graecina,
> the wife of Aulus Plautius, who had commanded the expedition to Britain
> in A.D. 43, a lady whom Tacitus describes as "insignis femina," had come
> under the influence of Christianity: she was accused of "alien supersti-
> tion," but left to her husband's jurisdiction, and was tried and acquitted
> by a family council presided over by him just about the time that the
> Epistle to the Romans was written.[21]

The mention of the household of Narcissus (16:11) leads to a further
possibility. C. H. Dodd comments,

> There was a Tiberius Claudius Narcissus, a freedman of the imperial
> ΄ouse, who exercised great influence under Claudius, and was put to
> ΄eath shortly after the accession of Nero. We may assume that his
> ΄household" of slaves would pass, with his other property, to the Em-
> ΄eror; and they might then, as often happened in such cases, retain the
> ΄istinguishing name of *Narcissiani*. There is an inscription which seems
> to confirm this. It was a suggestion of Lightfoot (*Philippians*, p. 175) that
> some of these *Narcissiani* were among the "saints of Caesar's household"
> referred to in Phil. iv.22. The suggestion has been widely accepted, and
> seems probable.[22]

About a generation after Nero's time, in the reign of Domitian or at its
close, the letter known as 1 Clement was written from the Roman church
to the church at Corinth. In chapter 65 the names of the men who carried
the letter to Corinth are given. Concerning the names of the first two—
Claudius Ephebus and Valerius Biton—Johannes Weiss writes as follows:

> They are double names and their first members, Claudius and Valerius,
> permit us to conjecture, rather reasonably, a connection with two famous
> families, the *gens Claudia* and the *gens Valeria*. To the *gens Claudia*
> belonged the first imperial house, the Julian-Claudian, which died out
> with Nero in the year 68. Tiberius and Drusus were Claudians, as well as
> Germanicus, Claudius, Caligula, Britannicus, and Nero, and Suetonius
> has depicted the renown and nobility of the *gens Claudia* at the begin-
> ning of his biography of Tiberius. The *gens Valeria*, likewise very old and
> highly celebrated, became connected with the *gens Claudia* in the mar-
> riage which the emperor Claudius made with Messalina (executed in
> A.D. 48), a woman of the *gens Valeria*—that famous and proverbially
> savage amazon, whose deeds Tacitus (Annal. 11.2f, 12, 26, 38), Suetonius
> (*Claudius*, 26 ff), and the poet Juvenal (Satire 6:115–135) have portrayed.
> A good proportion of the slaves of the rich Valerian house came into

the palace as a dowry at the time of the nuptials, and among the freedmen of Claudius and his successors are frequently to be found, as the inscriptions show, people bearing the family names of their masters—and indeed the two gentile names often appear connected with each other on the same stone. It is thus no groundless conjecture to recognize in the two ambassadors whom the Roman church sent to Corinth, perhaps about the year 85, freedmen of the imperial household. They cannot have been members of the two ancient and proud patrician houses, and certainly not of the imperial house itself. It is impossible to assume that they are slaves, because of the form of their names. Moreover they were masters of their own time if they could consent to go on the embassy on behalf of the church of Rome. The people from the emperor's house have thus preserved their honorable position within the Roman church.[23]

We should think of the Roman church, then, even at the time Paul sent his letter, as a collection of house churches scattered throughout the city and yet possessing liaison among themselves and able to unite in a common endeavor. Unlike the church at Jerusalem, which was limited by poverty, this church could be of immense help to Paul in realizing his desire to carry the gospel farther west, even to Spain. With the exception of a few smaller churches in the area, as noted above, it was probably the only church in a position to serve as a missionary base for Gaul and Spain. This helps to explain why it was that Paul's westward vision seemed always to have been joined with the existence of a church at Rome (Acts 19:21; cf. 23:11; Rom. 15:24, 28).

The Roman Church under Persecution

Like the Jerusalem church, the Christian community at Rome suffered persecution, but unlike the Jerusalem church it was able to survive the ordeal and grow stronger, finally taking a dominant position in the West and throughout Christendom.

The first attack on the Roman church is connected with the name of Nero. Tacitus is the leading Roman source of information.

> But all the endeavors of men, all the emperor's largesse and the propitiations of the gods, did not suffice to allay the scandal or banish the belief that the fire had been ordered. And so, to get rid of this rumor, Nero set up as the culprits and punished with the utmost refinement of cruelty a class hated for their abominations, who are commonly called Christians. Christus, from whom their name is derived, was executed at the hands of the procurator Pontius Pilate in the reign of Tiberius. Checked for the moment, this pernicious superstition again broke out, not only in Judea, the source of the evil, but even in Rome, that receptacle for everything that is sordid and degrading from every quarter of the globe, which there finds a following. Accordingly, arrest was first made of those who confessed [that is, to being Christians]; then, on their evidence, an

immense multitude was convicted, not so much on the charge of arson as because of hatred of the human race. Besides being put to death they were made to serve as objects of amusement; they were clad in the hides of beasts and torn to death by dogs; others were crucified; others set on fire to serve to illuminate the night when daylight failed. Nero had thrown open his grounds for the display, and was putting on a show in the circus, where he mingled with the people in the dress of a charioteer or drove about in his chariot. All this gave rise to a feeling of pity, even towards men whose guilt merited the most exemplary punishment; for it was felt that they were being destroyed not for the public good but to gratify the cruelty of an individual.[24]

The earliest Christian testimony concerning this initial persecution of the Roman church comes from 1 Clement, written to the Corinthian church by Clement as the spokesman of the church in Rome. He says nothing about Nero, but blames the persecution on envy and jealousy, the very features that were threatening havoc in the church at Corinth. After citing the deaths of Peter and Paul (chap. 5), Clement goes on to say, "To these men with their holy lives was gathered a great multitude of the chosen, who were the victims of jealousy and offered among us the fairest example in their endurance under many indignities and tortures" (chap. 6).

These two accounts, so different in their viewpoint, agree respecting the large numbers of Christians who lost their lives at this time. It became customary from this period on to bury believers in the catacombs, the passageways which eventually became a network totalling hundreds of miles. The majority of the epitaphs in the oldest sections of the catacombs are in Greek rather than Latin. These epitaphs give no information about the wealth or rank of the deceased, but simply state the name, age, and some brief comment about the faith of the departed.

The terms *envy* and *jealousy* used in 1 Clement invite reflection. If the Christians were despised, it becomes a bit dubious to suppose that the pagan Romans were either envious or jealous of them, whereas the motive mentioned by Tacitus is fully understandable, since Christians were despised for their exclusiveness and their "atheism" (unwillingness to recognize the gods and especially the deified Caesar). It is, however, possible that jealousy could have played a part in the persecution of Paul. In the first chapter of Philippians, writing as a prisoner, he cites the fact that although he no longer has the freedom to preach (except to the Praetorian guard), others have taken up the responsibility, but that some of them preach Christ from envy and rivalry, thinking to afflict him thereby in his imprisonment (vv. 15, 17). The similarity in the use of the word *envy* between the accounts of Paul and Clement is striking, and we know that Clement is relating what has happened at Rome ("among us"). It is just possible, then, that Paul at least was turned over to the authorities, perhaps on the promise of immunity from persecution, by those of a Judaizing tendency in the Roman church.

It is not necessary to assume that Paul suffered shortly after writing Philippians, for this was early in the 60s, before the conflagration in the city. There is evidence that makes it probable, if not certain, that the apostle was set free after the two years of imprisonment and enjoyed a short period of missionary activity. Whether he was able to go to Spain is not certain; it remains a possibility. More certain is his return to the East (Philem. 22). The pastoral epistles seem to reflect this late missionary activity as well as increasing opposition to the apostle (1 Tim. 1:3–7; 2 Tim. 1:15). Demas forsook him. Only Luke was with him when he was taken back to prison in Rome; his prospect on that occasion was not deliverance but rather an entrance into the heavenly kingdom (2 Tim. 4:6–9).

The case can be made that 1 Peter was written from Rome (5:13) in an atmosphere of impending trouble for believers both near and far (see, for example, 4:12). Possibly Peter sensed that severe trial was close at hand and might spread to saints in Asia Minor, and so he wrote to prepare them. There is archeological evidence that Peter and Paul were martyred in Rome.[25]

A generation after the Neronian persecution, the Roman church once again experienced the scourge of imperial disfavor during the reign of Domitian, reported by both Roman and Christian writers. Dio Cassius has this record:

> In the same year (95), Domitian had many executed, among many others Flavius Clemens, who was consul, although he was his cousin and was married to Flavia Domitilla, who likewise was a relative of the emperor. Both were accused of atheism, on account of which still many others, who had become perverted to Jewish customs, were condemned, some to death, and others to confiscation of property. Domitilla was however merely banished to Pandateria[26]

Eusebius also records that many Christians suffered martyrdom under Domitian. The reason this emperor afflicted the church was largely personal, a matter of his vanity and his insistence on being recognized as divine by all his subjects. Christians were unable to comply and remain true to their Lord.

The Roman church had just passed through this second bloodbath when 1 Clement was written. Right at the beginning, immediately after the salutation, the letter cites as the reason for delay in writing to the church at Corinth "the sudden and repeated misfortunes and calamities which have befallen us."

This letter not only prescribes a remedy for the troubles besetting the Corinthian church but also indirectly reveals the character and outlook of the Roman church of this period. Johannes Weiss has analyzed the letter from this standpoint and notes that the prevailing emphasis is on such matters as order, moderation, and a certain broad-mindedness, features that were needed to enable the church to assume the leadership it did in fact exercise through coming days.

Early in the second century, Ignatius, headed for Rome and martyrdom, wrote to the church there, but he was so preoccupied with his own prospect that he had little to say about the Roman church. However, he did commend it for teaching others and also said, "I do not order you as did Peter and Paul."[27]

Had it not been for the church at Rome, believers of subsequent centuries would have lacked this treasure, Paul's letter to the Romans, with its comprehensive exposition of salvation and its clear guidance for Christian living. The apostle spells out in some detail the gospel he has been proclaiming in the East in order that the Roman church may know just what sort of proclamation they will be expected to support if the author becomes their emissary to the unevangelized regions of the West.

Endnotes

Introduction

1. Bruce, "The History of New Testament Study," in *New Testament Interpretation*, ed. I. Howard Marshall (Grand Rapids: William B. Eerdmans, 1977), p. 51.

2. Goppelt, in *Current Issues in New Testament Interpretation: Essays in Honor of Otto A. Piper*, ed. William Klassen and Graydon F. Snyder (New York: Harper, 1962), p. 204.

3. Bornkamm, "Mimnēskomai," in *Theological Dictionary of the New Testament*, ed. Gerhard Kittel and Gerhard Friedrich, trans. Geoffrey W. Bromiley (Grand Rapids: William B. Eerdmans, 1964–76), 4: 676.

4. Schlatter, *Der Evangelist Matthäus* (Stuttgart: Calwer, 1929), pp. 477–78.

5. Marshall, "Orthodoxy and Heresy in Earlier Christianity," *Themelios*, September 1976, p. 7.

6. Goppelt, *Apostolic and Post-Apostolic Times*, trans. Robert A. Guelich (1962; London: Adam & Charles Black, 1970), p. 125.

Chapter I

1. Philo, *The Embassy to Gaius*, 36.281, 282.

2. Josephus, *Antiquities*, 14.7.2.

3. See Josephus, *The Jewish War*, 7.43–62, 110–11.

4. R. McL. Wilson, in *Peake's Commentary on the Bible*, ed. Matthew Black (New York: Thomas Nelson, 1962), p. 712b.

5. Erwin Rhode, *Psyche: The Cult of Souls and Belief in Immortality among the Greeks*, trans. W. B. Hillis (1925; London: Routledge & Kegan Paul, 1950), p. 130.

6. Tarn, *Hellenistic Civilization*, 3d rev. ed. (London: Edward Arnold, 1952), p. 337.

7. Fairweather, *The Background of the Epistles* (New York: Scribner's, 1935), p. 265.

8. Wilson, *The Gnostic Problem: A Study of the Relations between Hellenistic Judaism and the Gnostic Heresy* (London: A. R. Mowbray, 1958), pp. 69–70.

9. Piper, *God in History* (New York: Macmillan, 1939), p. 84.

10. Fairweather, pp. 25–26.

11. Angus, *The Environment of Early Christianity* (New York: Scribner's, 1921), p. 85.

12. Ethelbert Stauffer, *Christ and the Caesars: Historical Sketches*, trans. K. and R. Gregor Smith (Philadelphia: Westminster Press, 1955), p. 208.

13. Wolfson, *Philo: Foundations of Religious Philosophy in Judaism, Christianity, and Islam* (Cambridge: Harvard University Press, 1947), 1: 10–11.

Chapter II

1. Lietzmann, *The Beginnings of the Christian Church*, trans. Bertram Lee Woolf (New York: Scribner's, 1952), p. 251.

2. Baur, *Paul: His Life and Works* (Edinburgh: Williams & Norgate, 1873), 1: 132.

3. Holtzmann, in *The Beginnings of Christianity*, ed. F. J. Foakes-Jackson and Kirsopp Lake (London: Macmillan, 1920–33), 2: 383.

4. Hunkin, in *The Beginnings of Christianity*, 2:420.

5. Ramsay, *Pauline and Other Studies in Early Church History*, 2d ed. (London: Hodder & Stoughton, 1906), p. 199.

6. Conzelmann, *The Theology of St. Luke*, trans. Geoffrey Buswell (New York: Harper & Row, 1961), pp. 36–37.

7. Hengel, *Acts and the History of Earliest Christianity*, trans. John Bowden (1979; Philadelphia: Fortress Press, 1980), p. 55.

8. Thucydides, *History of the Peloponnesian War*, 1.22.1–2.

9. Gärtner, *The Aereopagus Speech and Natural Revelation*, Acta Senarii Neotestamentici Upsaliensis, no. 21, trans. Carolyn Hannay King (Uppsala: G. W. K. Gleerup, 1955), p. 9.

10. Jaeger, *Early Christianity and Greek Paideia* (Cambridge, Mass.: Belknap Press, 1961), p. 112.

11. Jaeger, p. 11.

12. Knox, *Some Hellenistic Elements in Primitive Christianity* (London: Oxford University Press, 1944), p. 28.

13. Gärtner, pp. 251–52.

14. Josephus, *Antiquities*, 1.222ff.

15. Moule, "The Christology of Acts," in *Studies in Luke-Acts*, ed. Leander E. Keck and J. Louis Martyn (Nashville: Abingdon Press, 1966), p. 170.

16. Burkitt, *Christian Beginnings* (London: University of London Press, 1924), p. 96.

17. Ramsay, *Was Christ Born at Bethlehem? A Study on the Credibility of St. Luke* (New York: G. P. Putnam, 1898), p. 40.

18. Haenchen, *The Acts of the Apostles: A Commentary*, trans. Basil Blackwell (Philadelphia: Westminster Press, 1971), pp. 136–37.

19. Haenchen, "The Book of Acts as Source Material for the History of Early Christianity," in *Studies in Luke-Acts*, p. 260.

20. Lightfoot, *Essays on Supernatural Religion* (London: Macmillan, 1893), p. 292.

21. James Hope Moulton and George Milligan, *The Vocabulary of the Greek New Testament* (Grand Rapids: William B. Eerdmans, 1930), p. 132.

22. Hanson, *The Acts*, in The New Clarendon Bible (Oxford: Clarendon Press, 1967), p. 6.

23. Sherwin-White, *Roman Society and Roman Law in the New Testament* (Oxford: Clarendon Press, 1963), pp. 154–55.

24. Sherwin-White, p. 173.

25. Sherwin-White, p. 55.

26. Sherwin-White, pp. 68–69.

27. See Joachim Jeremias, *Jerusalem in the Time of Jesus: An Investigation into Economic and Social Conditions during the New Testament Period*, trans. F. H. and C. H. Cave (1967; Philadelphia: Fortress Press, 1969), p. 27.

28. See Josephus, *Antiquities*, 20.98–102.

29. Sherwin-White, p. 189.

Chapter III

1. Schlatter, *The Church in the New Testament Period*, trans. Paul P. Levertoff (1926; London: S.P.C.K., 1955), p. 7.

2. Schlatter, p. 13.

3. Bauer, *A Greek-English Lexicon of the New Testament*, 4th ed., trans. and ed. William F. Arndt and F. Wilbur Gingrich, rev. F. Wilbur Gingrich and Frederick W. Danker (Chicago: University of Chicago Press, 1979), p. xxiv.

4. Schlatter, pp. 12–13.

5. Schlatter, p. 16.

6. Caird, *The Apostolic Age* (London: Gerald Duckworth, 1955), p. 50.

7. For more on this, see David W. Wead, "The Centripetal Philosophy of Mission," in *Scripture, Tradition, and Interpretation*, ed. W. Ward Gasque and William Sanford LaSor (Grand Rapids: William B. Eerdmans, 1978), pp. 176–86.

8. Goppelt, *Apostolic and Post-Apostolic Times*, trans. Robert A. Guelich (1962; London: Adam & Charles Black, 1970), pp. 81–82.

9. Jaeger, *Early Christianity and Greek Paideia* (Cambridge, Mass.: Belknap Press, 1961), p. 108.

10. Caird, p. 87.

11. Goppelt, pp. 68–69.

12. Dix, *Jew and Greek: A Study in the Primitive Church* (London: Dacre Press, 1953), pp. 61ff.

13. Goppelt, *Jesus, Paul and Judaism: An Introduction to New Testament Theology*, trans. Edward Schroeder (New York: Thomas Nelson, 1964), p. 104.

14. Goppelt, *Apostolic and Post-Apostolic Times*, p. 59.

15. See Bo Reicke, *The New Testament Era: The World of the Bible from 500 B.C. to A.D. 100*, trans. David E. Green (Philadelphia: Fortress Press, 1968), pp. 190–92.

16. Goguel, *The Birth of Christianity*, trans. H. C. Snape (1946; London: Allen & Unwin, 1953), p. 108.

17. Peter Richardson, *Israel in the Apostolic Church*, Society for New Testament Studies Monograph Series, no. 10 (London: Cambridge University Press, 1969), pp. 46–47.

18. Goppelt, *Jesus, Paul and Judaism*, p. 118.

19. Josephus, *Antiquities*, 20.200–203.

20. See Eusebius, *Ecclesiastical History*, 2.22.4–18.

21. Goguel, p. 124.

22. Goguel, p. 131.

23. Eusebius, *Ecclesiastical History*, 3.5.3.

24. See S. G. F. Brandon, *The Fall of Jerusalem and the Christian Church: A Study of the Effects of the Jewish Overthrow of A.D. 70 on Christianity* (London: S.P.C.K., 1957), pp. 169ff.

25. Goguel, 133.

26. McGavran, *The Bridges of God: A Study in the Strategy of Missions* (London: World Dominion Press, 1955), pp. 18–19.

27. Adolf von Harnack, *The Expansion of Christianity in the First Three Centuries*, ed. and trans. James Moffatt (London: Williams & Norgate, 1904–5), 2: 285.

28. Latourette, *A History of the Expansion of Christianity*, vol. 1, *First Five Centuries* (New York: Harper & Bros., 1937), p. 102.

29. Harnack, 2: 330.

30. Harnack, 2: 387.

31. Harnack, 2: 441.

32. Eusebius, *Ecclesiastical History*, 2.16.1.

33. Eusebius, *Ecclesiastical History*, 2.24.

34. See L. W. Barnard, "The New Testament and the Origins of Christianity in Egypt," in *Studia Evangelica*, ed. F. L. Cross (Berlin: Akademie-Verlag, 1968), 4: 277–80.

35. See F. F. Bruce, *New Testament History* (Garden City, N.Y.: Doubleday, 1969), pp. 276–78.

36. See Brandon, p. 178.

37. See Günther Bornkamm, Intro. to *The Acts of Thomas*, in *New Testament Apocrypha*, ed. Edgar Hennecke and Wilhelm Schneemelcher, trans. R. McL. Wilson (1964; Philadelphia: Westminster Press, 1965), 2: 425–31.

38. From *The Preaching of Peter* (v. 3), in *The Apocryphal New Testament*, trans. Montague Rhodes James (Oxford: Clarendon Press, 1924), p. 17.

39. Caird, p. 103.

40. Reicke, p. 304.

41. For a refutation of this position, see J. A. T. Robinson, *Redating the New Testament* (Philadelphia: Westminster Press, 1976), pp. 150–63.

42. Oscar Cullmann, *The State in the New Testament* (London: SCM Press, 1957), p. 35.

43. Ethelbert Stauffer, *Christ and the Caesars: Historical Sketches*, trans. K. and R. Gregor Smith (Philadelphia: Westminster Press, 1955), p. 125.

44. Stauffer, pp. 130, 131.

45. Stauffer, pp. 133–34.

46. Karl Barth, *A Shorter Commentary on Romans*, trans. D. H. van Darlen (1956; London: SCM Press, 1959), p. 158.

47. See Oscar Cullmann, "The Question of World Affirmation or World Denial in Light of the New Testament Redemptive History," in *Christ and Time: The Primitive Christian Conception of Time and History*, trans. Floyd V. Filson (Philadelphia: Westminster Press, 1964), pp. 191–210; see also Cullmann, *The State in the New Testament*, pp. 95–114.

48. Simeon L. Guterman, *Religious Toleration and Persecution in Ancient Rome* (London: Aiglon Press, 1951), p. 44.

49. Wilder, "Social Factors in Early Christian Eschatology," in *Early Christian Origins: Studies in Honor of Harold R. Willoughby*, ed. Allen Wikgren (Chicago: Quadrangle Books, 1961), p. 69.

50. F. J. A. Hort, *The First Epistle of St. Peter* (London: Macmillan, 1898), p. 76.

51. See E. M. Blaiklock, *The Christian in Pagan Society* (London: Tyndale Press, 1951), p. 9.

52. Gardner-Smith, "The Church in the Roman Empire," in *The Expansion of the Christian Church*, by P. Gardner-Smith and F. J. Foakes-Jackson (Cambridge: Cambridge University Press, 1934), p. 49.

53. Cadoux, *The Early Church and the World: A History of the Christian Attitude to Pagan Society and the State down to the Time of Constantinus* (Edinburgh: T. & T. Clark, 1925), pp. 90–92.

54. Sanders, *A Commentary on the Gospel according to John,* Harper's New Testament Commentaries, ed. B. A. Mastin (New York: Harper & Row, 1968), p. 317.

55. Daube, *The New Testament and Rabbinic Judaism* (London: Athalone Press, 1956, pp. 346–49.

56. See S. Scott Bartchy, "First-Century Slavery and the Interpretation of 1 Corinthians 7:21," Ph.D. diss., Harvard University, 1971, p. 88.

57. See Samuel Dickey, "Some Economic and Social Factors Affecting the Expansion of Christianity," in *Studies in Early Christianity,* ed. Shirley Jackson Case (New York: The Century Co., 1928), p. 404.

58. Rengstorf, *"Doulos,"* in *Theological Dictionary of the New Testament,* ed. Gerhard Kittel and Gerhard Friedrich, trans. Geoffrey W. Bromiley (Grand Rapids: William B. Eerdmans, 1964–76), 2: 271.

59. Gardner-Smith, p. 50.

60. Bevan, *Hellenism and Christianity* (London: Allen & Unwin, 1921), p. 87.

Chapter IV

1. Bultmann, *Theology of the New Testament,* trans. Kendrick Grobel (New York: Scribner's, 1951), 1: 93–94.

2. Flew, *Jesus and His Church: A Study of the Idea of the Ecclesia in the New Testament* (New York: Abingdon Press, 1938), p. 90.

3. For more on this topic, see Oscar Cullmann's *Peter: Disciple, Apostle, Martyr,* 2d rev. ed., trans. Floyd V. Filson (1953; London: SCM Press, 1962), pp. 220–28.

4. Schmidt, *"Ekklēsia,"* in *Theological Dictionary of the New Testament,* ed. Gerhard Kittel and Gerhard Friedrich, trans. Geoffrey W. Bromiley (Grand Rapids: William B. Eerdmans, 1964–76), 3: 526.

5. Goppelt, *Apostolic and Post-Apostolic Times,* trans. Robert A. Guelich (1962; London: Adam & Charles Black, 1970), p. 180.

6. Goppelt, p. 180.

7. See F. F. Bruce, *New Testament History* (Garden City, N.Y.: Doubleday, 1969), p. 371.

8. Thomas M. Lindsay, *The Church and the Ministry in the Early Centuries* (New York: George H. Doran, 1903), p. 116.

9. Moule, "The Christology of Acts," in *Studies in Luke-Acts,* ed. Leander E. Keck and J. Louis Martyn (Nashville: Abingdon Press, 1966), pp. 159–85.

10. Moule, p. 161.

11. Betz, *What Do We Know about Jesus?* trans. Margaret Kohl (London: SCM Press, 1968), p. 82.

12. Moule, p. 164.

13. Bruce, *The Acts of the Apostles* (Grand Rapids: William B. Eerdmans, 1951), p. 96.

14. See Ehrhardt's *The Framework of the New Testament Stories* (Cambridge: Harvard University Press, 1964), p. 151.

15. Rufinus, in J. N. D. Kelly, *Early Christian Creeds* (London: Longmans, Green, 1950), pp. 1–2.

16. Rufinus, in J. N. D. Kelly, p. 4.

17. Schaff, *The Creeds of Christendom,* vol. 1, *The History of Creeds,* 3d rev. ed. (New York: Harper & Bros., 1881), pp. 14–23.

18. Stauffer, *New Testament Theology*, trans. John Marsh (London: SCM Press, 1955), pp. 338–39.

19. Goppelt, p. 161

20. Schweizer, "Two New Testament Creeds Compared," in *Current Issues in New Testament Interpretation: Essays in Honor of Otto Piper*, ed. William Klassen and Graydon F. Snyder (New York: Harper, 1962), p. 171.

21. See Joachim Jeremias, *The Eucharistic Words of Jesus*, trans. Norman Perrin (Philadelphia: Fortress Press, 1977), pp. 129–31.

22. See A. M. Hunter, *Paul and His Predecessors* (1940; London: SCM Press, 1961).

23. See Thomas F. Torrance, "Proselyte Baptism," *New Testament Studies*, 1 (1954): 154.

24. Flemington, *The New Testament Doctrine of Baptism* (London: S.P.C.K., 1953), p. 75.

25. Daube, *The New Testament and Rabbinic Judaism* (London: Athalone Press, 1956), p. 112.

26. Lake, in his inaugural lecture at Leiden, January 1904.

27. Lampe, *The Seal of the Spirit: A Study in the Doctrine of Baptism and Confirmation in the New Testament and the Fathers* (London: Longmans, Green, 1957), p. 57.

28. Lampe, pp. 34–35.

29. Dunn, *Baptism in the Holy Spirit* (Philadelphia: Westminster Press, 1970), p. 128.

30. Hans Bietenhard, "*Onoma*," in *Theological Dictionary of the New Testament*, 5: 274.

31. Scott, *The Beginnings of the Church* (New York: Scribner's, 1925), p. 181.

32. Denney, *The Death of Christ*, ed. and rev. R. V. G. Tasker (1902; Tyndale Press, 1951), p. 185.

33. Schlatter, *The Church in the New Testament Period*, trans. Paul P. Levertoff (1926; London: S.P.C.K., 1955), p. 63.

34. Justin Martyr, *First Apology*, chap. 67.

35. Moule, *The Birth of the New Testament* (New York: Harper & Row, 1962), p. 27.

36. Cullmann, *Early Christian Worship*, trans. A. Stewart Todd and James B. Torrance (1953; Philadelphia: Westminster Press, 1978), p. 21.

37. Cullmann, *Early Christian Worship*, p. 27.

38. Lindsay, pp. 43ff.

39. Goguel, *The Primitive Church*, trans. H. C. Snape (1947; London: Allen & Unwin, 1964), p. 257.

40. Jeremias, pp. 72–87, 105ff.

41. Jeremias, p. 129. Jeremias notes other un-Pauline elements as well (see p. 131).

42. Jean-Jacques von Allmen, *The Lord's Supper*, Ecumenical Studies in Worship, no. 19 (Richmond: John Knox Press, 1969), pp. 32–33.

43. Manson, *Jesus and the Christian* (Grand Rapids: William B. Eerdmans, 1967), p. 98.

44. Barth, *Church Dogmatics*, vol. 4, pt. 4, *The Christian Life*, trans. Geoffrey W. Bromiley (Edinburgh: T. & T. Clark, 1969), p. 22.

45. A. B. Davidson, *The Epistle to the Hebrews* (Grand Rapids: Zondervan, 1950)

46. Beyer, "*Diakoneō* outside the New Testament," in *Theological Dictionary of the New Testament*, 2: 83.

47. *Theological Dictionary of the New Testament*, 1: 407–45.

48. Manson, *The Church's Ministry* (London: Hodder & Stoughton, 1948), p. 47.

49. Bromiley, *Christian Ministry* (Grand Rapids: Eerdmans, 1959), p. 24.

50. Ignatius, Epistle to the Trallians 7:2, in *The Apostolic Fathers*, trans. Kirsopp Lake (Cambridge: Harvard University Press, 1912), 1: 219.

51. Käsemann, "Ministry and Community in the New Testament," in *Essays on New Testament Themes*, trans. W. J. Montague (1960; London: SCM Press, 1964), pp. 63–94.

52. Käsemann, pp. 71–72.

53. Bruce, in *A New Testament Commentary*, ed. G. C. D. Howley, et al., p. 95.

54. Floyd V. Filson, *Three Crucial Decades: Studies in the Book of Acts* (Richmond: John Knox Press, 1963), p. 43.

55. Beyer, "*Katēcheō*," in *Theological Dictionary of the New Testament*, 3: 639.

56. Dodd, *Gospel and Law: The Relation of Faith and Ethics in Early Christianity* (New York: Columbia University Press, 1951), pp. 17, 19n.3.

57. Dodd, pp. 20–22.

58. Alfred Plummer, *An Exegetical Commentary on the Gospel according to S. Matthew*, 2d ed. (Grand Rapids: William B. Eerdmans, 1956), p. 252.

59. See Nigel Turner, *Grammatical Insights into the New Testament* (Edinburgh: T. & T. Clark, 1965), p. 80.

60. Lampe, "Church Discipline and the Interpretation of the Epistles to the Corinthians," in *Christian History and Interpretation: Studies Presented to John Knox*, ed. W. R. Farmer, C. F. D. Moule, and R. R. Niebuhr (Cambridge: Cambridge University Press, 1967), p. 351.

61. F. J. Foakes-Jackson, *Studies in the Life of the Early Church* (New York: George A. Doran, 1927), p. 42.

62. Foakes-Jackson, pp. 41–42.

Chapter V

1. Scott, *Christianity according to St. Paul* (Cambridge: Cambridge University Press, 1932), p. 160.

2. See Joachim Jeremias, *Jerusalem in the Time of Jesus: An Investigation into Economic and Social Conditions during the New Testament Period*, trans. F. H. and C. H. Cave (1967; Philadelphia: Fortress Press, 1969), p. 131.

3. Josephus, *The Jewish War*, 7.3.3.

4. See Bousset, *Kyrios Christos: A History of the Belief in Christ from the Beginnings of Christianity to Irenaeus*, trans. John E. Steely (Nashville: Abingdon Press, 1970).

5. See Glanville Downey, *Ancient Antioch* (Princeton University Press, 1963), p. 90.

6. Johannes Weiss, *Earliest Christianity: A History of the Period A.D. 30–150*, trans. and ed. Frederick C. Grant (New York: Harper, 1959), 1: 171.

7. Cadbury, *The Book of Acts in History* (London: Adam & Charles Black, 1955), p. 58.

8. See W. M. Ramsay, *St. Paul the Traveller and the Roman Citizen* (New York: G. P. Putnam, 1896), pp. 200–205.

9. Ramsay, p. 219.

10. Lightfoot, *Biblical Essays* (London: Macmillan, 1893), p. 259.

11. Lightfoot, *St. Paul's Epistle to the Philippians* (London: Macmillan, 1879), p. 56.

12. Jean Juster, *Les Juifs dans l'empire Romain* (Paris: P. Geuthner, 1914), 1: 188–94.

13. Schlatter, *The Church in the New Testament Period*, trans. Paul P. Levertoff (1926; London: S.P.C.K., 1955), p. 163.

14. Longenecker, *The Christology of Early Jewish Christianity*, Studies in Biblical Theology, 2d ser., vol. 17 (London: SCM Press, 1970), p. 56.

15. Ambrosiaster, *Epistula ad Romanos*, Intro., sect. 2, 3.

16. Seutonius, *Claudius*, 25.

17. Weiss, 1: 365.

18. Philip Schaff, *History of the Christian Church*, vol. 1, *Apostolic Christianity, A.D. 1–100* (1910; Grand Rapids: William B. Eerdmans, 1980), p. 372.

19. Robinson, *Redating the New Testament* (Philadelphia: Westminster Press, 1976), pp. 206–7.

20. Orr, *Neglected Factors in the Study of the Early Progress of Christianity* (London: Hodder & Stoughton, 1899), p. 100.

21. Cranfield, *A Critical and Exegetical Commentary on the Epistle to the Romans*, International Critical Commentary, 6th ed. (Edinburgh: T. & T. Clark, 1975), 1: 218.

22. Dodd, *The Epistle of Paul to the Romans* (London: Hodder & Stoughton, 1932), p. xxii.

23. Weiss, 2: 845.

24. Tacitus, *Annales*, 15.44.

25. See Jack Finegan, *Light from the Ancient Past: The Archeological Background of Judaism and Christianity* (Princeton: Princeton University Press, 1959), pp. 297–304.

26. Dio Cassius, *Roman History*, 67.14.

27. Ignatius, Epistle to the Romans, 3:1, 4:3.

Selected Bibliography

Chapter I, Section 1

Angus, Samuel. *The Environment of Early Christianity*. New York: Scribner's, 1921. Pp. 68–139.

Bruce, F. F. *New Testament History*. 1969. Garden City, N. Y.: Doubleday, 1971. Pp. 1–40.

Fairweather, William. *The Background of the Epistles*. New York: Scribner's, 1935. Pp. 201–91.

Grant, Frederick C. *Roman Hellenism and the New Testament*. London: Oliver & Boyd, 1962. Pp. 1–31.

Halliday, W. G. *The History of Roman Religion*. Liverpool: University Press of Liverpool, 1922. Pp. 1– 167.

Pfeiffer, R. H. *History of New Testament Times*. New York: Harper, 1949. Pp. 5–45.

Schürer, E. *A History of the Jewish People in the Time of Jesus Christ (175 B.C.–A.D. 135)*. Revised and edited by Geza Vermes and Fergus Millar. 1898. Edinburgh: T. & T. Clark, 1973. Div. II, vols. 1–3.

Tenney, Merrill C. *New Testament Times*. Grand Rapids: William B. Eerdmans, 1965. Pp. 25–98.

Chapter I, Section 2

Angus, Samuel, *The Religious Quests of the Graeco-Roman World: A Study in the Historical Background of Early Christianity*. New York: Scribner's, 1929. Pp. 1–46.

Caird, G. B. *The Apostolic Age*. London: Gerald Duckworth, 1955. Pp. 21–35.

Cumont, Franz. *The Oriental Religions in Roman Paganism*. Chicago: Open Court Publishing, 1911.

Davies, W. D. "Contemporary Jewish Religion." In *Peake's Commentary on the Bible*. Edited by Matthew Black. New York: Thomas Nelson, 1962. Pp. 705–11.

Halliday, W. G. *The History of Roman Religion*. Liverpool: University Press of Liverpool, 1922. Pp. 131–78.

Hengel, Martin. *Judaism and Hellenism*. 2 vols. Translated by John Bowden. London: SCM Press, 1974.

Macgregor, G. H. C., and A. C. Purdy. *Jew and Greek, Tutors unto Christ: The Jewish and Hellenistic Background of the New Testament*. New York: Scribner's, 1935. Pp. 273–329.

Nock, A. D. *Conversion: The Old and the New in Religion from Alexander the Great to Augustine of Hippo*. Oxford: Clarendon Press, 1933.

Stauffer, Ethelbert. *Christ and the Caesars: Historical Sketches*. Translated by K. and R. Gregor Smith. Philadelphia: Westminster Press, 1955.

Sweet, Louis Matthews. *Roman Emperor Worship*. Boston: R. G. Badger, 1919.

Tenney, Merrill C. *New Testament Times*. Grand Rapids: William B. Eerdmans, 1965.

Chapter II, Section 1

Aune, David E. "The Significance of the Delay of the Parousia for Early Christianity." In *Current Issues in Biblical and Patristic Interpretation: Studies in Honor of Merrill C. Tenney Presented by His Students*. Edited by Gerald F. Hawthorne. Grand Rapids: William B. Eerdmans, 1975. Pp. 87–109.

Barrett, C. K. *New Testament Essays*. London: S.P.C.K., 1972. Pp. 101–15.

Burkitt, F. C. *Christian Beginnings*. London: University of London Press, 1924.

Cadbury, Henry J. *The Making of Luke-Acts*. New York: Macmillan, 1927.

Cullmann, Oscar. *The Early Church: Studies in Early Christian History and Theology*. Translated by A. J. B. Higgins and S. Godman. Edited by A. J. B. Higgins. Philadelphia: Westminster Press, 1956. Pp. 3–16.

Gasque, W. Ward. *A History of the Criticism of the Acts of the Apostles*. Beiträge zur Geschichte der biblischen Exegese, no. 17. Tübingen: J. C. B. Mohr, 1975.

Hengel, Martin. *Acts and the History of Earliest Christianity*. Translated by John Bowden. 1979. Philadelphia: Fortress Press, 1980.

Machen, J. Grescham. *The Origin of Paul's Religion*. London: Hodder & Stoughton, 1921.

McGiffert, A. C. In *The Beginnings of Christianity*. Edited by F. J. Foakes-Jackson and Kirsopp Lake. London: Macmillan, 1920–33. 2: 363–433.

Marshall, I. Howard. "Early Catholicism in the New Testament." In *New Dimensions in New Testament Study*. Edited by Richard N. Longenecker and Merrill C. Tenney. Grand Rapids: Zondervan, 1974. Pp. 217–31.

Ropes, James Hardy. *The Apostolic Age in the Light of Modern Criticism*. New York: Scribner's, 1906.

Chapter II, Section 2

Bowker, J. W. "Speeches in Acts." *New Testament Studies* 14 (October 1967): 96–111.

Bruce, F. F. *The Speeches in Acts*. Tyndale New Testament Lecture, 1942. London: Tyndale Press, 1943.

Cadbury, Henry J. In *The Beginnings of Christianity*. Edited by F. J. Foakes-Jackson and Kirsopp Lake. London: Macmillan, 1920–33. 5: 402–27.

Conzelmann, Hans. "The Address of Paul on the Aereopagus." In *Studies in Luke-Acts*. Edited by Leander E. Keck and J. Louis Martyn. Nashville: Abingdon Press, 1966. Pp. 217–30.

Dibelius, Martin. "The Speeches in Acts and Ancient Historiography." In *Studies in the Acts of the Apostles*. Edited by Heinrich Greeven. Translated by Mary Ling and Paul Schubert. 1951. London: SCM Press, 1956. Pp. 138–85.

Gardner, P. "The Speeches of Paul in Acts." In *Cambridge Biblical Essays*. Edited by H. B. Swete. London: Macmillan, 1905. Pp. 380–419.

Gärtner, Bertil. *The Aereopagus Speech and Natural Revelation*. Translated by Carolyn Hannay King. Acta Senarii Neotestamentici Upsaliensis, no. 21. Uppsala: G. W. K. Gleerup, 1955.

Gasque, W. Ward. *A History of the Criticism of the Acts of the Apostles*. Beiträge zur Geschichte der biblischen Exegese, no. 17. Tübingen: J. C. B. Mohr, 1975. Pp. 210–34.

Ridderbos, H. N. *The Speeches of Peter in the Acts of the Apostles*. Tyndale New Testament Lecture, 1961. London: Tyndale Press, 1962.

Schubert, P. "The Final Cycle of Speeches in the Book of Acts." *Journal of Biblical Literature* 87 (March 1968): 1–16.

Schweizer, Eduard. "Concerning the Speeches in Acts." In *Studies in Luke-Acts.* Edited by Leander E. Keck and J. Louis Martyn. Nashville: Abingdon Press, 1966. Pp. 208–16.

Stonehouse, N. B. *The Aereopagus Address.* London: Tyndale Press, 1949.

Swamidoss, A. W. "The Speeches of Paul in Acts 13, 17, and 20." Ph.D. diss., Fuller Theological Seminary, 1979.

Chapter II, Section 3

Blaiklock, E. M. "The Acts of the Apostles as a Document of First Century History." In *Apostolic History and the Gospel: Biblical and Historical Essays Presented to F. F. Bruce on His 60th Birthday.* Edited by W. Ward Gasque and Ralph P. Martin. London: Paternoster Press, 1970. Pp. 41– 54.

Bruce, F. F. *The Acts of the Apostles: The Greek Text with Introduction and Commentary.* London: Tyndale Press, 1951. Pp. 15–18.

Burkitt, F. C. *Christian Beginnings.* London: University of London Press, 1924. Pp. 53–97.

Hanson, R. P. C. *The Acts.* The New Clarendon Bible. Oxford: Clarendon Press, 1967. Pp. 2–11.

Knox, Wilfred L. *The Acts of the Apostles.* Cambridge: Cambridge University Press, 1948. Pp. 54–68.

Longenecker, Richard N. *Paul, Apostle of Liberty.* New York: Harper & Row, 1964. Pp. 245–63.

Marshall, I. Howard. *Luke: Historian and Theologian.* London: Paternoster Press, 1970. Pp. 53–76.

Ramsay, W. M. *St. Paul the Traveller and the Roman Citizen.* New York: G. P. Putnam, 1896. Pp. 1–28.

————. *The Bearing of Recent Discovery on the Trustworthiness of the New Testament.* 4th ed. London: Hodder & Stoughton, 1920. Pp. 7–52.

Sherwin-White, A. N. *Roman Society and Roman Law in the New Testament.* Oxford: Clarendon Press, 1963.

Chapter III, Section 1

Bruce, F. F. *Commentary on the Book of Acts.* New International Commentary on the New Testament. Grand Rapids: William B. Eerdmans, 1954. Pp. 53–79.

Dunn, James D. G. *Baptism in the Holy Spirit: A Re-examination of the New Testament Teaching on the Gift of the Spirit in Relation to Pentecostalism Today.* Studies in Biblical Theology, 2d ser., no. 15. London: SCM Press, 1970. Pp. 38–54.

Hopwood, P. G. S. *The Religious Experience of the Primitive Church: The Period prior to the Influence of Paul.* New York: Scribner's, 1937. Pp. 122–206.

Lake, Kirsopp. In *The Beginnings of Christianity.* Edited by F. J. Foakes-Jackson and Kirsopp Lake. London: Macmillan, 1920–33. 5: 111–21.

Morgan, G. Campbell. *The Spirit of God.* New York: Revell, 1900. Pp. 129–41.

Moule, C. F. D. *The Phenomenon of the New Testament: An Inquiry into the Implications of Certain Features of the New Testament.* Studies in Biblical Theology, 2d ser., vol. 1. London: SCM Press, 1967. Pp. 1–20.

Purves, George T. *Christianity in the Apostolic Age.* The Historical Series for Bible Students, vol. 8. New York: Scribner's, 1902. Pp. 9–34.

Schlatter, Adolf. *The Church in the New Testament Period*. Translated by Paul P. Levertoff. 1926. London: S.P.C.K., 1955. Pp. 1–24.

Swete, Henry Barclay. *The Holy Spirit in the New Testament: A Study of Primitive Christian Teaching*. London: Macmillan, 1909. Pp. 63–80.

Weiss, Johannes. *Earliest Christianity: A History of the Period A.D. 30–150*. Translated and edited by Frederick C. Grant. New York: Harper, 1959. Pp. 14–40.

Chapter III, Section 2

Caird, G. B. *The Apostolic Age*. London: Gerald Duckworth, 1955. Pp. 83–115.

DeRidder, Richard R. *Discipling the Nations*. 1971. Grand Rapids: Baker Book, 1975.

Dix, Gregory. *Jew and Greek: A Study in the Primitive Church*. London: Dacre Press, 1953.

Filson, F. V. *Three Crucial Decades: Studies in the Book of Acts*. Richmond: John Knox Press, 1963. Pp. 91–114.

Foakes-Jackson, F. J. *The Rise of Gentile Christianity*. New York: George H. Doran, 1927. Pp. 60–83.

Goguel, Maurice. *The Birth of Christianity*. Translated by H. C. Snape. 1946. London: Allen & Unwin, 1953. Pp. 167–93, 292–303.

Green, Michael. *Evangelism in the Early Church*. London: Hodder & Stoughton, 1970. Pp. 112–43.

Goppelt, Leonhard. *Jesus, Paul and Judaism: An Introduction to New Testament Theology*. Translated by Edward Schroeder. New York: Nelson, 1964. Pp. 110–21.

Hengel, Martin. *Acts and the History of Earliest Christianity*. Translated by John Bowden. 1979. Philadelphia: Fortress Press, 1980. Pp. 69–126.

Longenecker, Richard N. *Paul, Apostle of Liberty*. New York: Harper & Row, 1964. Pp. 211–29.

Schlatter, Adolf. *The Church in the New Testament Period*. Translated by Paul P. Levertoff. 1926. London: S.P.C.K., 1955. Pp. 108–38.

Weiss, Johannes. *Earliest Christianity: A History of the Period A.D. 30–150*. Translated and edited by Frederick C. Grant. New York: Harper, 1959. Pp. 165–77, 203–18, 258–76.

Chapter III, Section 3

Caird, G. B. *The Apostolic Age*. London: Gerald Duckworth, 1955. Pp. 83–94.

Cullmann, Oscar. "Dissensions within the Early Church." In *New Testament Issues*. Edited by Richard Batey. London: SCM Press, 1970. Pp. 119–29.

Goguel, Maurice. *The Birth of Christianity*. Translated by H. C. Snape. 1946. London: Allen & Unwin, 1953. Pp. 106–48.

Goppelt, Leonhard. *Jesus, Paul and Judaism: An Introduction to New Testament Theology*. Translated by Edward Schroeder. New York: Nelson, 1964. Pp. 100–109.

Hort, Fenton John Anthony. *Judaistic Christianity*. London: Macmillan, 1904.

Moule, C. F. D. *The Birth of the New Testament*. New York: Harper & Row, 1962.

Munck, Johannes. *The Acts of the Apostles*. The Anchor Bible, vol. 31. Revised by W. F. Albright and C. S. Mann. Garden City, N.Y.: Doubleday, 1967. Pp. 285–304.

———. "Jewish Christianity in Post-Apostolic Times." *New Testament Studies* 6 (January 1969): 103–16.

Purves, George T. *Christianity in the Apostolic Age*. The Historical Series for Bible Students, vol. 8. New York: Scribner's, 1902. Pp. 169–76.

Schlatter, Adolf. *The Church in the New Testament Period.* Translated by Paul P. Levertoff. 1926. London: S.P.C.K., 1955. Pp. 79–87, 263–73.

Chapter III, Section 4

Allen, Roland. *Spontaneous Expansion of the Church and the Causes Which Hinder It.* London: World Dominion Press, 1956.

Blauw, Johannes. *The Missionary Nature of the Church: A Survey of the Biblical Theology of Mission.* New York: McGraw- Hill, 1962.

Filson, F. V. *A New Testament History.* Philadelphia: Westminster Press, 1964. Pp. 295–322.

Foakes-Jackson, F. J. *Studies in the Life of the Early Church.* New York: George A. Doran, 1927. Pp. 245–54.

Gardner-Smith, P., and F. J. Foakes-Jackson. *The Expansion of the Christian Church.* Cambridge: Cambridge University Press, 1934.

Harnack, Adolf von. *The Expansion of Christianity in the First Three Decades.* Edited and translated by James Moffatt. London: Williams & Norgate, 1904–5. 2: 147–82.

Latourette, Kenneth Scott. *A History of Christianity.* New York: Harper, 1953. Pp. 65–81.

Manson, William. *Jesus and the Christian.* Grand Rapids: William B. Eerdmans, 1967. Pp. 199–207, 208–26.

Neander, Augustus. *History of the Planting and Training of the Christian Church by the Apostles.* Translated by J. E. Leyland. New York: Leavitt, Trow, 1847.

Orr, James. *Neglected Factors in the Early Progress of Christianity.* London: Hodder & Stoughton, 1899.

Ropes, James Hardy. *The Apostolic Age in the Light of Modern Criticism.* New York: Scribner's, 1906. Pp. 37–64.

Streeter, Burnett Hillman. *The Primitive Church, Studied with Special Reference to the Origins of the Christian Ministry.* New York: Macmillan, 1929. Pp. 29–68.

Tenney, Merrill C. *New Testament Times.* Grand Rapids: William B. Eerdmans, 1965. Pp. 251–82.

Chapter III, Section 5

Barrett, C. K. *New Testament Essays.* London: S.P.C.K., 1972. Pp. 1–19.

Borg, M. "A New Context for Romans xiii." *New Testament Studies* 19 (January 1973): 205–18.

Cadoux, C. J. *The Early Church and the World: A History of the Christian Attitude to Pagan Society and the State down to the Time of Constantinus.* Edinburgh: T. & T. Clark, 1925. Pp. 97–115.

Caird, G. B. *The Apostolic Age.* London: Gerald Duckworth, 1955. Pp. 156–80.

Campenhausen, Hans von. *Tradition and Life in the Church: Essays and Lectures in Church History.* Translated by A. V. Littledale. 1960. London: Collins, 1968. Pp. 160–70.

Cranfield, C. E. B. "The Christian's Political Responsibility according to the New Testament." *Scottish Journal of Theology* 15 (1962): 178–92.

Cullmann, Oscar. *The State in the New Testament.* London: SCM Press, 1957. Pp. 50–92

Filson, F. V. *A New Testament History.* Philadelphia: Westminster Press, 1964. Pp. 333–36.

Guterman, Simeon L. *Religious Toleration and Persecution in Ancient Rome*. London: Aiglon Press, 1951.

Käsemann, Ernst. *New Testament Questions of Today*. Translated by W. J. Montague. 1965. London: SCM Press, 1969. Pp. 196–216.

Moule, C. F. D. *The Birth of the New Testament*. New York: Harper & Row, 1962. Pp. 105–24.

Schlier, Heinrich. *The Relevance of the New Testament*. New York: Herder & Herder, 1968. Pp. 215–38.

Stauffer, Ethelbert. *Christ and the Caesars: Historical Sketches*. Translated by K. and R. Gregor Smith. Philadelphia: Westminster Press, 1955. Pp. 112–91, 205–21.

Chapter III, Section 6

Bartchy, S. Scott. "First-Century Slavery and the Interpretation of 1 Corinthians 7:21." Ph.D. diss., Harvard University, 1971.

Blaiklock, E. M. *The Christian in Pagan Society*. London: Tyndale Press, 1951.

Cadoux, C. J. *The Early Church and the World: A History of the Christian Attitude to Pagan Society and the State down to the Time of Constantinus*. Edinburgh: T. & T. Clark, 1925. Pp. 70–84, 90–96, 131–36.

Deems, Mervin M. "Early Christian Asceticism." In *Early Christian Origins*. Edited by Allen Wikgren. Chicago: Quadrangle Books, 1961. Pp. 91–101.

Dobschütz, Ernst von. *Christian Life in the Primitive Church*. Translated by George Bremner. Edited by W. D. Morrison. New York: G. P. Putnam, 1904. Pp. 1–10.

Gardner-Smith, P., and F. J. Foakes-Jackson. *The Expansion of the Christian Church*. Cambridge: Cambridge University Press, 1939. Pp. 46–57.

Goguel, Maurice. *The Primitive Church*. Translated by H. C. Snape. 1947. London: Allen & Unwin, 1964. Pp. 529–32.

Grant, Robert M. *Early Christianity and Society: Seven Studies*. San Francisco: Harper & Row, 1977.

Judge, E. A. *The Social Pattern of Christian Groups in the First Century*. London: Tyndale Press, 1960.

Weiss, Johannes. *Earliest Christianity: A History of the Period A.D. 30–150*. Translated and edited by Frederick C. Grant. New York: Harper, 1959. Pp. 559–94

Zeisler, J. A. *Christian Asceticism*. Grand Rapids: William B. Eerdmans, 1973.

Chapter IV, Section 1

Davies, W. D. *Christian Origins and Judaism*. London: Darton, Longman & Todd, 1962. Pp. 199–229.

Fitzmeyer, J. A. "Jewish Christians in Acts in Light of the Qumran Scrolls." In *Studies in Luke-Acts*. Edited by Leander E. Keck and J. Louis Martyn. Nashville: Abingdon Press, 1966. Pp. 233–57.

Flew, R. Newton. *Jesus and His Church: A Study of the Idea of the Ecclesia in the New Testament*. New York: Abingdon Press, 1938. Pp. 99–120.

Goguel, Maurice. *The Primitive Church*. Translated by H. C. Snape. 1947. London: Allen & Unwin, 1964.

Harnack, Adolf von. *The Constitution and Law of the Church in the First Two Centuries*. New York: G. P. Putnam, 1910. Pp. 1–59.

Hopwood, P. G. S. *The Religious Experience of the Primitive Church: The Period prior to the Influence of Paul*. New York: Scribner's, 1937. Pp. 207–50.

Hort, Fenton John Anthony. *Christian Ecclesia*. London: Macmillan, 1908.

Johnston, George. *The Doctrine of the Church in the New Testament.* Cambridge: Cambridge University Press, 1943.

Lightfoot, J. B. "The Christian Ministry." In *St. Paul's Epistle to the Philippians.* 1868. London: Macmillan, 1879. Pp. 182–269.

Lindsay, Thomas M. *The Church and the Ministry in the Early Centuries.* New York: George H. Doran, 1903. Pp. 3–66.

Manson, T. W. *The Church's Ministry.* London: Hodder & Stoughton, 1948. Pp. 9–30.

Purves, George T. *Christianity in the Apostolic Age.* The Historical Series for Bible Students, vol. 8. New York: Scribner's, 1902. Pp. 35–46.

Schlier, Heinrich. *The Relevance of the New Testament.* New York: Herder & Herder, 1968. Pp. 193–214.

Schmidt, Karl Ludwig. "*Ekklēsia.*" In *Theological Dictionary of the New Testament.* Edited by Gerhard Kittel and Gerhard Friedrich. Translated by Geoffrey W. Bromiley. Grand Rapids: William B. Eerdmans, 1964–1976. 3: 501–36.

Schweizer, Eduard. *Church Order in the New Testament.* Studies in Biblical Theology, no. 32. Translated by Frank Clark. Naperville, Ill.: A. R. Allenson, 1961.

Stendahl, Krister, ed. *The Scrolls and the New Testament.* London: SCM Press, 1958. Pp. 18–32, 129–156.

Streeter, Burnett Hillman. *The Primitive Church, Studied with Special Reference to the Origins of the Christian Ministry.* New York: Macmillan, 1929. Pp. 29–101.

Chapter IV, Section 2

Bruce, F. F. *The Speeches in Acts.* Tyndale New Testament Lecture, 1942. London: Tyndale Press, 1943.

Dodd, C. H. *The Apostolic Preaching and Its Developments.* New York: Harper & Row, 1964.

Filson, F. V. *Three Crucial Decades: Studies in the Book of Acts.* Richmond: John Knox Press, 1963. Pp. 29–42.

Goppelt, Leonhard. *Apostolic and Post-Apostolic Times.* Translated by Robert A. Guelich. 1962. London: Adam & Charles Black, 1970. Pp. 33–41.

Green, Michael. *Evangelism in the Early Church.* London: Hodder & Stoughton, 1970. Pp. 48–138.

Longenecker, Richard N. *The Christology of Early Jewish Christianity.* Studies in Biblical Theology, 2d ser., vol. 17. London: SCM Press, 1970.

Marshall, I. Howard. *Luke: Historian and Theologian.* London: Paternoster Press, 1970.

Moule, C. F. D. "The Christology of Acts." In *Studies in Luke- Acts.* Edited by Leander E. Keck and J. Louis Martyn. Nashville: Abingdon Press, 1966. Pp. 159–85.

Mounce, Robert H. *The Essential Nature of New Testament Preaching.* Grand Rapids: William B. Eerdmans, 1960.

Ridderbos, H. N. *The Speeches of Peter in the Acts of the Apostles.* Tyndale New Testament Lecture, 1961. London: Tyndale Press, 1962.

Smalley, S. S. "The Christology of Acts." *Expository Times* 73 (1961–62): 358–62.

———. "The Christology of Acts Again." In *Christ and Spirit in the New Testament.* Edited by Barnabas Lindars and Stephen S. Smalley. Cambridge: Cambridge University Press, 1973. Pp. 79–93.

Chapter IV, Section 3

Cullmann, Oscar. *The Earliest Christian Confessions*. Translated by J. K. S. Reid. London: SCM Press, 1949.

Gundry, R. H. "The Form, Meaning and Background of the Hymn Quoted in I Timothy 3:16." In *Apostolic History and the Gospel: Biblical and Historical Essays Presented to F. F. Bruce on His 60th Birthday*. Edited by W. Ward Gasque and Ralph P. Martin. London: Paternoster Press, 1970. Pp. 203–22.

Hunter, A. M. *Paul and His Predecessors*. 1940. London: SCM Press, 1961.

Kelly, J. N. D. *Early Christian Creeds*. London: Longmans, Green, 1950. Pp. 1–29.

Kramer, Werner. *Christ, Lord, Son of God*. Studies in Biblical Theology, no. 50. Translated by Brian Hardy. London: SCM Press, 1966.

Neufeld, Vernon H. *The Earliest Christian Confessions*. New Testament Tools and Studies, vol. 5. Edited by Bruce M. Metzger. Grand Rapids: William B. Eerdmans, 1963.

Schweizer, Eduard. "Two New Testament Creeds Compared." In *Current Issues in New Testament Interpretation: Essays in Honor of Otto Piper*. Edited by William Klassen and Graydon F. Snyder. New York: Harper, 1962. Pp. 166–77.

Stauffer, Ethelbert. *New Testament Theology*. Translated by John Marsh. London: SCM Press, 1955. Pp. 235–57, 338–39.

Chapter IV, Section 4

Beasley-Murray, G. R. *Baptism in the New Testament*. London: Macmillan, 1962.

Cullmann, Oscar. *Baptism in the New Testament*. Studies in Biblical Theology, no. 1. Translated by J. K. S. Reid. London: SCM Press, 1950.

Dunn, James D. G. *Baptism in the Holy Spirit: A Re-examination of the New Testament Teaching on the Gift of the Spirit in Relation to Pentecostalism Today*. Studies in Biblical Theology, 2d ser., no. 15. London: SCM Press, 1970.

Flemington, W. F. *The New Testament Doctrine of Baptism*. London: S.P.C.K., 1953.

Goguel, Maurice. *The Primitive Church*. Translated by H. C. Snape. 1947. London: Allen & Unwin, 1964. Pp. 282–324.

Lambert, J. C. *Sacraments in the New Testament*. Edinburgh: T. & T. Clark, 1903. Pp. 1–239.

Lampe, G. W. H. *The Seal of the Spirit: A Study in the Doctrine of Baptism and Confirmation in the New Testament and the Fathers*. London: Longmans, Green, 1951. Pp. 46–63.

Manson, T. W. "Baptism in the Church." *Scottish Journal of Theology* 2 (1949): 391–403.

Oepke, Albrecht. "*Baptō*." In *Theological Dictionary of the New Testament*. Edited by Gerhard Kittel and Gerhard Friedrich. Translated by Geoffrey W. Bromiley. Grand Rapids: William B. Eerdmans, 1964–76. 1: 538–43.

Robinson, John A. T. "The One Baptism." In *Twelve New Testament Studies*. Studies in Biblical Theology, no. 34. London: SCM Press, 1962. Pp. 158–75.

Schlatter, Adolf. *The Church in the New Testament Period*. Translated by Paul P. Levertoff. 1926. London: S.P.C.K., 1955. Pp. 25–32.

Chapter IV, Section 5

Allmen, Jean-Jacques von. *The Lord's Supper*. Ecumenical Studies in Worship, no. 19. Richmond: John Knox Press, 1969.

Bornkamm, Günther. *Early Christian Experience*. Translated by Paul L. Hammer. London: SCM Press, 1969. Pp. 123–79.

Cullmann, Oscar. *Early Christian Worship*. Translated by A. Stewart Todd and James B. Torrance. 1953. Philadelphia: Westminster Press, 1978.

Delling, Gerhard. *Worship in the New Testament*. Translated by Percy Scott. London: Darton, Longman & Todd, 1962.

Goguel, Maurice. *The Primitive Church*. Translated by H. C. Snape. 1947. London: Allen & Unwin, 1964. Pp. 254–74.

Goppelt, Leonhard. *Apostolic and Post-Apostolic Times*. Translated by Robert A. Guelich. 1962. London: Adam & Charles Black, 1970. Pp. 202–21.

Hahn, Ferdinand. *The Worship of the Early Church*. Translated by David E. Green. Edited by John Reumann. Philadelphia: Fortress Press, 1973.

Higgins, A. J. B. *The Lord's Supper in the New Testament*. Chicago: H. Regnery, 1952.

Käsemann, Ernst. *Essays on New Testament Themes*. Translated by W. J. Montague. 1960. London: SCM Press, 1964. Pp. 108–35.

———. *New Testament Questions of Today*. Translated by W. J. Montague. 1965. London: SCM Press, 1969. Pp. 188–95.

Martin, Ralph P. *Worship in the Early Church*. Westwood, N.J.: Fleming H. Revell, 1964.

Moule, C. F. D. *The Birth of the New Testament*. New York: Harper & Row, 1962. Pp. 11–32.

———. *Worship in the New Testament*. Ecumenical Studies in Worship, no. 9. London: Lutterworth Press, 1961.

Reicke, Bo. "Some Reflections on Worship in the New Testament." In *New Testament Essays: Studies in Honor of Thomas Walter Manson*. Edited by A. J. B. Higgins. Manchester: Manchester University Press, 1959. pp. 194–209.

Schlatter, Adolf. *The Church in the New Testament Period*. Translated by Paul P. Levertoff. 1926. London: S.P.C.K., 1955. Pp. 63–74.

Schweizer, Eduard. "The Service of Worship: An Exposition of 1 Corinthians 14." In *Neotestimentica: German and English Essays, 1951–1963*. Zurich: Zwingli Verlag, 1963. Pp. 333– 43.

Taylor, Vincent. "The New Testament Origins of Holy Communion." In *New Testament Essays*. London: Epworth Press, 1970. Pp. 48–59.

Chapter IV, Section 6

Barth, Karl. *Church Dogmatics*, vol. 4, pt. 4: *The Christian Life*. Translated by Geoffrey W. Bromiley. Edinburgh: T. & T. Clark, 1962.

Bornkamm, Günther. *Early Christian Experience*. Translated by Paul L. Hammer. London: SCM Press, 1969. Pp. 71–86.

Campenhausen, Hans von. *Tradition and Life in the Church: Essays and Lectures in Church History*. Translated by A. V. Littledale. 1960. London: Collins, 1968.

Clogg, F. Bertram. *The Christian Character in the Early Church*. London: Epworth Press, 1944. Pp. 107–27.

Dobschütz, Ernst von. *Christian Life in the Primitive Church*. Translated by George Bremner. Edited by W. D. Morrison. New York: G. P. Putnam, 1904.

Furnish, Victor Paul. *Theology and Ethics in Paul*. Nashville: Abingdon Press, 1968. Pp. 207–41.

Goguel, Maurice. *The Primitive Church*. Translated by H. C. Snape. 1947. London: Allen & Unwin, 1964. Pp. 417–562.

Ladd, George Eldon. *A Theology of the New Testament*. Grand Rapids: William B. Eerdmans, 1974. Pp. 511–30.

McGiffert, A. C. *A History of Christianity in the Apostolic Age*. New York: Scribner's, 1897. Pp. 506–17.

Manson, T. W. *Ethics and the Gospel*. London: SCM Press, 1960.

Manson, William. *Jesus and the Christian*. Grand Rapids: William B. Eerdmans, 1967. Pp. 91–134.

Ropes, James Hardy. *The Apostolic Age in the Light of Modern Criticism*. New York: Scribner's, 1906. Pp. 169–206.

Schlier, Heinrich. *The Relevance of the New Testament*. New York: Herder & Herder, 1968. Pp. 127–41.

Thornton, L. S. *The Common Life in the Body of Christ*. 3d ed. London: Dacre Press, 1942. Pp. 1–126.

Weiss, Johannes. *Earliest Christianity: A History of the Period A.D. 30–150*. Translated and edited by Frederick C. Grant. New York: Harper, 1959. 1: 45–82, 546–79.

Chapter IV, Section 7

Beyer, Hermann W. "*Diakonos.*" In *Theological Dictionary of the New Testament*. Edited by Gerhard Kittel and Gerhard Friedrich. Translated by Geoffrey W. Bromiley. Grand Rapids: William B. Eerdmans, 1964–76. 2: 89–93.

Bittlinger, Arnold. *Gifts and Ministries*. Grand Rapids: William B. Eerdmans, 1973.

Bromiley, Geoffrey W. *Christian Ministry*. Grand Rapids: William B. Eerdmans, 1959.

Davies, W. D. *Christian Origins and Judaism*. London: Darton, Longman & Todd, 1962. Pp. 231–45.

Goguel, Maurice. *The Primitive Church*. Translated by H. C. Snape. 1947. London: Allen & Unwin, 1964. Pp. 116–63.

Käsemann, Ernst. "Ministry and Community in the New Testament." In *Essays on New Testament Themes*. Translated by W. J. Montague. 1960. London: SCM Press, 1964. Pp. 63–94.

Lindsay, Thomas M. *The Church and the Ministry in the Early Centuries*. New York: George H. Doran, 1903. Pp. 69–166.

Manson, T. W. *The Church's Ministry*. London: Hodder & Stoughton, 1948.

Riesenfeld, H. "The Ministry in the New Testament." In *The Root of the Vine: Essays in Biblical Theology*, by Anton Fridrichsen, et al. London: Dacre Press, 1953. Pp. 96–127.

Chapter IV, Section 8

Caird, G. B. *The Apostolic Age*. London: Gerald Duckworth, 1955. Pp. 106–15.

Carrington, Philip. *The Primitive Christian Catechism: A Study in the Making of the Marcan Gospel*. Cambridge: Cambridge University Press, 1952.

Daube, David. *The New Testament and Rabbinic Judaism*. London: Athalone Press, 1956. Pp. 106–40.

Dodd, C. H. *Gospel and Law: The Relation of Faith and Ethics in Early Christianity*. New York: Columbia University Press, 1951.

———. *More New Testament Studies*. Grand Rapids: William B. Eerdmans, 1968. Pp. 11–29.

Filson, F. V. "The Christian Teacher in the First Century." *Journal of Biblical Literature* 60 (1941): 317–28.

———. *Three Crucial Decades: Studies in the Book of Acts*. Richmond: John Knox Press, 1963. Pp. 29–48.

Goudge, H. L. *The Pastoral Teaching of St. Paul*. London: Edward Arnold, 1913.

Harrison, E. F. "Some Patterns of the New Testament Didache." *Bibliotheca Sacra* 119 (April 1962): 118–28.

Kuist, Howard Tillman. *The Pedagogy of St. Paul*. New York: George H. Doran, 1925.

Moe, Olaf Edvard. *The Apostle Paul*. Translated by L. A. Vigness. Minneapolis: Augsburg, 1950–54. 2: 40–59.

Moule, C. F. D. *The Birth of the New Testament*. New York: Harper & Row, 1962. Pp. 125–52.

Muirhead, Ian A. *Education in the New Testament*. Monographs in Christian Education, no. 2. Edited by C. Ellis Nelson. New York: Association Press, 1965.

Scott, Charles A. Anderson. *St. Paul: The Man and the Teacher*. Cambridge: Cambridge University Press, 1936.

Selwyn, Edward Gordon. *The First Epistle of St. Peter*. London: Macmillan, 1946. Pp. 363–488.

Sherrill, Lewis Joseph. *The Rise of Christian Education*. New York: Macmillan, 1944.

Wood, H. G. "Didache, Kerygma and Evangelion." In *New Testament Essays: Studies in Honor of Thomas Walter Manson*. Edited by A. J. B. Higgins. Manchester: Manchester University Press, 1959. Pp. 306–12.

Chapter IV, Section 9

Bertram, Georg. "*Paideuō*. . . . " In *Theological Dictionary of the New Testament*. Edited by Gerhard Kittel and Gerhard Friedrich. Translated by Geoffrey W. Bromiley. Grand Rapids: William B. Eerdmans, 1964–76. 5: 596–625.

Foakes-Jackson, F. J. *Studies in the Life of the Early Church*. New York: George A. Doran, 1927. Pp. 39–48.

Forkman, Göran. *The Limits of the Religious Community: Expulsion from the Religious Community within the Qumran Sect, within Rabbinic Judaism, and within Primitive Christianity*. Translated by Pearl Sjölander. Lund: Gleerup, 1972. Pp. 115–215.

Goguel, Maurice. *The Primitive Church*. Translated by H. C. Snape. 1947. London: Allen & Unwin, 1964. Pp. 224–46.

Lampe, G. W. H. "Church Discipline and the Interpretation of the Epistles to the Corinthians." In *Christian History and Interpretation: Studies Presented to John Knox*. Edited by W. R. Farmer, C. F. D. Moule, and R. R. Niebuhr. Cambridge: Cambridge University Press, 1967. Pp. 337–62.

Chapter V, Section 1

Aytoun, Robert Alexander. *City Centres of Early Christianity*. London: Hodder & Stoughton, 1915. Pp. 1–12.

Bruce, F. F. *New Testament History*. Garden City, N.Y.: Doubleday, 1971. Pp. 195–214.

Dobschütz, Ernst von. *Christian Life in the Primitive Church*. Translated by George Bremner. Edited by W. D. Morrison. New York: G. P. Putnam, 1904. Pp. 138–48.

Goguel, Maurice. *The Birth of Christianity*. Translated by H. C. Snape. 1946. London: Allen & Unwin, 1953. Pp. 89–148.

Goppelt, Leonhard. *Apostolic and Post-Apostolic Times*. Translated by Robert A. Guelich. 1962. London: Adam & Charles Black, 1970. Pp. 25–60.

Jeremias, Joachim. *Jerusalem in the Time of Jesus: An Investigation into Economic and Social Conditions during the New Testament Period*. Translated by F. H. and C. H. Cave. 1967. Philadelphia: Fortress Press, 1969.

Lietzmann, Hans. *The Beginnings of the Christian Church*. Translated by Bertram Lee Woolf. New York: Scribner's, 1949. Pp. 76–94.

Mann, C. S. "The Organization and Institutions of the Jerusalem Church in Acts." In The Anchor Bible, vol. 31: *The Acts of the Apostles*, by Johannes Munck. Revised by William F. Albright and C. S. Mann. Garden City, N.Y.: Doubleday, 1967. Pp. 276–84.

Purves, George T. *Christianity in the Apostolic Age*. The Historical Series for Bible Students, vol. 8. New York: Scribner's, 1902. Pp. 35–46.

Ramsay, W. M. *Pictures of the Apostolic Church: Studies in the Book of Acts*. London: Hodder & Stoughton, 1910. Pp. 24– 36.

Scott, Ernest F. *The Beginnings of the Church*. New York: Scribner's, 1925. Pp. 133–62.

Weiss, Johannes. *Earliest Christianity: A History of the Period A.D. 30–150*. Translated and edited by Frederick C. Grant. New York: Harper, 1959. 1: 45–82.

Chapter V, Section 2

Aytoun, Robert Alexander. *City Centres of Early Christianity*. London: Hodder & Stoughton, 1915. Pp. 81–112.

Christians, C. G. "The Church at Antioch." Th.M. thesis, Fuller Theological Seminary, 1967.

Downey, Glanville. *Ancient Antioch*. Princeton: Princeton University Press, 1963.

Goguel, Maurice. *The Birth of Christianity*. Translated by H. C. Snape. 1946. London: Allen & Unwin, 1953. Pp. 177–93.

Knox, Wilfred L. *St. Paul and the Church of Jerusalem*. Cambridge: Cambridge University Press, 1925. Pp. 156–98.

Metzger, Bruce M. "Antioch-on-the-Orontes." *Biblical Archeologist* 11 (December 1948): 70–88.

Purves, George T. *Christianity in the Apostolic Age*. The Historical Series for Bible Students, vol. 8. New York: Scribner's, 1902. Pp. 101–10.

Ramsay, W. M. *St. Paul the Traveller and the Roman Citizen*. New York: G. P. Putnam, 1896. Pp. 40–69.

Schlatter, Adolf. *The Church in the New Testament Period*. Translated by Paul P. Levertoff. 1926. London: S.P.C.K., 1955. Pp. 108–17.

Tenney, Merril C. "The Influence of Antioch on Apostolic Christianity." *Biblical Studies* 107 (July–September 1950): 298–310.

Weiss, Johannes. *Earliest Christianity: A History of the Period A.D. 30–150*. Translated and edited by Frederick C. Grant. New York: Harper, 1959. 1: 171–79.

Chapter V, Section 3

Blaiklock, E. M. *Cities of the New Testament*. London: Pickering & Inglis, 1965. Pp. 39–44.

Hayes, D. A. *Paul and His Epistles*. New York: Methodist Book Concern, 1915. Pp. 405–19.

Lightfoot, J. B. *St. Paul's Epistle to the Philippians*. London: Macmillan, 1879. Pp. 47–65.

Moe, Olaf Edvard. *The Apostle Paul*. Translated by L. A. Vigness. Minneapolis: Augsburg, 1950–54. 1: 260–69.

Ramsay, W. M. *St. Paul the Traveller and the Roman Citizen*. New York: G. P. Putnam, 1896. Pp. 198–226.

Schlatter, Adolf. *The Church in the New Testament Period.* Translated by Paul P. Levertoff. 1926. London: S.P.C.K., 1955. Pp. 139–46.

Weiss, Johannes. *Earliest Christianity: A History of the Period A.D. 30–150.* Translated and edited by Frederick C. Grant. New York: Harper, 1959. 1: 280–84.

Wright, William Burnet. *Cities of Paul: Beacons of the Past Rekindled for the Present.* New York: Houghton Mifflin, 1905. Pp. 58–78.

Chapter V, Section 4

Blaiklock, E. M. *Cities of the New Testament.* London: Pickering & Inglis, 1965. Pp. 45–49.

Denney, James. *The Epistles to the Thessalonians.* London: Hodder & Stoughton, 1903. Pp. 3–17.

Lightfoot, J. B. *Biblical Essays.* London: Macmillan, 1893. Pp. 253–69.

Milligan, George. *St. Paul's Epistles to the Thessalonians.* London: Macmillan, 1908. Pp. xxi-li.

Morris, Leon. *The First and Second Epistles to the Thessalonians.* Grand Rapids: William B. Eerdmans, 1959. Pp. 15–24.

Ramsay, W. M. *St. Paul the Traveller and the Roman Citizen.* New York: G. P. Putnam, 1896. Pp. 226–31.

Schlatter, Adolf. *The Church in the New Testament Period.* Translated by Paul P. Levertoff. 1926. London: S.P.C.K., 1955. Pp. 146–49.

Wright, William Burnet. *Cities of Paul: Beacons of the Past Rekindled for the Present.* New York: Houghton Mifflin, 1905. Pp. 79–115.

Chapter V, Section 5

Barrett, C. K. "Christianity at Corinth." *Bulletin of the John Rylands Library* 46 (March 1964): 269–97.

Dobschütz, Ernst von. *Christian Life in the Primitive Church.* Translated by George Bremner. Edited by W. D. Morrison. New York: G. P. Putnam, 1904. Pp. 11–80.

Glen, John Stanley. *Pastoral Problems in First Corinthians.* Philadelphia: Westminster Press, 1964.

Longenecker, Richard N. *Paul, Apostle of Liberty.* New York: Harper & Row, 1964.

Manson, T. W. *Studies in the Gospel and Epistles.* Edited by Matthew Black. Manchester: University of Manchester Press, 1962. Pp. 190–224.

Schlatter, Adolf. *The Church in the New Testament Period.* Translated by Paul P. Levertoff. 1926. London: S.P.C.K., 1955. Pp. 173–90.

Shaw, R. D. *The Pauline Epistles.* 1903. Pp. 127–62.

Weiss, Johannes. *Earliest Christianity: A History of the Period A.D. 30–150.* Translated and edited by Frederick C. Grant. New York: Harper, 1959. 1: 323–57.

Wright, William Burnet. *Cities of Paul: Beacons of the Past Rekindled for the Present.* New York: Houghton Mifflin, 1905. Pp. 116–62.

Chapter V, Section 6

Aytoun, Robert Alexander. *City Centres of Early Christianity.* London: Hodder & Stoughton, 1915. Pp. 13–31.

Blaiklock, E. M. *Cities of the New Testament.* London: Pickering & Inglis, 1965. Pp. 62–67.

Carrington, Philip. *The Early Christian Church.* Vol 1, *The First Christian Century.* Cambridge: Cambridge University Press, 1957. Pp. 126–47.

Dickey, Samuel. "Some Economic and Social Factors Affecting the Expansion of Christianity." In *Studies in Early Christianity*. Edited by Shirley Jackson Case. New York: The Century Co., 1928. Pp. 393–416.

Parvis, M. M., and F. V. Filson. *Biblical Archeologist* (September 1945): 62–73.

Ramsay, W. M. *The Church in the Roman Empire before A.D. 170*. London: Hodder & Stoughton, 1893. Pp. 112–45.

————. *Pauline and Other Studies in Early Church History*. London: Hodder & Stoughton, 1906.

Schlatter, Adolf. *The Church in the New Testament Period*. Translated by Paul P. Levertoff. 1926. London: S.P.C.K., 1955. Pp. 162–67.

Taylor, L. R. In *The Beginnings of Christianity*. Edited by F. J. Foakes-Jackson and Kirsopp Lake. London: Macmillan, 1920–33. 5: 251–62.

Weizsäcker, Karl von. *The Apostolic Age of the Christian Church*. 2d rev. ed. Translated by James Millar. New York: G. P. Putnam, 1894–99. 1: 376–405.

Wright, William Burnet. *Cities of Paul: Beacons of the Past Rekindled for the Present*. New York: Houghton Mifflin, 1905. Pp. 25–57.

Chapter V, Section 7

Francis, F. O., and W. A. Meeks, eds. and trans. *Conflict at Colossae: A Problem in the Interpretation of Early Christianity, Illustrated by Selected Modern Studies*. Missoula, Mont.: Scholars Press, 1975.

Martin, Ralph P. *Colossians, the Church's Lord and the Christian's Liberty: An Expository Commentary with a Present-Day Application*. Exeter: Paternoster Press, 1972.

Moule, C. F. D. *The Epistles of Paul the Apostle to the Colossians and to Philemon*. Cambridge: Cambridge University Press, 1957.

Radford, Lewis B. *The Epistle to the Colossians and the Epistle to Philemon*. London: Methuen, 1931.

Ramsay, W. M. *The Cities and Bishoprics of Phrygia*. Oxford: Clarendon Press, 1894. Pp. 208–16.

Robertson, A. T. *Paul and the Intellectuals: The Epistle to the Colossians*. Edited and revised by W. C. Strickland. Nashville: Broadman Press, 1959.

Westcott, B. F. *A Letter to Asia*. London: Macmillan, 1941.

Chapter V, Section 8

Aytoun, Robert Alexander. *City Centres of Early Christianity*. London: Hodder & Stoughton, 1915. Pp. 205–21.

Blaiklock, E. M. *Cities of the New Testament*. London: Pickering & Inglis, 1965. Pp. 83–88.

Bruce, F. F. *New Testament History*. Garden City, N.Y.: Doubleday, 1969. Pp. 373–93.

Edmundson, George. *The Church in Rome in the First Century*. London: Longmans, Green, 1913.

O'Callaghan, R. T. "Recent Excavations under the Vatican Crypts." *Biblical Archeologist* 12 (February 1949): 1–23.

————. "Vatican Excavations and the Tomb of Peter." *Biblical Archeologist* 16 (December 1953): 70–87.

Schlatter, Adolf. *The Church in the New Testament Period*. Translated by Paul P. Levertoff. 1926. London: S.P.C.K., 1955. Pp. 218–31.

Tucker, T. G. *Life in the Roman World of Nero and St. Paul*. New York: Macmillan, 1922.

Weiss, Johannes. *Earliest Christianity: A History of the Period A.D. 30–150*. Translated and edited by Frederick C. Grant. New York: Harper, 1959. 1: 358–68; 2: 837–66.

Weizsäcker, Karl von. *The Apostolic Age of the Christian Church*. 2d rev. ed. Translated by James Millar. New York: G. P. Putnam, 1894–99. 1: 358–68; 2: 837–66.